AN
ADDINGTON - CHALFANT
FAMILY HISTORY

WITH A

HISTORY OF THE ADDINGTON FAMILY

IN

RANDOLPH COUNTY, INDIANA

David Vern Addington

HERITAGE BOOKS
2024

HERITAGE BOOKS

AN IMPRINT OF HERITAGE BOOKS, INC.

Books, CDs, and more—Worldwide

For our listing of thousands of titles see our website
at
www.HeritageBooks.com

Published 2024 by
HERITAGE BOOKS, INC.
Publishing Division
5810 Ruatan Street
Berwyn Heights, MD 20740

Copyright © 1992 David Vern Addington

International Standard Book Number
Paperbound: 978-1-55613-609-2

Dedication

to Ashley and Carmen

and

to the next generation

and

to each generation to come

Table of Content

Acknowledgements

This book is about my paternal grandparents Harry Vern Addington and Alma Marguerite Chalfant. Harry Vern Addington died in a farm accident in 1930 so I never knew him but only heard those glowing comments that my grandmother made about him. My grandmother, Marguerite (Chalfant) Addington, was very much the stereotype doting grandmother and I still have fond memories of many days spent on the family farm between Farmland and Winchester in Randolph County, Indiana. I first developed an interest in the genealogy of our family in the mid 1970s when I sat down and had some very interesting talks with my grandmother. She gave me information on her direct knowledge of our family and also gave me several family photos which I treasure to this day and have included some in this book.

I hope my family as well as others enjoy the information contained in this book. I know that it is too factual and needs more family history and stories. Where I have used my best guess about relationships, I will so state or label with a question mark to indicate some doubt about the information.

Genealogy is tremendously interesting for some but can also be quite dry and tedious. The remains of our ancestors are but graves, old yellowed records, perhaps an old photo and memories of our most recent ancestors who we knew as children, but our fellow genealogists are as interesting and enthusiastic as we. This book would not be possible without the many published genealogies I have referenced and the help of many people with whom I have worked and corresponded over the many years of this project.

I would like to thank my wife Dixie and children, Ashley and Carmen, for their love, support and patience during this project. My parents, Vern and Louise Addington, were most helpful and visited many relatives and undertook some of the research work in Randolph County I was unable to do. I would like to thank my sister, Ann (Addington) Abel, for her suggestions and editing of the final text.

My thanks to Monisa Wisener, Randolph County Historian for her help, assistance and encouragement.

For their help on information on the Addington family and their descendents, I would like the many genealogists which I have corresponded with over the many years of this project. Specifically, I would like to thank Patricia Waltz (Portland, Indiana), Cecil Tharp (Eaton, Indiana), Joseph M. Patterson (Winter Haven, Florida), Harold W. Addington (Denver, Colorado), Joanne Moulton (Hussar, Alberta), William W. Addington (Fresno, California), Viola Hart (Lynn, Indiana), Anita Addington (Winchester, Indiana), Carolyn Garver (St. Joseph, Missouri), and Mrs. Ruth Addington (Red Key, Indiana). My thanks to Chester Addington (Westerville, Ohio) for his assistance and advice. I would also like to thank the officers and members of The Addington Association for their work in recording our history.

George Harcourt Bull (Mission Viejo, California) supplied much information on his knowledge of the Addingtons and had a major impact on this work. His expertise and friendship are gratefully acknowledged. My thanks for his review of the Addington section and descendents list.

My thanks to Joanne Ellis (Muncie, Indiana), Howard D. Chalfant, Sr. (Redford, Michigan), and Paul Chalfant (Colton, California) for their help on the Chalfant family. Robert Winders (East Waterford, Pennsylvania) was most helpful on the Winders family. Ruhana Shannon (Winchester, Indiana) helped me with the Bolinger and Feagans families. Mrs. Milo Kudobe (Mount Pleasant, Iowa) provided me with much information on the Townsend family.

David Vern Addington, PhD
January 1992

Harry Vern Addington Family History

Harry Vern Addington was born in White River Township, Randolph County, Indiana on 9 Mar 1893 to Joseph Leander and Dora Elizabeth (Feagans) Addington, the fourth child and third son. He had two older brothers, Cressie and Gilva, one older sister, Mabel and one younger brother, Cecil. Harry grew up on his father's farm located about one and a half miles south of Maxville which his father, Leander, had inherited from his father.

Alma Marguerite Chalfant was born on 9 Jun 1905 to Finley Ellsworth and Emma Alice (Fitzpatrick) Chalfant. She was the seventh of eight children and was considerably younger than some of her older siblings, her oldest sister being nineteen years older. The Chalfant family originally lived in southwestern Delaware County, but in 1900 they were living in Summitville in Madison County and then moved back to the city of Parker in Randolph County where Marguerite was born.

Harry Vern Addington and Alma Marguerite Chalfant were married in Randolph County, Indiana on 30 Sep 1922. They initially set up their household on a farm in section 29 of White River Township near his father's farm, about two miles south of Maxville. There, they had three sons: Leo Vern Addington, born 10 Apr 1923, Joseph Elsworth Addington, born 3 Apr 1925, and Murrie Alexander Addington, born 19 Apr 1927. In 1928, they moved to Green Township and rented a farm in section 21 from Martin Wood. The family was living there when tragedy struck. In August of 1930, Harry was helping a nearby farmer by the name of Les Melvin when Harry fell from a hay wagon and broke his neck, dying quickly. He was buried in the Woodlawn Cemetery at Maxville in the far eastern section. Later, his parents were buried beside him in an adjoining plot.

Marguerite and the three young boys then moved into Parker and lived with her parents for the next year. Harry had been very thoughtful and had taken out a life insurance policy on himself for $6,000. In 1931, Marguerite used the insurance money from Harry's death to buy a 93 acre farm on the northwest corner of section 27 in White River Township. This farm was originally owned by the Green family and is located about a miles south of Maxville and about one mile east. Marguerite married a second time on 12 Oct 1932 to Clarence Mason and they farmed this land with the help of the three boys. This marriage lasted for several years but eventually dissolved and they were divorced in the 1940s. Marguerite married a third time to a widower, Harry Puckett, on 10 May 1956. They enjoyed each others company for nine years until Harry died in 1965. Harry was buried in Buena Vista Cemetery next to his first wife.

Marguerite's house was a place of much warmth and was always a place of joy to visit. The farmhouse was located on about two acres of land and she had a riding lawn mower for that reason. It was always a great joy for her young grandsons to see that the yard had not been mowed when we drove up to the house so we could drive her little tractor. In the fall, several huge trees would cover the ground with layers of leaves. Visits would be spent raking leaves into large piles and promptly jumping in before they were set on fire. Eight Mile Creek went through the farm and much time was spent skipping rocks on the creek or walking along its banks. Marguerite's only granddaughter remembers making sugar cream pies with real cream and stirring everything with her fingers. Marguerite allowed a beekeeper to keep some hives in the small woods on the north edge of the farm. There were always numerous bees present in the woods but the hives also resulted in a supply of honey as rent.

After Harry's death, Marguerite continued living on the farm and reveled in her six grandchildren. Marguerite was particularly excited about her first great grandchild, Amy Louise Abel, born 6 Mar 1978, so much so that she arranged to show her off to her many friends in Winchester.

Marguerite died on 18 Aug 1979 at Ball Memorial Hospital in Muncie. She was buried on 22 Aug 1979 in Woodlawn Cemetery at Maxville next to her first husband, Harry Vern Addington, who had preceded her in death by 49 years.

The oldest son of Harry and Marguerite, Leo Vern Addington, was born on 10 Apr 1923 and goes by his middle name, Vern. He graduated in 1941 from the old Lincoln School which was located on State Road 32 about one mile east of Maxville. Vern enrolled in Ball State Teachers College the following fall and attended for two years. He was drafted into the Army in 1943 and served in the 63rd Infantry Division in Europe seeing action in southern France and Germany. He earned a Bronze Star Medal for valor in action on 25 Apr 1945 near Leipheim, Germany. He was discharged in late 1945 with the rank of Staff Sergeant. Vern returned to college at Ball State Teachers College where he graduated with a BS degree in Business in 1947.

Leo Vern Addington married Frances Louise Boggs, the daughter of Plummer and Hilda (Garringer) Boggs on 24 May 1946 in Cowan, Indiana. Vern and Louise have three children: Ann Frances Addington, born 11 Jun 1947, David Vern Addington, born 4 Aug 1948, and Dale Lee Addington, born 5 Dec 1950, all born in Winchester while the family was living in Farmland. Vern Addington taught school for three years and then accepted a job with the J. I. Case Company as a sales representative in farm implements. In 1952, the family moved to Twelve Mile, Indiana and spent five years there. In 1957, they moved to Greenwood, Indiana where they lived for two years. In 1959, they moved to the St. Louis, Missouri area where they lived in the northern suburbs. In 1962, they moved to Anderson, Indiana and bought a home on Dogwood Drive in the South Edgewood addition. All three children graduated from Madison Heights High School near Anderson.

Louise (Boggs) Addington graduated from Ball State Teachers College in 1944 with a BS degree in Home Economics. After teaching for many years, she returned to Ball State to earn a MS degree in 1965. She taught Home Economics at the high school and middle school level for over thirty-eight years, including the last twenty-five years in the Noblesville School System. Vern became an independent sales representative in 1973 and represented several farm implement companies. Vern and Louise are retired and still reside in Anderson, Indiana.

Of the children of Vern and Louise, Ann Frances Addington graduated from Ball State University in 1969 with a BA degree in English. She also earned a MS degree in Library Science from Indiana University in 1973. She has taught English and been a school librarian in the Kokomo area schools for over eighteen years. Ann married Capt. Richard Irwin Abel, the son

3

of Russell and Ethel (Peterson) Abel, on 24 Apr 1971 at Grissom Air Force Base, Indiana. They have one daughter, Amy Louise Abel, born 6 Mar 1978 in Kokomo, Indiana. The Abels still reside in Kokomo. The oldest son, David Vern Addington, graduated from Purdue University in 1970 with a BS degree in Chemical Engineering with Highest Distinction. He served in the U. S. Air Force from 1971 till 1974 in Germany and Alabama. He returned to graduate school and received MS and PhD degrees in Chemical Engineering from The University of Michigan. Since 1978, he has worked for The Atlantic Richfield Company in Plano, Texas. David married Dixie Carol Behr, daughter of Dick A. J. and Evelyn (Brammer) Behr on 29 Dec 1979 in Richardson, Texas. They have two children: Ashley Lynn Addington, born 20 Nov 1982 in Dallas, Texas and Carmen Elizabeth Addington, born 1 Nov 1985 in Dallas. The youngest son of Vern and Louise, Dale Lee Addington, graduated from Purdue University in 1972 with a BS degree in Economics. He married Mary Tammis "Tammi" Carson, the daughter of Joseph Albert and Elizabeth Suzanne (Klampper) Carson, on 10 Jun 1972 at West Lafayette, Indiana. Dale has worked in management for Sears, Roebuck and Company since 1972. Dale and Tammi (Carson) Addington have two sons: Stephen Carson Addington, born 16 May 1982 in Findlay, Ohio and James Michael Addington, born 28 Aug 1984 in Findlay. Dale and Tammi and their family still reside in Findlay, Ohio.

The second son of Harry and Marguerite (Chalfant) Addington, Joseph Elsworth Addington, grew up in White River Township and graduated from Lincoln School in 1943. Joe did some farming but eventually owned and operated the Ford farm dealership in Winchester for many years, part of the time in association with his brother Murrie. Joe Addington married on 10 Mar 1949 to Norma Jean Heniser and they have three sons: Wayne Alan Addington, born 26 May 1954, Michael Dean Addington, born 12 Feb 1957, and Kent Lee Addington, born 8 Jun 1961. Joe and Jean Addington bought a house in Winchester at 522 North Street where they raised their family. Joe took up flying as a hobby and was one of the founders of the annual Winchester Fly-In.

Of the sons of Joe and Jean, the youngest Kent married Angie Pigg on 31 Mar 1983. Kent and Angie have three children: Quinton Lee Addington, born 4 Sep 1983, Brandon Joseph Addington, born 17 Feb 1985, and Kayla Corrine Addington, born 9 Nov 1988. The oldest son, Wayne Alan Addington, married Judith Ann Gofort on 19 Jul 1990. Michael Dean Addington first married Peggy Lynn Himes but the marriage was later dissolved. Michael married second to Rebecca Ann McDavid on 28 Sep 1990 in Winchester. All three sons of Joe and Jean, still reside in Winchester with their families. Also, all three sons work for Lobdell Emory Manufacturing Company located in Winchester. Joe Addington retired from his farm implement store in 1987. Joe died on 11 Aug 1990 at the age of 65 and is buried beside his parents in the Maxville Cemetery.

The third son of Harry and Marguerite (Chalfant) Addington, Murrie Alexander Addington, grew up in White River Township and graduated from Lincoln School in 1945. Murrie took over the farming of his mother's land after school and also worked at Warner Gear in Muncie. He retired from Warner Gear in 1978 after 30 years of service. Murrie married on 16 Mar 1973 to Eunice Annette Barnett, and they own a farm across the road from his mother's farm. Eunice has two children: Timothy and Tamara and four grandchildren. Murrie and Eunice also own a winter home in Gibsonton, Florida where they spend the winter months.

Randolph County History

Randolph County plays such a key role in this family story that a review of its history seems appropriate. The land that is now Randolph County was part of the original Northwest Territory ceded to the struggling United States after the Revolutionary War. Numerous relics of the prehistory of Randolph County have been found. Several Indian burial mounds of various sizes were found in the county by the first settlers. Unfortunately, most were destroyed in the process of developing and cultivating the land. Before the appearance of white settlers in Indiana, the region was occupied by the tribes belonging to the Miami confederacy. The main tribes inhabiting Indiana were the Miamis, the Pottawatomies, the Weas, the Delawares and the Kickapoos. The Indians were quite prevalent and Indian trouble came to a head in 1812 and 1813. The trouble had settled down by 1814 and in a treaty made at Fort Wayne in 1818, certain tracts were reserved for the Indians.

The first settlers in central Indiana were in Wayne County which is located just south of Randolph County. Wayne County settlers started moving in about 1800. Many of these settlers who disliked slavery and were looking for a new land to settle were from North Carolina. The special 1807 census of the Northwest Territory shows only a few thousand settlers living in the state of what is now Indiana.

Randolph County lies in the eastern part of Indiana on the Ohio border. The county is about twenty-one and three quarters miles from east to west and twenty-one miles from south to north encompassing nearly 457 square miles. Randolph County is bounded on the north by Jay County, on the east by Mercer and Darke Counties in Ohio, on the south by Wayne County, and on the west by Delaware and Henry Counties. Two Indian boundaries pass through the county, both in a southwesterly direction. The first resulted from a treaty made at Greenville, Ohio in 1795 by Gen. Anthony Wayne and several tribes. The second line was drawn up for a treaty made with the Indians in 1809 by Gen. Harrison, the Governor of the Indiana territory. It was called the twelve mile boundary because the Indians ceded a strip twelve miles wide, just west of the previous boundary. When Randolph County was first created by the Legislature, it embraced only the land east of the twelve mile border. But in December 1819, the Legislature fixed the boundaries as they now stand.

There are no mountains nor even high hills in Randolph County. The land is mainly low and level and often needs drainage. Randolph County is drained by the start of two major rivers, the Mississinewa River in the northern part of the county and by the White River running through the center of the county. Many of the streams and the two rivers were used in the early days for water power for grist-mills, saw-mills and other machinery. When the first settlers arrived the county was thickly timbered with a tall, heavy forest, having a wonderful undergrowth of shrubs, wild grasses and weeds. The trees were beech, sugar tree, ash, oak, poplar, walnut, elm, hickory, buckeye, linn, wild maple, hackberry, coffeenut, honey locust and cottonwood. The main game were deer, squirrels, turkeys, pheasants and bears with some wolves, raccoons and various kinds of wild cats. Wild hogs became quite prevalent after the first settlers arrived and some of their domestic animals escaped to the wild.

The first white settlers in Randolph County starting moving into the southeastern townships in 1814, mainly moving up from Wayne County. The new county formed by the Legislature in 1818, was named Randolph from the old Randolph County in North Carolina, because many of the residents within its limits had come from that county in the "Old North State" and because a member of the Legislature, living within its bounds, was also a native of the same. Winchester was located as the county seat of Randolph County at the same time. The first acknowledged settlement in Randolph County was made in April 1814 in Greensfork Township by Thomas Parker (a Quaker from North Carolina) with his wife and three children. A considerable amount of land entries were made in 1814 and 1815, although often the owners did not occupy the land for several years. The land entries in the first two years were mostly in Greensfork, Washington and White River Townships in the southeastern portion of the county. There were even more land entries in 1816, 1817 and 1818 but then settlement slowed with almost no new growth from 1820 to 1828. Land entries were at a relative low level until 1831 when they increased and by 1837, almost all of the land had been "taken up." Land speculators had some of the land and many tracts laid unoccupied for many years. Whereas land entries for about 32,000 acres were entered on between 1816 and 1818, the years of 1832 through 1837 saw 172,000 acres claimed.

The early settlers were strongly religious people and churches were soon organized and built. Often a church would be convened at someone's house until a crude but suitable building could be built. It appears that the Friends and Methodists were probably the first to organize and build churches in Randolph County.

Winchester was the first town established in the county. Gov. Jennings appointed David Wright sheriff and asked him to organize the county. Five individuals donated 158 acres of land to help establish the site of Winchester, which was accepted by a set of commissioners appointed by David Wright. For several years after 1818, until the northern counties were organized, Winchester was the seat of justice for all the white people north, including those at Fort Wayne. Lots were laid out in the fall and winter of 1818 and sold the following spring. Contracts to build the first courthouse ($254.50) and the first jail ($125) were let in December 1818 and were accepted by the commissioners in October 1820. The first house was built in the spring of 1819 on lot no. 9 and was a round log-cabin, owned and occupied for many years by Martin Comer. Winchester grew slowly and by 1830, there were still but a dozen houses or so. It was still mainly just the seat of justice and little else. Most people lived a rural agricultural life and had no need of visiting the town.

The cabins that the early settlers built were crude and built from round logs of eight to ten inches in diameter. Sizes were from small cabins of twelve by fourteen feet to large cabins of maybe eighteen by twenty-five feet. Small cabins usually had one door and maybe one window while large cabins had two doors and several windows. Cabins were one story of about eight feet with a loft above in the roof. A fireplace and chimney occupied one wall and opened into the house. At the "raising", neighbors from miles around would come and lend their aid. The use of glass windows in houses was not

8

prevalent until about 1850. Eventually as saw mills were built, the quality and size of the cabins improved.

Early education in Randolph County was usually done at home since schools were few. The few schools that were available were usually associated with local churches. Before 1850 nearly all schools were supported by subscriptions and often times poorly supported. More public funds were allocated after this, but the school systems did not seem well organized until into the 1870s. The level of the education depended greatly on the family commitment to educate their children. The Union Literary Institute was founded in Ridgeville in the 1846 and educated blacks along with some white settler's children. Ridgeville College was founded in 1867 by the Free Will Baptists and survived until 1902.

The population of Randolph County by the 1840 census was 10,684. The county continued to grow to 14,785 by 1850, 18,997 by 1860 and to 26,768 by 1880. The population was evenly distributed but with a few towns of size. By 1880, only Union City (2,478), Winchester (1,965), Ridgeville (775) and Farmland (669) had substantial populations.

When the Civil War started in 1861, Randolph County showed its loyalty and devotion to that noble cause. Although exact numbers are not known, over 2,000 men from Randolph County served in the volunteer forces, this from a total population of about 19,000 in 1860. At least 250 of these brave volunteers lost their lives due to combat or disease in insuring the survival of the Union.

A majority of the above history is taken from *History of Randolph County, Indiana with Illustrations and Biographical Sketches* which was published by the Rev. Ebenezer Tucker in 1882. The Rev. Tucker spent over three years traveling around the county and interviewing numerous early settlers and gathering the early history of Randolph County. This oversize 512 page book is a monumental achievement and should be consulted to truly understand the hardships and environment of the early pioneers who settled Randolph County.

In more recent history, Randolph County has remained an agricultural based economy. The population of Randolph County has grown only slowly being about 28,900 in 1980. The population has shifted more to the cities as modern mechanization has resulted in larger farms.

Randolph County has taken pride in its history, its people and its accomplishments. The Historical and Genealogical Society of Randolph County has undertaken the task of organizing and recording this rich history. The Society published in 1990 an updated history of *Randolph County, Indiana* which covers the last one hundred years of the county's history.

The Ancestry of Harry Vern Addington

Harry Vern Addington was born 9 Mar 1893 to Joseph Leander and Dora Elizabeth (Feagans) Addington. The Addington family was of English origin and the Feagans family was of English or Irish origin. Both the Addington and Feagans families were very early settlers in Randolph County, Indiana. The Addington family arrived about 1835 and the Feagans family settled in Randolph County about 1838. The two families form the basis for this ancestral search but many other families are associated with them through marriage.

Families associated with the Addington line are the Bolinger and Goshorn families of Pennsylvania, the Townsend family of North Carolina and Pennsylvania, the Cain family of North Carolina and the Heaton family of Pennsylvania.

The Feagans family originally came from Virginia and passed through Ohio where they were associated with the McCracken family, also originally from Virginia. The Moore family originally from Delaware and the Wright family from North Carolina were also associated with the Feagans family.

The following is a listing of the direct line ancestors of Harry Vern Addington that are currently known. Numbering System - Father's name is always twice the number of the offspring. Mother's name is twice the offspring's number plus one.

4. Harry Vern Addington
   b. 9 Mar 1893, White River Twp, Randolph Co., Indiana
   m. 30 Sep 1922, Randolph Co., IN, Alma Marguerite Chalfant
   d. 13 Aug 1930, Green Township, Randolph Co., Indiana,
      bur. Maxville Cemetery
8. Joseph Leander Addington
   b. 15 Feb 1858, Randolph Co., Indiana
   m. 18 Feb 1880, Randolph Co., Indiana
   d. 11 Oct 1935, Randolph Co., Indiana, bur. Maxville Cem.
   16. David Addington
      b. 9 Mar 1828, Wayne Co., Indiana
      m. 27 Nov 1851, Randolph Co., Indiana
      d. 19 Jul 1902, Randolph Co., IN, bur. Maxville Cem.

32. Joseph Addington
  b. 21 Jul 1776, 96 District, Union Co., South Carolina
  m. (2nd) 22 Dec 1808, Preble Co., Ohio
  d. 20 Feb 1836, Randolph Co., Indiana
  bur. Sparrow Creek Cemetery
  64. John Addington
    b. 10 Nov 1749 (or 5 Oct 1745), Bucks Co., Pennsylvania
    m. (2nd) 3 May 1775, Newberry Co., South Carolina
    d. 1833 (will recorded 30 Aug 1833), Chester,
    Wayne Co., Indiana
    128. Henry Addington
      b. 1720/7, (family tradition says London, prob. PA)
      m. c1745/9, Pennsylvania
      d. 25 Jul 1787, 96 District, Union County, SC
    129. Sarah Elizabeth Burson
      b. 1723/6, Pennsylvania
      d. 14 Mar 1826, Chester, Wayne Co., Indiana
  65. Elizabeth Heaton
    b. prob. Pennsylvania
    d. bef. 1833, Wayne Co., Indiana
    130. Joseph Heaton
      b. 3 Feb 1699, Bucks Co., Pennsylvania
      m. c1730, Wrightstown, Bucks Co., Pennsylvania
    131. Leada (Lydia) Smith
      262. William Smith of Wrightstown, Pennsylvania
      263. Mary Croasdale
        526. Thomas Croasdale
        527. Agnes ?
33. Celia Townsend
  b. 22 Feb 1785, North Carolina
  d. 5 Mar 1852, Randolph Co., IN, bur. Sparrow Creek
  66. John M. Townsend
    b. 6 Nov 1763, Pennsylvania
    m. c1784, South Carolina
    d. 25 Aug 1853, 89y, 8m, 19d, Fountain City,
    Wayne Co., Indiana
    132. John Townsend
      b. c1725, Pennsylvania
    133. Elizabeth Pearson
      b. 8 Dec 1726, Middleton, Bucks Co., Pennsylvania
      266. Enoch Pearson
        b. 12 Mar 1690, prob. Pennsylvania
        m. 1712, Pennsylvania
        d. 1758, bur. Buckingham, Pennsylvania

12

532. Edward Pearson
 1064. Lawrence Pearson
 1065. Elizabeth ?
533. Sarah Burgess
267. Margaret Smith
534. William Smith
535. Mary Croasdale, see 263
67. Elvira Cain
b. 7 Mar 1768, Edgecombe, North Carolina
d. 11 Mar 1870, Elkton, Preble Co., Ohio
134. Jonathan Cain
135. Betty Harold
17. Huldah Ruth Bolinger
b. 20 Nov 1830, Pennsylvania, prob. Huntingdon Co.
d. 18 Sep 1907, Randolph Co., IN, bur. Maxville Cem.
34. Jacob Bolinger
b. 1810, Pennsylvania, prob. Huntingdon, Co.
m. 1829/30, Pennsylvania, prob. Huntingdon, Co.
d. 27 Dec 1860, Randolph Co., IN, bur. Maxville Cem.
35. Mary S. Goshorn
b. 24 Mar 1808, Pennsylvania, prob. Huntingdon, Co.
d. 20 Oct 1875, ae 67-6-27, Randolph Co., Indiana,
  bur. Maxville Cem.
70. ? Andrew or Nicholas Goshorn
140. Johann Jacob Goshorn
b. 4 Nov 1751, York Co., Pennsylvania
m. c1774
d. 1 Jul 1833, Huntingdon Co., Pennsylvania
280. Johann Georg Gansshorn
b. 19 Mar 1725, Bammental, Heidelberg, Baden,
  Germany
m. 6 Jan 1746, Germany
d. btw. 26 Jan 1806 and 11 Apr 1806,
  Huntingdon Co., Pennsylvania
560. Johann Phillip Gansshorn
m. 9 Nov 1706
d. 2 Mar 1744, Bammental, Germany
1120. Georg Wolf Gansshorn
b. c1628
m. (2nd) 6 Jul 1674
d. 30 Nov 1691, Bammental, Germany
2240. Clauss Nicholas Gansshorn
d. 18 Jun 1668, Waldhilsbach, Germany
2241. Catherina ?

1121. Margeretha Bender
   b. 1640, Reilsheim, Heidelberg, Baden, Germany
561. Appollonia Zielger
   1122. Hans Friedrick Zielger
   1123. Anna Ursula
281. Susanna Elisabetha Buckle
   b. 22 May 1723
   562. Johann Adam Buckle
      b. c1671, Wiesenbach, Neckargemund,
      Heidelberg, Germany
      m. 6 Apr 1706
      d. 7 Sep 1737
   563. Maria Veronika Wild
      1126. Hans Valentin Wild
         b. 10 Jan 1658, Neckargemund, Germany
         d. 7 Jul 1694
      1127. Maria Catherina Kueffer
         b. Aug 1658
         d. 12 Jan 1721
141. Susanna Fink
   b. 10 Apr 1753, Little York, York Co., Pennsylvania
   d. 10 Dec 1838, Huntingdon Co., Pennsylvania
   282. Andrew Fink
   283. Mary Markell
9. Dora Elizabeth Feagans
   b. 24 Oct 1862, Randolph Co., Indiana
   d. 19 Mar 1944, Randolph Co., Indiana, bur. Maxville Cem.
   18. Robert Wesley Feagans
      b. 13 Nov 1836, Ohio, prob. Licking Co.
      m. (2nd) 17 Jul 1862, Randolph Co., Indiana
      d. 8 May 1902, Randolph Co., IN, bur. Buena Vista Cem.
      36. James H. Figins
         b. 1814, Virginia, prob. Fauquier Co.
         m. prob. Licking Co., Ohio
         d. aft. 1870
         72. James Figins
            b. 1770/80, prob. Fauquier Co., Virginia
            d. 1830/40, Ohio, prob. Licking Co.
      37. Rebecca McCracken
         b. c1817, prob. Licking Co., Ohio
         d. 1842/3, Randolph Co., Indiana
         74. Robert McCracken
            b. 1785, Virginia
            d. 23 Sep 1858, Randolph Co., Indiana, ae 72-11-13

14

75. Urith ?
   b. c1787, Maryland
   d. 1 Aug 1861, Randolph Co., Indiana, ae 74 yrs
   bur. Buena Vista Cem.
19. Rebecca Jane Moore
   b. 10 Oct 1842, Wayne Co., Indiana
   d. 20 May 1878, Randolph Co., IN, bur. Buena Vista Cem.
   38. Benjamin Moore
      b. 1810, Delaware
      m. 30 Jul 1833, Wayne Co., Indiana
      d. 1858, Randolph Co., Indiana, bur. Buena Vista Cem.
      76. David W. Moore
         b. 6 Aug 1779, Philadelphia, Pennsylvania
         d. 1845, Wayne Co., Indiana
         152. Matthew Moore
            b. Jan 1753, Pettigoe, Donegal Co., Ireland
            m. 31 Aug 1776, Ireland
            d. Feb 1836, Wayne Co., Indiana
         153. Sarah McDowell
            b. Sep 1758, Scotland
            d. Nov 1845, Wayne Co., Indiana
      77. Mary Wilkins
   39. Hannah Wright
      b. 1813, Wayne Co., Indiana
      d. 1881, Randolph Co., Indiana, bur. Buena Vista Cem.
      78. Ralph Wright
         b. 19 Aug 1788, Springfield, North Carolina
         d. after 1850, prob. Huntington Co., Indiana
         156. Ralph Wright
            b. 24 Jul 1746, Prince George Co., Maryland
            m. c1770
            d. 23 Jul 1837, 90y 11m 30d, Wayne Co., Indiana
            312. James Wright
               b. 8 Jan 1718, Maryland, prob. Prince George Co.
               d. c1760
               624. James Wright
               625. Mary ?
            313. Lucy ?
               b. c1720, Prince George Co., Maryland
         157. Hannah ?
            b. 6 Jan 1752, Springfield, North Carolina
            d. 28 Feb 1826, Wayne Co., IN, bur. Whitewater Cem.

The Addington Family

The Addington family name is of English origin and references to Addingtons in England date back to the 1300s. The name "Addington" is of Anglo-Saxon origin and means the farm of Adda's people. Records show Addingtons in Oxfordshire as early as 1339 and an early reference shows a William Addington who witnessed a deed in 1351, near Potterspury in South Northhamptonshire. The Addingtons in Northhamptonshire can be continually traced from the will of a John Addington in 1514. There were also concentrations of Addingtons in Oxfordshire (in the early 1500s) and in London in the 17th and 18th centuries. It is not clear whether these Addington families are all related or not. The most famous of the Addington families come from Potterspury and leads down through Dr. Anthony Addington (1713-1790) and his son Henry Addington (1757-1844). Henry Addington was educated at Winchester College before graduating from Oxford University in 1778. He soon went into politics and was Speaker of the House of Commons and then in 1801 was called to be Prime Minister of England. He served in that post for three years and after resigning was raised to peerage as Viscount Sidmouth. He later held several cabinet positions including the post of Home Secretary from 1812-1822. Several books have been written about this Henry Addington and his work in government. *The Annals of the Addington Family* written by E. M. G. Belfield in 1959 gives a complete story of Henry's accomplishments and much information about the Addington lines in England.

The greatest concentrations of Addingtons in England have been in Bedfordshire and Northhamptonshire but significant numbers of Addingtons have been in Berkshire, Buckinghamshire, Lincolnshire and Oxfordshire. There are references to Addingtons in London as early as the 13th century and there appears many references in the 17th and 18th centuries. The two major Addington lines in America have not been directly linked up to any of these concentrations of Addingtons. The first name Henry is common only in the Potterspury-Fringford Addingtons. There was a Henry Addington baptized in London in 1606 and also one in 1627.

16

There are five villages named Addington in central England, in Cornwall, Kent, Buckinghamshire and (2) North-hamptonshire. On the east bank of the Thames River just across from Parliament is a very short street of no more than 100 yards named Addington Street.

North American Addington Lines

The earliest Addington to appear in American records was an Isaac Addington with a first reference when he was admitted to the first church in Boston in 1640. Isaac was a surgeon and married Anne Leverett. Isaac and Anne Addington had three daughters, Ann, born 10 Mar 1647 (m. Capt Samuel Mosely), Rebecca, born 15 Jan 1649 (m. Capt. Eleazer Davenport), Sarah, born 11 Feb 1652 (m. Judge Penn Townsend), and one son Isaac, born 22 Jan 1645. Isaac was evidently wealthy and owned more than one ship which traded to the West Indies. Isaac apparently died in 1653, perhaps while at sea. His son, Isaac Addington, Jr., was also a surgeon and was married twice but died on 13 Mar 1714 without any sons so the Addington name appears to disappear from this family line. Isaac's three daughters had children and descended some well-known Boston families. The Honorable Addington Davenport, the son of Capt. Eleazer and Rebecca (Addington) Davenport, was a judge on the Massachusetts Supreme Court from 1715-1736.

A majority of the North American Addingtons are descendants of two patriarchs, Henry Addington and William Addington. They migrated or first appeared at different times and there does not seem to be any tie between them. William Addington, who was born in London about 1750, immigrated to America in about 1770, and located in Culpepper County, Virginia where he married Margaret Cromwell in 1774. An account written by his grandson, John L. Addington, Sr. says that William joined the army of Gen. Washington during the Revolutionary War and served as Commissary and was present at the surrender of Cornwallis at Yorktown on 19 Oct 1781. After the war he moved to eastern North Carolina for a short while before moving to Russell County, Virginia in 1785. It is not clear how many children William had, but he had at least two sons, William Addington, Jr. and Charles Cromwell Addington. William Addington, the immigrant, evidently died in 1805 in a hospital in Williamsburg, Virginia. His two known sons, William and Charles, settled in the Scott and

Russell County area of Virginia. Son, Charles Cromwell Addington, is the father of a large number of descendants as described in Hugh Addington's book *History of the Addington Family in United States and England* published in 1931. Charles Cromwell Addington was married three times, raised sixteen children and died at age 104. His descendants generally remained in Virginia but some spread out into Kentucky and Tennessee. The other son, William Addington, Jr. was born in 1788 in North Carolina and had five sons and died in 1860 in Russell County, Virginia.

This William Addington of Virginia and Henry Addington of South Carolina are the ancestors of a majority of the Addingtons in North America but there were other immigrants. There are other references to Addingtons such as a John Addington of Connecticut and a Stephen Addington of New York plus several others. These Addingtons may have descendants or the family name may have died out, but either way, we currently know little of their history.

Stephen Addington of New York was born in 1757 in Welford, Northampton, England. Stephen married Sarah Rhoda Brookfield, migrated to New York and they had two sons, William R. and Stephen. A grandson of Stephen, Sr., also named Stephen, later moved to northern California where he was a newspaper editor. Apparently, there were no surviving sons so the Addington name died out from this line.

John Addington of Connecticut, who was born 1715/20 and married Hannah Hobby, had three daughters: Hannah, Sarah, and Elizabeth and five sons: John who remained in Connecticut, Thomas who died young, William who moved to Nova Scotia, Henry who later located at Ballston Spa, New York and Ebenezer who was a seaman. The New York Addingtons descend from son Henry. Ebenezer Addington fought in the Revolutionary War and was among the prisoners delivered at Rhode Island on 17 Mar 1778.

One other Addington line is found starting in Maryland with a reference to a Thomas Addington recorded in 1733 and a Richard Addington found in the 1790 census. Richard Addington married Eliza Clarke in 1787 in Prince George County, Maryland. A likely brother of Richard, William Henry Addington who was born in 1774 in Maryland, moved to Ohio

County, Kentucky where he raised a large family and died sometime after 1850. Henrietta Addington, a likely sister of Richard, married Washington Phipps and moved to Ohio County, Kentucky in 1800, the same year as her brother, William Henry. About 1850, some of William Henry Addington's children moved to Warrick County in southern Indiana but there appears to be no relationship or interaction with the Addingtons in Wayne and Randolph County, Indiana.

A Joseph Clarke Addington who first appears in the 1820 census in Norfolk County, Virginia, is probably the son of William and Eliza (Clarke) Addington of Maryland. Joseph conducted a wholesale shoe business in Norfolk. Joseph, who was born about 1790, married Elizabeth Leslie and they had ten children. Several of his children continued the shoe business and eventually the business spread to Richmond, St. Louis, Baltimore and Chicago. There are records of three marriages of female Addingtons in Anne Arundel County, Maryland in 1780 (Mary m. James Douglas) and in 1788 (Sarah m. George Paulk and Dorcus married Richard White) which probably relate to the Richard Addington described above.

The 1850 Wisconsin census lists a later Addington emigrant, John Addington, occupation "shoemaker" who was born in England in about 1815. By 1860, he is in Nebraska with a family including wife Harriet (possibly a second marriage for her) and children all born in Missouri.

The 1850 Missouri census for St. Louis lists another late emigrant, William Addington, age 53, born in England, occupation "confectioner" with his wife Doretta also born in England. William was born in 1796 in Northampton, England, the son of Samuel and Ann Addington. William and his wife had two sons (William and Joseph) and two daughters (Elizabeth and Ann). Son, Joseph Addington, later moved back east and lived in Albany, New York. Daughter Elizabeth married Elijah Saunders and lived in Allegan Town, Pennsylvania.

Another late Addington emigrant was a James Addington who was born in Hull, Yorkshire, England in 1863 and immigrated to California sometime around 1880. He married there to Valentina Sepulveda and had several children.

19

An Edward Addington who was born in Apr 1851 in England shows up in the 1900 Milwaukee County, Wisconsin census with wife Carrie who was also born in England. They had at least two daughter, Daisy born in c1877 and Violetta, born in c1883, both born in Wisconsin.

Another late emigrant is a Robert Addington born Jan 1863 in England or Canada who first appears in the 1900 Minnesota census in Washington County with wife Lend, who was born in Minnesota.

Henry and Sarah Addington of South Carolina

The patriarch for our family line is Henry Addington who family history says was born in London in 1720 and immigrated to North America sometime around 1740. This is family tradition that has been passed down from generation to generation. Henry's origin in England has not been confirmed by any official records. Some have claimed that Henry's parents were John and Elizabeth Addington of Pennsylvania but no records substantiate that. Bucks County, Pennsylvania records have been thoroughly searched and researchers have probably found all that is available. Another family story says that Henry came to America with his younger brother William, that they became separated and Henry never again heard from William. This may be a later story that tries to associate Henry of South Carolina with the William Addington of Virginia. The first name Henry is common only in the Potterspury-Fringford Addingtons so if he was born in England, he may be from this line. Hugh M. Addington of Virginia published *Addington, Volume II, U.S.A. and England* in 1960. This book is primarily about Henry Addington of South Carolina and his descendants.

Some researchers have given Henry's birthyear as 1727. References to Addingtons in Pennsylvania suggest that Henry may have been born in Pennsylvania. There is a record of a John Addington appearing in Bucks County, Pennsylvania in 1693 who may be an ancestor of Henry. John Addington and wife Elizabeth are recorded in 1704 in a land transaction when he bought 100 acres in Bristol Township, Bucks County, from Edmond Lovett. Our Henry Addington may be a son or

20

grandson of this John and Elizabeth Addington of Bucks County. The first known Pennsylvania record of our Henry Addington was when he paid the so called "poor tax" in Bucks County in 1742. The "poor tax" was only paid by unmarried males so it indicates he was not married by this date. Henry Addington is recorded as witnessing a will in Bucks County, Pennsylvania in 1749. Henry is later recorded near Philadelphia where family tradition says he married Elizabeth Burson. There were Bursons in Pennsylvania, some of whom came from Scarborough in Yorkshire, England. Later Henry's wife is only referred to as Sarah so it might be a second marriage or his wife's name might have been Elizabeth "Sarah" Burson. Many Addington genealogists accept Sarah and Elizabeth as being the same person but the issue is still open to debate. Henry evidently moved his young family to Loudoun County, Virginia where records show he rented a farm in 1765. Henry Addington, moved his family to 96 District, (now) Union County, South Carolina sometime between 1768 and 1774, where he received a land grant in 1774. Records also show that James Addington bought 153 acres of land in 96 District in 1785 and John Addington bought 217 acres of land in 1786.

Henry and his family settled on a 250 acre homestead on the Enoree River between Johns Creek and Frenchmans Creek. Henry and Sarah Addington had the following children:

(1) John Addington*, b. 10 Nov 1749 (also given as 5 Oct 1745), Pennsylvania, d. 1833, Wayne Co., Indiana
    m. c1769, Mary Lamb, d. 1774
    m. 2nd 3 May 1775, Newberry Co., SC, Elizabeth Heaton
(2) James Addington, b. c1750, Pennsylvania, d. 1799, SC
    m. Jan 1776, Rebecca Garrett
(3) Henry Addington, b. c1755, d. c1807, South Carolina
(4) Bethena Addington, b. c1757
    m. bef. 1787, Union Co., South Carolina, John McClain
(5) William Addington, b. c1759, d. 7 Sep 1845, Union Co., Georgia
    m. 23 Dec 1784, Delilah Duncan
(6) Elizabeth Addington, b. c1760, d. 1810/20
(7) Martha Addington, b. c1762, d. 1787
    m. c1782, Spartanburg Co., South Carolina, George Bruton
(8) Sarah (Sally) Addington, b. 1 Mar 1767
    m. c1787, Spartanburg Co., SC, George Bruton

(9) Charlota Addington, unmarried in 1787 at time of Henry's death

Henry died on 25 Jul 1787 and was buried in Union County, South Carolina. Sarah evidently then lived with her oldest son John. She was still alive and living with John when he moved north to Indiana in 1806. She died on 14 Mar 1826 in Wayne County, Indiana at the age of 100 according to one newspaper account or age 103 according to a later account. She is probably buried at the Friends Community Cemetery in Chester, Indiana.

Henry's will was written on 1 Mar 1787 and filed in court on 3 Aug 1787. (Transcription from *Addington, A Directory of the Descendants of Henry and Sarah Addington of Union County, South Carolina*)

Will of Henry Adington

In the Name of God Amen. I Henry Addington of Union County Ninety Six District and State of South Carolina, Farmer, being sick and weak in Body but of Perfect mind Memory Thanks be to Almighty God. Therefore Calling to mind the Mortality of my body and that it is appointed for all men once to die do think fit to make this my last will and Testament in manner and form following (that is to say) Principally, and first of all I commend my soul into the Hands of Almighty who gave it me, and my Body to the Earth to be Interred in a Christian and decend like manner at the Discretion of my Ex. Nothing doubting but at the General Resurrection I shall Receive it again by the Mighty Power of God, and as touching Such worldly Estate whereby it has Pleased God to bless me with, I give and Bequeath in manner and form following

Imprimas, I order that all my Just Debts and Burial Expenses be paid.

Secondly I give and Bequeath unto my well Beloved Son William Adington all my Plantation or tract of Land Whereon I now Live Provided also that he the Wm. Adington do give his Mother thirty Bushels of Corn two Hundred Pounds of Flower and one hundred Pounds of Pork and fodor for two Cows and that yearly During her Natural life or Widow Hood.

Item. My Desire is that my Loving wife Sarrah Adington shall have three Pounds Sterling Paid to her out of my personal Estate beside one Cow and a year old the Choice of my Stock with all my household furniture during her life or widowhood and at her Decease the sd furniture to be Equally Divided between my three Daughters, Elizabeth, Sarah and Charlota Adington only Reserving my wifes Bed and Chest of Drawers shall be given to my youngest Daughter Charlota.

Item. My Desire is that my two Daughters Elizabeth and Sarah is Each of them to have a bed and a Cow at their Marriage.

Item. My Desire is that my grand son Henry Adington shall have three Pounds Sterling and it to be put to Interest until he arrives to the age of Twenty one years.

Item. I give and Bequeath unto my three sons and two Daughters John, James and Henry Adington, Bethena McClain and Martha Bruton, each and Every one of them one Shiling Sterling.

Item. My Desire is that if there should be anything Remain in paying of this Legasays as above listed, my Son Wm. Adington take it for his trouble. whome I Constitute and appoint with my trusty friend John Odell my Extors. to see to and faithfuly Comply with this my Last will and Testament. Utterly Revoking and By annulling all former wills by me made. In Witness whereof I have hereunto set my hand affixed my Seal this 1st day of March 1787.

Signed, Sealed, Published and
declared by Henry Adington to be
his last Will and Testament
in Presence of us.
   his
John Garrett
  mark
  his
Jess Rush
  mark

      his
Henry Adington
    mark

State So Carolina
Union County

23

personly came John Garrett & Jess Rush and being duly
sworn on the hold Evenglist of almight God, saith the seen
Henry Adington sign and acknowledg the with in will as
his Last wil & testament and was in his senses and proper
undr standing at the time and Each of them was subscribing
witness to the same swore subscribe to this 3th August 1787

                                          his
                                    John   Garrett
Thos Brandon J. P.   mark
                                          his
                                    Jess   Rush
                                       mark

Three of the daughters of Henry Sr. married in South Carolina.
Martha married George Bruton but evidently died in the latter
part of 1787. It is thought that George Bruton then married her
sister Sarah. Henry's daughter Elizabeth evidently did not
marry but had at least one son Benjamin, born about 1785 and
probably another son, Vardy, also born out of wedlock. She is
listed in the 1800 and 1810 census as head of her own
household. Little is known of Henry Addington, Jr. other than
he was born in 1755 and died in 1807 in South Carolina. He is
not known to have any descendants. One report says Henry
was a loyalist during the war and moved north to Canada after
the war. Daughter Charlota is mentioned in Henry's will but
no other records on her have been found. She probably died
unmarried sometime after 1787.

Of this Addington line, the name William is probably the most
popular and common male name. Henry was of course
common in the early generations but has survived only in one
or two branches to this time. John and James were also
common male names along with Joseph. Female names
which were popular were Elizabeth, Sarah and Mary. In
families which had a large number of children almost all had a
daughter named Elizabeth. Biblical names such as Abraham,
Joshua, Jesse, Abijah, Isaac and Noah were often used in the
1800s. Some of the more unusual names have been Bishop,
Nacon, Burtie Lee, Oris, Leander, Meshach, Cressie and Gilva
for men and Karenhappuch "Carrie", Lorena, Hulda, Drusila,
Elsie, Diehless and Aner for women.

William Addington, son of Henry and Sarah

William Addington was born in Pennsylvania in the year 1759 or 1760. William married after moving to South Carolina on 23 Dec 1784 to Delilah Duncan. William and his wife had twelve children and first lived in South Carolina, then North Carolina and later moved to Georgia about 1836. Their children were:

(1) Jane Addington, b. Jan 1786, South Carolina, d. 1845/8
   m. William Shettlesworth
(2) John Addington, b. 10 Nov 1787, South Carolina, d. 30 Aug 1861, Jackson Co., Georgia
   m. 1 May 1808, Buncombe Co., NC, Rachel Miller
(3) Henry Addington, b. 28 Feb 1789, South Carolina, d. 19 Apr 1878, Macon Co., North Carolina
   m. 17 Jun 1818, Mary Weaver
(4) Sarah Addington, b. c1790, South Carolina, d. bef. 2 Dec 1848, Murray Co., Georgia, m. Rev. Jeremiah Harrison
(5) Moses Addington, b. 10 Feb 1793, South Carolina, d. 11 Oct 1858, Macon Co., North Carolina
   m. 24 Oct 1814, Buncombe Co., NC, Lydia Duckett
(6) William Addington, b. 1795, Newberry Co., South Carolina, d. 1850/8 Monroe Co., MS
   m. c1814, Mary ?
   m. 2nd 15 Jan 1843, Tuscaloosa Co., AL, Mary Ann Townsend
(7) James Addington, b. 15 Feb 1799, North Carolina, d. 11 Oct 1861, Fannin Co., Georgia
   m. Winifred Woodfin
(8) March Addington, b. 30 Mar 1802, North Carolina, d. 10 Jan 1881, Union Co., Georgia
   m. Sarah Moor, m. 2nd Emily Eliza White
(9) Martha Addington, b. 30 Mar 1802, North Carolina, d. 16 Jun 1881, Coryell Co., Texas
   m. James Hicks
(10) Delilah Addington, b. 2 Mar 1805, Buncombe Co., North Carolina, d. 29 Dec 1876, Morgan Co., Alabama
   m. 17 Jan 1822, Buncombe Co., NC, John Huckaby
(11) Mary "Polly" Addington, b. 23 Dec 1808, North Carolina, d. 23 Dec 1871, Union Co., Georgia
   m. 13 Sep 1828, Macon Co., North Carolina, Drury Logan

(12) Elizabeth F. Addington, b. 1810, Buncombe Co., North
    Carolina, d. aft. 1880, Clay Co., North Carolina
    m. 11 Aug 1832, Macon Co., NC, Asbury Curtis

William Addington fought in the Revolutionary War in Col.
Thomas Brandon's South Carolina state militia. He fought in
the Battle of Ninety Six and was discharged with the rank of
Lieutenant in 1782.

SOUTHERN LIVING magazine gave the following account
of Ninety-Six, South Carolina: Ninety-Six, S. C., was an
18th century Indian trading post, site of two Revolutionary
War battles and an important stop on one of South
Carolina's earliest highways, seat of colonial government.

Ninety-Six was a village on the Cherokee Path, a trade route
between Charlestown and the upcountry of South Carolina.
Ninety-Six was exactly ninety-six miles to Keowee, the
major Cherokee town in the Blue Ridge foothills. A
trading post opened about the year 1752 and was soon
followed by businesses and plantations.

In the French and Indian War, a hastily constructed fort
withstood two Indian attacks. At the time of the
Revolutionary War, Ninety-Six was the seat of government
for Ninety-Six District. In 1775, loyalists and patriots fought
a three-day battle at Ninety-Six with inconclusive results.
Ninety-Six was occupied by the British in 1781. General
Nathaniel Greene laid siege to the British who were
defending two redoubts, but despite a twenty-eight day
battle, Gen Greene failed to dislodge the defenders and
withdrew upon the arrival of British reinforcements. The
British burned Ninety-Six when they evacuated. "Ninety-
Six played its role in the course of a few decades, took a bow
and faded away."

At his father's death, William inherited his father's farm but
later sold it and moved to the Cartoogechaye River in
Buncombe County, North Carolina. In the early 1820s, they
moved to Macon County, North Carolina. About 1836
William and Delilah moved to Blairsville, in Union County,
Georgia and spent their later years with one of their daughters
living there. William died on 7 Sep 1845 in Union County but
was buried at Franklin, Macon County, North Carolina.

William's son Moses stayed in North Carolina but several of Moses' sons moved further west. Son Lorenzo Dow Addington moved on to Arkansas and later Oklahoma. Son Moses Henley Addington later moved west and died in Texas. Another son, William Askew Addington, after the Civil War moved his family north to Wisconsin and later into Minnesota. His sons and daughters married in Wisconsin and Minnesota.

William's son, James, stayed in Georgia where he died in 1861. However, James' son, James M. Addington, first settled in Arkansas and later moved to Idaho.

William's son, March Addington, stayed in Georgia but March's son, John March Addington, moved to Colorado about 1870/1. William's son William who married twice, raised five children and moved to Mississippi. William's son, Henry, who married Mary Weaver had a son Jacob Weaver Addington who moved his family to Alabama sometime before 1853. A majority of the southern Addingtons appear to be descended from this William Addington with most of the remainder being descendants of his brother James.

James Addington, son of Henry and Sarah

James Addington, the second son of the immigrant Henry, married in South Carolina to Rebecca Garrett and they had four sons and six daughters. Their children were:
(1) Thomas Addington, b. 12 Feb 1777, 96 District, SC
    m. Mary Stubbs
(2) Mary Addington, b. 30 Sep 1778, 96 District, SC
    m. ? Roberts
(3) Sarah Addington, b. 6 Sep 1781, nfi
(4) Henry Addington, b. 2 Jul 1784, 96 District, SC, d. 18 Aug
    1855, Miami County, Indiana
    m. 29 Mar 1804, Cane Creek MM, SC, Elizabeth Randel
(5) Rebecca Addington, b. 10 Jan 1787, nfi
(6) Martha Addington, b. 28 Aug 1789, 96 District, South
    Carolina, d. aft. 1850, Madison Co., Arkansas
    m. 4 Jun 1812, Kentucky, John H. William
(7) James Addington, Jr., b. 15 Jan 1792, 96 District, South
    Carolina, d. 25 Oct 1869, St. Claire Co., Missouri
    m. c1818, Elizabeth ?

m. 2nd 18 Nov 1855, Ann Wright
(8) Karenhappuch (Carrie) Addington, b. 5 Mar 1795, SC
    m. James Brown
(9) John Addington, b. 2 May 1797, South Carolina
    m. South Carolina, Rachel Miller
(10) Rachel Addington, b. 1798, South Carolina
    m. John McElreath

Family stories say that James Addington first fought in the Royalists forces but then resigned and fought with the Revolutionary Army. James was the first of the sons of the immigrant Henry to die. In his will signed 28 Jul 1798 and probated 3 Feb 1801, James' brother John was appointed guardian of his younger children and executor of his estate. When John moved North to Indiana in 1806, he took the younger children of his brother James with him.

The oldest children of James Addington, Thomas, Mary and Sarah were of age when he died and stayed behind in South Carolina. Daughter Martha ended up in Kentucky where she married in 1812. The next son, Henry, married on 29 Mar 1804 at the Cane Creek Monthly Meeting in South Carolina to Elizabeth Randel. He moved north with his uncle John and settled in Darke County, later Butler County, Ohio just across the state line from Wayne County, Indiana. Henry and Elizabeth (Randel) Addington had the following children: Rebecca, Sarah ("Sally"), Lydia, Hannah, Thomas, Martha Ann, Mary Ann and William Sherman. Around 1837, Henry moved his family to Grant County, Indiana where most of his children married. Henry died on 18 Aug 1855 in Miami County, Indiana. His son Thomas married in Grant County on 27 Feb 1840 to Mary Ann Mason. They had ten children: Mary Ann, Isaac, Nathan, Elizabeth, William, Edith ("Callie"), Milton, Rebecca, Lydia and Malinda. Thomas died in 1896 in Henry County, Indiana. Apparently most of the Addingtons who lived in the Indiana counties of Grant, Henry and Howard are from this line.

James' son, James Addington, Jr., married first Elizabeth, family name unknown, and settled in Darke County, Ohio. About 1855 he moved to Missouri where he remarried twice and later died in 1869 at Osceola, St. Claire Co., Missouri. His grandson William married in Missouri but later moved back to Darke County, Ohio.

James' son, John Addington, was born on 2 Mar 1797 in Union County, South Carolina and moved north with his uncle in 1806. However, by 1824, he had moved back to South Carolina and soon after was married to Rachel Miller.

John Addington, oldest son of Henry and Sarah

John Addington, the eldest son of the patriarch Henry, was born in Pennsylvania before the family moved south to South Carolina. His birth date have been given as both 5 Oct 1745 and 10 Nov 1749. John Addington is said to have served in the Revolutionary Army in North Carolina. His brothers, William and James, have been confirmed as serving in the War and fighting at the Battle of Ninety-Six which took place in 1781. There is no direct evidence that John served in the revolutionary forces but he is listed as a Revolutionary War soldier in the book entitled *Roster of Soldiers and Patriots of the American Revolution Buried in Indiana* by Margaret R. Water. John first married about 1769 to Mary Lamb, a Quaker, as recorded in the Bush River Monthly Meeting in Newberry County, South Carolina. John and Mary had two children, William, born 14 Apr 1770, and Alice, born 8 Mar 1773. Alice in one record is written Alcie so that may be the correct spelling. She married a Garrett at the Cane Creek Monthly Meeting in Union County, South Carolina, raising her family there and died sometime before 1833.

After the death of Mary (Lamb) Addington, John married at the Bush River Monthly Meeting in South Carolina on 3 May 1775 to Elizabeth Heaton. The Rev. Thomas Addington in his 1910 address on Addington family history says that Elizabeth Heaton was the daughter of Joseph Heaton of Bucks County, Pennsylvania and gives his birth date as 3 Feb 1699. The same reference gives her mother as Leada or Lydia Smith, a daughter of William and Mary (Croasdale) Smith of Wrightstown, Pennsylvania. There is a marriage record of Joseph Heaton to a Lydia Smith in 1730 in Bucks County, Pennsylvania. There were two different branches of Heaton families in Bucks County, Pennsylvania around 1700. One family was of a John Heaton who came to America in about 1685, settled in Bucks County and had one known son, also named John, who was born in 1690. This son John was in Burlington, New Jersey by

29

1718. The second Heaton family was descended from a Robert Heaton who was born between 1640 and 1645 in Yorkshire, England. He married in England about 1666 and immigrated to America in 1682. He became a large land owner in Bucks County, served in the Pennsylvania Assembly in 1698 and 1700 and died in 1717 in Bucks County. He had at least three known sons but Joseph was not listed among them. Joseph Heaton, our ancestor who was born in 1699 in Bucks County, is probably descended from this Robert Heaton family since a Robert Heaton was present at the marriage of William Smith and Mary Croasdale.

Joseph Heaton's wife, Lydia Smith, was one of the younger daughters of William and Mary (Croasdale) Smith and was probably born about 1710. According to the Josiah Smith history of Bucks County, William Smith came from Yorkshire, England as a young man in 1684 and bought land at Wrightstown, on which he spent the rest of his life. He married on 20 Sep 1690 to Mary Croasdale, the daughter of Thomas and Agnes Croasdale. William and Mary (Croasdale) Smith had eight children, including Lydia. The oldest daughter, Margaret, born 20 Aug 1691, married on 25 Sep 1712 to Enoch Pearson of Solebury. Their daughter Elizabeth married John Townsend whose granddaughter Celia later married into the Addington line. Mary (Croasdale) Smith died in 1716 and is buried in the old graveyard at Logtown. William Smith remarried and had seven children by his second wife Marcy.

John and Elizabeth (Heaton) Addington had seven children:
(1) Joseph Addington*, b. 21 Jul 1776, 96 District, South
    Carolina, d. 20 Feb 1836, Randolph Co., Indiana, bur.
    Sparrow Creek Cemetery
    m. 21 Dec 1799, South Carolina, Rachel Randel, d. c1806
    m. 2nd 22 Dec 1808, Preble Co., Ohio, Celia Townsend
(2) John Addington, b. 13 Oct 1777, 96 District, South Carolina,
    d. 1857 (will probated 15 Oct 1857), Hancock Co., Indiana,
    bur. Wayne Co., Indiana
    m. 1st ?
    m. 2nd 25 Jan 1837, Wayne Co., Indiana, Rebecca Thornton
    (Johnson)
(3) Thomas Addington, b. 1 Dec 1778, 96 District, SC, d. 8 Mar
    1839, Randolph Co., Indiana, bur. Sparrow Creek Cemetery
    m. 11 Oct 1807, Mary Smith

30

(4) Mary Addington, b. 2 Nov 1780, South Carolina, d. 12 Mar
1866, Hancock Co., Indiana
m. 26 Sep 1801, Newberry Co., SC, Thomas Roberts
(5) Sarah Addington, b. 9 Dec 1783, South Carolina, d. 26 Aug
1814, Wayne Co., Indiana
m. 6 Nov 1806, Phineas Roberts
(6) Elizabeth Addington, b. 9 Feb 1787, South Carolina, d. 8 Mar
1841, Wayne Co., Indiana
m. 1 Oct 1807, Warren Co., Ohio, James Martindale
(7) James Addington, b. 6 Feb 1789, South Carolina, d. Oct 1859,
Anderson Co., Kansas
m. 15 Jun 1809, Preble Co., Ohio, Nancy Lewallyn

John and Elizabeth (Heaton) Addington moved their family to
Indiana from South Carolina sometime in 1806. Some say that
they first moved to Butler County, Ohio but this is probably not
so. Cane Creek Monthly Meeting records in South Carolina
show John and his family received a certificate of transfer on 20
Sep 1806. John did settle his family on the Whitewater River
north of Richmond in Wayne County, Indiana. John entered
on land on four quarter sections, the first on 4 Dec 1806 and last
on 3 May 1808. John's name shows up in the records of the
Miami Monthly Meeting on 11 Jun 1807 and later in the
records of the West Branch Monthly Meeting on 22 Aug 1807.
John Addington's name along with his son Joseph, appears in
the 1807 special census of the Northwest Territories (recorded 4
Mar 1807) so he was with the first wave of immigrants to settle
in Indiana. John and Elizabeth Addington later sold one acre
of their land to the Society of Friends for the purpose of
building a meeting house. The meeting house was built and
along side was a cemetery. Today only a few grave markers
still exist from this Quaker church. John Addington evidently
also brought the younger children of his deceased brother
James with him. Most of John's children married in Wayne
County. Several of James' children also married in Wayne
County or just across the border in Darke or Preble County,
Ohio. One early source listed John as dying at Chester, Indiana
in 1819, however this is incorrect. The 1820 and 1830 census
data imply that he was probably living with the family of his
youngest son James. The 1820 census shows a 70-80 year old
male and a 70-80 year old female in James' household so this
must be John and his second wife, Elizabeth. The 1830 census
shows a male age 80-90 but does not show an older female in
the household so Elizabeth must have died during this decade.

John Addington's will was recorded in Wayne County records on 30 Aug 1833 so he must have died shortly before this date. His will reads:

Will of John Addington Deceased

Knowing that it is appointed of God that all men have to dey being weak in body but in full strength of mind, have thought right to make this my last Will and Testament. That is to say that my sons John & Thomas Addington are to settle my estate as Executors. That they collect & pay my son William Addington the sum of twenty dollars, that they pay to my daughter Alice Garrett's children one dollar each if they call for it, that my son Joseph Addington have the oldest fifty dollar note. That my son John Addington have the next oldest fifty dollar note. That they pay my daughter Mary Roberts twenty dollars. That they pay my daughter Sarah Roberd's children five dollars each. That they pay my daughter Elizabeth Martendel eighty dollars, that they pay my son James Addington twenty dollars. if after filling the above there remains any balance of my estate that my sons John and Thomas Addington divide the balance equal between themselves. signd and sealed in the presents of us 30th of 8th month 1833.

Phinehas Roberds   John Addington   Seal
Jesse Walker

It is believed that John and Elizabeth (Heaton) Addington are buried in the Quaker Cemetery on the edge of their land along with John's mother Sarah.

Of John's daughters, Alice married a Garrett and evidently stayed in South Carolina. The Garrett children are mentioned in John's will in 1833 so Alice must have deceased by 1833. Daughter Mary married Thomas Roberts and died in 1866 in Hancock County, Indiana. Daughter Sarah married Phineas Roberts in 1806 but died later in 1814. Phineas Roberts (spelled Roberds in the will) was a witness to John's will. Daughter Elizabeth married John Martindale and had two sons and later died in Wayne County in 1841. Descendents of John and Elizabeth (Addington) Martindale moved to Utah and had many descendents.

The 1830 census shows the five sons of John still clustered in Wayne Township in Wayne County. In the early 1830s four of the sons of John Addington moved their families from Wayne County to Randolph County as new lands were being opened. Franklin Township records show that James Addington first entered on land in section 10 on 20 Sep 1828 but he probably did not occupy it until later. James Addington entered on additional land in Franklin Township on 17 Mar 1832 as did a John Addington, probably a son of William, on 28 Apr 1832. James and his brother William probably moved into Franklin Township in 1832. Thomas Addington entered on land in section 26 in Franklin Township on 27 May 1834 and Jesse Addington, a son of Thomas, entered on land in section 22 on 25 Jun 1834. The following year, James entered on more land in section 34 on 25 Apr 1835, Joseph entered on land in section 34 on 12 Aug 1835 and Thomas entered on more land in section 35 on 19 Aug 1835. Thomas Addington also entered on some land in White River Township south of Maxville. Thomas and his brother Joseph probably moved into Randolph County sometime in 1835.

The fifth son of John Addington, John Addington, Jr., born in 1777 apparently stayed behind in Wayne County since he shows up there in the 1840 and 1850 census, but he later moved to Hancock County before dying there in 1857. In the 1830s and 1840s there appears to have been significant movement from Wayne to Randolph County but family ties were still strong to relatives remaining in Wayne County. The 1850 and 1860 census records show many Addington families in Randolph County and a few in Wayne County. The 1874 Plat map of Randolph County shows the Addington families clustering in the same areas in Franklin Township and in White River Township. The 1880 Soundex to the Indiana Census shows that most of the Addingtons had moved out of Wayne County and into Randolph County or into other surrounding counties.

From all the evidence gathered to date, it appears that all of the Addingtons in Wayne and Randolph Counties are descended from John Addington, the eldest son of Henry and Sarah Addington of South Carolina. Two nephews of John, Henry and James, sons of his brother James, moved into the adjoining counties of Ohio where they raised their families. Henry, the son of John's brother James, eventually died in

Miami County, Indiana in 1855 and some of his descendants moved into Grant and Howard Counties, including one line which still lives in Kokomo, Indiana. James lived in Darke County, Ohio but eventually moved to Missouri where he died in 1869. Some of his family remained in Darke County and some evidently moved back there from Missouri. No evidence has been found that indicates that any of the descendants of the brothers Henry and James ever settled in Wayne or Randolph County.

William Addington, son of John and Mary

William Addington, son of John and Mary (Lamb) Addington, was born 14 Apr 1770 and married twice. His first wife's name was Elizabeth, family name unknown, and he married her about 1790 in South Carolina. His family probably moved to Wayne County, Indiana along with his father John in 1806, although for some reason he does not appear in the 1807 census of the territory. William is listed in the 1820 and 1830 censuses as living in Wayne Township in Wayne County. William moved to Randolph County, Indiana sometime between 1832 and 1834. He was a miller by trade and soon bought a mill near Ridgeville. The mill had originally been built by a Meshach Lewallyn (most commonly spelled as Lewallyn but also spelled as Lewellen, Lewellan, Lewallen, or Lewellyn) who was the first settler in Franklin Township in about 1817. Lewallyn build this mill in 1819 and it was the first grist-mill built in the county. After buying the mill, William operated it with his son Joab who continued to operate the mill after his father's death. The mill is sometimes referred to as the "Whipple Mill" after a later owner. William and John (presumedly his son) Addington helped lay out the town of Ridgeville. They were proprietors of one section east and west of Main Street, recorded in 1837. The lots did not sell for many years and the town consisted of only a few houses until 1853 when a railroad project was announced. The town grew rapidly after 1858 when the railroad was completed.

William's wife Elizabeth evidently died sometime before 1840 because he married a second time on 23 Nov 1840 in Randolph County to Sarah Norton. Sarah Norton was probably an older widow since Maxville Cemetery records lists a Sarah Addington, w/o William Addington as dying in 1864, age 76.

34

This would have made her birth year, 1788, or age 52 when she married William.

William and Elizabeth Addington had the following children:
(1) Joshua (or Joseph) Addington, b. c1790, SC, d. c1848
    m. 28 Jan 1814, Wayne Co., Indiana, Rebecca Morgan
(2) Bishop Addington, b. 1795, SC, d. bef. 1840, Wayne Co., IN
    m. 15 Apr 1816, Wayne Co., Indiana, Betsy Cain
(3) Patsy Addington, b. 1800, South Carolina
    m. 23 Jan 1820, Wayne Co., Indiana, Samuel Prevoe
(4) John Addington, b. 1802, South Carolina, d. 1 May 1849,
    Randolph Co., Indiana
    m. 12 Sep 1822, Wayne Co., Indiana, Lucretia Roberts
    m. 2nd 18 Apr 1845, Randolph Co., Indiana, Louisa (Gray)
    Atkinson
(5) Jacob Addington, nfi
(6) William Addington, b. 1807, d. 1860
    m. 1828, Sudie (?Mary) White, d. bef. 1850
    m. 2nd 18 Oct 1853, Nancy Rash
(7) Elsie Addington, m. 1830, James Seagraves
(8) Elizabeth Addington, b. 1810, d. 1877, Winchester, Indiana
    m. 22 Mar 1832, Wayne Co., Indiana, Martin Seagraves
(9) Joab Addington, b. 1814, Wayne Co., Indiana, d. 6 Feb 1853,
    Randolph Co., Indiana
    m. 2 Feb 1843, Randolph Co., Indiana, Elizabeth Edwards
    m. 2nd 17 Jun 1847, Randolph Co., IN, Barbara Harshman

William Addington's death date has been reported as both 20 Nov 1844 and 1 Jan 1845 in Randolph County. The only children listed in William's will were John and Joab along with his second wife Sarah.

William's oldest son Joshua or sometimes listed as Joseph was born about 1790 and married Rebecca Morgan on 28 Jan 1814 in Wayne County. He raised his family in Wayne County as shown by the 1830 and 1840 census before dying in 1848. His widow Rebecca is shown in the 1850 census living in Delaware County with three children. Hugh M. Addington's 1960 book lists seven children, Wiley William, David, Betsy, Nancy, Anderson, Seravie and Jane, but they are difficult to find in county records. Son Jonathan moved to Wabash County where he is found in the 1850 census. Son Wiley Addington is also found in Wabash County, Indiana in the 1860 census. Son David Addington married 1 May 1859 to Eliza Jane Thompson in Wayne County, Indiana. He married second to Martha Ann Guard and eventually moved west to Kansas, later to Washington state, living to an old age and dying in Washington in 1922. Daughter Betsy married Richard (or Richmond) West and they moved to Iowa.

William's second son Bishop was born about 1795 in South Carolina and married Betsy Cain on 15 Apr 1816 in Wayne County, Indiana. Evidently the Cain family moved from South Carolina to Wayne County, Indiana about the same time as the Addington family. Bishop and Betsy (Cain) Addington had six known children: Nancy, Samuel, Abijah, Cane, Leander and Bishop, Jr. Bishop died sometime before 1840 since his wife Betsy is shown in both the 1840 and 1850 as head of the household. Of their children, Nancy married William Parsons and stayed in Wayne County. Abijah married twice in Wayne County, first to Huldah Moore and then to Ann Adams in 1850. Abijah and his second wife Ann had six children, two of whom died as young adults, while the other four, Henry, Virginia, Fred and Frank, married and raised families in Wayne County. Abijah died in 1870 while his second wife Ann survived till 1916. There is very little data on Bishop's sons Samuel, Cane and Leander. Leander evidently did not marry and died in Richmond, Indiana in 1888. Bishop's youngest son, Bishop, Jr., married on 12 Oct 1848 to Delilah Weyl. They had eight children: Elizabeth Jane, Sarah Caroline, Martha Alice, Mary Ann, Edward B., Charles Louis, Theodore, and Mirrilla May. Bishop Addington, Jr. moved his family to Iowa about 1860 since he is shown in the census there and his son Charles Louis was born in Iowa. Evidently things did not work out there since he moved back to Wayne County before 1867 and his children married there. Bishop, Jr. and his wife Deliah both died in 1904 in Jay County, Indiana.

William's daughter Patsy, born about 1800, married Samuel Prevoe on 23 Jan 1820 in Wayne County. The family can not be found in later censuses so they either moved off or died. We have little record of William's son Jacob so he either died young or is an error in an earlier reference.

William's son, John Addington born 1802, first married on 12 Sep 1822 to Lucretia Roberts in Wayne County. John migrated with his family to Randolph County as shown by the 1840 census. John and Lucretia had eight children from 1824 to

1842: Bishop, Benjamin, Kathern, William, Eliza, Drusila, Nacon and John, Jr. Lucretia must have died in or soon after 1842 since John remarried to Louisa (Gray) Atkinson on 18 Apr 1845. John and Louisa had two daughters, Susan and Miriam. John died on 1 May 1849 and Louisa is shown to be head of the household in the 1850 census. Louisa apparently married second to one of John's older sons, Benjamin in 1852. Most of the older children of this John Addington stayed in Wayne County.

William's next son, William, Jr. born 1807, married Sudie White in 1828. They had six known children: Joel, Bishop, William Louis, Matilda, Elizabeth and Zachariah. William's wife died before 1850 since in 1850, he was living with two of his children in the household of Martin Seagraves who married his sister. William probably married second to Nancy Rash on 18 Oct 1853 in Randolph County. They had one son, William, born in 1855. William died in early 1860 and unfortunately his widow Nancy and son William were living in the Randolph County poor house according to the 1860 census. Of the other children of William, Jr., Matilda died young. The oldest son Joel, moved west to Oregon by 1860 where he married Mary Jane Lewallyn. Joel and Mary had five children, all born in Oregon. The second son of William, Bishop, moved to Tazewell County, Illinois where he married Lucinda Falcor in 1857. They had nine children all born in Illinois. The third son of William, William Louis, married in 1865 to Elizabeth Ullom and they had eight children. The youngest son of William, Zachariah Addington, married in 1872 to Susan Lefevre and lived in Winchester, dying there about 1908.

William Addington, Sr.'s next daughter, Elizabeth, was born in 1810 and married on 22 Mar 1832 to Martin Seagraves and they had six children, William, Martha, James, Sarah, Anna and John. Elizabeth's sister Elsie had earlier married James Seagraves, a brother to Martin. Numerous descendants of Martin and Elizabeth (Addington) Seagraves still live in Randolph County.

William's youngest son, Joab, was born on 29 Aug 1814 and moved with his father to Randolph County. He married Elizabeth Edwards on 2 Feb 1843 and they had one child Polly (sometimes called Molly). Elizabeth died sometime around

1846 because Joab married second Barbara Ann Harshman on 17 Jun 1847. Joab and Barbara had four children: Elizabeth, Malinda Alice, John and Joanna. Joab died on 6 Feb 1853. Barbara later married a second time to John Wilson. Joab and Barbara's son John later migrated to Iowa where he married Mary Elizabeth Roberts in 1873. They had two sons: Joab and John Calvin. John died in 1875/6. The descendants of Joab and John Calvin Addington later migrated through Colorado, Idaho and into Alberta. Mrs. Joanne Moulton of Hussar, Alberta is a descendant of this Joab Addington.

John Addington, third son of John, Sr.

Of the five sons of John Addington, we know the least about John Addington, Jr., who was born on 13 Oct 1777 in South Carolina. We do not know much about John's first wife but after she died, John married second Rebekah Johnson Thornton in Wayne County on 25 Jan 1837. John's other four brothers, William, Joseph, Thomas and James all moved north from Wayne County into Randolph County, Indiana in the early 1830s but John appears to have stayed behind in Wayne County as indicated by the 1840 and 1850 censuses. The 1820 Indiana census shows John's family to be 2M<10, 3M10-16, 3F<10, 1F16-26 and wife. The 1830 Indiana census shows John Addington's family to be 1M<5, 1M5-10, 2M10-15, 1F<5, 1F10-15, 1F15-20 and wife 40-50. The 1840 Wayne County, Indiana census shows a John Addington, age 60-70, which fits his recorded birthyear of 1777. The 1850 Indiana census shows John, age 72 with wife Rebecca age 55, living next to his son, John, Jr. John evidently moved out of Wayne County after 1850 into Hancock County where he died in 1857 with his will dated on 10 Jan 1854 and probated on 15 Oct 1857. Rebecca died on 21 Aug 1862 and is buried in the Maxville Cemetery in Randolph County. John's will lists sons Noah, John, Jr., Morgan, Charles, Silas and daughters Delila Betsey, Mary Eliza and Rebecca. The will also lists Martin S. Addington but it does not specifically say he is a son but it is assumed. The following were known children of John Addington:

(1) Silas Addington, b. 1800/10, d. 1836, Wayne Co., Indiana
   m. 17 Nov 1828, Wayne Co., Indiana, Polly Davis
(2) Delilah Addington
   m. 1 Apr 1819, Wayne Co., Indiana, James Smith
(3) Morgan Addington, b. c1805, d. c1843
   m. 12 Sep 1822, Wayne Co., Indiana, Jane Mendenhall

(4) Charles Addington, b. c1808, d. aft. 1860
    m. 10 Feb 1825, Wayne Co., Indiana, Elizabeth Hunt
(5) Mary Addington
    m. 11 Dec 1828, Wayne Co., Indiana, Thomas Jordan
(6) Rebecca Addington, b. ? c1816, Ohio,
    m. 28 Feb 1833, Wayne Co., Indiana, James Walker, b. 1816
(7) Noah Addington, b. 1818, Wayne Co., Indiana, d. Feb 1863,
    Jefferson Barracks, Missouri
    m. 18 Jun 1837, Wayne Co., Indiana, Miriam Roberts
    m. 2nd 5 Jun 1856, Ringgold Co., Iowa, Mary Jane Garrett
    m. 3rd 4 Jul 1861, Phoebe Ann Roberts
(8) John Addington, Jr., b. c1820, d. 1908
    m. 3 Mar 1844, Sabrah Ann Sails
(9) Martin S. Addington, b. 1823
    m. 19 Sep 1844, Nancy King

There were probably more daughters, but they were married before 1850 so we can not confirm their names and they may have died before John's will in 1857. The following list of Addington females who can not be related to other Addington families were married in Wayne County and are probably daughters of John Addington: Betsey (m. 1822, Ichabod Gifford), Alice (m. 1825, James Graver) and Louisa (m. 1833, Nason Roberts).

Most of the sons of John did not stay in Wayne County but spread out in many directions. Son John, Jr. was an exception and stayed in Wayne County, marrying twice and raising several children before dying in 1908 at Chester, Indiana. One son of John, Jr., Benton C. Addington, married Martha Benham and moved to Cincinnati. On 6 Apr 1891, their daughter Sarah was born in Cincinnati. Sarah Addington went to Earlham College where she received a A. B. degree in 1912. She married Howard Reid on 20 Mar 1917 and they later moved to New York City. Sarah, writing under her maiden name, Sarah Addington, wrote a series of children's book which became quite popular in their day. Her books were: *The Boy Who Lived in Pudding Lane* (1922), *The Pied Piper in Pudding Lane* (1923), *The Great Adventure of Mrs. Santa Claus* (1923), *Round the Year in Pudding Lane* (1924), *Pudding Lane People* (1926), *Jerry Juddikins* (1926), *Tommy Tingle Tangle* (1927), *Grammar Town* (1927), *Dance Team* (1931) and *Hound of Heaven* (1935). Sarah Addington is listed in *Who's Who in America 1897-1942*. Sarah died on 7 Nov 1940.

Noah Addington, son of John Addington, moved to Iowa, later to Missouri where he died in 1863. Noah's son, Branson, moved on to Iowa and was in Jefferson County, Kansas in 1870. A biography of Branson Addington and his son Alexander Addington in a Kansas history book says that Noah and three of his sons including Branson enlisted during the Civil War in the Fourth Iowa Regiment. Its says that Branson was the only one of the four to survive the war. Noah is reported to have died at Jefferson Barracks near St. Louis. Two of Noah's sons, Joseph Clinton Addington, who died 22 Jul 1865 in Kentucky and Sylvester H. Addington, who died 27 Feb 1863 in Arkansas are probably the other brothers referred to in the biography.

Morgan's descendants later appeared in Hamilton County, Indiana. A son of Charles, Morgan Jr., born in 1827, later moved to Missouri where he died sometime after 1900. Charles' descendants moved to Grant County, Indiana while Martin's descendants apparently moved to Howard County, Indiana.

Thomas Addington, fourth son of John

Thomas Addington, son of John Addington, married on 11 Oct 1807 in South Carolina to Mary Smith. He may have moved north later than his father since his family is not listed in the 1807 special census. We know he was in Indiana by 1814 but he does not appear in the 1820 Indiana census (probably was just missed). Thomas probably moved to Wayne County, Indiana about 1808 and then migrated to Randolph County about 1834/35. Tucker's History of Randolph County lists one of Thomas' sons George as having moved in 1832 so they may have arrived in that year. Thomas entered on land in Franklin Township but he may have also taken some land in White River Township south of Maxville. Thomas and his wife were members of the Society of Friends. Their names are in the records of the Friends Monthly Meeting at Chester in Wayne County and the Sparrow Creek Monthly Meeting in Randolph County. Thomas Addington, Sr. died 8 Mar 1839 in Randolph County and his wife died on 25 Apr 1845. They are buried in the old abandoned Sparrow Creek Cemetery, located in section 33, of White River Township. The sons and daughters of Thomas and Mary (Smith) Addington stayed in Randolph

County and have many descendants there. Their children were:

(1) Hannah Addington, b. 15 Nov 1808, d. 1854, dnm
(2) Matilda Addington, b. 29 Aug 1810, d. 15 Mar 1811
(3) David Smith Addington, b. 24 Feb 1812, d. 25 Feb 1813
(4) Jesse Addington, b. 22 Jun 1814, Indiana, d. 1891
    m. 17 Jul 1834, Wayne Co., Indiana, Margaret Sullivan
(5) James Addington, b. 12 Jul 1816, d. 1881
    m. 12 May 1836, Randolph Co., Indiana, Susan Kelly
(6) Mercy Addington, b. 12 May 1819, d. 1894/5
    m. Littleberry Diggs, d. Dec 1849
    m. 2nd Joseph Hawkins
(7) Joseph Addington, b. 12 Oct 1820, d. 12 Oct 1871
    m. 30 Oct 1845, Wayne Co., Indiana, Susan Sullivan
(8) George Addington, b. 19 Sep 1822, d. 1885
    m. 6 Apr 1854, Priscilla Horn
    m. 2nd 11 Jul 1857, Priscilla Clinton
(9) Mary Addington, b. 23 Jan 1825, d. 20 Jun 1896
    m. William Roberts
(10) Elizabeth Addington, b. 28 Sep 1827, d. 25 Dec 1903
    m. 26 Sep 1851, Randolph Co., Indiana, Marshall Diggs
(11) Thomas Addington, b. 5 Dec 1829, d. 1 Feb 1912
    m. 8 Feb 1851, Randolph Co., IN, Martha Ann Hughes
    m. 2nd 11 Sep 1887, Margaret (Ellis) Painter
(12) d. in infancy
(13) d. in infancy

Thomas' son, Jesse, born 22 Jun 1814, in Wayne County, married 17 Jul 1834 in Wayne County to Margaret Sullivan. They moved to Randolph County and had two sons, Thomas, born 1836, died 1854 and James M., born 1839. James M. Addington married on 11 Jul 1857 to Henrietta Holloway and they had two sons Solomon and Thomas Jefferson. James M. Addington later moved to Jay County, Indiana.

Thomas' son, James born 12 Jul 1816, married on 22 Jun 1836 in Randolph County to Susan Kelly. James and Susan had children: Mary, William S., George Wesley and John Kelly. James died in 1881 at the age of 65. George Wesley Addington was a farmer in Randolph County while John Kelly Addington moved to Jay County. The third son, William S. Addington, married in Randolph County on 28 Aug 1867 to Mary Underwood. They had three sons and later moved west to Kansas, although their sons later returned to Indiana.

Thomas' daughter, Mercy, born 12 May 1819, married Littleberry Diggs in Randolph County. They had at least one son, Calvin, born 13 Sep 1843, but unfortunately Littleberry died in mid age in December 1849. In 1862 during the Civil War, Calvin Diggs enlisted in Company A of the 84th Indiana Infantry. At the Battle of Chickamauga, he was captured by the rebels while trying to help a wounded comrade. He was first transferred to Libby Prison in Richmond for one month, then to a prison at Danville, Virginia for five months and then he was transferred to the notorious prison at Andersonville, Georgia. He spent eight months there surviving horrible conditions. He was exchanged in Nov 1864 and rejoined his regiment after a 40 day furlough. He was mustered out with his regiment at the end of the war. After the war he taught school for three or four years and then served as a county deputy and then as county auditor and clerk. In 1880, he was appointed an Assistant Attorney General for the 6th and 11th Congressional districts. He married on 28 Oct 1877 to Harriet Edgar and they had two children: Bessie (who died young) and Nellie.

Thomas' son, Joseph, born 12 Oct 1820, is the ancestor of a considerable number of Addingtons still residing in and around Randolph County. Joseph married on 31 Oct 1845 in Wayne County to Susan Sullivan. Joseph and Susan Addington had the following children: Calvin, Martha Ellen, Robert Nelson, Franklin Madison, Mary Jamima, George Emerson, Carrie and Alvin Waldo. Of these children Carrie died young. Martha Ellen Addington married Elias Wright.

Joseph's son, Robert Nelson Addington, married Rebecca Jane Wright and they had children: George Elvin (the Rev. George), Charles Wesley, Luther Elsworth, Russell Wilson and Lena Gertrude. This Rev. George Addington, son of Robert Nelson Addington and grandson of Joseph Addington, collected genealogical information on the Addingtons. His research was the basis of much of the information on the Indiana Addingtons published in Hugh M. Addington's second book on the Addington family. The Rev. George Addington often told a story about the meaning of the name Addington. He said that the base of the name was Adda, presumingly a person's name. As there got to be more descendants, the name became Adding and when there were even more descendants, the "ton" was added on to become Addington. There is probably no basis for this interpretation but it makes an interesting story. Patricia Waltz of Portland, Indiana and Harold W. Addington of Aurora, Colorado are descendants of this Addington line.

Joseph's son, Franklin Madison Addington, married Anna Vanilla Wright and had seven children: John "Rufus", Harry, Hattie, Earl, Esta, Willard Clayton and Lyra. Franklin Madison Addington's children also had numerous children and many descendents still reside in Randolph County. Chester Luther Addington of Westerville, Ohio is a descendant of Willard Clayton and has done genealogy on the early Addington family, both in America and in England.

Joseph's son, George Emerson Addington, married Indiana Rose Bolinger and was an influential farmer in Randolph County but died with no issue.

Joseph's son, Alvin Waldo Addington, married on 4 Apr 1893 to Laura May Allen and they had one son, Archie. Alvin Waldo died soon after that. Archie Addington married in 1914 at Saratoga, Indiana to Mary Hitchcock and they later lived in Bloomington, Indiana, before migrating to California. Archie died in Fresno, California, in 1972. Their son William and daughter Madonna still live in California.

Thomas' son, George Addington, was born on 19 Sep 1822 and married Priscilla Horn on 6 Apr 1854 in Randolph County. She died soon after and he married second Priscilla Clinton. They had two children: Mercy Ellen and Nora. George operated a farm in Franklin Township and served as a Township Trustee from 1878-1880.

Thomas' daughter, Mary, born in 1825, married William Roberts and they had fourteen children. They later moved to Hamilton County where Mary died in 1895 and William in 1896. There are many descendents but they have not been traced. Thomas' daughter, Elizabeth, born in 1827, married Marshall Diggs and they had nine children. Marshall Diggs was for many years the pastor of the Congregational Church at Pisgah near Fort Recovery, Ohio.

Thomas' youngest son, Thomas, Jr. married on 8 Feb 1851 to Martha Ann Hughes and they had five children: Zeruiah, Emerson, Alfred M., Calvin T. and Jesse M. Martha died and Thomas remarried in 1887 to Margaret (Ellis) Painter. Thomas, Jr., often referred to as Rev. Thomas, was an influential minister and community leader in Randolph County. The 1914 Randolph County History gives the following information about Thomas:

"Thomas's parents settled on a farm near Maxville, where his boyhood days were passed on a farm, and where he went to school in one of the old-fashioned rude, log structures. Later he became a member of the Union Literary Institute, near Spartanburg, Ind., afterwards attending Liber college for a short time. At the age of nineteen he began teaching, continuing through five or six winter terms. Subsequent to his parent's death, he received as his share of the estate the homestead, which he occupied after marriage, living there until 1860, when he removed to Liber, Jay County, Indiana.

On August 7, 1862, he enlisted in company A, 84th Indiana infantry, his regiment being at once sent to Cincinnati, without arms or uniforms, to aid in the defense of that city when threatened by Kirby Smith, Gov. Morton afterwards procuring them arms. Mr. Addington participated in the battle of Chickamauga and numerous skirmishes. Although his face was several times scorched by bullets, he was never wounded. During the five months prior to the time of his discharge, March 19, 1864, he served as chaplain. He returned to his farm, which in 1885, he traded for another in Franklin township, which he still owns. In April 1885, he removed to Ridgeville, where, with the exception of one year spent with his son, he has since resided.

Mr. Addington has been a member of the Christian or New Light church from boyhood, and was ordained a minister in August, 1855, since when he has been in charge of from one to four churches, most of the time, until a year ago, when he retired from ministerial work. Mr. Addington has been engaged in the insurance business and at the present time presents four fire companies. Mr. Addington is a republican and a member of the G. A. R."

44

Rev. Thomas was also the self-appointed Addington family historian. Shown on the following pages is a printed copy of the address and attendance at the 1910 Graham-Addington Family Reunion held at Mills' Lake. Mills' Lake is located about two miles southeast of Farmland along Indiana highway 32. Mills' Lake was a resort area in the early 1900s where the White River was dammed up and several lakes were created. It was a very popular meeting place for various family events but later declined when the lakes were emptied. It is not clear how the Graham family is connected to the Addingtons, but it must be by marriage somewhere along the way. Only two Grahams, a John (age, 64) and Laura Graham, who were living in Laura, Ohio, at the time, attended the 1910 reunion.

HISTORY OF THE

ADDINGTON FAMILY

COMPILED AND READ BY

THE REV. THOS. ADDINGTON

AT THE MEETING OF THE

GRAHAM-ADDINGTON

REUNION ASSOCIATION

-------------AT-------------

MILLS' LAKE, RANDOLPH COUNTY

-------------O N-------------

LABOR DAY, SEPTEMBER 5, 1910

46

For several years past I have been repeatedly urged by various per sons to collect and formulate a history of the Addington family, tracing its history back as far as authentic records will warrant. These requests have been emphasized by my connection with the Graham-Addington Re union Association.

As a response I have written the following. But at the best I can give only a limited sketch of the most prominent facts. The family is known in English history for centuries, and was directly connected with the English government at a critical period of its history. More than two hundred years ago a branch of the family crossed the ocean and joined its destiny with that of the struggling colonies of the new world.

Isaac Addington was born in 1645, one author says at Suffolk, England, and another says at Boston, Mass. The latter is probably correct. His father bore the same name and was doubtless the one who emigrated from England. He served a term each as judge of the Probate Court and chief justice of the Supreme Court. He was then made secretary of the province of Massachusetts and held that position for twenty-five years, dying in office in 1715, at the age of 70 years. Dr. Anthony Addington, M. D., was the medical advisor of Lord Chatham, and was also called as counsel in a critical malady of his magesty. Henry Addington, Viscount Sidmouth, Prime Minister of England, was the oldest son of Anthony Addington, M. D. He was born at Reading, May 30, 1757. Was educated at Winchester, and at Braserose College, Oxford. He was called to the bar at Lincoln's Inn Fields 1784 and elected to Parliament the same year. He was on terms of familiar intimacy with the younger Pitt, and through his influence was in 1789 elected speaker of the house as successor to Lord Grenville. He filled that position for twelve years to the general satisfaction of all parties. In 1801 he succeeded Pitt as prime minister and chancellor of the exchequor. He was of the party known as "The King's Friends," and accepted the office at the urgent personal solicitation of "His Majesty." The most memorable event of his administration was the "Treaty of Armiens," which was concluded on terms considered favorable to English interests. Pitt now joined with Fox in opposition to Addington and as a result was restored to power in May 1804. But in January 1805, Lord Sidmouth again joined the cabinet as president of the council, and was made a Teer of the Realm, a dignity which he had heretofore declined to accept. In 1806 he became lord privy seal, and subsequently lord president in the cabinet of Fox and Grenville. He resigned in 1807. In 1812 he was a third time made lord president under Percival, and in June of the same year received the seal of the home office, under the administration of Lord Liverpool. He held this position for ten eventful years. His administration has been characterized as "vigorous, fearless and consistent. He resigned office in 1822 but retained his seat in the cabinet, however, until 1824. He died February 15, 1844, aged 87 years.

The Addington in America, in Canada and in England are conceded to be of one common family, but I have not been able to get very definite records of the first of the name to settle in the new world, and many points are left to inference and conjecture.

I quote first from manuscript written by John L. Addington, now deceased:

"The first representative of the family in America was Henry Addington, who was born in England about 1737 and who on emigrating to America took up his abode near Philadelphia. He became separated from a younger brother from whom he never afterward heard. He married Elizabeth Broson, by whom he had three sons, John, William, and James. About the year 1755 the family removed to South Carolina, where the eldest son married a Miss Lamb, by whom he had two children, William and Alsie. After the death of the first wife he married Elizabeth Heaton."

William S. Addington of Hot Springs, S. D., gives the following:

"My great grandfather came from England and settled in the state of New York. Moved from there to South Carolina where my grandfather was a captain in the British army. He somehow left the British army, and raised a company of volunteers and fought with the Whigs for the freedom of the States. He had three brothers, Thomas, James and John. My father, Thomas Addington, was in the war of 1812-14. He was born in South Carolina and moved from there to Butler county, Ohio. There I and my brother Thomas were born. We were both in the Civil War. I was in several hard battles besides skirmishes." Signed, William S. Addington, late sergeant Fourth Illinois Cavalry, of General Sherman's body-guard.

John W. Graham, of Laura, Ohio, gives this explanation as to how Captain Addington got out of the British army: He came over with Braddock, at the time of the French and Indian War. Was present at the time of "Braddox defeat," and with Washington in the rear guard, on the retreat. When Braddock came to embark to return to England, he found that the shipping facilities at his command could not carry all his men. On this account he offered an honorable discharge to all soldiers who might choose to remain in America. Captain Addington was one of those who accepted this proposition, and in this way secured an honorable discharge from the British service.

I make the following extract from a little booklet published by John L. Addington, Sr., of Nicholsville, Va.:

"William Addington was a man of great wealth; he was born in London, England in 1750. Was educated in the best institutions of learning of that country at the time. When a young man he imigrated to America, and after traveling extensively in this country, he finally settled at Culpepper, Va., where he married Margaret Cromwell in 1774. He fought through the Revolution under General Washington; was present when Cornwallis surrendered at Yorktown, October 19, 1781. Charles C. Addington, son of William and Margaret Cromwell Addington, was born in Culpepper county, Virginia, October 10, 1777. He married Anna Doty, January 2, 1802, and the same year settled on the Gillawater farm, on the Clinch river, in Culpepper county. He left there and settled on Copper creek, in Scott county, in 1805. The day he was 100 years old his descendents made him a birthday dinner. He had raised sixteen children; had 107 grand children; 443 great grandchildren, and seventeen great, great grandchildren; 557 in all; not counting the descendents of the oldest daughter who had married when yet young and emigrated to the west.

Of our branch of the family I think the following is correct: Henry Addington, born in England in 1737. Came to the United States in 1750; married Elizabeth Burson, who bore him three sons, John, William and James. Moved to South Carolina in 1755. John Addington married first a Miss Lamb. His second wife was Elizabeth Heaton, daughter of Joseph Heaton. Joseph Heaton was born in Bucks county, Pa., February 3, 1699, Married Lydia Smith, daughter of William Smith of Wright;s Town, Pa. John and Elizabeth Heaton Addington were the parents of seven children, viz. Joseph Addington, born July 21, 1776; John Addington, born October

48

13, 1777; Thomas Addington, born December 1, 1778; Mary Addington Roberts, born November 2, 1780; Sarah Addington Roberts, born September 21 1783; Elizabeth Addington Martindale, born February 9, 1787; James Addington, born February 6, 1789.

John Addington with his entire family as given above (except the daughter Alsie of whom we have no account except for her birth) came to Wayne county, Ind., in 1806 and settled on Whitewater, north of Richmond. In 1834 my parents came to Randolph county in company with my uncle Joseph and settled on Sparrow creek, one and one-half miles southeast of Macksville. My uncles, William and James, had settled somewhat earlier on the Mississinewa river where Ridgeville is now located.

From the foregoing we gather the following facts: Isaac Addington, Sr., was the first of the name to emigrate to the new world. So far as we have been able to learn Isaac Addington, Jr. was born in 1645, the first of the name born in this country. Henry Addington, William Addington and another brother, whose name I have not been able to get, came in 1750. Their descendents are found perhaps in every state in the Union and in Canada.

The following is registry of person attending the Graham-Addington family reunion at Mill's Lake, near Winchester, Monday, Sept 5, 1910:

Rev. Thomas Addington, Ridgeville, age 80; Margaret Addington, Ridgtville, 69; Magdalena Addington, Winchester, 58; Geo. W. Addington, Winchester, 66; John W. Malott, Decatur, 62; Zeruah A. Malott, Decatur, 58; Calvin T. Addington, Winchester, 48; Dora Addington, Winchester, 45; Everett R. Addington, Winchester, 16; Asa S. Freel, Muncie, 37; Josie M. Freel, Muncie, 32; Margaret Freel, Muncie, 8; Joseph Cox, Richmond, R. 4, 75; Jane Cox, Richmond, R. 4, 73; Pauline Murray, Richmond, R. 4, 12; Wm. J. Addington, Winchester, 74; Jennie Addington, Winchester, 59; Hazel Addington, Winchester, 17; Arthur Addington, Winchester, 17; Rev. A. M. Addington, Winchester, 55; Meek Addington, Winchester; Clyde W. Addington, Winchester, 30; Flora Addington, Winchester, 30; Helen Addington, Winchester, 7; Cecil T. Addington, Winchester, 3 ; Elmer W. Jay, Fairmont, 48;, Minnie E. Jay, Fairmont, 48, Carmen W. Jay, Fairmont, 21; Harry R. Jay, Fairmont, 14; Mrs. Harley Valentine Arcanum, O., R. 3, 23; Lulu Addington, Geneva, 23; Granville Williams, Richmond, 54; S. M. Williams, Winchester, R. 4, 65; Mary E. Miles, Geneva, 53; U. E. Pursley, Farmland, 30; Asa. R. Addington, Winchester, 44; Pearl Addington, Winchester, 37; Perry O. Addington, Winchester, 20; Kathlen Addington, Winchester, 12; Ernest Addington, Winchester 21; Arthur Addington, Bryant, 28; Louisa McIntire, Farmland, 70; Louis M. Addington, Marion, 22; Emerson Addington, Winchester, 50; Rosa Addington, Winchester, 47; Angie Addington, Marion, 57; H. R. Addington, Marion, 29; R. H. McIntire, Farmland, 30; Emma Pursley, Farmland, 30; Wanda Pursley, Farmland, 10; Kenneth Pursley, Farmland, 7; Mary Pursley, Farmland, 2; Robert C. Addington, Farmland, 64; Angie Addington, Farmland, 57; Mamie Addington, Farmland, 19; Elverson Driver, Winchester, 26; Hermieone Driver, Winchester, 21; Everett E. Gantz, Farmland, 24; Inez Addington-Gantz, Farmland, 25; Ollie Painter, Winchester, 46; Rosa Painter, Winchester, 40; Mary E. Pursley, Farmland, 57, F. M. Addington, Winchester, 56; Mrs. Arthur Gutbeil, Winchester, 36; Elva Durr, Winchester, 42; Wm. S. Diggs, Cincinnati, 48; Flora A. Fraze, Winchester, 44; Olive Fraze, Winchester, 19;

Pearl Taylor, Monon, 18; Helen Addington, Monon, 12; Clare Mote, New Madison, O., 17; John W. Graham, Laura, O., 65; Rachael E. Graham, Laura, O.; Nora B. Jackson, Farmland, 39: Mattie E. Jackson, Parker City, 32; Alice Addington Macy, Syracuse, N. Y., 69; Liberty Penney, Dayton, O., 72; Sarah A. Penney, Dayton O., 67; Robert P. Horn, Monon, 72; Benj. F. Addington, Ridgeville 54; Rev. Luther E. Addington Ridgeville, 31; James Addington, Ridgeville, 76; Lona Addington-Mitchell, Ridgeville, 26; James M. Addington, Ridgeville ,71; Cora Addington-Fraze, Ridgeville, 57; Jane Addington, Ridgeville, 55; Anna Addington, Winchester, 53; Elsie Addington, Ridgeville, 31; Hattie Cox, Muncie, 29; Lura Addington, Winchester, 17; U. S. Wright, Winchester, 44, Laura Wright, Winchester, 38; Elizabeth Ross, Muncie; Thomas L. Addington, Ridgeville, 82; Sarah Riddlebarger, Ridgeville, 55; Jesse Jackson, Farmland, 38; Nellie Jackson, Farmland, 34; O. D. Hayworth, Laura, O., 53; Mrs. David L. Mote, Greenville, O.; Edwin K. Addington, Lynn, 40; Mrs. Jack Addington, Ridgeville, 37; Gertrude Fraze, Ridgeville 27; Rose Addington-Cadwallader, Ridgeville 50; Martha I. King, Winchester; Rufus King, Winchester; Albert J. McGuire, Winchester, 40; Edward Addington, Farmland, 23; Jerrie Painter, Ridgeville, 68; Milford Addington, Redkey, 56; Everett Addington, Redkey, 17; Isaac B. Addington, Farmland, 84; Ivory H. Addington, Farmland, 36; Nancy J. Addington, Farmland, 72; Sarah S. Addington, Redkey, 53; L. L. Williams, Winchester, 64; Alice Addington-Wells, Geneva, 31; S. C. Williams, Winchester, 42; Effie Addington-Williams, Winchester, 42; Clinton Jackson Parker City, 33; James M. Pursley, Farmland, 61; Mary Jane Diggs, Winchester, 26; Leander Addington, Winchester, 52; Dora Addington Winchester, 48; Edna Wall, Winchester, 29; Lavina C. French, 59; Della Clevenger, Parker City, 28; Wm. Green, Ridgeville, Mrs. Wm. Green, Ridgeville; Gale Green, Ridgeville, Jesse D. Cox, Muncie, 31; Cal. W. Addington Diggs, Winchester, 69; Noel E. Addington Winchester, 28; Forest Addington, Redkey, 22; Gilva Addington, Winchester 25; Harry Addington Winchester, 17; Carl Addington, Ridgeville, 15; Verne F. Addington, Ridgeville, 37; Ed A. Cadwallader, Ridgeville, 52; Pearl O. Zimmerman, Muncie, 33; Mrs. Pearl Zimmerman, Muncie, 28; Edna Addington, Redkey; Myrtle Addington, Winchester, Ray Armstrong, Ridgeville 23; Gertrude Armstrong, 23; Harold Tompson, Winchester, 22; Kester Pike, Winchester, 68; Estie Pike, Winchester, 28; Geo. Pike, Winchester, 17; Nora Pike, Winchester, 13; Russell Payne, Winchester, 11; Emma M. Addington, Lynn, 15; E. Elsworth Addington, Chicago, 47; Mabel Addington, Winchester, 20; Edward Dull, Ridgeville, 30; Olive Addington-Dull, Ridgeville, 29; Asa Bond, Jonesboro, 80; Levi Bond, Farmland, 77; Salmon H. Addington, Ridgeville, 52; Archie R. Addington, Albany, 16; Earl Jackson, Farmland, 18; Elden Jackson, Farmland, 20; Norval Jackson, Farmland, 16; G. Tom Riddlebarger, Ridgeville, 49; W. C. Bosworth, Farmland, 38; Zellie Bosworth, Farmland, 37; Chester O. Bosworth, Farmland, 15; Benj. F. Addington, Ridgeville, 42; W. R. Herron, Farmland, 58; Inez M. Addington, Winchester, 24; Lizzie Barker, Winchester, 46; Alfretta Kolp, Winchester, 41; Clona Kolp, Winchester, 17; Phoebe P. Allen, Albany, 63; Henry T. Addington, Farmland, 66; Mrs. J. M. Johnson, Winchester, 87; Earl Pursley, Winchester, 23; Opal Pursley, Winchester, 22; Ellsworth Addington, Winchester, 49; Mabel Addington, Winchester, 24; Grace Addington, Winchester, 22; Frank W. Addington, Hagerstown; Cecil C. Fisher, Winchester; Cora P. Fisher, Winchester; Guy Fisher, Winchester; Ermann Fisher; Winchester; Mary A. Helms, Winchester.

James Addington, fifth son of John

The youngest son of John Addington, James Addington was born 6 Feb 1789 in South Carolina and moved with his father to Wayne County, Indiana in 1806. James married Nancy Lewallyn on 15 Jun 1809 in Preble County, Ohio although he was living in Wayne County, Indiana at the time. All five of their sons carried Lewallyn as their middle name although it is often spelled in its many variations. James Addington first entered on land in Randolph County in 1828 in Franklin Township and again in 1832 and most likely moved to Franklin Township that year. James shows up in the 1840 and 1850 Indiana censuses with his wife Nancy in Franklin Township. Their children were:

(1) John Lewallyn Addington, b. 1810, Wayne Co., Indiana, d. 1 Mar 1878, Hardin Co., Iowa
    m. 8 Nov 1832, Randolph Co., IN, Sally (Sarah) Stephens
    m. 2nd 7 May 1848, Randolph Co., IN, Nancy Fansher
(2) Rachel Addington, b. 15 Apr 1814, Wayne Co., IN, d. Iowa
    m. 27 Dec 1838, Randolph Co., Indiana, David Wilson
(3) William Lewallyn Addington, b. 1818, Wayne Co., Indiana, d. 4 Aug 1853, Randolph Co., Indiana (killed by lightning)
    m. 22 Sep 1840, Randolph Co., Indiana, Mary Hughs
(4) Benjamin Lewallyn Addington, b. 2 Dec 1826, Wayne Co., Indiana, d. 1885, Sibley, Ford Co., Illinois
    m. 9 Mar 1846, Randolph Co., IN, Margaret Mariah Hughs
(5) Thomas Lewallyn Addington, b. 26 Jan 1829, Wayne Co., Indiana, d. 7 May 1914, Randolph Co., Indiana
    m. 11 Sep 1852, Marybeth Woodward
    m. 2nd 26 Jul 1857, Nancy Alice Pierce
    m. 3rd 28 Aug 1885, Hannah M. Ward
(6) Isaac Lewallyn Addington, b. 1832, d. 9 May 1903
    m. 7 Dec 1854, Piety Horn
(7) Mary Addington, b. 1834, nfi

James and Nancy probably had other children who died young given the spacing of their children's birthyears. Nancy (Lewallyn) Addington died in Randolph County on 9 Nov 1851. James and his sons, John L. and Benjamin L. Addington, moved their families to Kansas about 1858. James, the father, died in Anderson County, Kansas in October 1859 at the age of 71 due to chronic disease according to 1860 Mortality Census records. Some of James' other offspring later moved to Kansas but some stayed behind in Randolph County. The second of the Addington books written by Hugh M. Addington goes into extensive detail about the Kansas and Missouri Addingtons that descend from James A. Addington, the son of John Lewallyn Addington.

John L. Addington and his second wife, Nancy Fansher, had three sons, two of whom moved to Iowa and one, Thomas F. Addington, who later moved to Oklahoma. This Thomas F. Addington left his home in 1873 and made his way to Texas where he joined the Texas Rangers. He hunted buffalo for three years until the herds were almost gone. He married Myrtle Maxey in 1883 and in Apr 1889 made the run for land in Oklahoma. Thomas was the postmaster of Yukon, Canadian County, Oklahoma for many years before his death in 1916.

Hugh M. Addington states in his 1960 book that the three sons of John L. and Nancy (Fansher) Addington founded the city of Addington, Oklahoma. This assertion is incorrect. The city of Addington is located in Jefferson County in the southern part of the state and currently has a population of about one hundred. There were several Addington families in Oklahoma from the southern branch of the Addington family. The city of Addington was founded by four sons of Jarrett Addington, who was born in South Carolina in 1817 and is thought to be a descendent of Henry and Sarah Addington of South Carolina through their son James.

James' second son, William L. Addington, married Mary Hughs in 1840 and they had four children, Nancy, Isaac, David and Meshach. William was killed by lightning in 1853. One of their sons, Isaac, had moved to Kansas by 1880 but the two other sons, David and Meshach, moved east across the border into Ohio. Meshach later moved to Kentucky where he died.

James' son, Benjamin L. Addington, moved west to Anderson County, Kansas with his father and older brother in 1858. Sometime later he moved back east since he died in Illinois in 1885. Benjamin's son, Randolph, remained in Illinois while his brother James Monroe was in Montana by 1900 and later died in California in 1925.

James' next son, Thomas L. Addington, remained in Randolph County. He married three times and had six children, Melissa,

52

William, Marybeth, Elizabeth, Elmer Elsworth and Anthony "Jack". He was one year older than his cousin the Rev. Thomas Addington and their records are often confusing. Thomas L. Addington was a Justice of the Peace for Franklin Township as was his older brother John L. Addington. Thomas L. Addington lived a very full life of 85 years, dying in Randolph County in 1914.

James' youngest son, Isaac L. Addington, remained in Randolph County where he married twice and had eight children. Isaac first married Piety Horn and they had eight children, Sarah, Benjamin Franklin, Jacob, Rose, Mary, Florence, Cora and Minnie. After his first wife died, he married Eliza Frances Pogue.

Joseph Addington, second son of John

Joseph Addington was born on 21 Jul 1776 in 96 District of South Carolina, now Union County. Joseph first married Rachel Randel on 21 Dec 1799 according to Quaker records. Joseph and Rachel (Randel) Addington had three sons, all born in South Carolina:
(1) John Randel Addington, b. 18 Oct 1800, 96 District, South Carolina
(2) William Randel Addington, b. 25 Aug 1802, 96 District, South Carolina, d. 5 Oct 1875, Randolph Co., Indiana
    m. 28 Sep 1825, Wayne Co., Indiana, Dorcas Mendenhall
(3) Joseph Randel Addington, b. 27 Feb 1804, 96 District, South Carolina, d. 3 May 1889, Pilot Grove, Lee Co., Iowa
    m. 27 Oct 1825, Wayne Co., Indiana, Mary Barker

Joseph along with his father moved their families to Wayne County, Indiana about 1806. They settled in the northeast township of present day Wayne County along the Whitewater River near the city of Chester. John and his son Joseph are listed in the special 1807 census of males over 21 years of age in the Indiana territory. At that time there were only a few thousand settlers in Indiana so they were at the forefront of the movement west.

Rachel (Randel) Addington died about 1806. It is thought that she died after the family moved to Wayne County, Indiana. Joseph married second on 22 Dec 1808 to Celia Townsend, the daughter of John M. and Elvira (Cain) Townsend. The marriage is recorded in Preble County, Ohio even though they were living in Indiana. The children of Joseph and Celia (Townsend) Addington were:

(1) Rachel Addington, b. 19 Mar 1810, d. before 1850
m. 3 Nov 1828, Wayne Co., Indiana, Seth Elliott
(2) Thomas Addington, b. 14 Jul 1811, Wayne Co., IN, d. c1840
m. 16 May 1833, Wayne Co., Indiana, Beulah Hunt
(3) Jonathan Addington, b. 18 Mar 1813, Wayne Co., Indiana, d. 15 Sep 1891, Randolph Co., Indiana
m. 4 Jul 1839, Randolph Co., Indiana, Sarah Rule, b. 11 Aug 1817, d. 7 Jul 1899
(4) Elvira Addington, b. 20 Apr 1815, Wayne Co., Indiana, d. 30 Aug 1837
m. 30 Apr 1834, Wayne Co., Indiana, Robert Cox
(5) Elisha Addington, b. 11 Sep 1817, Wayne Co., Indiana, d. 4 Mar 1839, Randolph Co., Indiana
(6) Elihu Addington, b. 21 Jan 1820, Wayne Co., Indiana, d. 17 Feb 1898, Grant Co., Indiana
m. 1 Sep 1842, Hannah Cox, d. 19 Apr 1859
m. 2nd 25 Nov 1860, Delaware Co., Indiana, Eliza Branson
(7) Stephen Addington, b. 12 Jan 1822, Wayne Co., Indiana, d. 1 Mar 1839, Randolph Co., Indiana
(8) Benjamin Robert Addington, b. 28 Jun 1824, Wayne Co., Indiana, d. 6 Nov 1906, Randolph Co., Indiana
m. 30 Oct 1850, Randolph Co., Indiana, Rebecca Harold
m. 2nd Jun 1878, Randolph Co., Indiana, Sarah Jane Day
(9) David Addington*, b. 9 Mar 1828, Wayne Co., Indiana, d. 19 Jul 1902, Randolph Co., Indiana
m. 27 Nov 1851, Huldah Ruth Bolinger, b. 20 Nov 1830, Pennsylvania, d. 18 Sep 1907, Randolph Co., Indiana

The 1882 Tucker History of Randolph County also lists a daughter Celia but no other records have been found for a daughter with this name.

Of the three sons from Joseph's first marriage to Rachel Randel, we know very little about the first son, John Randel Addington. His birth is listed in the Friends records as 18 Oct 1800 but he is not listed in Joseph's 1834 will. His name is listed in 1812 in Friends records when he was admitted to membership with his family. Some earlier Addington researchers have stated that John Randel Addington moved to Coles County, Illinois by 1840 and died there in 1853. There is a John Addington, age 40-50, with family in the 1840 Coles

County census but further research revealed that this John usually spelled his name Edington, was born in Ohio and apparently his name was misspelled only in this one census. The John Addington who married Lucretia Roberts in Wayne County in 1822 is the son of William Addington and not this John Randel Addington as often listed. I believe John Randel Addington died sometime between 1812 and 1834 with no issue. This assumption is based on the evidence currently available.

The second son of Joseph and Rachel (Randel) Addington, William Randel Addington, was married in Wayne County on 28 Sep 1825 to Dorcas Mendenhall, daughter of Absalom Mendenhall. William Randel moved to Randolph County in the mid 1830s and was a farmer in Franklin Township until his death in 1875. William and Dorcas (Mendenhall) Addington had the following children:
(1) Jesse Addington, b. Mar 1827, Indiana, d. 7 Dec 1908, Modoc Co., California
    m. Martha Ann Harshman
(2) Joseph Mendenhall Addington, b. 6 Oct 1829, Wayne Co., Indiana, d. 3 Feb 1898, Randolph Co., Indiana, dnm
(3) Rachel Addington, b. 1831, Wayne Co., Indiana
    m. 5 Sep 1850, Randolph Co., Indiana, Julian Green
(4) Absolum Addington, b. 1833, d. 26 Sep 1864, Boise, ID
(5) James Addington, b. 9 Mar 1834, d. 5 Oct 1912
    m. 27 Sep 1863, Randolph Co., Indiana, Sarah Ann Tharp
(6) John Addington, b. c1836, nfi
(7) Warren Addington, d. before 1850
(8) Thomas Addington, b. 1839, nfi
(9) Sarah J. Addington, b. c1843
    m. J. Malott
(10) Elizabeth "Betsey" Addington, b. c1843
    m. 8 May 1867, Randolph Co., Indiana, Nelson Barnesly
(11) Elmira Addington, b. c1854, nfi
+ three who died in infancy

Most of their children remained in Randolph County but their first son Jesse was quite a wanderer. He is found in the 1850 census in Fulton Co., Indiana, in the 1860 census in Iowa, in the 1870 census in Walla Walla County, Washington, in the 1880 census in Lake County, Oregon and in the 1900 census in Modoc County, California where he died in 1908. William Randel Addington's second son, Joseph Mendenhall

55

Addington ventured west to the Oregon territory where he spent nineteen years engaged in mining, working on government surveys and fighting Indians. He participated in the war with the Rogue River Indians in 1866. He returned to Randolph County in 1870 and was a very successful and well respected farmer until his death in 1898.

The third son of Joseph and Rachel (Randel) Addington, Joseph Randel Addington, married in Wayne County on 27 Oct 1825 to Mary Barker. Joseph moved his family to Randolph County in the early 1830s and resided in Franklin Township until about 1846 when he moved to near Pilot Point, Iowa in Lee County. Joseph Randel and Mary (Barker) Addington had the following children:

(1) Isaac Barker Addington, b. 21 Oct 1826, d. 19 Feb 1914
    m. 25 Sep 1873, Nancy J. Flood, b. 10 Feb 1838, d. aft 1914
(2) Rachel Addington, b. 29 Nov 1828, nfi
(3) Louise (or Louisa) Addington, b. 9 Feb 1830, m. ? Benford
(4) Celia Addington, b. 9 Jun 1832, d. 2 Nov 1899, Idaho
(5) William J. Addington, b. 21 Nov 1835, d. 17 Sep 1917, Randolph Co., Indiana
    m. 16 Feb 1869, Randolph Co., Indiana, Annis L. Pike
(6) Willis G. Addington, b. 31 Oct 1838, Indiana, d. 17 May 1919, Riverside, California
    m. 21 Feb 1864, Mary Melissa Jessup, b. c1843, Iowa
(7) Hannah Ann Addington, b. 14 Nov 1841, d. young
(8) Amos T. Addington, b. 29 Apr 1845, Wayne Co., Indiana, d. 26 Feb 1891, Tacoma, Washington
    m. 8 Apr 1866, Elizabeth Jessup
(9) Alfred Benjamin Addington, b. 25 Dec 1849, Iowa, d. 14 Sep 1924, Arnett, Oklahoma
    m. Rosanne Jessup
(10) Albert David Addington, b 25 Dec 1849, Iowa, d. 1 Oct 1875, Lee Co., Iowa
    m. Mary E. Jessup

At least two of Joseph Randel Addington's sons, Isaac and William J., moved back to Randolph County and raised their families there. William spent some time in Illinois, fought in an Illinois regiment in the Civil War and then moved back to Randolph County where he married in 1869. William's first son was born in Iowa and by 1880 he had moved his family to Montgomery County, Kansas. He moved his family back to Randolph County sometime after that and remained there till he died in 1917. Many descendants of this William J. Addington still live in Randolph County, including his great granddaughter Anita Addington who supplied much of the information about this family.

Joseph Randel Addington's son, Willis, moved on to Kansas, later to Washington, then back to Idaho and eventually to California where he died in 1919. Son Amos moved further west and died in Washington in 1891. Twin sons Alfred Benjamin Addington and Albert David Addington married and raised their families in Iowa. Albert David Addington died in Iowa in 1875 but Alfred Benjamin Addington later moved to Washington, and then to Oklahoma. Descendants of Alfred Benjamin Addington lived in Oregon, Washington and Oklahoma.

Returning to Joseph Addington who was born in 1776, he entered on land in section 34 in Franklin Township, Randolph County in 1834. He apparently moved his family unto that land sometime in 1835. Unfortunately, tragedy struck and Joseph died of milk sickness less than a year after moving.

Two dates have been listed for Joseph's death. Sparrow Creek Monthly Meeting records list 9 Feb 1836 but his gravestone says 20 Feb 1836. He gave a verbal will shortly before his death which was later recorded in Probate Court:

Last Will of Joseph Addington, Deceased

The will by word of mouth of Joseph Addington, made and declared by him on the 7th and 9th day of February, in the year of our Lord 1836, in the presence of us, who have subscribed our names as witnesses hereto:

My will is that William R. Addington; Thomas Addington; Joseph R. Addington; Rachel Elliott, formerly Rachel Addington; have had their share of the estate, and Jonathan Addington has had his share of land and one horse, beast, it not being his full share as had gone to the others, some personal property as full share, and not to Jonathan Addington.

The balance of my estate after paying my just debts to be equally divided among the other heirs of mine, except that

57

my son Elihu Addington, shall live with Robert Cox, to learn the Will Wright trade, if the said Robert Cox agrees to give him 80 acres of land when he comes of age, and that my wife live on the place where I now live during her life of widow-hood to raise the children on, and that my youngest son David Addington, have the same when he comes of age and it is my will that my brother Thomas Addington be executor of this my last will and testament due date by the said Joseph Addington, in his last sickness to be his last will and testament in the presence of us whom he requested to bear witness that the same was his last will and testament as to that fact, February 23, 1836.

Jonathan Addington

his
Joseph R. Addington
mark

State of Indiana
Randolph County
This day the within verbal will of Joseph Addington, deceased, was probated before me, Charles Conway, Clerk of the Randolph Probate Court, by the affirmation of Jonathan Addington, and Joseph R. Addington, the subscribing witnesses to the said will who have been by me duly affirmed as the law directs, witness that the matters and facts stated in said will are true to the best of their knowledge and being affirmed before me this 19th day of March, A. D. 1836

C. Conway, Clerk

After Joseph's death, his widow, Celia (Townsend) Addington, sent one or two of the children to live with relatives but somehow kept the rest of the family together. At the time of Joseph's death, son David was not quite eight and Benjamin was but eleven so it must have been quite a struggle. In June 1836, Celia entered on land in section 29 in White River Township about one and one half miles south of Maxville in the name of her youngest son, David, and she moved her family there. Two of Joseph's sons, Elisha and Stephen, died within four days of each other in 1839 from an epidemic of milk sickness. They are both buried in the Sparrow Creek Cemetery. Daughter Rachel had married Seth Elliott on 3 Nov 1828 in Wayne County. They had four children before she died early in life sometime probably before 1840. Son Thomas also married in Wayne County on 16 May 1833 to Beulah Hunt. They had one son, Henry, and three daughters, Anna, Hanna and Kentia. Beulah died in 1838 and Thomas died a little later. Thomas is buried in the Sparrow Creek Cemetery, only a birth date being given on the stone, no death date. Joseph and Celia's daughter Elvira married Robert Cox on 30 Apr 1834 in Wayne County. They had two sons and one daughter before she died in 1837.

The Sparrow Creek Cemetery is located in section 33 of White River Township about 3 miles south and 1 mile east of Maxville. It has been abandoned for decades and even was reported as such in Tucker's 1882 History of Randolph County. It was originally next to a Friends Meeting House which was built about 1840 but burned down about a year later. The cemetery is located on land originally entered on by Daniel Beals. The cemetery which is little more than a small clump of trees is located about 300 yards west of county road 500W and about 500 yards north of county road 200S. The author visited the cemetery in 1990 and found about 12 stones, all overturned and many partially buried. However, a single stone spire (see photo) marks the site of Joseph's grave, his second wife Celia and four of their children.

The single stone spire reads:

Side 1	Side 2	Side 3	Side 4
Father	Thomas	Elisha	Rachel
Joseph	Addington	Addington	Elliott
Addington	14th 7th mo	11th 9th mo	13th 10th mo
21st 7th mo	1811	1817	1800
1776		4th 3rd mo	
20th 2nd mo		1839	
1836		-	
-		Stephen	
Mother		Addington	
Celia		12th 1st mo	
Addington		1822	
22nd 2nd mo		1st 3rd mo	
1785		1839	
5th 3rd mo			
1852			

Rachel Elliott's birth year was 1810 not 1800 but all of the other dates appear to be correct. A similar gravestone was found for Joseph's brother Thomas and his wife Mary.

After the death of his father, Elihu Addington, then about fifteen, was boarded out to his brother-in-law, Joseph Cox in Wayne County. Cox was a millwright and Elihu spent six years learning that trade. Elihu married Hannah Cox, a daughter of Jeremiah Cox, on 1 Sep 1842 in Randolph County. He moved to Randolph County in 1843 and purchased land about a mile south of Maxville, where he developed a fine farm. Elihu and Hannah had four daughters and two sons, Ruth Ellen, Martha Ann, Lindsey, Wilson, Mary and Lilly, before she died in the mid 1850s. Elihu married second Eliza Branson and they had one daughter and three sons, Minnie, Ellsworth, Burtie Lee and Waldo. About 1868 he sold his farm and bought another farm nearer Winchester. Two years later, he moved into Winchester. Elihu later moved to Grant County, Indiana where he died in 1898.

Joseph's son, Jonathan Addington, married Sarah Ruble on 4 Jul 1839 in Randolph County. They had three daughters, Louise, Sarah and Ida Bell, and three sons Henry Taylor, Robert G. and Benjamin. Jonathan was a miller by trade and operated a mill near Maxville besides farming in Franklin Township until his death on 15 Sep 1891. Jonathan's son, Henry Taylor Addington, first worked at his father's mill before enlisting in the 147th Indiana Infantry near the end of the Civil War. After the war Henry purchased a farm in section 19 of White River Township and became a well known farmer and stock raiser. He introduced the breeding of fine Jersey cattle into the neighborhood along with a superior breed of swine, Duroe Jersey. Henry married first to Emily C. Green and they had three children, Lilly, Ellsworth and Minnie. After Emily's death, he married Nannie E. Edgar and they had five children, Bertha, Harry, Edward, Laura and Russell.

Joseph's son, Benjamin, married on 6 Nov 1850 in Randolph County to Rebecca Harold, the daughter of Macy and Leah Harold. They had five sons and two daughters, Cornelius, Sylvester, Milford, Elvira, Emma, Henry L. and Asa Robert. Benjamin was a Quaker and bought and donated the land for the Quaker Friends Church at Bear Creek, known then as Benny's half acre. The cemetery near the church is now known as the New Dayton Cemetery. Rebecca died on 4 Mar 1876 at the age of 47. Benjamin later married in 1878 a widow, Sarah Jane Day, with six children. This second marriage created quite a large family but one which integrated easily and with much warmth. Uncle "Benny" and Aunt "Sarah" were very well known and respected residents of Franklin Township. When Sarah died in 1904, her children wrote a very moving tribute to her in the local newspaper. Benjamin was a farmer in Franklin Township until his death on 6 Nov 1906, the last of Joseph's children to die. Benjamin Addington has many descendants still living in Randolph County, mainly from his son Milfred. One son of Milfred, Evert Asa Addington, served as the State Representative from Randolph County in 1923 and 1924. Evert Asa was blind either from birth or from early childhood, but he attained a fine education including going to law school and was so respected by his neighbors that he was elected to represent Randolph County. Evert was also the nominee for Randolph County prosecutor in 1924 when he feel ill to typhoid fever and died at age 31. Joseph Milton Patterson of Winter Haven, Florida is a descendant of this Addington line through Benjamin's son Asa Robert.

The Civil War

Civil War records for Indiana list several Addingtons who served in Union forces during the war and two who gave their lives in that war. The first of the two who gave the supreme sacrifice was Henry Addington, a son of Thomas and grandson of Joseph. He served in the 84th Indiana Infantry and died on 7 Oct 1863 of wounds received in the Battle of Chickamauga. John Addington, also a member of the 84th Indiana Infantry, died on 12 Sep 1864 of wounds received on Lookout Mountain near Chattanooga. This John is probably the son of John Addington and grandson of William Addington, but his identity has not been positively confirmed. Three other Addingtons served in this regiment: Nason Addington (son of John and grandson of William) in Company A, Thomas Addington (son of Thomas and grandson of John) in Companies A and F, and William S. Addington (son of James and grandson of Thomas). William S. Addington according to his son's story was wounded in the hip during the Civil War, the wound never fully healing and bothered him for the rest of his life. The Rev. Thomas Addington served as chaplain of the regiment for his last five months of service.

The 84th Indiana Infantry was mustered into federal service on 3 Sep 1862 at Richmond, Indiana under the command of Col. Nelson Trusler. Their first work was to go to aid in the defense of Cincinnati against the legions under Kirby Smith. Then the regiment participated in the West Virginia campaign. In March 1863, they moved to Nashville and were present at the Battle of Chickamauga, the regiment participating on both days, fighting bravely and losing heavily. Holding the key to Rosecran's retreat, their division stood stubbornly and helped save the army. The regiment drove with Sherman to Atlanta in the spring 1864 campaign during which they were engaged in fifteen battles. They were assigned back to Nashville fighting at the Battle of Franklin on the way. The regiment participated in the Battle of Nashville where Hood's army was decimated. Then, they moved into Alabama around Huntsville in pursuit of Hood's army. They ended the war on duty in Nashville and were mustered out there 14 Jun 1865.

Other Civil War records showed a James Addington and Nason Addington (son of Bishop and grandson of William) served in the 8th Indiana Infantry, a three month unit serving early in the war. Lewis Addington and George W. Addington both served in the 9th Indiana Calvary. George W. is a son of James Addington and grandson of Thomas Addington and Lewis is a son of William and grandson of his father William.

James Addington and William Addington served in the 55th Indiana Regiment. This regiment was formed in Jun 1862 to help repel the invasion of Kirby Smith and served for three months. Three Addingtons served in the 147th Indiana Infantry: Henry T. (son of Jonathan and grandson of Joseph), James A. (son of John L. and grandson of James) and Nathan (son of John L. and grandson of James). The 147th was formed late in the war in 1865 for the final push to victory and did mainly support and guard duty in Virginia.

William J. Addington, a son of Joseph Randel Addington and grandson of Joseph Addington, had moved to Illinois before the Civil War. There he enlisted in the 19th Illinois Infantry and was mustered out with that regiment.

David Addington, youngest son of Joseph

David Addington was born on 9 Mar 1828 in Wayne County and was but seven when the family moved to Randolph County. His birth has also been reported as 9 Mar 1827 but I believe 1828 to be the correct date based on cemetery and census records. He was not quite eight when his father died. He learned the farming business very early in life and eventually took over the family farm in White River Township about a mile and a half south of Maxville. On 27 Nov 1851, he married Huldah Ruth Bolinger, the daughter of Jacob and Mary (Goshorn) Bolinger. David and Huldah Ruth (Bolinger) Addington had four children:

(1) Mary Elizabeth Addington, b. Dec 1852, d. 20 Jan 1943, bur. Maxville Cem.
   m. 1870, James M. Pursley, b. May 1849, Indiana, d. 24 Nov 1912, bur. Maxville Cem.
(2) Cecilla Addington, b. c1854, died age 2
(3) Joseph Leander Addington*, b. 15 Feb 1858, d. 11 Oct 1935, bur. Maxville Cem.
   m. 18 Feb 1880, Dora Elizabeth Feagans, b. 24 Oct 1862, d. 19 Mar 1944, bur. Maxville Cem.
(4) Nora Bell Addington, b. c1868, d. c1872

David Addington was brought up as a Quaker but later the family took membership in the Methodist Episcopal Church at Maxville. The first church at Maxville was built in 1838. It burned in 1847 and was completely rebuilt in 1856. David Addington died in 1902 and is buried in the old portion of the Woodlawn Cemetery at Maxville, just across the street from the church there. Huldah Ruth (Bolinger) Addington died on 18 Sep 1907 and is buried in Maxville Cemetery next to her husband. The following obituary on David Addington gives a better description of his life than can the author. It was written by the Rev. Thomas Addington, a cousin of David and self-appointed family historian. Published obituaries of this period were often short if written at all. The length and detail of this obituary reflects the impact that David Addington must have had on his family and community.

ADDINGTON:- David, son of Joseph and Celia Townsend Addington, was born at Chester, Wayne county, Indiana, March 9th, 1828, and died at his home one mile south of the Maxville church, July 19th, 1902, at the age of 74 years, 4 months and 10 days.

He leaves a devoted wife, one son, one daughter, eleven grandchildren, twelve great-grandchildren, and one surviving brother, with many other relatives and friends to mourn their loss. Father, mother, all of his brothers and sisters with one exception were waiting to welcome him on the other shore.

In 1807 his parents left South Carolina on account of their opposition to slavery and with his grandfather John Addington and two uncles, John and Thomas Addington settled at Chester, Wayne Co. Richmond was at that time a small village of log cabins, much of the land on which the beautiful city now stands being government property subject to entry at $1.25 per acre. The Indian had not yet left his native forests, which were full of game. About the same time two other uncles settled in Randolph county in the vicinity of Ridgeville.

His parents were life long members of the Friends, being perhaps charter members of the society at Chester, which after nearly a century of usefulness, still lives as a monument to the faithfulness of the early pioneer Christians who were willing to endure hardness and privation in the cause of Christ.

In the twenty-seven years spent in Wayne county, they saw the forest give way to productive farms, the blazen path replaced by good roads, and comfortable dwellings take the place of log cabins. Here all their children were born, and in the early spring of 1834, when David their youngest was a boy of six years old, they sold their farm at Chester and a second time braved the hardships of pioneer life that they might secure homes for all their children. They settled one and a half miles south of Maxville, on the farm on which David spent nearly his entire life and on which he died. But a sad affliction awaited them in their new home. The family was stricken with that mysterious poison known as milk sickness of which the father and two sons died.

The two young men who died were named Elisha and Stephen. One son, Thomas, and two daughters, Rachel and

Elvira, had married in Wayne county. Thus the widowed wife and mother was left in a new country on a farm yet to be redeemed from its native forest, with a family of three sons to provide for, Jonathan, then a young man, Benjamin and David, boys of perhaps seven and nine years; and one son Elisha, went to the home of an uncle in Wayne county, Isaac Commons, with whom he remained till grown to manhood. The wife of the married son soon after died leaving a babe, Henry, which was adopted by the widowed grandmother and cared for as her own. She also took to her home one of the children of her daughter, Rachel Elliott, who had died leaving a husband and four children.

Of the hardships, privation and toil through which the family fought its way at that time, the present generation can form no conception, and yet, in the midst of our rich abundance and our ten thousand opportunities we hear continual complainings and invectives against the hardness of their fate and their want of opportunity by many who have never learned the abcs of real hardship and struggle as known to these early pioneers.

With these surroundings, David grew to manhood, toiling late and early through spring, summer and autumn in helping to cultivate the little farm, gather in the ripened products, and subdue the forest. There were no public schools and he could attend the subscription school of the day only as time could be snatched from his necessary labor at home. Yet with these disadvantages he secured sufficient education for the intelligent management of the business affairs of life, and dearly loved to read good books, and his religious and political papers. In coming to their new home they did not leave their religion behind them, but transferred from Chester to Dunkirk, and the widowed mother and her family afterward became charter members of Sparrow Creek meeting where they attended services regularly not only on the first day of the week but one day in the middle of the week.

David Addington and Huldah R. Bolinger were married Nov. 27, 1851. Nov. 27, 1901 they celebrated their golden wedding by a pleasant and profitable family reunion. They were the parents of four children, three daughters and one son. Two daughter, Celia Ellen and Rosa Belle, both died at the ages of two and four years. One daughter, May E., wife of James Pursley, and the son Joseph L., are yet living on the old home farm and on one adjoining it. The M. E. church at Maxville was blessed with a gracious out-pouring of the Holy Spirit and revival of vital piety in the winter of 1858-9 under the pastoral labors of Rev. L. J. Templin able assisted by other ministers of the same and of sister denominations. More than one hundred being converts were added to the army of the Lord, and old professors were quickened into renewed spiritual life. The Friends meetings at Dunkirk and at Sparrow Creek had gone down and being without a church house nearer than Poplar Run and Cedar, he, to encourage the work of grace then in progress, cast his lot with them- the church waying their rule on baptism in his favor. He remained a faithful and consistent member to the time of his death, being, as long as able to attend an active worker in the church. At the same time he was broad and liberal in his spiritual life and loved to meet with the children of God, without regard to denomination. Wherever he found the spirit of the Master, there he felt at home. He always felt an especial attachment to the church of his father and of his own earlier religious life, and would often attend and participate in their meetings.

Through all his life he was an enemy of slavery and intemperance, and an earnest worker in the cause of liberty and sobriety. He was also intensely loyal and at the opening of the civil war seriously contemplated going into the army but circumstances however seemed to forbid. All could not become soldiers, someone had to look after affairs at home, not only for themselves but for their neighbors as well, who were in the tented field. This part of the work fell to the lot of David, among others, two families at least being under his especial care and oversight besides his own, as well as a general interest in the families of all soldiers in his vicinity.

I lived on an adjoining farm when I went into the service, and I left a wife and four small children, one a babe of two months old. I shall never cease to be grateful for the care he bestowed upon them in my absence of more than nineteen months. Besides this, his nephew, Henry Addington, whom his mother had cared for all his life had married and was the father of three girls and of one son born after the father had gone into the service. These, with their mother, David took charge of and cared for the same as his own family. And when the father died of disease in the hospital at Nashville, Tenn., he still gave them a home and looked after all their interests till the mother was taken away by death and the children had grown to maturity and were able to care for themselves. These are but a few of the many instances which might be given of his broad and liberal spirit and of the great benevolence of his heart.

He was an inveterate foe to the liquor traffic, and years ago cast in his lot with the Prohibition party; and being very plain spoken and earnest in his conviction and having never learned the arts by which hard things are sometimes spoken smoothly, he sometimes made enemies among those who differed from him. But even these will accord to him the honour of honest convictions and of answering fidelity to conscience at all hazards and regardless of cost.

Of his father's large family, consisting of father, mother, nine sons and two daughters, there is now living but one son, Benjamin robbed in so short a time of his companion and of his only remaining brother, his lot is surely a sad and lonely one. But he looks forward with answering faith to that glad reunion, which in nature cannot be distant in the future, when they shall meet again in the Eternal city.

Funeral services at the residence Monday, July 21st, at 1 o'clock p.m. conducted by Rev. W. R. Freeland, assisted by Rev. W. C. McKaig and the writer. Burial at Maxville.
THOMAS ADDINGTON.

Joseph Leander Addington, son of David

Joseph Leander Addington farmed for his entire life on the original Addington family farm about two miles south of Maxville. He was a breeder of championship pure bred registered Norman horses. He married on 18 Feb 1880, Dora Elizabeth Feagans, the daughter of Robert Wesley and Rebecca Jane (Moore) Feagans. Leander and Dora had four sons and one daughter:
(1) David "Cressie" Addington, b. 3 Jan 1881, d. 1966
   m. 25 Nov 1911, Jeanetta Clevenger
(2) Robert "Gilva" Addington, b. 4 Aug 1885, d. 18 Sep 1971
   m. 28 Feb 1914, Mary Ermel Clevenger
(3) Mabel Elizabeth Addington, b. 10 Jul 1890, d. 16 Oct 1977
   m. Sylvester Starbuck
(4) Harry Vern Addington*, b. 9 Mar 1893, d. 13 Aug 1930
   m. 30 Sep 1922, Alma Marguerite Chalfant
(5) Cecil Lester Addington, b. Oct 1898, d. 30 Aug 1980
   m. 20 Sep 1922, Osa Main, d. 11 Feb 1990

From their offspring, they had 16 grandchildren and more than 34 great grandchildren. Leander died in 1935 and Dora died in 1944 and are buried in Maxville Cemetery alongside their son Harry Vern, who died earlier in 1930 as the result of a farm accident.

David "Cressie" Addington, the first born son of Leander and Dora (Feagans) Addington, was born on 3 Jan 1881 and married Jeanetta Clevenger on 25 Nov 1911. They had seven children: Floyd, Doris, Mildred, Gerald, Dora Alice, Mary Alma and Gene Clay. Floyd Addington was born on 2 Jan 1913 and married Ethel Green and they had five children, Linda, Robert, Michael, Judy and Tammy. Doris Addington was born on 17 Sep 1915 and did not marry. Mildred Addington was born on 6 Feb 1917 and married Bud Oliver and they have one daughter, Marlene. Gerald Addington was born on 9 Dec 1919 and married Ruth Potter and they have seven children, Nila, Ardith, William, Marilyn Sue, Sandy, David and Mark. Dora Alice Addington was born 2 Nov 1921 and married Howard Thornburg and they have five children, Vern, Luetta Sue, Edward, Donna Jo and David. Mary Alma Addington was born 13 Mar 1923 and married John Pavey and they have 5 children. Gene Clay Addington was the last born and married June Shreves and they had three children, Millie, Ronnie and Bruce. Jeanetta (Clevenger) Addington died in 1946 and is buried in the Maxville Cemetery. Cressie then married a second time to Karen Bosworth. Cressie died in 1966 and is buried in Maxville Cemetery next to his parents.

Gilva Addington, the second son of Leander and Dora (Feagans) Addington was born on 4 Aug 1885 and married Mary Ermel Clevenger on 28 Feb 1914. They had three children: Dallas Eugene, Viola Elizabeth and Rosemary. Dallas Eugene Addington was born on 22 Nov 1917 and married Nell Oliver in 1940 and they have one daughter Pamela. Viola Addington was born on 7 Nov 1922 and married Marvin Hart on 29 Feb 1948, no children. Rosemary Addington was born on 22 Aug 1929 and married Henry Haworth and they have one son Lowell Anthony. Gilva was a farmer all of his life and first farmed south of Mills Lake and then later owned a farm about two miles south of Maxville.

Mabel Addington, the only daughter of Leander and Dora (Feagans) Addington, was born on 10 Jul 1890 and married Sylvester Starbuck. They had four sons, Murray, Glenn, Cecil and Irwin "Pete". Sylvester Starbuck died on 28 Aug 1972 and Mabel died on 16 Oct 1977. Son Murray died as an infant. Glenn married Ester Davis and they have three children, Sandra Sue, Shirley Suzanne and Sheldon Scott. Cecil married Dora May Archer and they have one son, Jerry. Pete married Bonnie Watson and they have two children, Stephen and Dane.

Cecil Addington, the youngest son of Leander and Dora (Feagans) Addington was born in Oct 1898 and married Osa Main on 20 Sep 1922, no children. Cecil and Osa lived on and continued to farm the original Addington homestead. Cecil died on 30 Aug 1980 and Osa died on 11 Feb 1990 and they are buried in Maxville Cemetery.

Harry Vern Addington, son of Joseph Leander

Harry Vern Addington was born 9 Mar 1893 to Joseph Leander and Dora Elizabeth (Feagans) Addington, the third son and fourth child. Harry grew up on the old Addington farmstead located about one and a half miles south of Maxville.

Harry Vern Addington and Alma Marguerite Chalfant were married in Randolph County on 30 Sep 1922. Alma Marguerite Chalfant was born on 9 Jun 1905 to Finley and Emma Alice (Fitzpatrick) Chalfant. She was the seventh of eight children and was considerably younger than some of her older siblings. The Chalfant family originally lived in southern Delaware County, but in 1900 they were living at Summitville in Madison County and later moved back to Parker in Delaware. Harry and Marguerite initially set up their household on a farm in section 29 of White River Township, about two miles south of Maxville. There they had three sons: Leo Vern, born 10 Apr 1923, Joseph Elsworth, born 3 Apr 1925, and Murrie Alexander, born 19 Apr 1927. In 1928 they moved to Green Township and rented a farm in section 5 from Martin Wood. The family was living there when tragedy struck. In August of 1930, Harry was helping a nearby farmer by the name of Les Melvin when he fell from a hay wagon and broke his neck, dying quickly. He was buried in the Woodlawn

Cemetery at Maxville in the far eastern section. Later his parents were buried beside him. The following Obituary reported Harry's death:

Harry Vern Addington was the fourth child of a family of five children born to Leander and Dora Addington, being born on the farm south of Maxville in Randolph county, Ind., March 9, 1893.

His entire life was lived in the county of his birth and came suddenly to a close near his home, northeast of Parker, Ind., August 13, 1930 at the age of 37 years, 5 months and 4 days.

Harry, in his childhood days, was a quiet, agreeable and dutifull boy, and highly esteemed by all who knew him. He was united in marriage to Marguerite Chalfant, September 30, 1922, to this union were born three sons, Leo Vern, Joseph L. and Murry A. To this family Harry gave his deepest love and best providence.

Harry was clean in habbits, and industios, though having never engaged in the more active religious customs of common faith, he maintained a standard of regard for principle worthy of more than a passing notice.

Owing to condition resulting from an accident a few years ago, the manner of his death was no surprise to him, having made statements at various times which led us to this conclusion, thus the extent of his prepardness as a matter wholy between him and his God is very much unknown to us. Who can know the heart of man there is a spirit in man and the inspiration of the Almighty mighty giveth him understanding.

In the face of these facts we are content to leave the destiny of our dead with the mercy and love of Him who gave His life a ransome for sinners, I come not to call the righteous, but sinners unto repentance.

He leaves to mourn his sudden passing his youthful wife, the three above named sons, father and mother, three brothers, Cressie, Gilvia and Cecil, one sister, Mrs. Mable Starbuck, father and mother-in-law, sisters and brother-in-law, together with a large number of near relatives and hosts of friends.

The obituary must of have been written in some haste due to the numerous misspellings. The part about the previous illness is probably just a standard passage added as filler.

Marguerite and the three young boys then moved into Parker and lived with her parents for the next year. See the earlier section on Harry and Marguerite for details of their family.

Other Descendants

The descendants list in the back of this book lists the known children. Many times in local history books, family stories will list names of children of which there are no further records or will list just infant, died young. The mortality rate for infants was known to be significant. The Indiana Mortality Census taken in 1850 for that one year, lists three Addington children: Calvin S. Addington, died July, age, 3 months, of lung fever, Celia Addington, died May, age 2 months, of croup, and Martin L. Addington, died June, age 1 month, of inflammation of the brain. The death of infants was a part of life at this time in history but who knows how many died and what a loss the families felt.

Movement West

Many of the Addington descendants of John Addington have remained in Randolph County with a few still in Wayne County. Many families have moved to the surrounding counties of Jay, Delaware and Henry. However, some moved further west.

No sooner had the Addington families moved into Randolph County, but some of the more adventurous thought about moving further west to newer lands just opening up. A John N. Addington, age 23, born Indiana, shows up in the 1850 Will County, Illinois census but his ancestry is not clear. By 1857, Bishop Addington, the son of William Addington and grandson of William, moved to Illinois since he is recorded as marrying Lucinda Falcor in Tazewell County. Bishop lived in Tazewell County for at least the next twenty years. William Lewis Addington, the son of Joseph Randel Addington and grandson of Joseph Addington moved over into Illinois sometime before the Civil War. He fought in the Civil War as a member of the 19th Illinois Infantry. He later returned to Indiana to marry in 1869. His first son was born in Iowa in 1870 and by 1880 he was in Montgomery County, Kansas. He returned to Indiana sometime before 1900 and remained in Randolph County until he died in 1917. Benjamin L. Addington, a son of James Addington moved to Iowa before 1860 but moved back to Illinois sometime in the 1870s and he is recorded as dying in Sibley, Ford County, Illinois in 1885. The 1900 Illinois census lists two Addingtons in Cook County (Elmer, age 28 and Homer, age 34) and one in Logan County (Carl, age 28) who were all born in Indiana and probably descendents of John Addington.

The first of the Indiana Addingtons to move into **Missouri** was probably Noah Addington, a son of John Addington, Jr. Noah moved first to Howard County, Indiana and then about 1855 moved to Iowa, where he married for a second time in Ringgold County to Mary Jane Garrett. He married a third time to Phoebe Ann Roberts in 1861 and died at Jefferson Barracks, near St. Louis in 1863. Jesse Addington, a son of William Randel Addington and grandson of Joseph Addington, moved from Fulton County, Indiana to Missouri where his oldest son was born in 1856 but by 1860 he had already moved on to Iowa. In 1870 he is found in the Walla Walla County, Washington census, in 1880 he is found in the Lake County, Oregon census and in 1900 he is found in the Modoc County, California census. Barbara (Harshman) Addington, the widow of Joab Addington (the youngest son of William Addington), remarried after Joab's death in 1853 and later moved to McDonald County, Missouri where son John was married in 1873 at Pineville. Lindsey Addington, a son of Elihu Addington and grandson of Joseph Addington moved to

Missouri before 1870 since he married Angeline Scott in Worth County in 1870.

The state of Iowa seems to have held a popular appeal to westward immigrants from Indiana. Bishop Addington, Jr., a son of Bishop Addington and grandson of William Addington moved to Iowa sometime before 1859 when his son Edward was born in Iowa. It appears that sometime before 1867 he must have moved back to Indiana when a daughter was married in Wayne County in 1867. Bishop, Jr. died in Jay County, Indiana in 1904. Joseph Randel Addington, a son of Joseph Addington moved to Iowa about 1846 and resided there until his death in Lee County, Iowa in 1899. Two of his sons, Isaac Barker and William J. later returned to reside in Randolph County. However, four other sons, Willis G., Amos T., Alfred Benjamin and Albert David, either remained in Iowa or moved further west. John L. Addington first moved to Kansas but later to Iowa where he died in Hardin County in 1878. Two of John L. Addington's younger sons, Samuel and John, raised families in Iowa while one other son, Thomas F., later moved to Oklahoma where he died in 1916. Branson Addington, a son of Noah Addington, and grandson of John Addington, Jr. was in Iowa by 1858 but moved on to Cherokee County, Kansas by 1870.

Kansas was also a popular destination for some of the Indiana Addingtons. James Addington, the youngest son of John Addington, moved to Kansas in 1858 and died there in October 1859 in Anderson County, Kansas. James' sons John L. Addington and Benjamin L. Addington were living in Anderson County, Kansas during the 1860 census. John L. Addington's son, James A. Addington, moved to near Kansas City, Kansas about 1880 and he is the ancestor of most of the Addingtons in that area. David Morgan Addington, a son of Joshua Addington and grandson of William Addington was in Montgomery County, Kansas in 1880. Also in the same county was William J. Addington, a son of Joseph Randel Addington and grandson of Joseph Addington. William J. Addington later moved back to Randolph County while David Morgan Addington moved further west and died in Seattle, Washington in 1922. William S. Addington, a son of Joseph Addington and grandson of Thomas Addington, married Mary Underwood in Randolph County in 1867 but moved to Butler County, Kansas by 1880. Later his family must have moved

73

back to Randolph County since his sons married in Randolph and Jay Counties.

California showed one very early Addington immigrant, Absalom M. Addington, a son of Morgan Addington, and grandson of John Addington, Jr. Absalom is shown in 1850 living in Placerville, El Dorado County, California as age 21, born Indiana and his occupation was listed as miner. He must have caught "gold fever" and took off on his own to find his fortune. He stayed in California where he raised a family in Sacramento County. Jesse Addington, a son of William Randel Addington and grandson of Joseph Addington, is found in the 1900 Modoc County, California census. Modoc County is in the far northwest part of California in a very rural area. Willis G. Addington, a son of Joseph Randel Addington and grandson of Joseph Addington, was in California sometime after 1900, and later died in 1919 in Riverside.

The first movement of Addingtons into **Washington** state was sometime before 1870 with Jesse Addington, a son of Joseph Randel Addington and grandson of Joseph Addington. Jesse is shown as living in Walla Walla County in the 1870 census as is his son Isaac Addington and his family. Willis G. Addington, a son of William Randel Addington and grandson of Joseph Addington is shown in Columbia County, Washington in 1880. Willis' brother Amos also moved to Washington where he died in 1891 in Tacoma.

Joel Addington, a son of William Addington and grandson of William Addington, moved to **Oregon** sometime before 1860 since he married Mary Jane Lewellen in Lane County in that year. He remained in Oregon, raising a family of six children before dying in Portland in 1921. Joseph Mendenhall Addington, a son of Joseph Randel Addington and grandson of Joseph Addington was in Lane County, Oregon by 1870 and his brother Jesse had moved to Lake County by 1880. Joseph Mendenhall Addington later moved back to Randolph County where he died in 1898. Jesse later moved south to California.

Several Addington families moved west looking for that elusive "new frontier." Systematic tracing of the movement of Addington families since 1910 is difficult due to lack of census indexes and some confidentiality of records. The increased movement of families, especially since World War II, has made the task even greater. Hopefully, today's generation can connect their own family history to a family already mentioned and see how they fit into the Indiana Addingtons.

More Recent History

The 1908 Randolph County Indiana Directory lists forty-one Addington households in the county with many families in Ridgeville. The occupations listed included farmer (numerous), retired, widow, miller, grocer, clerk, R. R. mail carrier (2), barber, merchant, insurance agent, carpenter and butcher.

In the 1910 Randolph County census, there were twenty-seven Addington households (plus of course many others into which Addington daughters had married). Of the sons of John Addington who migrated from South Carolina, eleven of the household were head by descendants of Joseph Addington as were eleven descendants of Thomas Addington. Five household heads were descendants of son James Addington and but one of son William Addington. None were known to be descendants of the other son John since his sons migrated to surrounding counties very early.

The recent history of Randolph County lists six Addingtons who served in World War I: Earl, Edward C., Orval A., Ray R., Russell and Willard C. Earl is a great grandson (thru George Wesley, James) of Thomas Addington as is Willard C. (thru Franklin Madison, Joseph). Edward C. and Russell were great grandsons of Joseph Addington (thru Henry Taylor, Jonathan). Orval is a great grandson of James Addington (thru Elsworth, Thomas L.) Ray R. is believed to be the great great grandson of James Addington (thru Newton, James A., John L.)

The Addington family has not had a tradition of being political office seekers, although several Addingtons were Justices of the Peace in the early 1800s. However, Evert Asa Addington, the son of Forest Addington and grandson of Benjamin Addington and great grandson of Joseph Addington, served as the Indiana State Representative from Randolph County from 1923 to 1924. A descendent of Noah Addington, William H. Addington who was born 8 Mar 1924, Elkhart, Morton County, Kansas did run for governor of Kansas several years back.

The history of Randolph County lists three Addingtons who served in World War II: Chester L., Isadora and L. Vern. Chester Luther Addington is a great great grandson of Thomas Addington (thru Willard Clayton, Franklin Madison, Joseph). Isadora is a great great granddaughter of Thomas Addington (thru Evert Ray, Calvin, Rev. Thomas) L. Vern Addington, the author's father, is a great great grandson of Joseph Addington (thru Harry Vern, Joseph Leander, David).

At the time of the writing of this book, many Addington families still live in and around Randolph County. The 1988 Winchester phone book lists eighteen Addington households in central Randolph County. Many of the descendants of Joseph Leander Addington, a son of David Addington and grandson of Joseph Addington still live in and around Winchester. Several Addington families still living around Winchester trace their ancestry through Henry Addington who was born in 1897 and he is currently still alive at the time this book is written. Henry is a descendant of Edwin Kester Addington, a grandson of William Addington, a great grandson of William Randel Addington, and great great grandson of Joseph Addington. This Henry was called to military service in 1918 and was waiting at the train station to report for duty when a phone call came saying that the war was over and that he did not have to report.

Addington reunions have been held for many years in Randolph County. In the 1900-1910 era, large family reunions were common as shown by the report on the 1910 Graham-Addington Reunion shown earlier. In more recent years, the descendants of Franklin Madison Addington have held an annual reunion, usually at Saratoga. The descendants of Leander Addington have also held annual reunions, usually near Winchester.

The Feagans Family

Harry Vern Addington's mother was Dora Elizabeth Feagans, a daughter of Robert Wesley and Rebecca Jane (Moore) Feagans. Robert Wesley Feagans was a son of James H. and Rebecca (McCracken) Feagans. The Feagans family is often hard to trace because of the many different ways the family name has been spelled. It has been seen spelled as Feagans, Feagan, Feagins, Figens, Figgens, Figgins, Figins, Fegan and Fagan. The original ancestry of the Feagans family is probably English or Irish. Our James H. Feagans family moved to Randolph County, Indiana sometime in 1837 or 1838. The 1850 and 1860 census data show James Feagans (often spelled Figins) was born in 1814 in Virginia.

We first pick up the trail of the Feagans family in Ohio. James Figins first married about 1834 in Licking County, Ohio to Rebecca McCracken, the daughter of Robert and Urith McCracken. Unfortunately, the marriage records for Licking County are not available from 1820 to 1840. Rebecca's father, Robert McCracken, moved his family to Randolph County, Indiana about the same time as the Feagans and they lived near each other in Stony Creek Township (sometimes spelled Stoney Creek). James and Rebecca (McCracken) Feagans had the following children:
(1) Alexander Feagans, b. c1835, Ohio
(2) Robert Wesley Feagans*, b. 13 Nov 1836, Ohio, d. 8 May 1902
(3) Sarah E. Feagans, b. 12 Nov 1838, Indiana
(4) James H. Feagans, b. 1 Feb 1841, Indiana

Rebecca (McCracken) Feagans evidently died sometime in 1842/3 and then James married second Julia Cowgill on 15 Mar 1843 in Randolph County. Julia was born 25 Mar 1818, the daughter of Elisha and Rebecca Cowgill. James Figins died some time after 1870. Julia died in Dec 1877.

Trying to pick up the trail of James Figins, we see that the 1830 Ohio census for Hopewell Township of Licking County lists a James Figgins 1M<5, 2M10-15, 1M15-20 (age of son James. H., b. 1814 VA), 1M40-50 (b. 1780-1790), 1F<5, 2F10-15, 1F40-50. From this data it indicates that James H. Feagans' father was probably also named James. Also listed in Hopewell Township is Robert McCracken (2M 20-30, 1M40-50, 2F10-15, 1F15-20, 1F40-50). This Robert McCracken was the father of Rebecca McCracken who married James H. Figins. Census data indicates that Robert McCracken was born in 1784 in Virginia. His wife, Urith, family name unknown, was born in Maryland. Robert McCracken evidently was in Pennsylvania around 1810 before moving to Licking County, Ohio. Robert McCracken later moved to Randolph County where he died in 1858 at the age of 74 and is buried in the Buena Vista Cemetery.

The 1820 Ohio Census lists no Fegans of any spelling in Licking County so they were probably still in Virginia but it still lists Robert McCracken in Hopewell Township. There are some Feagans in Fayette County, Ohio but this is a different unconnected family which consistently spells their family name as "Feagans."

The 1820 Virginia Census lists four James Fagan in Fauquier County while the 1810 Census lists but a single James Fagan. The LDS International Genealogical Index lists 30 references to the Fagan/Feagan family in Fauquier County, Virginia from 1777 to 1850. Only one of these is for James, a James born in 1807 to William and Jane (McClenachann) Feagan. However one reference is for a Mahala Feagan who was born in 1811 to the above. Mahala is not a common name but we do find a record of a Mahala R. Feagans, a granddaughter of James H. Feagans, marrying a David B. Strahan on 2 Jul 1871 in Randolph County, Indiana indicating that there may be a connection between the Fagans of Fauquier County and the James H. Figins who migrated to Randolph County.

The early records of Fauquier County show a 1780 will of a Edward Feagins with children Cleary, Edward, Frances, John, Mary, Sarah, Susanna and William. This Edward Feagins could be the patriarch of this entire Feagans family of Fauquier County.

The Indiana trail of the Feagans show James H. Figins to be in Randolph County, Indiana by 1840 as his family is listed in West River Township as 2M<5, 1M20-30 and 1F20-30.

The 1850 Indiana Census lists in the same township:

James Figins	36	VA
Julyemy	33	Ohio
Alexander	14	Ohio
Robert W.	12	Ohio
Sarah E.	11	Indiana
James H.	9	Indiana

Listed directly below the James Figins family is Robert McCracken, Jr., age 39, born PA, who is a brother to James' first wife, Rebecca McCracken. Robert McCracken, Sr. is also listed nearby in West River Township.

Of the children of James Feagans, Alexander Feagans was the first son married when he wed Rachel Moore on 14 Sep 1854. Robert Wesley Feagans married first Elizabeth Starbuck on 26 Aug 1858. James H. Feagans, born 1 Feb 1841 married Abigail Harris on 17 Mar 1863 in Randolph County. They had at least two children: Charles C. Feagans, born 19 Sep 1865 and Orin G. Feagans, born 11 Aug 1867. An item in an 1879 Union City newspaper reported that James Fegans was moving to Missouri but he has not been traced there.

The 1860 Indiana Census in Stony Creek Township of Randolph County lists:

James Figgens	46	VA
Julia E.	41	Ohio
James	19	Indiana
Mary Cowgill	8	Indiana
Wm Ogden	7	Indiana
Robert W. Feagans	23	Ohio
Elisabeth	19	
Mary E.	1	
Alex Figgins	26	Ohio
Rachel	22	
Rebecca M.	4	
Geo. W.	2	

Tucker's History of Randolph County states that Alexander Feagans served in the 105th Indiana Regiment of Minutemen which was organized in 1863 during the raid of General John Morgan into southern Indiana and Ohio.

The first child of Robert Wesley and Elizabeth (Starbuck) Feagans was Elizabeth Feagans, born in 1859 and their second child was Mary E. Feagans, born 30 May 1861, married Isaac Smith, had four children and died 22 May 1936 in Farmland. Evidently, Elizabeth (Starbuck) Feagans died sometime between mid 1861 and mid 1862, since Robert Wesley Feagans married second on 17 Jul 1862 to Rebecca Jane Moore, the daughter of Benjamin and Hannah (Wright) Moore. Rebecca Jane Moore was a cousin to Rachel Moore who married Wesley's brother, Alexander. Robert Wesley and Rebecca Jane (Moore) Feagans had three daughters:

(1) Dora Elizabeth Feagans*, b. 24 Oct 1862, d. 19 Mar 1944
    m. 18 Feb 1880, Joseph Leander Addington
(2) Ella Feagans, m. ? Sayers (or Sears)
(3) Pearl Feagans, d. aft. 1940, m. ? Powell

In the photo section there is a picture of Pearl (Feagans) Powell with her sister Dora and their husbands. The Powells eventually moved to Michigan.

The 1865 and 1874 Plat maps show James H. Figgins owning 40 acres in section 6 of Stony Creek Township. The 1870 census shows the family name to be spelled Fagans with James H., age 55, Guiliuemy, age 52 and Mary Cowgill, age 18 probably a niece of Julianna.

Also, in the 1870 census:

Alex Feagans	35	Ohio
Rachel	34	IN
Mahala R.	15	IN
George W.	12	IN
Mary E.	9	IN

Mahala married David B. Strahan on 2 Jul 1871. Robert Wesley Feagans' family can not be found in the 1870 census so they were probably not recorded. One family story says the family broke up but no records have been found to that effect. Rebecca Jane (Moore) Feagans died on 20 May 1878 and is buried in the Buena Vista Cemetery, her grave marked by a very nice gravestone. Robert Wesley Feagans evidently married a third time to Mary, family name unknown, in 1879 since the 1900 census shows his family to be:

Wesley Feagans	Nov 1837	62	m21	OH	VA	IN
Mary	May 1848	52	m21	IN	VA	KY
Otto	20			IN		

Burley	15	IN
Orvil	13	IN
Iva K.	11	IN
Claude	6	IN
Alfred Moore	56	IN

Robert Wesley Feagans died on 8 May 1902 and is buried in the Buena Vista Cemetery in West River Township a short distance from his second wife, Rebecca and his gravesite is covered with a matching stone. The Feagans family name is not currently found in Randolph County so any descendants probably moved off.

The Bolinger Family

Harry Vern Addington's paternal grandmother was Huldah Ruth Bolinger, the daughter of Jacob and Mary (Goshorn) Bolinger. Huldah was born in Pennsylvania and married David Addington on 27 Nov 1851 in Randolph County, Indiana. David and Huldah Addington farmed the land in section 36 of White River Township that was the original Addington farmstead in White River Township. Huldah's exact birthdate is not known. Her death record lists 20 Nov 1820, but this must be a mistake meaning 1830. However, the 1850 (age 20), 1860 (27), 1870 (38), 1880 (49) and 1900 (Oct 1831) censuses (generally taken in mid-year) give very conflicting dates. The Maxville Cemetery records list only the years 1830-1907, ae 76-9-29. Taking her age at death and death date of 18 Sep 1907, would give a birth date of 20 Nov 1830.

The Bolinger family moved to Randolph County, Indiana between 1835 and 1840. This was a time of rapid growth for the county and land was taken up very rapidly. Data indicate that the family of Jacob Bolinger moved into Stony Creek Township before 1840 as shown in that census. The 1850 census shows their son Moses to have been born in Pennsylvania in 1835 and their daughter Sophia to have been born in Indiana in 1839. Generally families moved as family groups but no records of any other Bolingers or Goshorn families in Randolph County have been found so Jacob's family may have made this move entire on their own. A family story says that Jacob's father also accompanied the family on their migration west but then returned to Pennsylvania.

The 1840 census lists Jacob Bolinger in Stony Creek Township as age 30-40, wife age 30-40 and 1M<5, 1F<5 and 1F5-10. The children would correspond to Huldah, Moses and Sophia listed below. It also lists in White River Township the family of John Bolinger, age 50-60 and wife age 50-60. This John Bolinger whose name was spelled Bolander (or sometimes Bolender) was born in Germany and does not appear to be related to our Jacob Bolinger. The 1882 Tucker History of Randolph County says this John Bolander was a soldier in the army of Napoleon.

He appears to have arrived in Randolph County about 1838. Later the family spelling of the name became commonly spelled as Bolinger.

The 1850 Randolph County census shows the Jacob Bolinger family with Jacob being 42, born in Pennsylvania and wife Mary S. age 40, also born in Pennsylvania, and children including
Hulda*, age 20, b. PA
Moses, 15, b. PA
Sophia, 11, b. IN
Elizabeth J., 8, b. IN
Martha E., 5, b. IN
Samuel R., 3 b. IN
Mary J. Grow, 25
They lived in White River Township south of Maxville. Huldah Ruth Bolinger married on 27 Nov 1851 to David Addington, the youngest son of Joseph and Celia (Townsend) Addington. Moses E. Bolinger married Mariah Louisa Miller on 22 Jul 1858. Sophia Bolinger married on 25 Jul 1855 to Henry Addington, the son of Thomas and Beulah (Hunt) Addington and a nephew of David Addington. Two of Jacob's daughters, two of his granddaughters and one great granddaughter married Addingtons so there was a close tie between the families for several generations.

The 1860 census shows the Jacob Bolinger (misspelled as Billinger in the census) family in Stony Creek Township:
Jacob Billinger, age 50, PA
Mary S., 52, PA
Mary Jane, 35, PA
Elizabeth, 17, IN
Martha, 15, IN
Samuel R., 14, IN
Hannah, 9, IN

Jacob and Mary Bolinger are living in Stony Creek township so they must have moved to another farm sometime after 1850. It is not known what relationship Mary Jane was to the family but by her age, she is probably not their natural daughter but adopted into the family. There is a Randolph County marriage record of a Mary J. Grow marrying Lucas Ullum on 20 Dec 1851. Evidently he must have died and Mary Jane moved back in with the Bolinger family. Shortly after the 1860 census, Jacob

Bolinger died on 27 Dec 1860 and is buried in the old section of the Maxville Cemetery.

The 1870 census lists two Bolinger households. Moses Bolinger is listed as age 33, born Pennsylvania with wife Mariah, age 29, born Indiana. Children are:
Waldo B., 10, b. IN
Indiana, 7, b. IN
Charles P., 5, b. IN
Minnie, 2, b. IN
Samuel, 23, b. IN (Moses' brother)

In a separate household nearby are:
Mary S. Bollinger, 61, b. PA
Mary J. Grow, 44, PA

Mary Bolinger died on 10 Oct 1875, age 67 years, 6 months, and 27 days, and is buried in Maxville Cemetery about five graves away from her husband in the oldest part of the cemetery. This would make her birthday 23 Mar 1808.

The 1874 Randolph County Plat map shows M. E. Bolinger owning land in Section 20 of Stony Creek Township. Moses E. Bolinger, the son of Jacob and Mary (Goshorn) Bolinger, was born on 17 May 1836 in Pennsylvania and was still a very young boy when he accompanied his family west to Indiana. He married Mariah Louisa Miller on 22 Jul 1858 in Randolph County. Moses and Mariah had the following children:

(1) Waldo Rosco Bolinger, b. 12 May 1861, Indiana, d. 1922
    m. 10 Jul 1888, Randolph Co., Indiana, Rosa Smith
(2) Indiana Rosa Bolinger, b. 9 Aug 1893, Randolph Co., Indiana, d. 23 Dec 1920
    m. 20 Jun 1887, Randolph Co., Indiana, George Emerson Addington
(3) Charles T. Bolinger, b. 30 Mar 1865, Indiana, d. 4 Oct 1912
    m. 16 Jun 1887, Randolph Co., Indiana, Nettie A. Barnes
(4) Minnie E. Bolinger, b. 9 Aug 1867, Indiana
    m. 29 Mar 1889, Randolph Co., Indiana, Kelly S. Smithson
(5) Lilly Pearl Bolinger, b. 29 May 1873, d. 2 Jul 1931
    m. 30 May 1889, Asa Robert Addington

The oldest son of Moses, Waldo Rosco Bolinger, and his wife Rosa Smith had a large family of nine children:

(1) Carl Bolinger, d. 24 Jul 1892
(2) Hattie Bolinger, d. 20 Jul 1894
(3) Fleety G. Bolinger, b. 15 Dec 1892
    m. 25 Jan 1915, Delaware Co., Forest Morris Addington
(4) Neal W. Bolinger, b. 14 Jan 1895
(5) Wilbur Bolinger, b. c1901, m. Dorothy Current
(6) Madonna Bolinger, b. 7 Oct 1902
(7) Mildred Bolinger, b. c1903
(8) Edith U. Bolinger, b. c1905
(9) Louise Adaline Bolinger, b. 2 Dec 1907

Moses' daughter Indiana Rosa Bolinger married on 20 Jun 1887 to George Emerson Addington but they had no children. She died on 30 Dec 1920 in Randolph County. Moses' son Charles T. Bolinger married on 16 Jun 1887 to Nettie A. Barnes and they had one son, Ernest E. Bolinger who married Inez Wise and they had four children. Charles Bolinger died on 4 Oct 1912 in Randolph County.

Moses' daughter Minnie E. Bolinger married on 29 Mar 1889 to Kelly S. Smithson and had at least one daughter Ruby who married George Chalfant.

The youngest daughter, Lilly Pearl Bolinger, married on 30 May 1889 to Asa Robert Addington. They had four children:
(1) Perry Orvil Addington, b. 8 Mar 1890, d. 13 Feb 1967
    m. Mae Veirl Jones
(2) Cleo Louisa Addington, b. 22 Mar 1895, d. 6 Dec 1904
(3) Kathleen Rebecca Addington, b. 28 Sep 1897, Randolph Co., Indiana, d. 28 Jan 1986, Clawson, MI
    m. 27 Aug 1919, Randolph Co., IN, George Russell Patterson
(4) Paul O. Addington, b. 12 Nov 1905, d. 14 Nov 1905

Samuel Bolinger, the youngest son of Jacob and Mary, was born on 9 Oct 1846 in Randolph County. He married on 7 Nov 1874 to Samatha Clevenger and they had children:
(1) Lily G. Bolinger, b. 1873
(2) Leuela Bolinger, b. 1875
(3) Charles W. Bolinger, b. 1879

The 1880 Randolph County census lists two Bolinger households:
Moses E. Bolinger, age 45, PA
Marian, 39, IN

Waldo, 19, IN
Rosa, 16, IN
Charles T., 15, IN
Miney E. 12, IN
Lily P., 7, IN

Samuel Bolinger, age 31, IN
Samatha, 28, IN
Lily G., 7, IN
Leuela, 5, IN
Charles W., 1, IN

In trying to trace the Bolinger family, the 1830 Indiana census lists no Bolingers in Randolph County or in any surrounding county, and since Huldah was born in 1830 in Pennsylvania, the families must still be there. The death record for Huldah lists her mother as Mary Goshorn and the death record for Moses Bolinger lists his mother as Mary Goosehorn.

The 1830 Pennsylvania census lists five Jacob Bolingers of various spellings with Bolinger/Bollinger families in Huntingdon, Alleghany, Lancaster and York counties. There are also ten Gooshorn (sometimes spelled Gosham) families in Huntingdon County with two families in Mifflin County and two families in Beaver County. All of the Gooshorn families living in Huntingdon County are in Tell Township as are four of the nine Bolinger families in Huntingdon County. One of the two Jacob Bolinger families in this county is shown as 1M<5, 1M20-30, 1F5-10 and 1F20-30. This could be our Jacob Bolinger but the ages of the children are too old. Either the ages of the children are in error or perhaps Jacob and his family are still living with his parents or her parents.

The Bolinger families in 1830 in Huntingdon County are headed by Jacob (age 20-30), Peter (age 50-60), John (age 40-50), Peter (age 50-60), Benjamin (age 50-60), Adam (age 70-80), Michael (age 20-30), Jacob (age 60-70) and Abraham (age 40-50). It would appear that Adam and Jacob are brothers and are the patriarchs of the family in this county. The 1790 Pennsylvania Head of Households shows three Adam Bolander families in Northumberland County along with four other Bolander families head by Frederick, Henry, John and Michael so the family appears to be concentrated there in 1790. One of these Adam Bolanders is probably Adam Bolander, Sr.

who is listed in DAR records as an outstanding patriot. Adam Bolander, Sr. was born on 22 May 1735 in Germany and immigrated to Pennsylvania before the revolution. During the Revolutionary War he was a member of the Committee of Public Safety from Pennsylvania Township in Northumberland County, Pennsylvania. He married Elizabeth Krespie and had known children: Adam, Jr., John, Frederick, John, Henry and Elizabeth. Adam Bolander, Sr. died in 1820 in Snyder County, Pennsylvania.

The Goshorn Family

Huldah Ruth Bolinger's mother was Mary Goshorn (Harry Vern Addington's great grandmother) according to Huldah's death record. Mary (Goshorn) Bolinger is buried in the Maxville Cemetery and records say she died 20 Oct 1875 at the age of 67 years, 6 months and 27 days. This would make her birthdate to be 23 Mar 1808. Census records indicate she was born in Pennsylvania. This birthdate is consistent with the ages recorded in the 1850 and 1860 census.

Mary Goshorn evidently married Jacob Bolinger in 1829 or early 1830 since their first born, Huldah Ruth was born in Oct 1830 according to the 1880 census records or 20 Nov 1830 based on her death record. Unfortunately marriage records for Huntingdon County are not available for this time period so confirmation of their marriage location and date are not available. The 1830 Pennsylvania census does not list a Jacob Bolinger family of the appropriate ages so it is assumed that this Jacob Bolinger family is still living with his or her parents.

The 1830 Pennsylvania census shows ten Gooshorn (sometimes spelled Gosham) families in Huntingdon County with two families in Mifflin County and two families in Beaver County. The Gooshorn families in Huntingdon County are headed by Nicholas (age 20-30), John (age 20-30), Andrew (age 40-50), Jacob, Jr. (age 50-60), William (age 40-50), Jacob, Sr. (age 70-80), John (age 50-60), Samuel (age 40-50), Nicholas (age 40-50) and George (age 50-60). Seven of these families are living in Tell Township and are listed next to three Bolinger families. It is assumed that Mary and Jacob come from these families. From the ages of the family members in the 1830 census, it looks like Jacob and Mary could be living with either the Nicholas or Andrew Gooshorn families, indicating that Nicholas or Andrew may be her father.

A published genealogy by Marjorie Carter entitled *Goshorn Descendants of Johann Georg and Susannah Gansshorn* gives details on this German family. The original name of this family in German is Gansshorn but it is later standardized as

Goshorn although it has also been written as Goosehorn or Gooshorn.

Andrew and Nicholas Gooshorn were both sons of Johann Jacob and Susannah (Fink) Goshorn. Johann Jacob Goshorn was born on 4 Nov 1751 in York County, Pennsylvania. He married Susannah Fink about 1774 and was listed in the first census in 1790 in Huntingdon County. Johann Jacob and Susannah (Fink) Goshorn has the following children:

(1) George Goshorn, b. 22 Sep 1775, d. May 1850
    m. Mary Vaughn
(2) Jacob Goshorn, b. 10 Dec 1778, m. Margaret ?
(3) Samuel Goshorn, b. c1778, m. Ellen Traxler
(4) John Goshorn, b. c1779, d. 1857, m. Elizabeth Baughman
(5) Andrew Goshorn, b. 3 Mar 1871, d. 11 Apr 1861
    m. Margaret Gooshorn
(6) Nicholas Goshorn, b. 26 Oct 1782, d. 3 Feb 1868
    m. 2nd Jane Traxler
(7) William Goshorn, b. c1789, m. Elizabeth ?
(8) Mary Goshorn, b. c1790, m. James Jones
(9) Elizabeth Goshorn, b. 1 Jun 1791, d. 20 Oct 1863
    m. 15 Jan 1810, Jacob Jones

Jacob and Susannah probably had other daughters but we do not know their names.

All of the Goshorn families in Huntingdon County were headed by sons or grandson of Jacob so I feel Mary Goshorn is almost surely his granddaughter. Jacob made out his will on 12 Sep 1829 and he died on 1 Jul 1833. His will was registered for probate on 13 Aug 1833.

Johann Jacob Goshorn was the son of Johann Georg Gansshorn who was born on 19 Mar 1725 in Bammental, Heidelberg, Baden, Germany. Johann Georg Gansshorn married on 6 Jan 1746 in Wiesenbach, Heidelberg, Baden, Germany to Susanna Elisabetha Buckle. Susanna was born on 22 Mar 1723, the daughter of Johann Adam and Maria Veronika (Wild) Buckle. Johann Georg Gansshorn with his wife Susanna and their daughter Maria Katharina immigrated to America on the ship BROTHERS from Rotterdam by way of Cowes on the Isle of Wright and landed in Philadelphia on 24 Aug 1750. They first settled in York County, Pennsylvania where the remainder of their children were born. Their children were:

(1) Johann Bartholomaeous Gansshorn, b. 30 Jan 1747,
    d. ? young
(2) Maria Katharina Gansshorn, b. 12 Jun 1729, Bammental
    m. Jacob Grim
(3) Johann Jacob Gansshorn*, b. 4 Nov 1751, York Co.,
    Pennsylvania, d. 1 Jul 1833, Huntingdon Co., Pennsylvania
    m. c1774, Susannah Fink
(4) Johann Nicholas Gansshorn, b. 14 May 1753, York Co.,
    Pennsylvania, d. 5 Mar 1835
    m. Sarah Vaughn
(5) Johann Georg Gansshorn, bap. 1 Feb 1756, York Co., PA
    m. 2nd Margaret McKnight
(6) Johann Phillip Gansshorn, bap. 25 Jun 1758, York Co., PA
(7) Maria Barbara Gansshorn, bap. 3 Aug 1760, York Co., PA
    m. George Fink
(8) Leonard Gansshorn, b c1761, d. c1812
    m. Rachel Stillwell

Johann Georg is listed as George Goosehorn in Huntingdon
County, Pennsylvania in the 1790 census and in Dublin
Township of the same county in 1800. Johann Georg
Gansshorn's will was dated 26 Jan 1806 and entered for probate
on 1 Apr 1806 so he must have died between these dates. In his
will he disowned his children from receiving any property but
the other devisees signed over the estate to "his lawful heirs."

The Gansshorn genealogy also lists several more generations
of this family with the first known ancestor being a Clauss
Nicholas Gansshorn who was first recorded in Neckargemund,
Germany. His wife's name was Catharina and they settled in
Waldhilsbach, Heidelberg, Baden, Germany sometime after
1647. Clauss Nicholas died on 18 Jun 1668 in Waldhilsbach.
Clauss and Catharina had six known children including:
Georg Wolf Gansshorn*, b. 1628

Georg Wolf Gansshorn first married on 7 Jul 1647 Anna
Barbara Fromm and they had four children. Georg married
second on 6 Jul 1674, Margaretha Bender who was born about
1640 in Reilsheim, Heidelberg, Baden, Germany. Georg and
Margaretha had six children including:
Johann Phillip Gansshorn*, b. 1 Dec 1678
Georg Wolf Gansshorn died on 30 Nov 1691 in Bammental.

Johann Phillip Gansshorn married on 9 Nov 1706 to Appollonia Ziegler. Appollonia was born on 3 Feb 1684 in Bammental, the daughter of Hans Friedrick Zielger and Anna Ursula. Johann Phillip and Appollonia had eight children including:

Johann Georg Gansshorn*, b. 19 Mar 1725 who immigrated to America in 1750.

Johann Phillip Gansshorn died on 2 Mar 1744 in Bammental. Appollonia died on 23 May 1744.

Susanna Elisabetha Buckle who married Johann Georg Gansshorn was the daughter of Johann Adam Buckle and his second wife Maria Veronika Wild. Johann Adam Buckle was born about 1671 in Wiesenbach, Germany and married Maria on 6 Apr 1706. They had ten children including their second youngest daughter Susann Elisabetha* who was born 22 Mar 1723. Johann Adam Buckle died on 7 Sep 1737 in Wiesenbach.

Maria Veronika Wild, born on 28 Oct 1683, was the oldest daughter of Hans Valentin Wild who married Maria Catherina Kueffer. Hans Valentin Wild was born on 10 Jan 1658 in Neckargemund, Heidelberg, Baden, Germany and died on 7 Jul 1694. Maria Catherina Kueffer was born in Aug 1658 in Keckarelz and died on 12 Jan 1721.

The Moore Family

Harry Vern Addington's maternal grandmother was Rebecca Jane Moore who married Robert Wesley Feagans. The earliest identifiable Moore ancestor of this family is Matthew Moore who was born in January 1753 in Pettigoe in Donegal County in the north of Ireland. The Moore family name is quite common in Ireland and is recorded in many ancient records. Matthew Moore married about 1775 to Sarah McDowell. Sarah was born in September 1758 of Scottish-Irish background. One letter describes Sarah as tall and prepossessing in appearance, neither large nor spare in figure, quiet, and dignified in action, benevolent by nature but unforgiving of wrong, with a character as firm as the everlasting hills, she cast an influence on all around her.

Matthew and Sarah immigrated to America shortly after they were married, for their first child, Ann, was born in Philadelphia on 6 Aug 1777. A younger brother of Matthew named Jonathan Moore also immigrated with him. Jonathan Moore married Elizabeth Long and had at least six children. Jonathan Moore eventually settled his family in Bartholomew County, Indiana. One of their sons, Hosea Moore, born 1803 was said to have been killed at the Alamo.

One record says that Matthew Moore was an off-and-on soldier in the Continental Army, joining up when there was trouble and then going home when the immediate trouble subsided. Matthew moved his family quite frequently in the next thirty years with records finding them in Philadelphia, New Castle County, Delaware, Chester County, Pennsylvania and Lancaster County, Pennsylvania. From Lancaster County, Pennsylvania, the Moore family started their westward migration in 1817. Some of their children were grown by this time but they all migrated except one daughter who was married and remained in Delaware. The family halted for a year near Jamesville (believed to be Zanesville in Muskingum County), Ohio where one daughter died and another was left my marriage. The family finally settled in Wayne County, Indiana in 1818.

Matthew and his oldest son David settled on a tract of land about two miles west of Middleboro and six miles north of Richmond. There they raised their family and saw their children married. Matthew Moore died in February 1836 at the age of eighty-three. Sarah then lived with her son Matthew who had moved to Darke County, Ohio. She died there in Nov 1845. Both Matthew and Sarah are buried in the Woodbury Quaker Meeting Cemetery about two miles south of Whitewater, Indiana.

Matthew and Sarah (McDowell) Moore has the following children:
(1) Ann Moore, b. 6 Aug 1777, Philadelphia
    probably married and remained in Delaware
(2) David Moore*, b. 6 Aug 1779, prob. Philadelphia, d. 1845, Wayne Co., Indiana
    m. c1803, Mary Wilkins
(3) Alexander Moore, b. 25 Mar 1781, nfi
(4) Mary "Isabella" Moore, b. 26 Apr 1783
    died or remained in Muskingum Co., Ohio
(5) Margaret Moore, b. 19 Aug 1785, m. Gideon Garrison
(6) George Moore, b. 23 Dec 1787, nfi
(7) Sarah Moore, b. 19 Apr 1790, m. Henry Davis
(8) Hannah Moore, b. 26 Mar 1794, m. Moses Woods
(9) Jane Moore, b. 17 Oct 1796, d. 1874, Randolph Co., Indiana
    m. John Bishop
(10) Robert Moore, b. 16 Sep 1799
(11) Matthew Moore, Jr., b. 31 Jul 1802, d. 4 Oct 1845, Drake Co., Ohio, dnm

All eleven of their children appear to have survived to adulthood, quite a feat in this frontier era when childhood diseases often took the lives of young children. Not all of these lines have been traced but there are numerous descendants.

Mathew Moore's first born son David married Mary Wilkins, about 1803 probably in Delaware although no marriage record has been found. David's family accompanied his father's family west to Wayne County, Indiana in 1817-18 and entered on land next to his fathers. When Mathew died, his farm passed to David.

David and Mary (Wilkins) Moore had the following children:
(1) Henry W. Moore, b. 1804, Wilmington, Delaware, d. 1879,
    Randolph County, Indiana
    m. 10 Feb 1831, Wayne Co., Indiana, Mary Wright
(2) George Moore, b. 1806, Delaware, d. 4 Apr 1897
    m. 1839, Mary Hiatt
(3) Sarah Moore, b. 1807
(4) Benjamin Moore*, b. c1810, Delaware, d. 1857, Randolph
    Co., Indiana
    m. 30 Jul 1833, Wayne Co., Indiana, Hannah Wright
(5) Lydia V. Moore, b. 1812
    m. John Martin
(6) Mary Moore
    m. Jonathan Commons
(7) Rachel Moore
    m. Eli Townsend
(8) Elizabeth J. Moore, b. 19 Sep 1821, d. 26 Feb 1885
    m. 11 Nov 1845, Chandler Graves
(9) Alexander Moore, nfi

Of the children of David and Mary Moore, we known that
several migrated to Randolph County. Eli and Rachel (Moore)
Townsend settled in Stony Creek Township by 1840. George
Moore settled in West River Township and raised his family
there. Henry Moore also moved to Randolph County and
farmed there until his death in 1879. Besides farming, David
Moore was a blacksmith by trade. David Moore died in 1845 in
Wayne County. Mary (Wilkins) Moore died sometime before
that date.

George Moore grew up in Wayne County and married in 1839
Mary Hiatt, a daughter of Isaac and Hannah (Sulgrove) Hiatt.
He moved to Randolph County in 1839 and settled on forty
acres of land in West River Township. Later he received from
his father and bought acreage up to a total of one hundred and
seventy-two acres. George and Mary (Hiatt) Moore had six
children: Mahala, William A., Rachael, David, Martha and
Henry A. Rachael Moore married in 1846 to Alexander
Feagans, a brother to Robert Wesley Feagans. David Moore
was a soldier in the Civil War serving in Company D, 147th
Indiana Volunteers.

Our direct line ancestor is Benjamin Moore, who was born in
Delaware in 1810 and was a young boy when his family made

the big move west to Indiana. He grew up in Wayne County and married Hannah Wright, the daughter of Ralph and Hannah Wright, on 30 Jul 1833. Hannah was born in 1813 in North Carolina and her sister Mary married Henry Moore, Benjamin's brother. Benjamin was a school teacher and a splendid wood workman. He made furniture of high quality. About 1848, he moved his family to Huntington County where they are recorded in the 1850 census. Sometime after that they must have moved back to Randolph County to a small farm in White River Township near where his brothers Henry and George were living. Benjamin died in 1857 at the age of forty-seven from consumption (tuberculosis). Hannah evidently remarried in 1858 or 1859 to a John Morrison, 14 years her junior, since she is listed in the 1860 Randolph County census as Hannah Morrison, with children Rebecca J, William H., Mary Ann, and George A. Moore in the household. However, by the 1870 census, she is listed again as Hannah Moore with only son George still in the household. Hannah died in 1881 and is buried besides her first husband, Benjamin, in Buena Vista Cemetery.

Benjamin and Hannah (Wright) Moore had the following children:
(1) Lydia Wright Moore, m. Robert Liverton
(2) Jonathan Wright Moore, b. 1836, d. 1884
(3) Armeda Ann Moore, b. 1841, d. 1907
    m. ? Fulhart
    m. 2nd James Spray
    m. 3rd B. P. Cougill
(4) Rebecca Jane Moore*, b. 10 Oct 1842, d. 20 May 1878
    m. 17 Jul 1862, Randolph Co., IN, Robert Wesley Feagans
(5) William Henry Moore, b. 1844, m. Clara Mercer
(6) Mary Hannah Moore, b. 1848, d. 1939
    m. William Wallace Phelps
    m. 2nd James Moune
    m. 3rd Isaac Mills
    m. 4th W. W. Wiles
(7) George Arthur Moore, b. 1851, d. 1937
    m. Malissa Small
    m. 2nd Olive Mendenhall

Mary Hannah Moore married William Wallace Phelps and they had seven children. One daughter, India Wilma Phelps, married in 1894 to George Thomas Larkin Murphy. They had eight children and four of their daughters, Doris, Bonnie, Olive and Ethel, wrote a genealogy on the Mathew Moore family from whence most of this information is taken.

Rebecca Jane Moore married Robert Wesley Feagans on 17 Jul 1862 in Randolph County. Wesley's first wife, Elizabeth Starbuck, had born him one daughter and then died about a year later. Wesley and Rebecca Jane (Moore) Feagans had three daughters, Dora Elizabeth, Ella and Pearl. Ella married Orville Sayers (or Sears) and they had five children. Pearl married a Powell and they later moved to Michigan and there are no known children. Rebecca Jane (Moore) Feagans died on 20 May 1878 and is buried in Buena Vista Cemetery.

The Wright Family

Our direct line ancestor from the Wright family is Hannah Wright (great grandmother of Harry Vern Addington) who was born on 1813 in Wayne County, Indiana and married Benjamin Moore on 30 Jul 1833 in Wayne County, Indiana. The Wright family is most likely English in origin but that has not been confirmed. They are first identified in Maryland in the early 1700s. The family later moved to North Carolina sometime before 1771 and then moved to Indiana about 1806.

Benjamin and Hannah (Wright) Moore raised their family in Wayne County until the late 1840s when they moved to Huntington County as shown by the 1850 census. Benjamin Moore died in 1857. The family had evidently moved to Randolph County before his death. Benjamin's brothers George and Henry were living in Stony Creek Township. In the 1860 census, Hannah was living in Stony Creek Township and had remarried to John Morrison, fourteen years her junior.

Hannah Wright's parents were Ralph and Hannah Wright, Jr. and were living in Huntington County next door to the Benjamin Moore family as shown by the 1850 census data. Ralph Wright was born on 19 Aug 1788 in North Carolina. We do not know Hannah's family name but she was born in 1799 in North Carolina. The Wrights were Quakers and were members of the Whitewater Monthly Meeting in Wayne County. Records from this Monthly Meeting showed the Wright family to have come to Wayne County early since in 1809, Ralph, Sr. was appointed an elder. Ralph, Jr. is listed as being received into membership in 1816. References also list a Jonathan Wright, son of Ralph, Sr. as coming from the Springfield MM in North Carolina.

No marriage record has been found for Ralph Wright but he is shown in the 1820 Wayne County census in Wayne Township with one son under 10 and two daughters under 10 (one of which should be Hannah) and wife age 16-25. Ralph raised his family in Wayne County until the late 1840s. He then moved with his son-in-law Benjamin Moore to Huntington County where he appears in the 1850 census. There were many Wright families in Randolph County but most are unrelated to our Wright family which came from North Carolina. Ralph and Hannah Wright stayed in Huntington County as shown by the 1860 census. It is assumed they died in that county sometime after 1860.

Ralph Wright, Jr., born 1788, was the son of Ralph Wright, Sr. who was born 24 Jul 1746 in Prince George County, Maryland. It is not known when Ralph, Sr. moved to North Carolina but he was there by 1771 since his first child was born there. His wife's name was also Hannah but the family name is not known. Ralph Wright, Sr., moved his family north to Wayne County, Indiana sometime around 1806. They settled in Wayne Township along with their married children. Ralph Wright, Sr. lived a long life and died in Wayne County on 23 Jul 1837 at the age of 90 year, 11 months and 30 days. Hannah had died before him on 28 Feb 1826 at Whitewater in Wayne County. Ralph and Hannah Wright, Sr. had the following children:

(1) James Wright, b. 9 Sep 1771, d. 5 Dec 1833, Wayne Co., IN
(2) William Wright, b. 1 Jan 1773, d. 4 Nov 1780, bur. Springfield, North Carolina
(3) Jane Wright, b. 18 Oct 1774
(4) Elijah Wright, b. 12 Oct 1776, d. 29 Dec 1845, Wayne Co., IN
(5) John Wright, b. 7 Nov 1778, d. 27 Oct 1778, bur. Springfield, North Carolina
(6) Richardson Wright, b. 6 Nov 1780
(7) Hannah Wright, b. 4 Jan 1783
(8) Lydia Wright, b. 6 Jan 1785, d. 27 Jun 1785, bur. Springfield, North Carolina
(9) Jonathan Wright, b. 24 Apr 1786, d. 28 May 1862, Wayne Co., Indiana
    m. 28 Feb 1810, Lydia Hawkins
(10) Ralph Wright*, b. 19 Aug 1788, North Carolina, d. aft. 1860, prob. Huntington Co., Indiana
    m. Hannah ?
(11) David Wright, b. 17 Oct 1790, d. 20 Aug, 1870, Wayne Co., Indiana
    m. 4 Aug 1813, Hepsa Coffin
(12) Ruth Wright, b. 9 Sep 1792, d. 28 Jul 1797, bur. Springfield, North Carolina
(13) Mary Wright, b. 24 Jul 1795, d. 22 Jan 1799, bur. Springfield, North Carolina

Quakers records in North Carolina show the Wright family to belong to the Deep River Monthly Meeting in Guilford County. The first meeting of the Deep River Monthly Meeting was held on 7 Sep 1778. Hannah Wright and her daughter Jane were received into membership on that day. The Deep River Meeting was located in the western part of Guilford County, about 12 miles from Greensboro. Midweek meetings had been held there as early as 1753 and a preparative meeting established in 1758. The meeting enjoyed great growth through immigration from the North during the latter half of the 18th century but suffered great losses by migration to the Northwest during the first half of the 19th century. One report in the book *Southern Quakers and Slavery* says: "Deep River is, and has been, one of the strongest monthly meetings. Its record of migration begins with 1811 and extends to 1860. As usual, they are all to Indiana except ten, which are divided between Tennessee, Ohio and Illinois. Between 1811 and 1845 the movement was quite uniform. The favorite objective point was the White Water Meeting, Indiana."

The Whitewater Monthly Meeting minutes say Ralph Wright was received of membership from the Back Creek Monthly Meeting in Randolph County, North Carolina. No record of Ralph Wright has been found in those records but he may have had some connections there.

Ralph Wright, Sr. parents were a James and Lucy Wright. James Wright was born on 8 Jan 1718 probably in Prince George County, Maryland. We do not know the family name for Lucy but she was also born in Prince George County about 1720. James and Lucy Wright had the following children, all born in Prince George County:
(1) Ralph Wright*, b. 25 May 1746, d. 23 Jul 1837
(2) Elizabeth Wright, b. 15 Oct 1747
(3) James Wright, b. 1 Dec 1748
(4) Ann Wright, b. 25 Oct 1750
(5) Susanna Wright, b. 19 Mar 1753
(6) Boyster Wright, b. 13 Sep 1755
(7) Micajah Wright, b. 24 Apr 1758

Lucy may have died sometime around 1760 since James evidently married a second time to Phoebe, family name unknown. James Wright moved his family to North Carolina and died there at some later date.

The parents of James Wright, born 1718, are listed in one reference as a James and Mary Wright. There is no further data on them so they may have been born in Maryland or could have been the original Wright immigrants to America. This Wright family was obviously among the early settlers in America.

The Townsend Family

The Townsend family is connected to the Addington family through the marriage of Celia Townsend to Joseph Addington in 1808. The Townsend family is of English origin and is first referenced in Pennsylvania in the early 1700s. The early information on this Townsend family comes from the Townsend Newsletter published by the Townsend Society of America.

The first identified John Townsend of our line of Townsends was born about 1725 in Pennsylvania. Some genealogists have said that his father was also named John Townsend who was born in England and came to America on the ship "Welcome" but this has not been proved.

John Townsend married in Pennsylvania to Elizabeth Pearson. Elizabeth was born 8 Dec 1726 in Pennsylvania, the daughter of Enoch and Margaret (Smith) Pearson.

Elizabeth's father, Enoch Pearson, was born in 1683 and married Margaret Smith in 1712. Margaret was the daughter of William and Mary (Croasdale) Smith. Both Enoch and his wife were noted Quaker preachers. Enoch and Margaret (Smith) Pearson had the following known children:
(1) William Pearson, b. 1713, m. Elizabeth Duer
(2) Thomas Pearson, b. 1714, d. 1719
(3) Mary Pearson, b. 1716, m. John Hulme
(4) Enoch Pearson, Jr., b. 1718, m. Tabitha Jay Cox
(5) Thomas Pearson(twin), b. 1718
(6) Sarah Pearson, b. 1720
(7) Phebe Pearson, b. 1721
(8) Margaret Pearson, b. 1723
(9) Rachel Pearson, b. 1724
(10) Elizabeth Pearson*, b. 8 Dec 1726, m. John Townsend
(11) John Pearson, b. 1728, m. Sarah Hill
(12) Samuel Pearson, b. 1730

Enoch Pearson died in 1758 and is buried in Buckingham, Pennsylvania. After the death of Enoch Pearson, Jr. in 1775, his wife Tabitha Cox is reportedly to have married second John

Townsend. Evidently Elizabeth (Pearson) Townsend died sometime after 1775 and Tabitha then married John Townsend, Sr. A Tabitha Townsend is recorded in the 1800 South Carolina census as head of the household, indicating John Sr. must have died before then.

John and Elizabeth (Pearson) Townsend had the following children:
(1) James Townsend
    m. 6 Apr 1775, Newberry Co., South Carolina, Mary Cook
(2) Elizabeth Townsend
    m. 12 Apr 1775, Newberry Co., South Carolina, Amos Cook
(3) William Townsend, b. c1759
    m. Margaret ?, d. 4 Sep 1824, Darke Co., Ohio
(4) John M. Townsend*, b. 6 Nov 1763, Bucks Co.,
    Pennsylvania, d. 25 Aug 1853, Fountain City, Indiana
    m. 6 May 1783, South Carolina, Elvira Cain
(5) Margaret Townsend
    m. 11 Feb 1789, Newberry Co., SC, Samuel Hunt
(6) Ruth Townsend, m. ? Hunt
(7) Sarah Townsend, m. ? Cain
(8) Esther Townsend
    m. 11 Feb 1784, Bush River MM, SC, James Parnell

It is not clear when the Townsend family moved south to the 96th District area of South Carolina, now Union County. There John M. Townsend married on 6 May 1783 to Elvira Cain who was born 7 Mar 1768 in Edgecombe Co., North Carolina. The Townsend and Cain families must have been very close since it appears that they moved north together to Indiana and Ohio about 1803.

Fox's *Memoirs of Wayne County* published in 1912, gives the following biography of John Townsend:

John Townsend was born in Pennsylvania of English parentage, in 1758. At the age of seventeen, he joined the Revolutionary army under General Greene and served four years. While with this command in South Carolina he contracted smallpox and was given a furlough for treatment. While yet in the early stage of the disease he started on foot across the country to reach a place where he might receive treatment, but after walking a few days fell exhausted from travel and the weakness caused by the

102

disease. As fate would have it, while thus lying in the woods, he was discovered by Miss Elvira Cain, a young girl of twelve, who in company with a negro servant, was hunting the cows. She insisted the stricken soldier accompany her to her father's home and there be taken care of. Mr. Townsend objected to going to the house, for fear of spreading the disease among the members of the family, but he stopped at an unoccupied cabin on the plantation and there was cared for by one of Mr. Cain's slaves who was immune.

After his recovery, he returned to his command and served out his term of enlistment, receiving an honorable discharge. Immediately thereafter he returned to the home of the girl who had saved his life and asked for and received her hand in marriage. They began their married life together in North Carolina and lived there a number of years, coming to Indiana in 1803. Mr. Townsend settled upon and cleared a tract of land adjoining the present city of Richmond on the south, and lived there until about 1830, when he removed to a farm two miles north of Centerville. He died at the residence of his daughter, Mrs. Isaac Commons at the age of 89 years, 9 months and 19 days.

During the last twenty years of his life he was afflicted with blindness. One of his eyes having been lost while a soldier in the Revolutionary war. While living in North Carolina he and his wife became converted to the principles of peace as taught and practiced by the Society of Friends. As an evidence of their supreme faith in these teachings there are two incidents that deserve mention. Mr. Townsend was entitled to a government pension, and during the last twenty years of his life was tendered a pension payment every three months. But although stricken with blindness he steadfastly refused to accept it, saying it was blood money, and that he had enlisted under a Captain of Peace and was no longer serving under General Greene. At the time of the death of the father of Mrs. Townsend, she inherited seven full grown slaves, worth from $700 to $1,000 each. The administrator of her father's estate came to Indiana, where she and her husband were living in humble circumstances, and offered to buy the slaves and pay her the market price. She refused the offer and asked to have the slaves sent to her, and upon their arrival in Indiana she gave them their freedom. The grandparents were thus numbered among the pioneer settlers of eastern Indiana, where they took up their abode a number of years prior to the admission of the state to the Union.

Another story says that while John Townsend had smallpox, he was captured by the British along with six other soldiers. The other six were hanged. Because he had smallpox the British were afraid of him. They said, "Let him go. He will die anyway."

John Townsend enlisted from Guilford County, North Carolina at the age of 17 in 1780 with the rank of private 2nd class. John Townsend is shown in Quakers records as being eased out on 28 Dec 1782 for "taking up arms and going out in a warlike manner." It appears that John Townsend spent some time in both North and South Carolina. John Townsend with wife and ten children were received by certificate from Cane Creek Monthly Meeting in South Carolina on 19 Mar 1803. The 1800 Union County, South Carolina census shows five Townsend households, John, William (younger and probably John's son), plus two households lead by Martha and one by Tabitha.

The Townsends were Quakers and were opposed to slavery and joined the movement north from South Carolina in the 1800s. John M. Townsend moved north to Wayne County, Indiana in 1802 or 1803. Evidently his older brother William also moved his family at the same time but he settled in Darke County, Ohio where he later died.

John M. and Elvira (Cain) Townsend had the following children:
(1) Celia Townsend*, b. 22 Feb 1785, d. 5 Mar 1852, Randolph Co., Indiana, bur. Sparrow Creek Cemetery
    m. 22 Dec 1808, Preble Co., Ohio, Joseph Addington, b. 21 Jul 1776, d. 20 Feb 1836
(2) James Townsend, b. 17 Dec 1787
    m. 16 Dec 1807, Warren Co., Ohio, Rosannah Smith
(3) Rachel Townsend, b. 29 Oct 1790
    m. 18 Dec 1807, William Harvey
(4) Jonathan Townsend, b. 1793, South Carolina, d. 13 Jul 1862, Pilot Grove, Iowa
    m. 28 Sep 1814, Wayne Co., Indiana, Polly Clawson

104

(5) Mary Townsend, b. 7 Mar 1794
m. 29 Nov 1809, Wayne Co., Indiana, Isaac Commons
(6) William Townsend, b. 10 Apr 1795, d. bef. 1850,
m. 29 May 1816, Elizabeth Morrow
(7) Esther Townsend, b. 4 Feb 1798
m. 1 Mar 1815, Preble Co., Ohio, William Stubbs
(8) Sarah Townsend, b. 28 Dec 1800
m. 8 Apr 1818, Joseph Stubbs
(9) Elizabeth Townsend, b. 28 Dec 1802, d. 11 Apr 1871
m. Sep 1819, Elisha Stubbs
(10) John Townsend, b. 1804, Wayne Co., Indiana,
m. 8 Mar 1827, Wayne Co., Indiana, Martha Jones
(11) Barbara Townsend, b. 6 Feb 1807
(12) Stephen Townsend, b. 31 Dec 1810, d. 15 Jul 1884, Fountain
City, Indiana
m. 19 Nov 1835, Mary Griffin

The 1820 Wayne County, Indiana census lists five Townsend households, John and his sons James, Jonathan, and William plus another William, probably John's brother. In addition, the 1820 Ohio census lists some Townsends living across the Ohio border from Wayne County, James, Joseph and William, sons of John's older brother William.

The 1830 Indiana shows John M. Townsend and four of his sons in Wayne County. The Ohio census shows three Townsend families in Darke County, James, Jonathan and Margaret, two Townsend families in Warren County, Jesse and John and Eli Townsend in Preble County.

The Townsend family continued to live in Wayne County as shown by the 1850 census. John and Elvira, ages 86 and 83 are listed as a separate household indicating they must have remained in good health. Their son James died before 1840 since his widow Rosannah is shown as head of the household in both 1840 and 1850. John M. Townsend died on 25 Aug 1853 and is buried in Willow Grove Cemetery at the south edge of Fountain City, Indiana.

The 1860 Indiana census lists ten Townsend households in Wayne County but only two in Randolph County, Eli and Uriah Townsend.

Eli Townsend and Uriah Townsend, grandsons of John M. Townsend, appear to be the only Townsend descendants to move over to Randolph County. Eli was born on 20 Apr 1817 in Wayne County, Indiana and married Rachel Moore. Eli owned a farm in Stony Creek Township and was a leader in the Society of Friends in the Popular Run Monthly Meeting, first set up in 1846. Hiram Townsend, a son of Eli, was born on 6 Apr 1840 and fought in the Civil War in Company A of the 84th Indiana Infantry. He survived the war and was mustered out of the regiment on 14 Jun 1865. Hiram was a farmer in Randolph County and died sometime after 1900.

Several female descendants of this John M. Townsend have used John as their Revolutionary War ancestor to join the Daughters of the American Revolution. Laura Addington who married Hovey Thornburg, joined the DAR in 1956 and is a great granddaughter of Joseph and Celia (Townsend) Addington.

The Ancestry of Alma Marguerite Chalfant

Alma Marguerite Chalfant was born 9 Jun 1905 to Finley Ellsworth and Emma Alice (Fitzpatrick) Chalfant and married Harry Vern Addington on 30 Sep 1922 in Randolph County, Indiana. The Chalfant family was of English origin and the Fitzpatrick family was of Irish origin. The Chalfant family originally was from Pennsylvania, moved to Ohio and then settled in Perry Township in the southeastern part of Delaware County in 1840. Some descendents later moved over into Stony Creek Township of Randolph County. The Fitzpatrick family came from North Carolina through Wayne County and into Randolph County about 1855.

These two families form the basis for this ancestral search but many other families are associated with them through marriage. Families associated with the Chalfant line are the Winders family of New Jersey, Pennsylvania and Ohio and the Templin family of Ohio and Pennsylvania.

The Fitzpatrick family originally came from North Carolina but may have been in Virginia before that. Other families associated with this Fitzpatrick line are the Terrell family of Virginia and Ohio, the Moore family of Virginia, the Seany family of North Carolina and the Johnson family of Virginia.

The following is a listing of the direct line ancestors of Alma Marguerite Chalfant that are known. Numbering System - Father's name is always twice the number of the offspring. Mother's name is twice the offspring's number plus one.

5. Alma Marguerite Chalfant
   b. 9 Jun 1905, Randolph Co., Indiana
   m. 30 Sep 1922, Randolph Co., IN, Harry Vern Addington
   d. 18 Aug 1979, Muncie, Indiana
   bur. Maxville Cemetery

   10. Finley Ellsworth Chalfant
      b. 18 Aug 1866, Randolph Co., Indiana
      m. 25 Jul 1884, Randolph Co., Indiana
      d. 9 Feb 1940, Randolph Co., Indiana
      bur. Union Cemetery, Windsor, Indiana

20. Alexander Chalfant
  b. 14 Jan 1840, Mt. Pleasant, Delaware Co., Indiana
  m. 27 Jun 1858, Delaware Co., Indiana
  d. 29 May 1930, Indiana, bur. Union Cemetery
  40. Jesse Chalfant, Jr.
    b. c1797, Pennsylvania
    m. 21 Sep 1826, Highland Co., Ohio
    d. 16 Sep 1873, Delaware Co., Indiana
    bur. Mt. Pleasant Cem., Delaware Co., Indiana
      80. Jesse Chalfant, Sr.
        b. 1744/7, Pennsylvania
        m. c1790
        d. 1827, Ohio, prob. Belmont Co.
        160. James Chalfant
          b. 20 Feb 1717, Pennsylvania
          m. c1744
          d. 1808, Pennsylvania
          320. John Chalfant
            b. 14 Apr 1690, England
            d. 7 Sep 1729, Pennsylvania
            640. Henry Chalfant
              b. 13 May 1663, England
              1280. Robert Chalfant
                b. 24 Feb 1626, England
                m. 9 Jun 1658
                2560. Christopher Chalfont
                  b. 4 Nov 1574, Oxfordshire, England
                  m. 3 May 1625
                  5120. Thomas Chalfont
                    b. 5 May 1520
                    m. 28 Jun 1570, Chepping, Wycombe
                    10260. William Chalfont
                      b. c1460
                      d. 7 Feb 1543, Chepping Wycombe, Eng.
                      20520. William Chalfont
                    10261. Margaret Artbroke
                      20522. Robert Artbroke, Chepping
                        Wycombe
                  5121. Margaret Bennett (Cornwallis)
                2561. Elizabeth Paynter (Chilton)
                  d. 11 Jan 1628
                1281. Lydia Barnard
                  2562. Thomas Barnard
                  2563. Elizabeth Bayes
108

5126. John Bayes
5127. Perryn Ralphe
641. Elizabeth Chandler
321. Martha ?
161. Hannah Harris
81. Rachael Ann Bailey
162. Joel Bailey
b. 1734
m. 24 Nov 1757
d. 1825
324. Josiah Bailey
d. 1791
648. Joel Bailey
bap. 29 Jan 1658, England
m. 1687, Pennsylvania
d. 1732
1296. Daniel Bailey
b. 1601, Westbrook, Parish of Bromham
d. 1674
2592. Thomas Bayley, Chitto, Parish of
Bromham, Wiltshire
b. 3 Jul 1567
5184. William Bayley
2593. Anne ?
1297. Mary ?
649. Ann Short
325. Sarah Marsh
163. Hannah Wickersham
326. William Wickersham
b. 3 Feb 1706, Chester Co., PA
m. 26 Mar 1730
652. Thomas Wickersham
b. c1660, Bolney, Sussex, England
m. 2nd 27 Jun 1700, Cowford, Sussex, Eng.
d. Jun 1730, Chester Co., Pennsylvania
653. Alice Hogge
b. 1677, Ifiels, Sussex, England
1306. Richard Hogge
2612. Richard Hogge
1307. Alice Pannell
2614. John Pannell
327. Rachel Haynes
654. Henry Haynes
b. 1667, Oxfordshire, England

1308. Richard Hayes
   d. 1676
655. Isabella ?
41. Elizabeth Winders
  b. 30 Oct 1806, Fayette Co., Pennsylvania
  d. 1896, Indiana
  82. Daniel Winders
    b. c1785
    m. 29 Jan 1806
    d. 1839/52
    164. James Winder
      b. c1747
      m. c1770
      d. 1831 Fayette Co., Pennsylvania
      328. James Winder
        m. 9 May 1743, All Saints Parish, Fayette Co., MD
        d. 1789, Washington Co., Maryland
        656. Thomas Winder
          m. 5 Jun 1704, London
          d. 1746, New Jersey
        657. Sara Bull
      329. Elizabeth Sherwood
    165. Elizabeth Grable
      d. bef 1830, Redstone Twp, Fayette Co., PA
      330. Samuel Grable
        b. 17 Sep 1725, Germany
        d. 17 Sep 1811, Fayette Co., Pennsylvania
        660. Nicholas Grable
      331. Hannah Earhart
        b. 29 Jan 1733
        d. 29 Jun 1804, Fayette Co., Pennsylvania
        662. Philip Earhart
          b. Germany
  83. Mary Kennedy
21. Elizabeth Templin
  b. 24 May 1843, Delaware Co., Indiana
  d. 1 Apr 1870, bur. Blountsville, Henry Co., Indiana
  42. Terry (Terah) Templin
    b. 26 Oct 1806, Highland Co., Ohio
    m. 25 Oct 1827, Highland Co., Ohio
    d. 23 Jan 1855, Henry Co., IN, bur. Blountsville, IN
    84. Robert Templin
    b. 18 Mar 1776, Pennsylvania
    d. 23 Jun 1849, Blountsville, Indiana

168. James Templin
  b. Pennsylvania
  d. Ross Co., Ohio
  336. Richard Templin
    b. 1688
    d. 1775, Warwick, Pennsylvania
  337. Mary ?
169. Mary Salmon
  b. Pennsylvania
  d. Ross Co., Ohio
85. Eunice Beals
  b. 2 Jan 1785, Surrey Co., North Carolina
  d. 26 Jun 1859, Howard Co., Indiana
  170. John Bowater Beals
    b. 26 May 1764
    m. 4 Feb 1784, Surrey Co., North Carolina
    340. Bowater Beals
      b. 1725
      m. 2 Oct 1752, Warrington MM, Pennsylvania
      d. 9 Feb 1781
      680. John Beals, Jr.
        b. 28 Jan 1685, Nottingham, Chester Co., PA
        m. 14 Sep 1711 Chester Meeting House
        d. c1748, Prince George Co., Maryland
        1360. John Beals, Sr.
          b. c1650
          m. 1 Nov 1682, Chester Co., Pennsylvania
          d. 1726
          2720. William Beals
        1361. Mary Clayton
          b. 29 Jun 1665, Sussex Co., England
      681. Sarah Bowater
        b. c1690, Chester Co., Pennsylvania
        d. Prince George Co., Maryland
        1362. Thomas Bowater
        1363. Sarah Edge
    341. Sarah Ann (Cook) Myers
  171. Lois Branson
    b. 4 Jan 1765, Virginia
    342. Thomas Branson
    343. Jane ?
43. Rachel Johnson
  b. Jun 1812, Ohio
  d. 17 Apr 1884, Wells Co., Indiana

111

86. Enos Johnson, prob. descendent of William
     Johnson, see 1476
87. Sarah ?
11. Emma Alice Fitzpatrick
  b. 26 Nov 1866, Randolph Co., Indiana
  d. 14 Feb 1946, Randolph Co., Indiana, bur. Union Cem.
  22. William F. Fitzpatrick
    b. 1839, Wayne Co., Indiana
    m. 22 Feb 1865, Randolph Co., Indiana
    d. 9 Sep 1915, Randolph Co., Indiana, bur. Union Cem.
    44. William Fitzpatrick
      b. 1815, North Carolina
      m. 25 Mar 1837, Wayne Co., Indiana
      d. 1854/60, Randolph Co., Indiana
    45. Hannah Seany
      b. c1818, Wayne Co., Indiana
      d. 1854/1860, Randolph Co., Indiana
      90. Jacob Seany
        b. 1794, North Carolina
        d. after 1850, Indiana
        180. Owen Seany
          b. 1750/60
          d. 1830/40, Wayne Co., Indiana
      91. Susanna ?
        b. c1795, North Carolina
        d. after 1850, Indiana
  23. Jemima Emily Terrell
    b. 3 Dec 1837, Randolph Co., Indiana
    d. 7 Jun 1916, Randolph Co., Indiana, bur. Union Cem.
    46. George Wesley Terrell
      b. 1804, Virginia
      m. 27 Nov 1825, Highland Co., Ohio
      d. 22 Mar 1878, Randolph Co., IN, bur. Union Cem.
      92. prob. William Terrell
        b. 24 Mar 1779, Virginia
        m. 25 Feb 1802, Campbell Co., Virginia
        d. bef 1834, Ohio, prob. Highland Co.
        184. Benjamin Terrell
          b. 7 Nov 1750, Louisa Co., Virginia
          d. 15 Jun 1834, Clinton Co., Ohio
          368. David Terrell II
            b. 1729, Golansville, Caroline Co., Virginia
            m. 19 Jan 1749, Louisa Co., Virginia
            d. 14 Feb 1805, Campbell Co., Virginia

736. David Terrell I
   b. 1695/1700, prob. Caroline Co., Virginia
   m. c1727
   d. 1757, Virginia
   1472. William Terrell
      b. 1675, Virginia
      d. 1743, Hanover County, Virginia
      2944. Richmond Terrell
         bap. 17 Oct 1624, St. Giles Parish, Reading,
         England
         5888. Robert Terrell
            m. 29 Jun 1617, St. Giles Parish, Reading,
            England
            11776. William Terrell
            11777. Margaret ?Richmond
         5889. Jane Baldwin
            d. 30 Jan 1661
            11778. Robert Baldwin
               m. 5 Oct 1590, Reading, England
            11779. Joan Pigeon
      1473. Susannah Waters
737. Agatha Chiles
   d. 1766
   1474. Micajah Chiles
      d. bef 1760, Caroline Co., Virginia
      2948. John Chiles
         d. 1723
         5896. Lt. Col. Walter Chiles
         b. England
         d. bef 15 May 1672, Virginia
            11792. Walter Chiles, Sr.
               d. 1653, Virginia
            11793. Elizabeth ?
         5897. Mary Page
            11794. Col. John Page of York Co., VA
               b. 1627, England
               d. 1691/2, Virginia
               23588. Francis Page, Bedford,
                  Middlesex Co., Eng.
            11795. Alice Lukens
               23590. Baron Lukens, Essex County, Eng.
      2949. Mary Boucher
   1475. ? Terrell
      2950. Joel Terrell, Sr.
113

369. Sarah Johnson
  b. 10 Apr 1729
  d. 1775/80
  738. Benj Johnson
    b. 1705
    m. 1728
    d. 1754
    1476. William Johnson
      2952. James Johnston
      2953. Jean Oglive
    1477. Sarah Massie of St. Peter's Parish,
      Norfolk Co.,Virginia
      2954. ? Massie
      2955. ? Ashley
        5910. Lord Ashley, (Baron of Winbourne, St.
        Giles in 1601)
  739. Agnes Clark
    b. 1712
    d. 1754
    1478. Christopher Clark
      b. England
    1479. Millicent (or Mildred) Terrell
      2958. Joel Terrell, Sr.
185. Sarah Parrott
  b. 19 Nov 1756
  d. 21 Jun 1848
93. Jemima Smithson
  b. 1780/83, Virginia
  d. 1830/40 Randolph Co., Indiana
  186. Drummond Smithson
    b. 12 Jul 1754, Virginia
    d. 31 Dec 1844, Randolph Co., Indiana
      bur. Union Cemetery, Windsor, Indiana
  187. Mary ?
    b. c1754
    d. 16 Jan 1851, 97 yrs
      bur. Union Cemetery, Windsor, Indiana
47. Sarah Moore
  b. 1804, Virginia
  d. 8 Jul 1884, Randolph Co., IN, bur. Union Cem.
  94. William Moore
    b. c1767, Surrey Co., Virginia
    m. 30 Nov 1789, Campbell Co., Virginia
    d. 7 Oct 1855, Randolph Co., IN, bur. Union Cem.

188. John Moore
189. Mary ?
95. Winnifred Terrell
  b. 14 Oct 1760, Virginia
  d. 17 Oct 1855, Randolph Co., IN, bur. Union Cem.
  190. David Terrell, see 368

The Chalfant Family

Alma Marguerite Chalfant was born on 9 Jun 1905, the seventh child and fourth daughter of Finley Ellsworth and Emma Alice (Fitzpatrick) Chalfant. She married Harry Vern Addington on 30 Sep 1922 in Randolph County, Indiana. They had three sons, Leo Vern, Joseph Elsworth and Murrie Alexander. Harry Vern Addington died in a farm accident in 1930 and Marguerite was left to raise the family alone. She married a second time on 12 Oct 1932 to Clarence Mason and they moved to a farm in White River Township about two miles southeast of Maxville. Marguerite divorced Clarence Mason in the late 1940s and later married a third time on 10 May 1956 to Harry Puckett, a widower. Harry Puckett died in 1965 and was buried in Buena Vista Cemetery. Marguerite (Chalfant) Addington died on 18 Aug 1979 and was buried beside her first husband in the Maxville Cemetery.

Marguerite's parents, Finley Ellsworth and Emma Alice (Fitzpatrick) Chalfant, were married in Randolph County on 25 Jul 1884 and had eight children:
(1) Pearl Maude Chalfant, b. 25 Jan 1886, d. 19 May 1958
    m. 3 Sep 1904, Tessie Dudley
(2) Shirl Milford Chalfant, b. 26 Mar 1888, d. 25 Mar 1956
    m. 7 Aug 1909, Elsie Effie Gable
(3) Earle Melvin Chalfant, b. 22 Dec 1894, d. 10 Jan 1947
    m. 21 Sep 1912, Lola Gunkle
(4) Mabel Meryl Chalfant, b. 22 Dec 1894, d. 1982
    m. 28 Dec 1912, William Clevenger
(5) Verle Murtle Chalfant, b. 12 Oct 1897, d. 20 Apr 1970
    m. 27 Apr 1914, Earl James
(6) Marvin Hurley Chalfant, b. 3 Apr 1901, d. 29 Jul 1974
    m. 11 Jun 1921, Mary Winget
(7) Alma Marguerite Chalfant*, b. 9 Jun 1905, d. 18 Aug 1979
    m. 30 Sep 1922, Harry Vern Addington
(8) Harry Marshall Chalfant, b. 14 Jan 1911, d. 5 Aug 1922

The youngest son, Harry Marshall Chalfant, was killed at the age of 11 in an early automobile accident in the city of Parker. His obituary says he was a newscarrier for the Muncie Press and died 5 Aug 1922 as a result of injuries he received when he was run over by the automobile of C. A. Wood of Winchester, who was on his way to Muncie hospital with his wife who was ill. The accident occurred that Tuesday evening at the west Parker crossing, when the boy who had waited until the interurban car had passed, rode from the side street into the Hub highway when he was hit by the auto. The passing car obstructed the view of both parties so that neither saw the other until it was too late to avoid the accident. The funeral was held the following Thursday with interment in Union Cemetery.

The Chalfant family had migrated to Delaware County, Indiana in 1840 and lived in Perry Township and later around the city of Windsor in Randolph County. Finley Ellsworth Chalfant was the son of Alexander and Elizabeth (Templin) Chalfant. Alexander Chalfant was born 14 Jan 1840 in Ohio according to the 1850 census but in Indiana according to the 1860 and 1880 census. He married Elizabeth Templin (born 24 May 1843), daughter of Terah and Rachael (Johnson) Templin on 27 Jun 1858 in Delaware County. Elizabeth (Templin) Chalfant died 1 Apr 1870 and is buried in the Blountsville Cemetery in northern Henry County.

Alexander Chalfant served for a short time in the Civil War in Company E of the 147th Infantry of Indiana Volunteers. The regiment was mustered in on March 13, 1865 at Indianapolis under the command of Col. Milton Peden. It first went to Harper's Ferry, Virginia and was later assigned to the Army of Shenandoah. It was delegated to guard and garrison duty at several points and was mustered out on August 4, 1865. Records show Alexander Chalfant was mustered out on May 7, 1865 so he may have come down with some illness and been discharged early.

The 1860 Indiana Census shows Alexander Chalfant in Perry Township of Delaware County with wife Elizabeth Templin (age 19) and one daughter Ora (age 6 months). The children of Alexander and Elizabeth (Templin) Chalfant were:
(1) Ora Chalfant, b. 1859
(2) Alice Melissa Chalfant, b. 5 Aug 1862, Randolph Co., IN
    m. 4 May 1881, Adolph Hill
(3) Finley Ellsworth Chalfant*, b. 18 Aug 1866, Randolph County, Indiana, d. 9 Feb 1940
    m. 25 Jul 1888, Emma Alice Fitzpatrick

(4) Charles Chalfant, b. c1869, d. 24 Aug 1911

After the death of his first wife, Alexander Chalfant married a second time on 25 Oct 1870 in Jay County, Indiana to Susannah Puckett and they had the following children:
(5) Ethel Chalfant, b. 1873
(6) Leroy Chalfant, b. 1875
(7) Edna Chalfant, b. 1877
Susannah evidently died about 1880. It has been difficult to find records on Alexander's children so several of them may have died young. Some of Alexander's children were brought up by other families since he could not care for all of them after the death of his second wife.

Alexander Chalfant was the son of Jesse Chalfant, Jr. and Elizabeth Winders. The 1860 census shows Alexander's father Jesse, Jr., age 64, born in Pennsylvania and wife Elizabeth, age 59, born Ohio. Jesse had married Elizabeth Winders on 21 Sep 1826 in Highland County, Ohio. The History of Delaware County says that Jesse Chalfant came to Perry Township in 1833 along with many other settlers. The census data, based on the birth locations of his children, would indicate he came sometime in 1839. He is listed in the 1830 census as residing in Adelphia Township, Ross County, Ohio. The 1840 census lists him as Jessee Chaffer in Delaware County, Indiana.

Jesse Chalfant, Jr. and Elizabeth Winders had the following children:
(1) Albert Chalfant, b. c1827, Ohio
    m. Rachel Beamer, b. c1829
    m. 2nd 1878, Rebecca Ellen Clevenger
(2) Joel Chalfant, b. 1827, Ohio, d. 11 Feb 1899
    m. 30 Jan 1849, Cynthia Jackson, b. c1833
    m. 2nd 17 Oct 1872, Nancy J. Gibson
(3) Robert Chalfant, b. 5 May 1830, Ohio, d. 15 Feb 1855
    m. 3 Sep 1851, Priscilla Weir
(4) George Chalfant, b. 28 Oct 1832, Ohio, d. 25 Mar 1909
    m. 7 Sep 1854, Julia Hutchings
    m. 2nd Zerilda Jackson
(5) John Chalfant, b. 22 Sep 1835, Ohio, d. 14 Feb 1896
    m. 13 Dec 1853, Sarah Thackara, b. 1837, d. 14 Jul 1911
(6) Rachel Chalfant, b. 1837, Ohio
    m. 16 Aug 1855, Thomas Thornburg
(7) Phoebe Jane Chalfant, b. 8 Feb 1839, Ohio

m. 10 Sep 1870, Riley Felton
(8) Alexander Chalfant*, b. 14 Jan 1840, Indiana, d. 29 May 1930
    m. 27 Jun 1858, Delaware Co., Indiana, Elizabeth Templin
    m. 2nd 25 Oct 1870, Jay County, Indiana, Susannah Puckett
(9) Lavina Chalfant, b. 18 Apr 1842, Indiana
    m. 8 Mar 1860, Thomas W. Newcomb
(10) Elizabeth Chalfant, b. 12 Mar 1842, Indiana, d. 1914
    m. 15 Dec 1859, Samuel Hutchings
(11) Jesse Bailey Chalfant, b. c1846, Indiana, d. 17 Dec 1932
    m. 1866, Pauline Benbow
(12) Levi Chalfant, b. 18 Apr 1848, Indiana
    m. 8 Nov 1866, Sarah A. Felton
    m. 2nd 1911, Nellie Essa Morris
(13) John B. Chalfant, b. c1853, Indiana
    m. 19 Jan 1872, Ellen Stanford

Jesse Chalfant, Jr. died on 16 Sep 1873. Elizabeth (Winders) Chalfant died in 1896.

Jesse's son, Joel Chalfant, was a widely known and well respected farmer in Delaware County. He married Cynthia Jackson and had children:
(1) Martha Chalfant, b. 1853
(2) Emma Chalfant, b. 1856
(3) Finley Hanaway Chalfant, b. 1859
(4) Olive Chalfant, b. 1862
(5) Viola Chalfant, b. 1866
(6) Serena Chalfant, b. 1869
After Cynthia died, Joel married Nancy J. Gibson on 17 Oct 1872 in Delaware County and had children:
(7) Chadd B. Chalfant, b. c1875
(8) Jesse G. Chalfant, b. c1879
(9) Cynthia Chalfant, b. 1881
(10) Glennie C. Chalfant, b. 8 Mar 1886
(11) Marshall H. Chalfant

Finley H. Chalfant, son of Joel Chalfant, married Phebe B. Shaw on 13 Jun 1878 in Delaware County. They had two children and son Memphis Chalfant, born c1879, married Fromin M. Campbell on 27 Jan 1906 in Delaware County. They had at least two children: Bernice, born 1907 and Dorothy, born 1909. A majority of the descendents of Jesse Chalfant, Jr. have remained in the Delaware and Randolph County area.

A Jesse Chalfant, presumed to be the son of Jesse Chalfant, Jr. served in Company G of the 121th (Ninth Cavalry) Indiana Regiment during the Civil War. This regiment was mustered into federal service in March 1864 at Indianapolis. It proceeded first to Nashville and then to Pulaski, Tenn. It participated in the Forrest and Wheeler campaigns and fought at Sulpher Branch Trestle in Alabama on Sep 25, 1864 where the regiment suffered heavy losses. It then spent some time in Alabama before being sent to New Orleans and then later garrison duty at Vicksburg. Jesse Chalfant was mustered out on August 28, 1865 with his regiment. Several of the members of this regiment were lost on the steamer Sultana when a boiler blew up on April 17, 1865.

The 1840 Indiana census lists the Jesse Chalfant family as 1M<5, 3M5-10, 2M 10-15, 1M40-50, 2F<5, 1F30-40. The 1830 Ohio census shows Jesse Chalfant to be in Adelphia Township of Ross County where he had married Elizabeth Winders on 21 Sep 1826. There is also a marriage record of a Jesse Chalfant to Ann Webster on 26 Jun 1822 in Belmont County, Ohio in the Stillwater MM records. This may have been a first marriage for our Jesse or perhaps this is a cousin also named Jesse. There were also two other Chalfants, James and Robert, in Belmont County.

The 1820 Ohio census shows Jesse Chalfant, Sr. in Goshen Township of Belmont County (3M16-26 (Jesse, Jr. age 24), 1M45+, 1F16-26 and 1F45+). James and Robert Chalfant were also listed in Belmont County. This James Chalfant was born about 1770/5 and this Robert Chalfant was born about 1775/80. They may be cousins or nephews of Jesse Chalfant, Sr.

Jesse Chalfant, Sr. was born in 1747 (some places listed as 1744) in Pennsylvania, the son of James Chalfant. Jesse married late in life to Rachel Ann Bailey in or about 1790. Rachel Ann Bailey was the daughter of Joel and Hannah (Wickersham) Bailey. Joel Bailey was born in Pennsylvania about 1734 and married Hannah Wickersham on 24 Nov 1757. Joel Bailey was the son of Josiah and Sarah (Marsh) Bailey. Josiah Bailey was the son of Joel and Ann (Short) Bailey. This Joel Bailey was born in England where he was baptized on 29 Jan 1658. He immigrated to America sometime before 1687 when he married Ann Short in Pennsylvania. Joel's father was Daniel Bailey who was born in 1601 in Westbrook in the Parish of

Bromham. Daniel's father was Thomas Bayley and his father was named William Bayley. Rachel Ann Bailey's mother was Hannah Wickersham who was a daughter of William and Rachel (Haynes) Wickersham. Rachel Haynes was the daughter of Henry (born 1667, Oxfordshire, England) and Isabella Haynes. William Wickersham was born on 3 Feb 1706 in Chester County, Pennsylvania, the son of Thomas and Alice (Hogge) Wickersham. Thomas Wickersham was born about 1660 in Bolney, Sussex, England and married on 27 Jun 1799 at Cowford, Sussex to Alice Hogge before they immigrated to America. Alice Hogge was the daughter of Richard and Alice (Pannell) Hogge.

Jesse and Rachel Ann (Bailey) Chalfant had the following known children:
(1) Jesse Chalfant, Jr.*, b. 1794, d. 16 Sep 1873
(2) Ezekial Chalfant, b. 1800, d. Dec 1881, m. Mary ?

The 1790 Pennsylvania census shows two Jesse Chalfants in Chester County. No James Chalfant is listed but a James Chaffin is listed in Chester County so his name was evidently misspelled. Family records say James died in 1808 so this is probably the correct James. The 1800 Pennsylvania census lists a Jesse Chalfant in Chester County with 3M<10, 1M26-45 and 1F 26-45. If this is correct this would indicate that Jesse Sr. may have been born later than first thought. The 1810 Pennsylvania census again shows Jesse in Chester County.

Jesse Chalfant's father, James Chalfant was born in 1717 in Pennsylvania and married Hannah Harris about 1744. It appears he lived his entire life in Chester County. James and Hannah (Harris) Chalfant had the following children:
(1) Lydia Chalfant, m. ? Bentley
(2) Phebe Chalfant
(3) Hannah Chalfant
(4) James Chalfant
(5) John Chalfant
(6) Elizabeth Chalfant, m. ? Crawford
(7) Jesse Chalfant*, b. c1744
      m. c1790, Rachel Ann Bailey
Hannah (Harris) Chalfant died sometime before 1770 when James Chalfant married second to Elizabeth Martin.

James died on 1 Jan 1808 and his will in Chester County listed him as living in East Fallowfield Township. Paul S. Chalfant of Colorado Springs, Colorado did extensive work on the ancestry of this Chalfant line and says that James Chalfant's father was John Chalfant, born 1690 in England. John Chalfant emigrated on the ship "Canterbury", arriving in the Port of Philadelphia on 30 Nov 1699 with his uncle John Chalfant and cousins John Chalfant, born 1689, and Robert Chalfant, born 1688. John settled with his uncle John on the Brandywine near Birmingham, in Chester County, Pennsylvania. They named this land "Rockland Manor". John Chalfant, born 14 Apr 1690, is often identified as John Chalfant of West Marborough where he settled. John and his wife, name unknown, had sons:

(1) Joseph Chalfant
(2) Isaac Chalfant
(3) Henry Chalfant
    m. 15 Aug 1742, Elizabeth Jackson
(4) James Chalfant*, b. 20 Feb 1717, d. 1 Jan 1808
    m. Hannah Harris
(5) William Chalfant
(6) John Chalfant

John Chalfant's father was Henry Chalfant, born 13 May 1663, who married in 1687 in England to Elizabeth Chandler, a daughter of Thomas Chandler. Thomas Chandler immigrated to Chester County, Pennsylvania where he appears on the tax rolls in 1715. Henry Chalfant and his family apparently stayed in England but his son John immigrated to America with his Uncle John. Henry and Elizabeth (Chandler) Chalfant had children:

(1) Robert Chalfant, b. 26 Sep 1688, d. 13 May 1693
(2) Henry Chalfant, b. 3 Jul 1689, d. 7 Sep 1728
(3) John Chalfant*, b. 14 Apr 1690, d. 7 Sep 1729, Pennsylvania
(4) Elizabeth Chalfant, b. 12 Mar 1691
    m. 4 Jul 1712, Caleb Swayne
(5) Ruth Chalfant, b. 28 Jun 1692, died young.

Henry Chalfant's father was Robert Chalfant who was born 24 Feb 1626 in England. Robert Chalfant married Lydia Barnard on 9 Jun 1658. Lydia was the daughter of Thomas and Elizabeth (Bayes) Barnard of St. James, London. Elizabeth Bayes was the daughter of John and Perryn (Ralphe) Bayes. This Robert Chalfant is the ancestor of apparently all the

Chalfants in America. Robert and Lydia Chalfant has three children of record:
(1) John Chalfant, b. 8 May 1660, England, d. Aug 1725, Chester Co., Pennsylvania
    m. Ruth Chandler
        son Robert Chalfant, b. 12 May 1688, England, d. 6 Apr 1767, Chester Co., Pennsylvania
        son John Chalfant, b. 7 Mar 1689, England
(2) Henry Chalfant*, b. 13 May 1663
    m. Elizabeth Chandler
(3) Margaret Chalfant, b. 8 Apr 1665
    m. Jonathan Compton
Robert Chalfant died on 15 May 1684.

Robert Chalfant's father was Christopher Chalfont who was born 4 Nov 1574 and married on 3 May 1625 to Elizabeth (Paynter) Chilton, widow of Edward Chilton. In the license he is described as a "schoolmaster about 50" and she a "widow about 40". The marriage was at St Mary, Sandwich where Christopher taught school. They had two children: Robert* and William Chalfant. Elizabeth died on 11 Jan 1628 shortly after the birth of her second son and the two infants were left with Samuel Paynter, Elizabeth's brother, by whom they were raised. Christopher returned to Aylesbury, Bucks and remarried in 1632 to Margaret (Harris) Alcock, widow of Thomas Alcock. It was about this generation that the spelling of the family changed from Chalfont to Chalfant.

Christopher Chalfont's father was Thomas Chalfont who was born on 5 May 1520 and married on 28 Jun 1570 Margaret (Bennett) Cornwallis, the widow of Francis Cornwallis.
They had five known children:
(1) William Chalfont, b. 19 Jun 1571, of Love-end, Oxford County, d. 9 Mar 1629.
(2) Christopher Chalfont*, b. 4 Nov 1574
    m. 3 May 1625, Elizabeth (Paynter) Chilton
(3) Margaret Chalfont, b. 2 Sep 1575
(4) John Chalfont, b. 14 Jan 1577
    m. 23 Dec 1602, Elizabeth Burrell
(5) Richard Chalfont, b. 27 Mar 1578

Thomas Chalfont's father was William Chalfont who was born sometime before 1500 and married Margaret Artbroke, daughter of Robert Artbroke of High Wycombe. William

Chalfont had been appointed Mayor of Wycombe in the 6th, 8th and 12th years of Henry VIII (1515, 1517, 1521) and was still apparently mayor in 1533. He owned property in Bemynster, Dorsset County and died 7 Feb 1543 and is buried at High Wycombe. Wycombe is situated a few miles west of Chalfonte-St. Giles. William's father was also named William and is the first recorded Chalfant that can be traced.

This William Chalfont, the patriarch of the family, is first mentioned in English records on 5 Jun 1485. William Chalfont was born about 1460 and was associated with the town of Aylesbury and the manor of Chalfonte-St. Giles. He had at least two sons, William* and Christopher. Christopher was the VICAR of Upton cum Chalvey, Bucks as recorded in Oct 1548. William Chalfont was also the last Master of the Hospital of St. John the Baptist at the date of its suppression by Henry VIII in 1541.

There are no records of this first William Chalfont's father but a hundred years earlier in the same area was a Henry deChalfunte born around 1360. Henry's father was a Thomas deChalfunte born about 1335 and died in 1374. Thomas' father was Sir Henry deChalfunte who married Maude Garound in 1333 and was Sheriff of Buckinghamshire. Sir Henry's father was a John deChalfunte born about 1290 and his father was William deChalfunte born about 1265 and in 1288 was living near Chalfonte-St. Giles.

The Fitzpatrick Family

Alma Marguerite Chalfant's mother was Emma Alice Fitzpatrick who was born in Randolph County, Indiana on 26 Nov 1866, the daughter of William F. and Jemima Emily (Terrell) Fitzpatrick. The Fitzpatrick family was originally of Irish origin and came through North Carolina before they moved to Indiana. Emma Alice Fitzpatrick married Finley Ellsworth Chalfant on 25 Jul 1884 and they had eight children. Emma died on 14 Feb 1946 and is buried in the Union Cemetery, south of Windsor in Randolph County.

William F. Fitzpatrick was born in 1839 in Wayne County, Indiana to William and Hannah (Seany) Fitzpatrick. William and Hannah were married on 25 Mar 1837 in Wayne County. They are listed in the 1840 census with one son (William). By 1850, William Fitzpatrick had moved his family to Stony Creek Township in Henry County. Henry County borders on the southern boundary of Randolph County and Stony Creek Township is in the northwest part of Henry County. The 1850 census lists:
Wm Fitzpatric, age 35, NC
Hannah, 32, IN
Wm, 10, IN
John, 7, IN
Pleasant, 1, IN
William's occupation is shown as shoemaker. The next record of this Fitzpatrick family is found in the 1860 census in Stony Creek Township of Randolph County. William Fitzpatrick, age 21, born Indiana, is listed as the head of the household with three younger brothers: John, age 17, Pleasant, age 11, and Lewis, age 6, all born in Indiana. Evidently their parents, William and Hannah, had both died sometime between 1854 when their last child was born and the 1860 census. County death records were not kept during this time period and cemetery records have not been found so we may never know exactly what happened to them.

Little information has been found on William F. Fitzpatrick's three brothers. John Fitzpatrick, who was born on 15 Dec 1842, married Mary L. Smith and died on 11 Aug 1922. Little is known about Pleasant Fitzpatrick, who was born about 1849, other than one photo showing him still alive in 1923. The Fitzpatrick Reunion photo, taken about 1910, shows a rather large gathering but many of these descendents may come from Emma Alice (Fitzpatrick) and Finley Ellsworth Chalfant who had a large family.

William F. Fitzpatrick enlisted in the 84th Indiana Infantry and served with that regiment throughout the Civil War. The history of the 84th Regiment is related in the Addington Family section. William Fitzpatrick was discharged on 14 Jun 1865 along with the rest of the regiment. One photo in this book shows him much later in life with two old comrades from the 84th Regiment, Isaac P. Watts and Isiah Puckett. The trio had developed a friendship while serving in the war and retained close ties throughout the rest of their lives.

William F. Fitzpatrick was married to Jemima Emily Terrell on 22 Feb 1865 in Randolph County. This is interesting since his discharge date is given as 14 Jun 1865. He could have been on leave when he married or the discharge date may be incorrect. Emily Terrell was the daughter of George Wesley and Sarah (Moore) Terrell. William and Emily Fitzpatrick lived on a farm in Stony Creek Township near the city of Windsor. They had the following children:
(1) Emma Alice Fitzpatrick*, b. 26 Nov 1866, d. 14 Feb 1946
    m. 25 Jul 1888, Randolph Co., IN, Finley Ellsworth Chalfant
(2) Sarah M. Fitzpatrick, b. c1875
(3) George W. Fitzpatrick, b. c1879, d. 1951

After the death of George Wesley Terrell, Emma's mother Sarah lived with the Fitzpatrick family as shown by the 1880 census. William F. Fitzpatrick was a farmer in Stony Creek Township all of his life. He died on 9 Sep 1915 and is buried in Union Cemetery near Windsor. Emily died within nine months on 7 Jun 1916 and is also buried in Union Cemetery. Their son, George Fitzpatrick, was a carpenter and lived in the Windsor area until dying at the age of 72 in 1951. Their daughter, Sarah, married a Bailey and lived in Desoto.

Tracing the ancestry of William F. Fitzpatrick has been difficult. The 1880 Randolph County census states that his father, William Fitzpatrick, was born in North Carolina and his mother, Hannah Seany, in Indiana. Information on the

126

Seany family follows below. Wayne County marriage records show a James Fitzpatrick married on 31 Dec 1841 to Mary Hillander. The 1850 Wayne County census shows a James Fitzpatrick, age 33, born North Carolina with wife Nancy, age 28. Delaware County records and a biography list a James Fitzpatrick who was born in North Carolina and moved to Delaware County so this is probably the same one although that biography says his wife's name was Sallie Thomas. This James Fitzpatrick was probably a younger brother to our William Fitzpatrick, Sr.

William Fitzpatrick, Sr. was born in 1815 in North Carolina. The 1830 Indiana census shows no Fitzpatricks in Wayne County or any surrounding counties. The 1820 Ohio census lists a Wm Fitzpatrick in Preble County age 16-26, wife age 16-26 and one son age < 10, which would fit William's birthdate of 1815 so his father's name may have also been William. If so, his father would have been born about 1794/8 probably in North Carolina. The 1820 North Carolina census lists on only one Fitzpatrick, a widow names Polly, age 45+ in Rowan County. The 1810 North Carolina census lists a Hugh Fitzpatrick in Stokes County and a Mary Fitzpatrick (widow age 45+) in Rowan County. Hugh is shown as age 45+, wife age 45+ and one female <16. The 1800 North Carolina census lists Mary Fitzpatrick and Edward Fitzpatrick in Rowan County; Hugh Fitzpatrick in Stokes County; Thomas Fitzpatrick with a large family in Wilkes County and James Fitzpatrick in Lincoln County. The 1790 North Carolina census lists Thom Fitspatrick in Wilkes County, John Fitzpatrick in Dobbs County, James Fitzpatrick in Rowan County, John Fitzpatrick in Stokes County and Sam. Fitzpatrick, in Stokes County. There were only a few Fitzpatrick families in North Carolina before 1815, the date of William Fitzpatrick's birth so he is probably a descendent of one of them. Future research may someday tell us the relationships.

The Seany Family

Hannah Seany was a great grandmother of Alma Marguerite Chalfant on her mother's side. Hannah was married to William Fitzpatrick on 25 Mar 1837 in Wayne County, Indiana. Hannah was born in 1818, in Indiana, probably in Wayne County. Her father was apparently Jacob Seany and his wife Susanna.

Jacob's family is found in the 1830 Wayne County census as 1M5-10, 1M30-40, 3F<5, 2F5-10, 1F10-15, and 1F30-40. On the same census page is the listing for Owen Seany with 1M70-80 and 1F60-70 so it is assumed that Owen is Jacob's father.

Jacob Seany is found in the 1840 census but no Owen indicating he died in that decade. In the 1850 Wayne County census, we find:
Jacob Seany, age 56, Farmer, NC
Susanna, 57, NC
Maria, 18, IN
Susanna, 13, IN
John Molder, 13, IN
Isaac Seany, 10, IN

The 1860 Indiana census lists:
Jacob Seany, age 65, b. North Carolina
Elizabeth, 63, NC

Owen Seany, 59, NC
Martha, 60, Penn
Sarah J., 16, IN
John W., 15, IN

This Owen Seany is probably a younger brother to Jacob and was born in North Carolina and came to Wayne County at an early age. He married Martha Grimes and raised his family in Wayne County. He died on 17 Mar 1781 in Randolph County. His son, John W. Seany, was born on 5 Aug 1843 in Wayne County. He later moved to Ridgeville where he set up and operated a dry goods store.

The Seany family apparently moved up from North Carolina sometime around 1815. No Seany families appear in the 1820 Indiana census so they were either missed or the the name misspelled. Early Wayne County marriage records show a John Seany married Martha Chamber in 1817 and a Bryan Seany married a Sally Little also in 1817. These were probably brothers to Hannah's father, Jacob. Owen Seany, possibly another brother of Jacob, married Martha Grimes in 1825. Sarah Seany married Jessel Odell in 1834 and Elizabeth Seany married in 1838. These could be sisters or cousins to Hannah.

The 1810 North Carolina census lists two Seany families, Archabald and David Seany, both living in Mechenburg County. The 1790 North Carolina census shows Owen Seny living in the Salisburg District of Rowan County: 1M<16, 3M>16, 2F>16 and 1 slave. We lose track of Owen for several years and either his family was not enumerated in the census or the spelling has not been recognized. There were Fitzpatricks living in Rowan County according to the 1790 and 1830 census data so the Fitzpatrick and Seany families may have been associated in North Carolina.

The Templin Family

The Templin family is connected to the Chalfant family by the marriage of Elizabeth Templin to Alexander Chalfant. The Templin family was originally thought to be of English origin however one biographer of the family, Ronald Templin, in his book *The Templins of Indiana*, is firmly convinced that the family is of German origin. The first records of our Templin family are of a Richard Templin who was born in 1688 and located in East Nantmel Township in Chester County, Pennsylvania. Richard's wife's name was Mary, family name unknown, and they had eight known children including the youngest son and our ancestor, James Templin. Richard Templin died on 13 Apr 1775 and is buried with his wife, Mary, at St. Mary's Episcopal Church in Warwick, Pennsylvania.

Richard's son, James Templin, was living near Uniontown, Pennsylvania in the 1780s. James was originally a farmer in Chester County and fought in the Revolutionary War. James married Mary Salmon and they had the following children:
(1) Salmon Templin, b. 1775, PA, d. 11 Jun 1855, Highland, Co., Ohio
  m. Catherine White
(2) Robert Templin*, b. 18 Mar 1776, Pennsylvania, d. 23 Jun 1849, Blountsville, Indiana
  m. Eunice Beals
(3) Terah Templin, m. Esther Wilson
(4) Isaac Templin
(5) John W. Templin
(6) James Templin, Jr.
(7) Esther Templin
(8) Polly Templin

James Templin and his family migrated to near Washington, Mason County, Kentucky in the 1790s. He did not like slavery and therefore migrated back north to Ohio about 1796. His three sons, Salmon, Terah and Robert were members of the original party which settled Chillicothe and Station Prairie in Ross County in 1796. From 1796 to 1800, a malaria epidemic swept through Chillicothe so James Templin moved his family west to Highland County, Ohio. They settled there where their

130

sons and daughters married and they farmed the land and raised their families. Robert settled on a branch of Rocky Fork Creek in the southern part of Marshall Township.

Robert Templin, the second son of James, was born on 18 Mar 1776 in Pennsylvania. Robert was still unmarried when he moved with the family to Ohio but married Eunice Beals in Highland County about 1801. Eunice Beals was born on 2 Jan 1785 in North Carolina. Society of Friends records show Eunice being dismissed for marrying out of unity. Robert and Eunice (Beals) Templin had the following children:
(1) James Templin, b. 12 Oct 1802, Hillsboro, Highland, Co., Ohio
    m. 26 Apr 1827, Highland Co., Ohio, Catherine Swan
(2) Polly Templin, b. 26 Jan 1805?
    m. 31 Aug 1822, John Fletcher
(3) Terah Templin*, b. 26 Oct 1806, Highland, Co., Ohio, d. 23 Jan 1855, Henry Co., Indiana, bur. Blountsville, Indiana
    m. 25 Oct 1827, Highland Co., Ohio, Rachel Johnson
(4) Timothy Templin, b. 22 Jul 1809
    m. 8 Sep 1831, Delilah Goode
(5) Isiah Templin, b. 22 Mar 1810
    m. 11 Mar 1830, Elizabeth Clevenger
(6) Nancy Templin, b. 27 Mar 1812
    m. 14 Dec 1831, Martin Oder
(7) Katie Templin, b. 28 Mar 1814
    m. John Lenington
(8) Delilah Templin
(9) Eunice Templin
(10) Richard Templin
(11) Jane Templin
(12) Cyrus Templin
(13) Isaac Templin

Elizabeth Beals was born in Surrey County, North Carolina on 2 Jan 1785 to John Bowater and Lois (Branson) Beals. The Beals family moved to New Hope, Tennessee about 1795 and then are recorded in the Ohio Miami Monthly Meeting records in 1804. John Bowater Beals was the son of Bowater and Sarah Ann (Cook) Beals. Bowater Beals was born about 1725 in Pennsylvania, married Sarah in 1752 in Pennsylvania and later moved his family to North Carolina. Bowater Beals was the son of John Beals, Jr. and Sarah Bowater. Sarah Bowater was the daughter of Thomas and Sarah (Edge) Bowater. John Beals,

Jr. was born on 28 Jan 1685 at Nottingham, Chester County, Pennsylvania. He married Sarah in 1711 and later moved to Prince George County, Maryland where he died about 1748. John Beals, Jr. was the son of John Beals, Sr. and Mary Clayton. John Beals, Sr. was born in England about 1650 and immigrated to America sometime before 1682 when he married Mary Clayton in Chester County, Pennsylvania.

In 1829, Robert and Eunice (Beals) Templin moved their family to Perry Township in Delaware County, Indiana. Perry Township is located is the southeastern corner of the county only a few miles north of the village of Blountsville in Henry County. Robert Templin and his family were staunch Presbyterians and he was an elder in the Stony Creek Church near Blountsville. Robert Templin died on 23 Jun 1849 and was buried on his farm north of Blountsville. One story says that the subsequent owner plowed up the graveyard where he was buried and threw Robert's headstone into the creek. Robert's stone was later recovered and placed with that of his wife in Hopewell Cemetery in Kokomo, Indiana. After Robert's death, Eunice lived with her son Timothy in Howard County and died there on 26 Jun 1859.

James Templin, the first born son of Robert Templin, was born on 12 Oct 1802 near Chillicothe, Ohio. On 26 Apr 1827, he married Catherine Swan, a daughter of John and Sarah (Wilson) Swan. He was a tanner by trade and set up business in Highland County. In 1829, he migrated with his father to Delaware County, Indiana. While Robert and his sons were building cabins in the wilderness of Delaware County, their families stayed in the small village of Blountsville in northwest Henry County. Catherine died about 1843 and James married a second time to Elizabeth Gilbert and they had four children. In 1853, James moved his family from Henry County to Delaware County and later to Grant County.

Our direct line ancestor, Terah Templin, was born on 26 Oct 1806 in Highland County, Ohio and was named in honor of his uncle Terah. He grew up in Highland County and on 25 Oct 1827 married Rachel Johnson who was born Jun 1812 in Ohio. Rachel was the daughter of Enos and Sarah Johnson. See the following section on the Johnson family, which was a numerous and influential family in Highland County. Terah Templin moved with his father to Indiana in 1829 and

132

established a home near Blountsville in Henry County. Terah and Rachel (Johnson) Templin had the following children:
(1) Sara A. Templin, b. 23 Feb 1829, Ohio
(2) Nancy J. Templin, b. 5 Dec 1832, Indiana
(4) Lancey J. Templin, b. 20 Dec 1834
(5) Eunice Templin, b. 30 Dec 1836
    m. 18 Jul 1856, Henry Hill
(6) Catherine Templin, b. 5 Mar 1838
    m. Ephraim Carey
(7) Elizabeth Templin*, b. 24 May 1843, d. 1 Apr 1870
    m. 27 Jun 1858, Delaware Co., Indiana, Alexander Chalfant
(8) Grace A. Templin
(9) Sanford Hill Templin, b. 11 Oct 1845, Henry Co., Indiana
    m. 4 Feb 1865, Randolph Co., Indiana, Margaret Faulkner
(10) Rachael L. Templin, b. 17 Oct 1847
(11) Charles E. Templin, b. 10 Jul 1851
(12) A. Seneth Templin, b. 24 Jun 1854
(13) Letita Templin, b. 28 Dec 1859

Terah was a carpenter and wagon maker and set up his business in Blountsville. He had a very successful business going when he died of typhoid on 23 Jan 1855. He is buried in the Methodist Cemetery in Blountsville. Rachel (Johnson) Templin later moved with her son Sanford and his family to Wells County, Indiana where she died on 17 Apr 1884.

The Johnson Family

Rachel Johnson, who was born Jun 1812 in Highland County, Ohio and married on 25 Oct 1827 to Terah Templin, was a great grandmother of Alma Marguerite Chalfant. She was the daughter of Enos and Sarah Johnson. The book *Highland Pioneer Sketches* gives the following account of this Johnson family:

The Johnson family is descended from the Johnston or de Johnstone family of Scotland. The family is assumed to have begun with Stephen de Johnston who is said to have arrived in the north of Scotland around 1329. Stephen was a man of great learning and was honored by the title "The Clerk." He married into wealth and his estate became known as the "lands of Johnstone." Stephen had a son John, and he, a son Gilbert, and he, a son named Alexander de Johnstone. Alexander's son, William, married Margaret, daughter of Meldrum de Fyvie, "greatest barron for the tyme in the North pairt of Scotland." William died in battle when he accompanied King James IV to England in 1513. Land and titles went to James Johnston who married Jean Oglive. They were the parents of three sons, William, John and Alexander, and two daughters. The three sons arrived in America in 1696 in a vessel belonging to Charles Dun.

Of the three sons, Alexander married in Virginia and had three sons. Sons William and John married two girls by the name of Massie in St. Peter's Parish, New Kent County, Virginia. The Massie girls were descended from the Ashley family of England. The first identified patriarch of this family was Benedict Ashley who lived in the reigns of Henry II and Edward I. His son, Robert Ashley, acquired by marriage the manor Winbourne St. Giles in the County of Dorsset. Sir Henry Ashley, born in 1519, was knighted at the Coronation of Queen Mary, and married Catherine, daughter of Sir John Basset. Another descendent, Sir Anthony Ashley, became the first Earl of Shaftesburg and was created Baron Ashley of Winbourne St. Giles in 1661. The next year Lord Ashley and other influential men, appraised of the excellent soil of Virginia, formed a project and planned a colony. Charles II granted land from Lucke Island in Virginia to the river and extending west to the Pacific Ocean. Tradition states that two brothers by the name of Massie married daughters of Lord Ashley. The eldest daughters of these Massie families were married to William and John Johnson.

John Johnson, one of the three original emigrants, married Lucretia Massie in New Kent County, Virginia about 1700. They had the following children: Agnes, John, born 1702, Massie, born 1705, Robert, born 1708, Ashley, Thomas, born 1714, Charles, Margery, Benjamin and James. Their son John married Elizabeth Ellyson and they had eight children. One son, Ashley Johnson, fathered twelve children by two wives and four of his sons migrated to Highland County when it was opened up to settlement.

William Johnson, one of the three original emigrants, married Sarah Massie and they had five children: Anne, born 1699, William, born 1701, Benjamin, born 1705, Collins, and Cicely, born 1711. The third child, Benjamin, was born in 1705 and died in 1754. Benjamin married Agnes Clark. The Highland County History states she was a sister of Gen. George Rogers Clark, but this is believed to be incorrect. The Terrell Genealogy says she was born in 1712 and was the daughter of a Christopher Clark. Benjamin and Agnes (Clark) Johnson had nine children: Sarah, born 1729, Christopher, William, Benjamin, Penelope, Collins, Edward, Agnes and Newby. Their first daughter, Sarah Johnson, is a direct line ancestor, having married David Terrell (born 1729) on 19 Jan 1749 in Louisa County, Virginia. The third child, William married Susannah Johnson and they had twelve children, the first born being Ashley Johnson, born in 1756. Ashley Johnson was a soldier in the Revolution, enlisting at the age of fifteen. He later married Milley Johnson and they were the first Johnsons to migrated to Highland County, Ohio in April 1806. Ashley started a mass migration to Highland County with many Johnson families soon following. The original list of voters in 1807 contains the following members of the Johnson family, who were all related to the emigrants, William and John Johnson: New Market Township, William, Thomas, William and Enos; Liberty Township, William and Thomas; Fairfield Township, Charles, Jonathan, Ashley, Pleasant, William, Christopher, Sr., Christopher, Jr., Thomas A., Thomas, Ashley, Samuel, James, Benjamin H. and Harrison Johnson. The Enos Johnson and his wife Sarah are the parents of Rachael Johnson who was born in Jun 1812 in Highland County and on 25 Oct 1827 married Terah Templin. Because of the great number of Johnson families in Highland County, it has not been possible to identify whether Enos is a descendent of William or John Johnson but he is certainly descended from this Scottish family.

Terrell and Associated Families

Jemima Emily Terrell is the maternal grandmother of Alma Marguerite Chalfant. The Terrell family is an old established family that was of importance in England and early Virginia. The first members of this family arrived in Virginia in the mid 1600s and settled in the central part of the state. In the early 1800s, a few Terrell families moved to Clinton and Highland Counties in Ohio in the very early period of settlement of that state. Around 1830 three Terrell families moved to Randolph County, Indiana and settled in Stony Creek Township.

Jemima Emily Terrell was born in Randolph County, Indiana on 3 Dec 1837 to the George Wesley and Sarah (Moore) Terrell and was called by the name Emily. The Terrell family lived in Stony Creek Township where she grew up near the town of Windsor. She married William F. Fitzpatrick on 22 Feb 1865 at the rather late age of 27. They had at least three children: Emma Alice Fitzpatrick (born 26 Nov 1866), Sarah M. Fitzpatrick (born 1875) and George W. Fitzpatrick (born 1879) as shown by the 1880 census. There may have been other children who died young.

George Wesley Terrell was born in 1804 in Virginia according to later census records and then migrated with his family to Ohio sometime before 1820 settling in Clinton or Highland County. On 27 Nov 1825 he married Sarah Moore (spelled Moor on the marriage record) in Highland County with Rev. David Terrell performing the ceremony. The Rev. David Terrell is probably Sarah's uncle. Sarah Moore is the daughter of William and Winnifred (Terrell) Moore, and by 1850 when they are in their 80s, they were living in the George Wesley Terrell household. Winnifred Moore is also a Terrell, the daughter of Benjamin and Sarah (Parrott) Terrell. Sarah Moore is a granddaughter of Benjamin Terrell while George Wesley Terrell is a great grandson, meaning George Wesley married his second cousin. The Terrell family had a history of intermarrying.

Winnifred Terrell was born on 14 Oct 1760 in Virginia. She first married on 26 Nov 1781 in Bedford County, Virginia to

Edward Woodham but he died soon afterwards. She married second on 3 Nov 1789 in Campbell County, Virginia, to William Moore. William Moore was a son of John and Mary Moore of Albemarle Parish of Surry County, Virginia and christened on 5 Apr 1767. This Moore family of Virginia is not related to the Moore family from Delaware also discussed in this book. The Moore family moved to the Clinton County, Ohio sometime between 1806 and 1820, probably with some of the Terrell families that moved there. There in 1825 Winnifred's daughter Sarah married George Wesley Terrell. The William Moores moved on to Randolph County at the same time as George Wesley Terrell. Cemetery records in Randolph County show William Moore died 7 Oct 1855 at age 88 years. Winnifred (Terrell) Moore died ten days later on 17 Oct 1855 at the age of 95 years. They are both buried near Windsor in Union Cemetery. This cemetery was originally called the Terrell Cemetery, possibly George Wesley Terrell donated the land for it.

George Wesley Terrell moved his family to Randolph County sometime around 1827 and is listed in the 1830 census in Stony Creek Township. George Wesley Terrell is listed in the Indiana censuses as George W. or as Wesley Terrell so he probably went by the name Wesley. He owned land about a mile and a half southeast of the town of Windsor and evidently farmed for the rest of his life the land he bought when he first moved to Randolph County. George Wesley Terrell died on 22 Mar 1878 and is buried in Union Cemetery, south of Windsor. Sarah (Moore) Terrell died on 8 Jul 1884 and is no doubt also buried in Union Cemetery but no stone has been found.

George Wesley and Sarah (Moore) Terrell had the following children:
(1) William Terrell, b. 13 Jul 1827, Indiana
   m. 22 Nov 1849, Rebecca Thornburg
   m. 2nd 27 Mar 1856, Delaware Co., IN, Mary A. Thornburg
(2) Martha Ann Terrell, b. c1830
   m. 4 Apr 1850, John Tilman Cox
(3) Jemima Emily Terrell*, b. 3 Dec 1837, d. 7 Jun 1916
   m. 22 Feb 1865, William F. Fitzpatrick
(4) George C. Terrell, b. c1842, d. 22 Mar 1865
   m. ? 30 Mar 1862, Delaware Co., Indiana, Sharon A. Glaze

There may have been others who died at a young age given the spread in birthdates for the children.

Martha Ann Terrell married John Tilman Cox on 4 Apr 1850 and they were living in the Terrell household when the 1850 census was taken. However, he must have died within a few years since Martha is listed in the 1860 census back in the Wesley Terrell household. Apparently they did not have any children.

William Terrell married Rebecca Thornburg on 22 Nov 1849. They had two children: Lucinda J. and John W. Rebecca evidently died sometime about 1854 or 1855 since William remarried to Mary A. Thornburg on 27 Mar 1856. William and Mary had children: Margaret, Sarah, George E., Ulysses, William "Grant", Susannah, Maude, Della and Lydia. William Terrell was a minister in the Christian Church around Windsor for over twenty years.

George C. Terrell, son of George Wesley and Sarah (Moore) Terrell, was born in 1842. He married Sharon A. Glaze on 30 Mar 1862 in Delaware County, Indiana. During the Civil War, George enlisted in the 124th Indiana Infantry and served with that regiment in its service in the western theater. He was wounded in one of the regiment's last battles at Goldsboro, North Carolina and died the following day on 22 Mar 1865.

Two other Terrells apparently migrated to Randolph County about the same time as George Wesley Terrell. Drummond S. Terrell, born about 1803 in Virginia and John M. Terrell, born about 1811, Virginia, are listed in the 1840, 1850 and 1860 Indiana census records, also in Stony Creek Township. Wesley, Drummond and John are most likely brothers but there is no confirming vital record data. The initial S. in Drummond's name probably stands for Smithson, since his maternal grandfather was named Drummond Smithson. A marriage record in Highland, County, Ohio, stated that Drummond Terrell married Judith Merrill on 4 Oct 1825. Drummond can not be found in the 1830 Ohio or Indiana census, however, he is found in the 1840 Indiana census in Stony Creek Township, age 30-40 in a household with 1F15-20 and 1F60-70. Evidently his wife died before 1840 and his mother, Jemima (Smithson) Terrell, may be living in his household. The 1850 Indiana census shows him as age 40 (probably a mistake) living in the Dudley household. A marriage record in Clinton County, Ohio states a Drummond S. Terrell married Sarah Ratcliff on 25 Sep 1850. The 1860 Indiana census shows a D. S. Terrell, age 47, born Virginia with wife Sarah and son John W. Terrell so evidently he married in Ohio but moved back to Indiana.

John M. Terrell was born about 1811 in Virginia according to later census data. He married in Randolph County in 1833 to Eliza Smithson, who is probably his cousin. John M. Terrell is listed in the 1840, 1850 and 1860 Randolph County census in Stony Creek Township. John and Eliza had the following children:

(1) William W. Terrell, b. c1835, IN, m. Elizabeth ?, b. 1847
(2) Drummond S. Terrell, b. c1837, Indiana, d. aft 1900
    m. 22 Feb 1859, Clinton, Co., Ohio, Louisa J. Taylor
(3) Isaac Terrell, b. c1839, Indiana
(4) Elizabeth A. Terrell, b. c1842, Indiana
(5) John E. Terrell, b. c1849, Indiana, m. Gertrude ?, b. 1856
(6) George H. Terrell, b. c1859, Indiana

I have no vital record data that indicate who was George Wesley Terrell's father, but several pieces of data indicate that it was William Terrell who was born on 24 Mar 1779 in Campbell County, Virginia. He married on 25 Feb 1802 in Campbell County to Jemima Smithson, the daughter of Drummond and Mary Smithson. They moved to Highland County, Ohio sometime between 1810 and 1820. William Terrell died there sometime in or before 1834. I believe George Wesley Terrell is the son of William Terrell for the following reasons: (1) William had a brother named George W. Terrell (born 1784) so those names are in the family, (2) Wesley named his first son William (a fairly common custom is this era to name your first son after your father), (3) Wesley also named a daughter Jemima, probably his mother's name and (4) the Drummond Smithson family also moved to Randolph County and lived near George Wesley Terrell. The 1840 Randolph County census shows Drummond Terrell, age 30-40 in a household with a female age 50-60. I believe this to be his mother Jemima (Smithson) Terrell. Also listed two lines below is Drummond Smithson, age 80-90, and wife, age 80-90 (Mary), Jemima's parents. Drummond Smithson died in 1844 at the age of 90. His wife, Mary Smithson, is shown in the 1850 Stony Creek Township census as age 95, living with her son Ira

Smithson's family. It appears that the Smithson, Moore and Terrell families all moved together from Highland County, Ohio.

The patriarch of the Smithson family was Drummond Smithson who was born 12 Jul 1754 in Virginia. The Tucker History of Randolph County makes the following remarks about Drummond: one year old when the French War broke out, 22 at the signing of the "immortal declaration", died age 90, 31 Dec 1844. Drummond's wife Mary died 16 Jan 1851 at the age of 97 years. They are both buried in the old section of Union Cemetery.

The 1820 Highland County, Ohio census shows William, David, Henry and Samuel Terrell to have sons of the age of George Wesley. One published genealogy on the Terrell family, by Cleste Jane Terrell Barnhill, does not list a George Wesley, Drummond or John Terrell as sons of David, Henry or Samuel. Unfortunately, that genealogy does not list the descendents of William Terrell and no other published list has been found. All I can conclude is that George Wesley Terrell is most probably the son of William and Jemima (Smithson) Terrell. Certainly if not the son of William, he is of this same Terrell line.

William Terrell was the son of Benjamin and Sarah (Parrott) Terrell. Benjamin Terrell was born in 1750 in Louisa County, Virginia and married Sarah Parrott in the same county. They later moved to the northern portion of Pittsylvania County where he acquired large land holdings. From 1814 to 1820 he sold this land and moved to Clinton County, Ohio. Benjamin Terrell died in Clinton County, Ohio on 15 Jun 1834. Sarah died on 21 Jun 1848. The children of Benjamin and Sarah (Parrott) Terrell were:
(1) William Terrell*, b. 24 Mar 1779, Pittsylvania Co., VA, d. bef 1834, Highland Co., Ohio
    m. 25 Feb 1802, Campbell Co., VA, Jemima Smithson
(2) Robert Terrell, b. 11 Feb 1780, d. 18 Jun 1864
    m. Nancy West
(3) Elizabeth Terrell, b. 26 Nov 1781, d. 14 Feb 1873
    m. Johnson Terrell
(4) George W. Terrell, b. 30 May 1784, d. 20 Mar 1871, Tipton, Indiana
    m. 27 Dec 1811, Martha Wayne

(5) Sarah Terrell, b. 11 Apr 1786, d. 23 Aug 1864
   m. Campbell Smithson
(6) Nancy Terrell, b. 24 May 1788
   m. Henry West
(7) John Terrell, b. 25 Jun 1790, d. 16 Aug 1865
   m. 27 Feb 1812, Jane West

Benjamin Terrell was born on 7 Nov 1750, probably in
Caroline County, Virginia, the son of David and Sarah
(Johnson) Terrell. David Terrell was born in 1729 and married
Sarah Johnson (born 10 Apr 1729) on 19 Jan 1749. Sarah
Johnson was the daughter of Benjamin and Agnes (Clark)
Johnson. See the separate Johnson family write up for the
history of this family. David and Sarah (Johnson) Terrell had
the following children:
(1) Agatha Terrell, b. 17 Dec 1749
   m. ? Pulliam
(2) Benjamin Terrell*, b. 7 Nov 1750, d. 15 Jun 1834
   m. Sarah Parrott
(3) Edward Terrell, b. 12 Feb 1753
   m. 17 Mar 1772, Mary Johnson
   m. 2nd 19 Oct 1794, Jane Johnson
(4) Sarah Terrell, b. 10 Jan 1755
   m. 26 Nov 1781, Benjamin Arthur
(5) Mary Terrell, b. 6 Apr 1757
   m. 29 Oct 1782, John Richardson
(6) Winnifred Terrell*, b. 14 Oct 1760, Virginia, d. 17 Oct 1855,
   Randolph County, Indiana
   m. 26 Nov 1781, Edward Woodham
   m. 2nd 3 Nov 1789, William Moore
(7) David Terrell, b. 11 Mar 1763, d. 27 Aug 1853, Clinton Co.,
   Ohio
   m. 25 Sep 1788, Mary Anthony
(8) Henry Terrell, b. 13 Aug 1767
   m. 1798, Charity Gordon
(9) Samuel Terrell, b. 12 Dec 1769, d. 6 Jul 1829
   m. 13 Sep 1796, Nancy Reynolds
(10) Susannah Terrell, b. 9 Aug 1771, d. 9 Jan 1857
   m. 17 Mar 1796, Charles Johnson
(11) Ann Terrell, b. 1773, m. John Fowler

Sarah (Johnson) Terrell died between 1775 and 1780 and David
remarried on 5 Oct 1782 to Sarah Goode. She died in 1788 and
he married for a third time to Patty Johnson on 25 Feb 1793. In

1781, David moved his family to Bedford (now Campbell County, Virginia) where he died in 1805. Four of his sons, Benjamin, Edward, David and Samuel moved their families to Clinton and Highland Counties in Ohio starting in 1806. Daughter Winnifred and her second husband William Moore also moved to Ohio about the same time.

David Terrell (born 1729) was the oldest son of David and Agatha (Chiles) Terrell. The elder David Terrell married about 1727 to Agatha Chiles, the daughter of Micajah Chiles. See the following section on the Chiles Family. David's brother Henry married Anne Chiles, a sister to Agatha.

David and Agatha (Chiles) Terrell made their home in Caroline County about 40 miles north of Richmond. David was born about 1695/1700. They had the following children:
(1) David Terrell*, b. 1729, d. 1805
    m. 19 Jan 1749, Louisa Co., Virginia, Sarah Johnson
(2) Henry Terrell, b. 1730, d. 1806, dnm
(3) Micajah Terrell, b. c1732, d. 1805
    m. 10 Feb 1745, Sarah Lynch
    m. 2nd Deborah Gardner
(4) Pleasant Terrell, d. 1803
    m. Catherine Farish
(5) Mary Terrell, m. 1755, Robert Cobb
(6) Milicent Terrell, b. 7 Jun 1741
    m. Christopher Clark
(7) Ann Terrell, nfi
(8) Chiles Terrell, m. Mrs. Margaret (Douglas) Meriwether
(9) Christopher Terrell, b. c1747
    m. Martha Wilson
(10) Rachel Terrell, b. 1749, d. 1781
    m. 1768, John Burress
(11) Susannah Terrell, b. 30 May 1752, d. 8 Dec 1828
    m. 1770, William Burress
(12) Jonathan Terrell, b. 1755
    m. Margaret Hunnicutt

David Terrell and his wife Agatha joined the Society of Friends. David Terrell was appointed one of the overseers of one of the first Quaker meetings set up in Virginia, the Cedar Creek Meeting on 12 Mar 1739. Later a meeting was set up in Caroline County and David and his brother Henry were leaders in that church.

David Terrell died in 1759. His will was dated 15 Mar 1751 and was proved 12 Apr 1759. Agatha died in 1766. They evidently accumulated a large amount of land because each son received at least 200 acres in the will.

David Terrell was the son of William Terrell who married Susannah Waters. They resided in Hanover County, Virginia after 1720 where William died in 1743. William and Susannah (Waters) Terrell had the following children (generally accepted as correct):

(1) William Terrell, Jr., d. c1755 Caroline Co., Virginia
(2) Joel Terrell, Sr., d. 1758, Hanover Co., Virginia
    m. Elizabeth Oxford
(3) Anne Terrell, m. David Lewis
(4) David Terrell*, b. c1695/1700. d. 1759, Caroline Co., Virginia
    m. Agatha Chiles
(5) Henry Terrell, d. 1760, Caroline Co., Virginia
    m. Ann Chiles
(6) Timothy Terrell, d.. 1763, Orange Co., North Carolina
(7) James Terrell, d. c1722 Caroline Co., Virginia
(8) John Terrell, d. c1785, Franklin Co., North Carolina
(9) Mary Terrell, m. Mathew Mills

There were probably other daughters but no one has confirmed their names. It is believed that William and Susannah's children were all born between 1690 and 1710 in New Kent County, later Hanover County.

This William Terrell is the son of Richmond Terrell who came to America in 1656. William was probably born about 1670/5 in Virginia. His father, Richmond Terrell, was baptized on 17 Oct 1624 at St. Giles Parish, Reading, England. It is not clear if he married in England or after he immigrated to North America in 1656. Besides William, he had two other sons, Richmond, Jr. and Timothy.

Richmond Terrell, Sr. was the son of Robert Terrell. Robert married Jane Baldwin, the daughter of Robert and Joan (Pigeon) Baldwin, on 29 Jun 1617 at St. Giles Parish. Jane died in 1661 and it is not known when Robert Terrell died.

One of the published genealogies on the Terrells takes this Robert Terrell's heritage back another seventeen generations to a Sir Walter Tyrrell of Normandy who married Adeliza, a daughter of Richard le Clare and Rohnese, his wife was a daughter of Walter Gifford, the Elder. Walter Gifford served England in many offices including Archbishop of Canterbury during the period of Henry III who died in 1272.

Another Terrell history says the name started out from the town of Tirel, in France. The founder of the English and Irish Terrell families was Sir Walter de Tirel who went to England with William, the Conqueror. The *Genealogy of Richmond and William Terrell* by Joseph Henry Terrell, of England, gives the descent of the Terrells in England and America from Edward I and Eleanor of Castile.

The Chiles Family

The Chiles family is associated with the Terrell family through the marriage of Agatha Chiles to David Terrell. The Chiles family was an old and prominent family in Virginia of Irish extraction, according to Susan Pruitt in her book *Some Descendents of Walter Chiles, the Immigrant in Virginia, until About 1800*. The family name was originally Child, became Childs, and after coming to Virginia was commonly written Chiles. The Immigrant Walter Chiles came to America in his own ship in the 1630s, accompanied by his wife, Elizabeth and sons William and Walter. He was a merchant by trade and obtained land in Charles City County (now Prince George County). He was a prominent citizen and represented Charles City in the House of Burgesses in 1642/3. He represented James City in 1645, 1649 and in 1652 was elected speaker of the House. After the death of his first wife, Walter Chiles married Alice Lukens. Walter Chiles died in 1653, a honored and respected Virginian. After his death, Alice remarried to Col. John Page.

Of Walter Chiles' two known sons, little is known about William. He either died young or returned to England. Walter Chiles, Jr., the oldest son of the Immigrant Walter Chiles, was born in England and accompanied his father to America. He first married Mary Page, the daughter of Col. John Page the Councillor, son of Francis Page of Bedford, Middlesex County, England. Col. John Page was born in 1627 in England and immigrated to York County, Virginia about 1650, and first settled in James Town. His second wife was Alice Lukens, daughter of Baron Edwin Lukens of Essex County, England and the widow of Walter Chiles, Sr. Col. John Page raised his family in York County and gave the site of the church building in Bruton Parish. Col. Page died in York County in 1691 or 1692.

Walter and Mary (Page) Chiles had two children:
(1) John Chiles*, d. 1723
(2) Elizabeth Chiles, m. 1683, Henry Tyler

Henry and Elizabeth (Chiles) Tyler were great-grandparents of President John Tyler through their son John Tyler who married Ann Contesse and their son John Tyler who married Mary Marot Armistead.

After Mary (Page) Chiles died, Walter Chiles married second Susannah, family name unknown. Walter and Susannah Chiles had one son: Henry Chiles who died about 1718.

Walter Chiles served in the House of Burgesses in 1658/9 and 1660/3. He was church warden of James Town Parish and owned land in James City County in 1661. He resided in "Kemp House" in James Town inherited from his father, probably the first brick dwelling erected in America. Walter Chiles, Jr. died some time shortly before 15 May 1672.

John Chiles, son of Walter and Mary (Page) Chiles was born about 1655/65. John first married Mary Boucher, sometime before 1690. Mary later died and he married second Eleanor Webber, the daughter of Henry Webber, of Gent, St. Joseph Parish of King William County. Between his two wives, John Chiles had eight children:
(1) Mary Chiles, (mother Boucher)
(2) Susannah Chiles, m. Joseph Martin (mother Boucher)
(3) William Chiles, d. 1778 (mother Boucher)
(4) Micajah Chiles*, d. bef 1760 (mother Boucher)
(5) Jane Chiles, m. John Wright
(6) Eleanor Chiles
(7) John Chiles, d. 1774, no heirs (mother Webber)
(8) Henry Chiles, d. 10 Jun 1763 (mother Webber)
    m. Mary Carr

John Chiles served in the Virginia government and was a messenger of the Council in 1693. He was church warden of St. Margaret's Parish and was a justice in King William County in 1714. In 1722, he was granted 300 acres in King William County. He was a member of the assembly from King William County in 1723, the same year in which he died.

Micajah Chiles was the son of John Chiles and it is believed that Mary Boucher was his mother. Micajah moved to Caroline County where he patented land, bordering on William Terrell's land, in St. Margaret's Parish in 1730. He married Elizabeth Terrell, a daughter of Joel Terrell Sr. and they had seven children:
(1) John Chiles

147

(2) Manoah Chiles
(3) Micajah Chiles, Jr.
(4) Thomas Chiles
(5) Sally Chiles
(6) Ann Chiles, m. Henry Terrell
(7) Agatha Chiles*, d. 1766, m. David Terrell

Micajah Chiles died sometime before 1760. His daughter Agatha Chiles married David Terrell and they had twelve children.

The Winders Family

Elizabeth Winders who married Jesse Chalfant, Jr. on 21 Sep 1826 in Highland County, Ohio was a great grandmother of Alma Marguerite Chalfant. R. Winder Johnson published in 1902 his book *Winders in America* which lists a Thomas Winder as the patriarch of the Winder family that first settled in New Jersey. Thomas Winder was born in England, probably in London sometime around 1680.

Thomas was in America by 1703 when he purchased land in Amwell Township, Hunterdon County, New Jersey. He evidently returned to London because he married Sara Bull on 5 Jun 1704 at St. Margaret's, Westminster. Since the first genealogy on Thomas Winder was published, there have been questions raised about whether this marriage record is correct or may have been later altered. Recent research has concluded that the marriage record is correct and is the Thomas Winder of our ancestral line. Thomas and Sara immigrated to New Jersey about 1705 and settled on their previously purchased land.

Thomas and Sara (Bull) Winder had five known children:
(1) John Winder, b. c1707, d. 9 Aug 1770
    m. Rebecca Richards
(2) Thomas Winder, nfi
(3) James Winder*, d. 2 Jul 1789
    m. 9 May 1743, Elizabeth Sherwood
(4) Jane Winder, m. John Slack
(5) Elizabeth Winder, m. Peter Phillips

Sara (Bull) Winder died sometime before 1731 since Thomas married second on 1 Apr 1731 to Rebecca Gregory in New Jersey. Thomas and Rebecca (Gregory) Winder has one child, Elinor Winder, who was later married on 31 Jul 1751 in Philadelphia to Thomas Guinnup.

New Jersey land of this era was often sold many times over by corrupt land speculators and it appears that Thomas Winder's rights to his land were in dispute. In 1732 and 1733 he acquired two tracts of land in Lower Makefield Township of Bucks,

County, Pennsylvania, probably with the intention of moving there.

It is believed that Thomas Winder drowned in 1734 in the Delaware River while attempting to board a ship. His estate records a payment for "taking deceased body out of the water, he having been drowned." An inventory of his estate in 1734 shows "a canoe, new rifle barreled gun, old ditto, old sword, two great Bibles and three small ones, negro Ben, valued at six pounds, negro Toby, valued at 30 pounds, wheat sold to Benjamin Pidcock, as well as 552 acres of land in Lower Makefield Township of Bucks Co., Pa." plus a listing of about ten individuals who owed Thomas. Records show Rebecca (Gregory) Winder was appointed administrator of the estate on 23 May 1734. Rebecca later remarried to a Collins since she is listed as Rebecca Collins in a final accounting of the estate in 1746.

James Winder, the son of Thomas and Sara (Bull) Winder, moved to Prince George County, Maryland sometime prior to 1743. There he married on 9 May 1743 to Elizabeth Sherwood in All Saints Parish. In 1752 James bought a hundred acre tract of land known as "Medcalfs' Meadow." This land was described as: Beginning at a bounded White Oak standing by the side of a little spring within half a mile of the Waggon Road that goes from Stulls Mill to the mountains." Stulls Mill was located on Antietam Creek, just shortly to the east of present-day Hagerstown, Maryland. James evidently lived on this land from 1752 until his death in 1789. James had written his will on 15 Mar 1785 and it was proved in Washington County on 15 Aug 1789. A tombstone inscription has been reported from Funkstown Cemetery, Maryland supposedly reading "James Winder, died 4 July 1782." This is possibly our James Winder with the date mis-copied as 1782 rather than 1789. James lived close to Funkstown as did several of his children. His will listed a complicated scheme of distributing his estate to his wife, five surviving daughters and seven sons.

James and Elizabeth (Sherwood) Winder had the following children:
(1) Thomas Winder, birthdate unknown, lived in Shenandoah County, Virginia
(2) James Winder*, b. c1747, d. Mar 1831, Fayette Co., PA
    m. c1770, Elizabeth Grable, d. bef. 1830

150

(3) John Winder
(4) Daniel Winder, birthdate unknown, d. 1795, Washington Co., Maryland
(5) Alexander Winder, b. 2 Nov 1765, d. 30 Aug 1789, Washington Co., Maryland
(6) Isaac Winder, birthdate unknown, in 1800 Washington Co. census
(7) George Winder, nfi
(8) Mary Winder, m. ? McCown
(9) Susanna Winder, b. c1760, d. 11 Apr 1844, m. John Orr
(10) Mercy Winder, m. ? Darling
(11) Rachel Winder, m. by 1785 John Snebely
(12) John Winder, m. by 1785 ? Bond

Our direct line ancestor is the second son, James Winder who was born about 1747. Records show that James Winder migrated to Fayette County, Pennsylvania sometime before 1768. He was an early settler in Redstone Township as reported in Ellis' *History of Fayette County*. The 1790 Fayette County census lists James Winder in Redstone Township with a family of 2 males under 16, 2 males over 16 and three females. He is also listed in Fayette County in the 1800, 1810 and 1820 census.

James Winder married Elizabeth Grable although it is not clear where the marriage occurred or the exact date. Elizabeth Grable was the daughter of Samuel and Hannah (Earhart) Grable who were early settlers in Redstone Township. Samuel Grable is reported to have been born 17 Sep 1725 in Germany. He immigrated to America some time before 1751, when his name first appeared on the tax roles in Chester County, Pennsylvania. A Nicholas Grable whose will was written 16 Apr 1774 in Frederick County, Maryland, names Samuel Grable as one of his sons. Nicholas Grable appears on the tax roles in Coventry Township, Chester County, Pennsylvania as early as 1729 and as late as 1760. A 1764 land deed in Frederick County, Maryland shows he bought a tract of land known as "Old Barrel."

Samuel Grable's will was written 12 Sep 1809 and probated in September 1811 in Fayette Co., Pennsylvania. He made bequests to:
the two children of my daughter Catherine Several the sum of $60 each

my daughter Elizabeth Winders the sum of $230
my son David Grable the sum of $320
son Samuel Grable $300
daughter Susannah Wells $230
daughter Mary Colvin $230 and one cow
daughter Hannah Ratcliff $230 and use of my plantation for
two years after my decease, rent free
my son Philip Grable $300
my daughter Sarah Stubaker $230

Returning to the Winder family, James and Elizabeth (Grable) Winder had the following known children:
(1) James Winder, b. 1775, d. 1861
(2) Daniel Winder*, b. c1785
    m. 29 Jan 1806, Fayette Co., PA, Mary Kennedy
(3) David Winder, nfi
(4) Sarah Winder, m. Elisha White
(5) Katherine Winder, m. James Laughlin
(6) Elizabeth Winder, m. Nathan McGrew

James and Elizabeth (Grable) Winder lived in Fayette County, Pennsylvania from 1780 until James's death in 1831. James wrote his will on 28 May 1829 and the will was probated on 8 Mar 1831 after his death. Well before his death, James had bought two tracts of land in what is now Harrison County, Ohio. He later sold these tracts to his sons James, Daniel and David.

James Winder's will reads: "In the name of God, amen, I James Winder of the township of Redstone, County of Fayette and Commonwealth of Pennsylvania, Yeoman, being of far advanced in years and of sound mind and memory thanks be to Almighty God, and calling to mind the uncertainties of this life, do make and ordain this to be my last will and testament.
First: burial and funeral expenses and all my just debts are to be paid.
Second- I give and bequeath unto my son James Winder the sum of $50
Third- I give and bequeath unto my son Daniel Winder the sum of $50
Fourth- Unto my son David Winder I bequeath the sum of $50
Fifth- I give unto my daughter Sarah White the sum of $100

Sixth- I give unto my grandchildren, namely Elizabeth White and James N. White, the sum of $100, divided equally among them.

Seventh- I give unto my daughters, Katherine Laughlin, Elizabeth McGrew, and Sarah White the residue of my estate to be sold at public sale and the proceeds equally divided among them.

Eighth- I appoint my confidential friends Philip Grable and Nimrod Grable to be my executors. Done 28 May 1829"

Witnesses: Salome Grable, Queen Esther Grable, Earhart Grable

Proved 8 Mar 1831, Fayette County, Pa.

Of the sons of James Winder, son James evidently stayed in Pennsylvania in Crawford County. Daniel and David Winder moved to Harrison County, Ohio but the date is uncertain. Daniel Winder was apparently the youngest son and married Mary Kennedy. One genealogical source gives a marriage date of 29 Jan 1806 in Fayette County. It is known for sure that Daniel and Mary (Kennedy) Winder were in Harrison County, Ohio by 1813.

Daniel and Mary (Kennedy) Winder had the following children:
(1) Elizabeth Winder*, b. 30 Oct 1806, prob. Fayette Co., PA, d. 1896, Delaware Co., Indiana
m. 21 Sep 1826, Highland Co., Ohio, Jesse Chalfant, Jr.
(2) Samuel Winder, b. 8 Mar 1808, prob. Fayette Co., PA
m. Ruth B. Hibbs
(3) Saloma Winder, b. 1 May 1810, prob. Fayette Co., PA
m. Horace Belknap
(4) Chelnessa Winder, b. 17 Jan 1813, Harrison Co., Ohio
m. 5 Oct 1835, John Gandy
(5) Dorcas Winder, b. 2 Mar 1815, Harrison Co., Ohio
(6) James Robert Winder, b. 4 Nov 1817, d. 16 Nov 1817
(7) Katherine Winder, b. 8 Feb 1820
(8) David Winder, b. 4 Apr 1820, d. 21 Jun 1881
m. Anne Holliday

Daniel Winder purchased his land in Harrison County from his father on 20 Oct 1813. Later deed records show he sold 2.5 acres to the trustees of the Nottingham Friends Meeting, the land that currently contains the Greenmont Cemetery. Daniel and his family may have been members of this Quaker Monthly Meeting but their names are not found in the surviving records. Daniel Winder's name is listed in another 1839 land deed. He apparently died sometime between 1839 and 1852 but the exact date is not known. Mary (Kennedy) Winder died sometime after 1832.

Daniel's first born, daughter Elizabeth, was married to Jesse Chalfant, Jr. on 21 Sep 1826 in Ross County, Ohio. Ross County is located in the central part of the state while Harrison County is in the far east bordering upon Pennsylvania. The Jesse Chalfant, Sr. family was living in Belmont County according to the 1820 census. Belmont County is directly south of Harrison County so Jesse and Elizabeth must have met there sometime before 1826. Why the marriage took place in Ross County is unclear. Perhaps the Chalfants moved on to Ross County and Jesse returned to woe Elizabeth but married her in Ross County. There were some other Winders families in Ross and Highland Counties, that were a couple of generations removed from Daniel's line. Maybe there still existed contact between these Winders. The 1830 Ohio census shows Jesse and Elizabeth (Winder) Chalfant to be in Adelphia Township of Ross County. Jesse Chalfant, Jr. moved his family to Delaware County, Indiana probably sometime in 1839. His son Alexander Chalfant was born on 14 Jan 1840 in Indiana according to later censuses.

Harry Vern and Alma Marguerite (Chalfant) Addington, 1922

Harry Vern Addington, age 2

Harry Vern Addington

Alma Marguerite (Chalfant) Addington

156

Grandchildren of Harry Vern and Alma Marguerite (Chalfant) Addington, 1962

Joseph Elsworth, Murrie Alexander and Leo Vern Addington, 1973

Alexander, Marshall, Alma Marguerite and
Emma (Fitzpatrick) Chalfant, about 1914

The Joseph Leander Addington Family about 1910
Front: Dora Elizabeth (Feagans), Joseph Leander
Harry Vern, David Cressie, Mabel Elizabeth, Robert Gilva, Cecil Lester

Finley Ellsworth and Emma Alice (Fitzpatrick) Chalfant

Civil War Comrades (from left):
Luther Puckett, William Fitzpatrick, Isiah P. Watts, about 1905

Alexander Chalfant

William F. and Jemima Emily (Terrell) Fitzpatrick

Cressie and Gilva Addington Family Reunion, about 1945

Cressie and Jeanetta (Clevenger) Addington
Floyd and Doris

Gilva and Ermel (Clevenger) Addington

Cecil and Osa (Main) Addington

David Vern and Dixie (Behr) Addington
Ashley and Carmen, 1991

L. Vern Addington Family, 1984

Elizabeth (Addington) Pursley

Joseph and Celia (Townsend) Addington gravestone
Sparrow Creek Cemetery

Joseph Leander and Dora Elizabeth (Feagans) Addington about 1930

Pearl (Feagans) Powell and husband
Leander and Dora Elizabeth (Feagans) Addington

Thrashing Day at Leander Addington's farm
about 1910

Fitzpatrick Family Reunion about 1910
Alma Marguerite Chalfant, probably in front row

167

Maps

Shown on the following pages are several maps of Randolph County and its townships. County history and county records are often divided by township and township designations have often been used in this book. The county map is provided for reference purposes in understanding the text. Several township maps have also been included to show the locations of various homesteads and the locations of various families.

All of the families discussed in this book in Randolph County were concentrated in the western half of Randolph County. Few if any located east of the city of Winchester. The Addington family was concentrated in Franklin Township and the western part of White River Township, south of Maxville. The Chalfant, Fitzpatrick and Terrell families were mostly in Stony Creek Township with some overlap into Delaware and Henry Counties.

Maps Shown:
    1865 Randolph County
    1865 White River Township, western part
    1865 Franklin Township
    1865 Stony Creek Township (sometimes written as
                                    Stoney Creek)

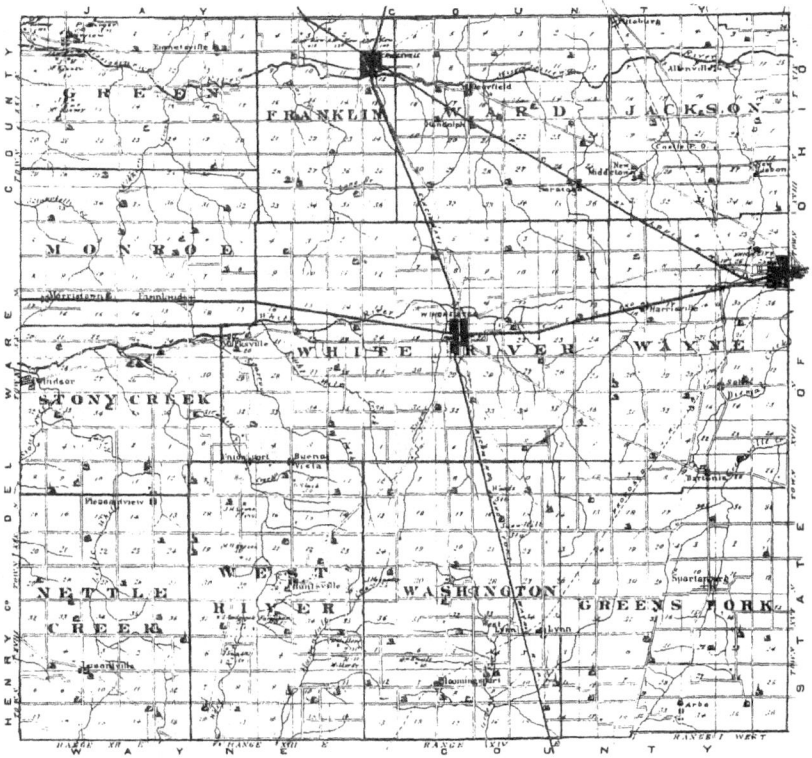

MAP OF RANDOLPH COUNTY.

WHITE RIVER TWP.

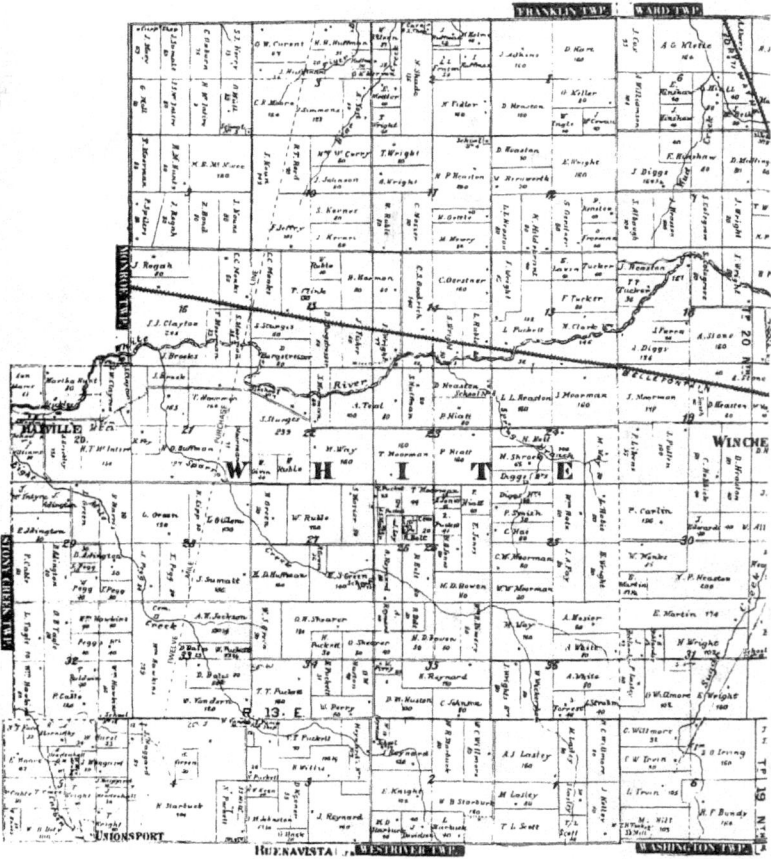

FRANKLIN TWP.

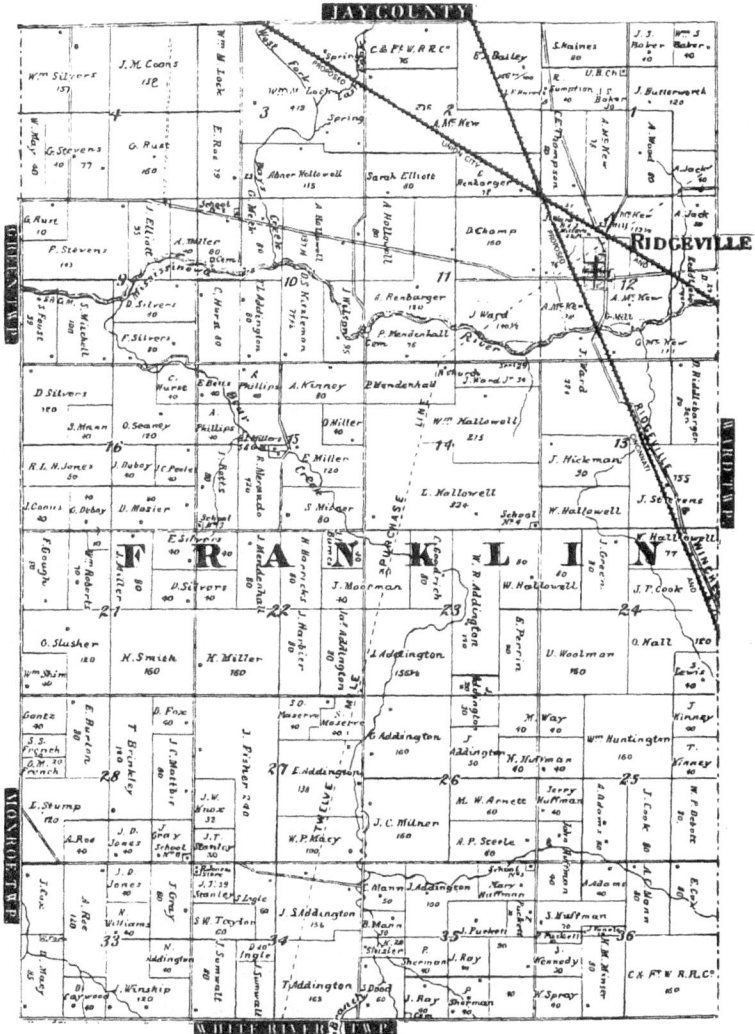

171

STONY CREEK TWP.

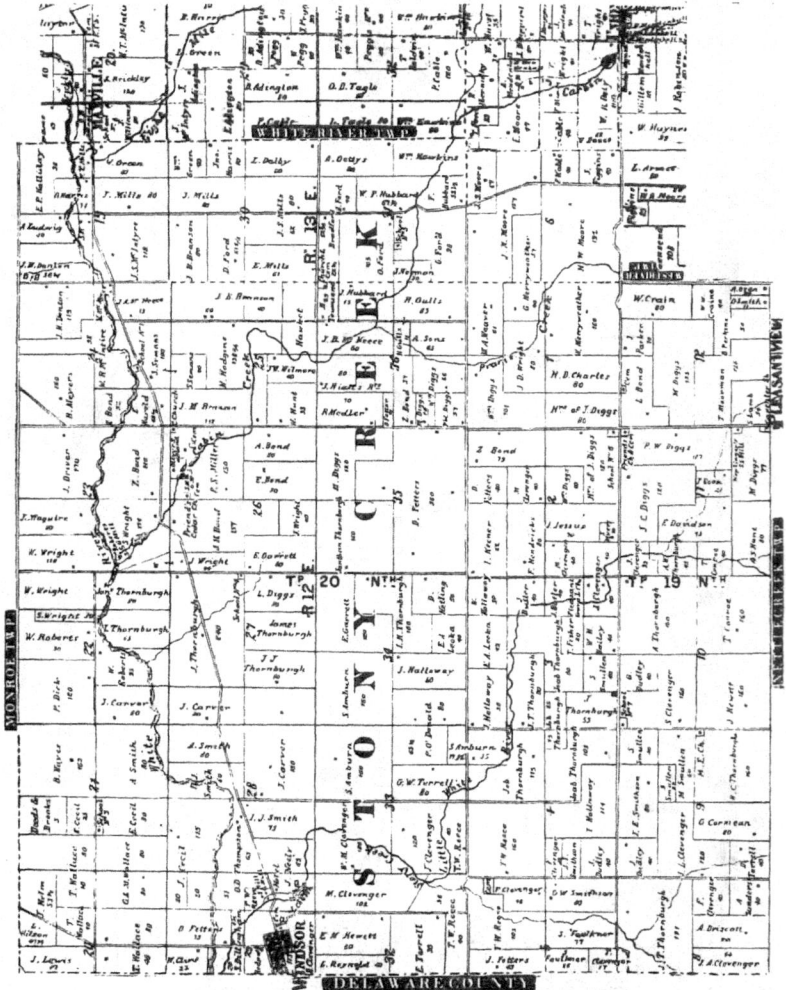

Migration Routes

One of the goals of my research has been to find out the nationality and migration paths for our ancestors. The families seem to be predominantly English with some English related such as Irish and Scottish. There is also some German heritage as brought in by the Bolinger and Templin families.

For most of the families we only have a general idea of when they immigrated from the "old" country or some legal reference that first records their presence in America. For the families with known immigration dates, the latest family to migrate was apparently the Moore family who migrated in 1775 or 1776. Walter Chiles immigrated to America sometime in the 1630s. The Terrell family immigrated to America in 1656 and was among the earliest. It appears the Wright family was here before 1700 and the Chalfants immigrated in 1699. Thomas Winder immigrated in 1705. The Addington family was in Pennsylvania by 1742 but may have roots back to a John Addington who was in Pennsylvania by 1692. For several of the families we do not have a specific time period of their immigration but none are known to have come after the Revolutionary War.

These families took several different routes to Randolph County. There was the southern route where the families (often Quaker related) of Addington, Townsend, Cain, Wright, Fitzpatrick and Seany came through Virginia and Pennsylvania to North and South Carolina and then north to Indiana. Many families came from Virginia with most first migrating to Ohio and then on to Indiana, the Terrells, Moores, Feagans, McCrackens and Winders. Pennsylvania was the starting point for the Bolingers who came directly to Indiana, and the Chalfants and Templins, who first moved to Ohio before proceeding on to Indiana. The Moore family came from Delaware through Pennsylvania and Ohio.

The earliest families to move into Randolph County were apparently the Terrells, Moores and Smithsons in 1828. The Templins came to northwest Henry County in 1829 but had close ties to Randolph County. The Addingtons moved to Randolph County in 1832/5 and the Feagans and Bolingers both came in 1838. The Chalfants came to Delaware County about 1840 and later moved over into Stony Creek Township of Randolph County. The other Moore family came about 1855 although other branches were here earlier. The Fitzpatrick family moved up from Wayne and Henry Counties into Randolph County in the late 1850s.

The following tables are a chronological listing of the families with the names of our direct line ancestors and their family locations as they can best be determined.

1750	1760	1770	1780	1790	1800	1810	1820	1830	1840	1850	1860	1870	1880	1890

ADDINGTON

1835 Randolph Co., Indiana ———
1806 Wayne Co., Indiana ——
1768/74 96 Dist., (Union Co.), SC -
1756 Loudoun Co., Virginia
1742 Philadelphia

1858 Joseph Leander ———— 1935
———— 1902
1828 David ————
1836
1833
1776 Joseph ————
1749 John ————
1727 Henry ————1787

FEAGANS (married into Addington family)

1837 Randolph Co., Indiana ———
Licking Co., Ohio –
? Fauquier Co., Virginia ———

1862 Dora Elizabeth ————1944
1836 Robert Wesley ———— 1902
———— about 1878
1814 James H. ————
James ————
about 1834

BOLINGER (married into Addington family)

abt 1838 Randolph Co., Indiana ———
Pennsylvania ———

1830 Huldah Ruth ———— 1907
1810 Jacob ———— 1860

MOORE (married into Feagans family)

abt 1855 Randolph Co., Indiana ———
1817 Wayne Co., Indiana ———
1776 Philadelphia and Delaware
Ireland ———

1837 Rebcca Jane ———— 1878
1810 Benjamin ———— 1858
1779 David W. ———— 1845
1745 Matthew ———— 1836

175

Family Name | 1750 1760 1770 1780 1790 1800 1810 1820 1830 1840 1850 1860 1870 1880 1890

TOWNSEND (married into Addington family)

  96 District, SC ————
  1725 Pennsylvania --
    1785 Celia ——————— 1852
    1763 John M. ——————— 1853
  1803 Wayne Co., Indiana ————
  Randolph Co., Indiana

McCRACKEN (married into Feagans family)

  1725 John ———— about 1790
  Pennsylvania --
  Virginia ————
  1817 Rebecca ——— 1838
  1786 Robert ——————— 1858
  about 1810 Licking Co., Ohio --
  1838 Randolph Co., Indiana --

WRIGHT (married into Moore family)

  Guilford Co., North Carolina ————
  Virginia --
  1746 Ralph ————
  1788 Ralph ——————— 1882
  1813 Hannah ——————— after 1860
  1837
  Wayne Co., Indiana ————
  Huntington Co., Indiana --

HEATON (married into Addington family)

  South Carolina ————
  Pennsylvania ————
  c1755 Elizabeth —————— 1820/30
  John ———— ?

CAIN (married into Townsend family)

  North Carolina ————
  1767 Elvira ——————————————————— 1869
  Jonathan ———— ?
  Wayne Co., Indiana ————

1750 1760 1770 1780 1790 1800 1810 1820 1830 1840 1850 1860 1870 1880 1890

CHALFANT (married into Addington family)

1840 Delaware Co., Indiana --------

abt 1815 Ohio ------

1699 Pennsylvania ------

1866 Finley Ellsworth ----1940

1840 Alexander ----1930

1873

1797 Jesse Jr. ---- 1827

1744 Jesse Sr. ----

1727 James----1808

TEMPLIN (married into Chalfant family)

Ross, Highland Co., Ohio ----

Pennsylvania --Kentucky

1843 Elizabeth ---- 1870

1808 Terah ----1855

1849

1776 Robert ----

abt 1750 James----

abt 1820

WINDERS (married into Chalfant family)

Harrison Co., Ohio --

Fayette Co., Pennsylvania ----

Maryland ----

1807 Elizabeth ---- ? aft 1860

c1785 Daniel ---- c1835

1831

1747 James----

1680 Thomas --1734

177

Family Name — 1750 1760 1770 1780 1790 1800 1810 1820 1830 1840 1850 1860 1870 1880 1890

FITZPATRICK (married into the Chalfant family)

Randolph Co., Indiana ------

Wayne Co., Indiana -

Ohio ----

North Carolina -

1866 Emma Alice --------- 1946

--------- 1915

1839 William -------

--------- 1856/1860

1815 William ---------

TERRELL (married into the Fitzpatrick family)

Randolph Co., Indiana ------

Highland Co., Ohio --

Campbell Co., Virginia -------

1837 Jemima Emily --------- 1916

1804 George Wesley --------- 1878

1779 William -------

bef. 1834

1760 Winnifred --------- 1855

MOORE (married into the Terrell family)

Randolph Co., Indiana -------

Highland Co., Ohio --

Surrey Co., Virginia --

Campbell Co., Virginia --

1804 Sarah --------- 1884

1767 William --------- 1855

SEANY (married into the Fitzpatrick family)

Wayne Co., Indiana -------

North Carolina -------

1817 Hannah --------- 1856/60

1794 Jacob --------- 1850/60

abt. 1750 Owen --------- 1820/30

178

Descendents Lists

I have included descendents lists on seven of the families covered in this book. There are presented starting with a key ancestor and contain all the information currently compiled on that ancestor's descendents. They are numbered as generations from the beginning ancestor so it is quite easy to identify how many generations each descendent is from the patriarch. The letter refers to the earliest ancestor with which the list begins and each subsequent dash and number refers to the order of the children in the next generation. Children are numbered in order of birth if that is known. A ? indicates that the relationship is probably correct but there is some uncertainty.

I present this data in this form since it would be extremely difficult to present it is a prose form and retain an overall grasp of the relationships. I present it to help others understand the family relationships.

Indiana Addingtons
A Partial Descendents List
of
Henry Addington of South Carolina

A. Henry Addington, b. 1720 or 1727 (family tradition says London but probably Pennsylvania), 1768/74 moved to 96 District, SC, d. 25 Jul 1787, Union Co., South Carolina
  m. 1745/9, prob. Bucks Co., Pennsylvania, "Sarah" Elizabeth Burson, b. 1723/6, d. 14 Mar 1826, Chester, Indiana
A-1 John Addington, b. 10 Nov 1749 (also given as 5 Oct 1745), Bucks Co., Pennsylvania, d. 1833, Chester, Wayne Co., Indiana (will recorded 30 Aug 1833)
  m. 1st c1769, Newberry Co., South Carolina, Mary Lamb, d. 25 Apr 1774, South Carolina
A-1-1 William Addington, b. 14 Apr 1770, 96 District, South Carolina, d. 1 Jan 1845 (or 20 Nov 1844) Ridgeville, Randolph Co., Indiana, bur. Ridgeville Cem.
  m. Elizabeth ?, b. <1775
A-1-1-1 Joshua (or Joseph) Addington, b. c1790, South Carolina, d. c1848, Ridgeville, Indiana
  m. 28 Jan 1814, Wayne Co., Indiana, Rebecca Morgan, b. 1799, SC, (1850 Delaware Co., IN), d. 1851, near Ridgeville
A-1-1-1-1 Maria "Polly" Addington, b. c1816, d. 1880
  m. 5 Jan 1832, Wayne Co., Indiana, Charles Wilmott
A-1-1-1-2 Wiley Addington, b. c1822
  m. Sarah ?, b. 1821, Virginia
A-1-1-1-2-1 Dona R. Addington
A-1-1-1-2-2 Mary E. Addington, b. 1855
A-1-1-1-2-3 Lyda J. Addington, b. c1858
A-1-1-1-3 Jonathan Addington, b. 1823, Wayne Co., Indiana, d. 1864, California
  m. Margaret ?, b. 1828, Indiana
A-1-1-1-3-1 Allen W. Addington, b. c1847, Indiana
A-1-1-1-3-2 William W. Addington, b. c1849, Indiana
A-1-1-1-3-3 Charles Addington, b. c1855, California
A-1-1-1-3-4 Lorena Addington, b. c1857, California
A-1-1-1-4 William Addington b. c1825/30, d. age 2
A-1-1-1-5 Elizabeth "Betsy" Addington, b. c1827
  m. 21 Jan 1849, J. Richard (or Richmond) West, (lived Davis Co., IA)
A-1-1-1-5-1 Minerva J. West, b. 1849

A-1-1-1-6 Nancy Morgan Addington, b. 1825/6, d. 1924, Eureka or Hill City, Kansas
m. 21 Mar 1847, Benjamin Franklin Anderson
A-1-1-1-6-1 William H. Anderson, b. c1847, Indiana
A-1-1-1-6-2 John C. Anderson, b. c1849, Indiana
A-1-1-1-7 Minerva Jane Addington, b. 1833, Indiana
m. 16 Sep 1850, Delaware Co., Indiana, William Alexander
A-1-1-1-8 David Morgan Addington, b. 9 Jul 1835, Richmond, Indiana, d. 3 May 1922, Seattle, Washington (1880, 1900 and 1910 Montgomery Co., Kansas)
m. 1 May 1859, Wayne Co., Indiana, Eliza Jane Thompson, b. 19 Dec 1840, Richmond, IN, d. 12 Dec 1863, Wayne Co., IN
A-1-1-1-8-1 William Wiley Addington, b. Mar 1861, Indiana
m. Ella J. Hosmer
A-1-1-1-8-1-1 Mabel J. Addington, b. c1885, Kansas
A-1-1-1-8-1-2 Martha "Mattie" Addington, b. Apr 1887, Kansas
A-1-1-1-8-1-3 Walter C. Addington, b. Mar 1889, Kansas
A-1-1-1-8-1-4 David M. Addington, b. Feb 1891, Kansas
A-1-1-1-8-1-5 Edith Addington
A-1-1-1-8-1-6 Minerva Addington, d. infancy
A-1-1-1-8 m. 2nd 3 Sep 1864, Wayne Co., Indiana, Martha Ann Guard, b. Jan 1840, Indiana, d. 20 Feb 1901
A-1-1-1-8-2 James A. Addington, b. Jun 1865, Indiana
m. Elizabeth E. Dison, b. Jul 1872, Iowa
A-1-1-1-8-2-1 Theodore Addington, b. Jun 1891, Iowa
A-1-1-1-8-2-2 Gertie Addington, b. Jan 1895, Missouri
A-1-1-1-8-3 Oliver M. Addington, b. May 1866, Indiana
A-1-1-1-8-4 Francis M. Addington, b. Jun 1869, Indiana
m. Nellie Powers, b. Apr 1872, IL
A-1-1-1-8-5 Elmer E. Addington, b. Apr 1872, Illinois (lived Bartlesville, Oklahoma)
A-1-1-1-8-6 Mary P. "Nellie" Addington, b. Apr 1872, Illinois
m. W. A. Logan
A-1-1-1-8 m. 3rd 1 Mar 1911, Randolph Co., Indiana, Lulla B. Alexander
A-1-1-1-9 Lorena Seravie Addington, b. 1840, IN, d. bef. 1903
m. 19 Sep 1860, Wayne Co., Indiana, Milton Catey, b. 1838
A-1-1-2 Bishop Addington, b. c1792, d. bef. 1840
m. 19 Apr 1816 Wayne Co., IN, Betsy Cain, b. 1799, SC
A-1-1-2-1 Nancy Addington, b. 15 Mar 1817, d. 20 Feb 1883
m. 15 Jul 1841, Wayne Co., Indiana, William Parsons
A-1-1-2-1-1 James Parsons, b. 1843, m. Sue Bennett, ni
A-1-1-2-1-1 m. 2nd Emma Edwards, ni
A-1-1-2-1-2 Elizabeth A. Parsons, b. c1846, m. James O. Neal
181

A-1-1-2-1-2-1 Clara Neal

A-1-1-2-1-2-2 Mattie Neal

A-1-1-2-1-2-3 William Neal

A-1-1-2-2 Samuel Addington, b. c1818
  m. 30 Nov 1837, Randolph Co., IN, Elizabeth Robinson
  m. 30 Oct 1842, Wayne Co., Indiana, Sarah Taylor

A-1-1-2-3 Abijah Addington, b. 20 May 1820, Wayne Co.,
  Indiana, d. 31 Dec 1870, Wayne Co., Indiana
  m. 30 Jan 1845, Wayne Co., Indiana, Hulah Moore
  m. 2nd 22 Dec 1850, Wayne Co., Indiana, Ann Adams, b. 22
  Sep 1834, d. 14 Aug 1916

A-1-1-2-3-1 Henry Bishop Addington, b. 24 Jul 1851, d. 10 Jan
  1915, Tarrant Co., Texas (1900 Jackson Co., MO)
  m. 15 Mar 1874, Mary Holmes

A-1-1-2-3-1-1 Charles Walter Addington, b. 25 Jun 1881, Kansas
  m. 30 Apr 1906, Ethel L. Ersman

A-1-1-2-3-1-1-1 George Richard Addington, b. 31 Aug 1908, Ft.
  Worth, Texas, m. 28 Jun 1931, Oklahoma, Francis Eline
  Sutton, b. 24 Jul 1911, Ft. Worth, Texas

A-1-1-2-3-1-1-1-1 William Gordon Addington, b. 11 Sep 1933, Ft.
  Worth, Texas, m. 8 Aug 1957, Charlotte Ann Caldwell

A-1-1-2-3-1-1-1-2 George Ronald Addington, b. 30 Nov 1934, Ft.
  Worth, Texas, m. Ruth ?

A-1-1-2-3-1-1-1-3 Infant, b. & d. 4 Jul 1932, Ft. Worth, Texas

A-1-1-2-3-1-1-2 Charles Walter Addington, Jr., b. 19 Aug 1912,
  Ft. Worth, Texas, m. 20 Feb 1945, Stella West Stephens

A-1-1-2-3-2 Laura Viola Addington, b. 18 May 1853, d. 28 Dec
  1871

A-1-1-2-3-3 Hulda Virginia "Jennie" Addington, b. 26 Jan 1856,
  d. 20 May 1875, m. Lon Hoover

A-1-1-2-3-3-1 Jessie Hoover, b. 12 Aug 1875, d. 4 Apr 1920
  m. Forrest Rosser

A-1-1-2-3-3-1-1 Marie Rosser, b. Jul 1893, m. Edwin Frick

A-1-1-2-3-3-1-1-1 Marian Frick, b. Feb 1916

A-1-1-2-3-3-1-1-2 Edwin Ross Frick

A-1-1-2-3-4 Edgar Harrington "Fred" Addington, b. 4 Jun 1858,
  Richmond, Indiana, d. 5 Mar 1920, Hamilton Co., Ohio
  m. 7 Nov 1878, Wayne Co., Indiana, Maggie Doulon, d. 1887

A-1-1-2-3-4-1 Blanch Addington, b. 20 Feb 1879, Indiana, d. 23
  Dec 1969, Nazarth, Pennsylvania
  m. 12 Jan 1905, St. Charles, Missouri, Albert Letts

A-1-1-2-3-4-1-1 Albert Edgar Letts, b. 11 May 1911, Dayton, Ohio,
  d. 24 Aug 1975, Easton, Pennsylvania

m. 18 Nov 1939, Kansas City, Missouri, Catherine Eileen Hawthorn

A-1-1-2-3-4-1-1-1 Carole Ann Letts, b. 22 Nov 1944, Ashland, KY, m. 6 Sep 1969, Irvin Greenberg, ni

A-1-1-2-3-4-1-1-2 Lois Eileen Letts, b. 25 Jun 1947, Ashland, KY m. 13 Dec 1975, Anthony Zettlemoyer

A-1-1-2-3-4-1-1-2-1 James Thaddeus Zettlemoyer, b. 24 Mat 1978, Harrisburg, Pennsylvania

A-1-1-2-3-4-2 William Saunders Addington, b. 26 Dec 1880, Hamilton Co., Ohio, d. 17 Jul 1947, Enid, Oklahoma
m. 24 Dec 1904, Newkirk, Oklahoma, Effie May Walker

A-1-1-2-3-4-2-1 William Sage Addington, b. 29 Oct 1905, Little Rock, Pulaski Co., Arkansas, d. 20 Sep 1938, Miami, FL
m. Myrtle Marie Tremain, b. 26 Oct 1905, Sumner Co., Kansas

A-1-1-2-3-4-2-1-1 Enid Maurine Addington, b. 25 Feb 1925, Enid, OK, m. 2 Aug 1947, Enid, Oklahoma, Rex Lile McSparrin

A-1-1-2-3-4-2-1-1-1 Madelyn Kay McSparrin, b. 29 Jun 1950, Cherokee, Oklahoma, m. 26 Dec 1971, Tonkawa, Oklahoma La Kirk Mittelstet

A-1-1-2-3-4-2-1-1-1-1 Staci Nicole Mittelstet, b. 18 Jun 1975, Enid, Oklahoma

A-1-1-2-3-4-2-1-1-1-2 Matthew Kirk Mittelstet, b. 9 Apr 1979, Stillwater, Oklahoma

A-1-1-2-3-4-2-1-1-2 Marcia Sue McSparrin, b. 29 Jun 1952, Enid, OK, m. 30 Aug 1975, Tonkawa, OK, Ralph Edward Seals, Jr.

A-1-1-2-3-4-2-1-1-2-1 Adam Blake Seals, b. 19 Apr 1979, Enid, OK

A-1-1-2-3-4-2-1-1-2-2 Ryan Alan Seals, b. 27 Jan 1982, Enid, OK

A-1-1-2-3-4-2-1-1-3 Meredith Ann McSparrin, b. 17 Apr 1956, Enid, OK, m. 10 Jun 1974, Stillwater, OK, Jet J. Williamson

A-1-1-2-3-4-2-1-1-3-1 Joshua Lile Williamson, b. 23 Jan 1975, Ponca City, Oklahoma

A-1-1-2-3-4-2-1-1-3-2 Summer Leigh Williamson, b. 29 Jan 1979, Ponca City, Oklahoma

A-1-1-2-3-4-2-1-1-3-3 Auburn Ann Williamson, b. 10 Aug 1981, Ponca City, Oklahoma

A-1-1-2-3-4-2-1-2 Gloria Mae "Dody" Addington, b. 27 May 1930, Ponca City, Oklahoma
m. 19 Jun 1948 Muskogee, OK, Kenneth Dwayne "Pete" Lewis

A-1-1-2-3-4-2-1-2-1 Linda Joy Lewis, b. 23 May 1949, Enid, OK
m. 18 Apr 1967, Anthony, Kansas, Michael Boyd Hemphill

A-1-1-2-3-4-2-1-2-1-1 Michael Todd Hemphill, b. 12 Jun 1968 Enid, Oklahoma, d. 17 Oct 1975, Enid, Oklahoma

A-1-1-2-3-4-2-1-2-1-2 Matthew Scott Hemphill, b. 7 Jun 1972, Enid, Oklahoma

A-1-1-2-3-4-2-1-2-1-3 Holly Lynn Hemphill, b. 25 Mar 1977, Enid, Oklahoma

A-1-1-2-3-4-2-1-2-1 m. 2nd 29 Jun 1980, Bruce Wayne Erbele

A-1-1-2-3-4-2-1-2-1-4 Garrett Blake Erbele, b. 11 Nov 1981, Enid, Oklahoma

A-1-1-2-3-4-2-1-2-2 Leslye Marie Lewis, b. 27 Dec 1952, Enid, OK m. 22 Nov 1974, Enid, Oklahoma, Rodney Van Buskirk

A-1-1-2-3-4-2-1-2-1 Christopher Bryan Van Buskirk, b. 10 Apr 1979, Enid, Oklahoma

A-1-1-2-3-4-2-1-2-3 Kenneth Earl Lewis, b. 5 Nov 1959, Enid, OK

A-1-1-2-3-4-2-1-3 William Ronald Addington, b. 15 Jun 1933, Ponca City, Oklahoma, m. Nancy Pearl Seiger, div.

A-1-1-2-3-4-2-1-3-1 William Michael Addington, b. 4 Aug 1957, Enid, Oklahoma, m. 30 Jul 1977, Virginia Lynn Barnes

A-1-1-2-3-4-2-1-3-1-1 Christopher Michael Addington, b. 10 Aug 1980, Enid, Oklahoma

A-1-1-2-3-4-2-1-3-1-2 Infant, b.and d. 1983

A-1-1-2-3-4-2-1-3-2 Gwendolyn Kay Addington, b. 16 Jul 1959, Tacoma, WA, m. 23 Oct 1976, Enid, OK, Daniel Lee Jellison, div., ni, m. 2nd Aug 1979, Enid, OK, James Louis Quiggle

A-1-1-2-3-4-2-1-3-3 Deborah Lynn Addington, b. 2 Jun 1963, Chinon, France, m. 8 Aug 1981, Enid, Oklahoma, Gary Gene Wehrenberg, div.

A-1-1-2-3-4-2-1-3-3-1 Tabitha Blythe Wehrenberg, b. 16 Jun 1982, Enid, Oklahoma

A-1-1-2-3-4-2-1-3-3-2 Kelsi Nicole Wehrenberg, b. 9 Jul 1983, Enid, Oklahoma

A-1-1-2-3-4-2-1-3-4 Stephen Wayne Addington, b. 13 Apr 1966, Fort Mommoth, New Jersey

A-1-1-2-3-4-2-1-3 m. 2nd Lois Kincade Henneke

A-1-1-2-3-4-2-1-4 Edward Sage Addington, b. 4 Jan 1939, Enid, OK, m. Linda Lou Winter, div.

A-1-1-2-3-4-2-1-4-1 William Curtin Addington, b. 30 Oct 1956, Ardmore, Oklahoma, m. 14 Oct 1977, San Antonio, Texas, Gloria Ann Villarreal, div.

A-1-1-2-3-4-2-1-4-1-1 Christopher Addington, b. 13 Mar 1979, San Antonio, Texas

A-1-1-2-3-4-2-1-4-1-2 Samantha Yolanda Addington, b. 21 Jan 1984, Dallas, Texas

A-1-1-2-3-4-2-1-4 m. 2nd Yolanda ?

A-1-1-2-3-4-2-1-4-2 Edward Eric Addington, b. 18 Jul 1960, Evreax, France

A-1-1-2-3-4-2-1-4-3 Lewis Brian Addington, b. 14 Sep 1963, Barksdale, Louisiana

A-1-1-2-3-4-2-1-4-4 Kenneth Lyle Addington, b. 17 Feb 1965, Barksdale, LA

A-1-1-2-3-4-2-1-4-5 Katherine Lynn Addington, b. 17 Feb 1965, Barksdale, LA

A-1-1-2-3-4-2-1-4-5-1 Adam Sage Arano, b. 27 Aug 1981, Del City, Oklahoma

A-1-1-2-3-4-2-1-4 m. 2nd Etta Sue Charles

A-1-1-2-3-4-2-2 Margaret Lucille Addington, b. 13 Jul 1908, Shawnee, Pottawatomie Co., Oklahoma
m. Zonnie Orris Hardy, b. 25 Feb 1906, Bibb Co., GA

A-1-1-2-3-4-2-2-1 Norma Jean Hardy, b. Jul 1931, d. Jul 1931

A-1-1-2-3-4-2-2-2 Doris Darlene Hardy, b. 17 Feb 1933, Ponca City, Oklahoma, m. Jack Winstel

A-1-1-2-3-4-2-2-3 Donald Orris Hardy, b. 11 Dec 1939, Cresent, OK

A-1-1-2-3-4-2-2-4 Judith Lorraine Hardy, b. 23 Jul 1944, Pasedena, Texas

A-1-1-2-3-4-2-2-5 Ellen Lynn Hardy, b. 5 Apr 1946, Pasedena, TX

A-1-1-2-3-4-3 Edith Ann Addington, b. 3 Oct 1884, d. 18 Jan 1958, Arkansas City, Kansas, dnm

A-1-1-2-3-4 m. 2nd 28 Dec 1893, Wayne Co., Indiana, Mary Agnes Stein

A-1-1-2-3-4-4 Laura Addington, b. Jan 1895, KS, d. 1945, dnm

A-1-1-2-3-4-5 Caroline Mary Addington, b. 27 Dec 1897, Arkansas City, KS, d. 27 Apr 1983, Arkansas City, KS, ni
m. 7 Jul 1931, Lawton, Oklahoma, James M. Marshall

A-1-1-2-3-4-6 Louise Elizabeth Addington, b. 14 Jul 1899, Arkansas City, Kansas, d. 27 Apr 1981, Wichita, KS, ni
m. 1 Jan 1925, Noble E. Wing, b. 20 Sep 1898, d. 14 Jan 1985

A-1-1-2-3-4-7 Henry Paul Addington, b. 10 Dec 1901, Arkansas City, Kansas, d. 18 Sep 1964, Salina, Kansas
m. 9 May 1925, Enid, Oklahoma, Mary Jo Coker, b. 7 Jul 1899, d. 26 Jul 1982

A-1-1-2-3-4-7-1 Paul H. Addington, b. 10 Dec 1932, Oklahoma City, Oklahoma, m. 26 Feb 1965, Elizabeth Duke Smith

A-1-1-2-3-4-7-1-1 Paul Craig Addington, b. 16 Aug 1966, Houston, Texas

A-1-1-2-3-4-7-1-2 Derek Brown Addington, b. 15 Aug 1968, Jackson, MS

A-1-1-2-3-4-7-1-3 Todd Duke Addington, b. 25 Feb 1970, Houston, Texas

A-1-1-2-3-4-7-2 Charles Edgar Addington, b. 29 Oct 1933, Hobart, Oklahoma

A-1-1-2-3-5 Walter W. Addington, b. 1862, d. 1871

A-1-1-2-3-6 Frank W. Addington, b. 5 Nov 1865, (?1910 Washington Co., Oklahoma)
m. 15 Dec 1886, Wayne Co., IN, Ardell Evans, b. Apr 1866
A-1-1-2-3-6-1 Irene E. Addington, b. 25 Sep 1887, Wayne, Co., Indiana, d. c1959, m. 24 Nov 1915, Edgar Nathan Davis
A-1-1-2-3-6-2 Edna Margaret Addington, b. 18 Jul 1894, Indiana
m. 22 Jan 1913, Wayne Co., Indiana, Lewis R. Kirby, b. 2 Dec 1890, d. 8 Feb 1960
A-1-1-2-3-6-2-1 Gretchen Irene Kirby, b. 25 Aug 1913, m. Robert Boren
A-1-1-2-3-6-2-1-1 Karen Boren
A-1-1-2-3-6-2-1 m. 2nd Howard Nutley
A-1-1-2-4 Bishop Addington, Jr., b. Mar 1826, Indiana, d. 12 Oct 1904, Jay Co., Indiana
m. 12 Oct 1848, Wayne Co., Indiana, Delilah Maria Wile (or Weyl), b. 15 Sep 1832, IN, d. 26 Feb 1904, Jay Co., Indiana
A-1-1-2-4-1 Elizabeth Jane Addington, b. 8 Sep 1849, Wayne Co., Indiana, d. 22 Oct 1930, Dunkirk, Indiana
m. 22 Dec 1867, Wayne Co., Indiana, George Hartup, b. 9 Sep 1842, Wayne Co., Indiana, d. Jul 1915
A-1-1-2-4-1-1 Ada M. Hartup, m. John N. Brooks
A-1-1-2-4-1-2 John G. Hartup, m. Martha Ray
A-1-1-2-4-1-3 Decatur Hartup, d. young
A-1-1-2-4-1-4 Luther Hartup, d. young
A-1-1-2-4-1-5 James Cliffton Hartup, b. Jay Co., Indiana
m. Madgelene "Lena" Hugo
A-1-1-2-4-1-5-1 Catherine Hartup, m. Emmett W. Yeiser
A-1-1-2-4-1-5-1-1 Catherine Yeiser, m. ? Hugo
A-1-1-2-4-1-5-1-1-1 Hugh Hugo, b. 1958
A-1-1-2-4-1-5-1-1-2 James Hugo, b. 1961
A-1-1-2-4-1-5-1-1-3 Louise Hugo, b. 1964
A-1-1-2-4-1-5-1-2 Emmett Yeiser, Jr.
A-1-1-2-4-1-4 Ernest Hartup, m. Nora Jormagin
A-1-1-2-4-1-5 Alva Luther Hartup, m. Inez McTyre
A-1-1-2-4-2 Sarah Caroline Addington, b. 7 Oct 1851, d. 28 Jun 1924, m. 9 Oct 1870, Wayne Co., Indiana, Henderson Oler, b. 9 Apr 1847, d. 24 Apr 1925
A-1-1-2-4-2-1 Daisy Oler
A-1-1-2-4-2-2 Cicero Oler
A-1-1-2-4-2-3 Ohmer Oler
A-1-1-2-4-2-4 Icy Oler
A-1-1-2-4-3 Martha Alice Addington, b. 8 Sep 1856
m. 8 Feb 1883, Jay Co., Indiana, Alvin Armitage
A-1-1-2-4-3-1 Oneida Armitage

A-1-1-2-4-3-2 Hazel Armitage

A-1-1-2-4-4 Mary Ann Addington, b. c1854
  m. 8 Feb 1883, Jay Co., Indiana, Asbury Cain

A-1-1-2-4-4-1 Fred Cain

A-1-1-2-4-5 Edward B. Addington, b. 22 Sep 1859, Iowa (1910 Jay
  Co., Indiana)
  m. 26 Sep 1889, Jay Co., Indiana, Adah Bell Geiger

A-1-1-2-4-5-1 Lola Addington, b. 3 Oct 1894, Jay Co., Indiana

A-1-1-2-4-5 m. 2nd 15 Nov 1911, Jay Co., Indiana, Ethel Sharp

A-1-1-2-4-5-2 Burnel Addington

A-1-1-2-4-5-3 Edward Addington, b. 13 Sep 1912, Jay Co., Indiana

A-1-1-2-4-5-4 Max Sharp Addington, b. 29 Dec 1918, Jay Co.,
  Indiana, d. 18 Jan 1919

A-1-1-2-4-6 Charles Louis Addington, b. 25 Sep 1860, nr.
  Fairfield, Iowa, m. Ida Baker

A-1-1-2-4-6-1 Oris Addington, b. 31 Jul 1890, Indiana
  m. 24 Oct 1914, Delaware Co., Olive Fern Jester

A-1-1-2-4-6-1-1 Florence M. Addington, b. 26 Feb 1916, Delaware
  Co., Indiana

A-1-1-2-4-6-1-2 Oris Howard Addington, b. 1 Jun 1918, Delaware
  Co., Indiana

A-1-1-2-4-6-1-3 Kenneth Earl Addington, b. 3 May 1920,
  Delaware County, Indiana

A-1-1-2-4-6-1-3-1 David Addington

A-1-1-2-4-6-1-3-2 James L. Addington

A-1-1-2-4-6-1-4 Robert Addington

A-1-1-2-4-6-2 Harold Addington, ? b. 9 Apr 1902
  m. Helen Florey

A-1-1-2-4-7 Theodore W. Addington, b. 4 Nov 1867
  m. 11 Dec 1898, Jay Co., Indiana, Margaret Andrews

A-1-1-2-4-8 Mirrilla May Addington, b. 18 Jan 1871
  m. 3 Oct 1892, Jay Co., Indiana, Amos J. D. Baker

A-1-1-2-4-8-1 Chloe Agnes Baker, b. 20 Jun 1895
  m. 25 Dec 1914, Marvin Babcock

A-1-1-2-4-8-2 Harry Leland Baker, b. 26 Sep 1897
  m. 12 Apr 1916, Marguerite Weaver

A-1-1-2-4-8-3 Dwight Wayne Baker, b. 15 Jan 1901

A-1-1-2-4-8-4 son, b. & d. 16 Jan 1904

A-1-1-2-5 Cane Addington, b. 1828, Indiana

A-1-1-2-6 Leander Addington, b. 1834, d. 28 Dec 1888,
  Richmond, Indiana

A-1-1-3 Patsy Addington, b. 1800
  m. 23 Jan 1820, Wayne Co., Indiana, Samuel Prevoe

A-1-1-4 John Addington, b. 1802, d. 1 May 1849, Randolph Co., Indiana, bur. Ridgeville Cem.

m. 12 Sep 1822, Wayne Co., Indiana, Lucretia Roberts, d. 30 Jan 1844, bur. Ridgeville

A-1-1-4-1 Bishop Addington, b. 17 Mar 1823, d. 30 Apr 1881

m. 8 Jan 1845, Randolph Co., Indiana, Amanda Paxton, b. 1825, Pennsylvania

A-1-1-4-1-1 Warren M. Addington, b. 25 Mar 1849, Indiana

m. Emma Edwards

A-1-1-4-1-1-1 Anne Addington, b. 1875, Indiana, (lived in Richmond)

A-1-1-4-1-1-2 Frank Addington, b. 1879, Indiana, (lived in NY, Chicago)

A-1-1-4-1-1-3 Lizzie Addington, b. 6 Jan 1884, Indiana, (lived in Chicago)

m. ? 29 April 1902, Wayne Co., Indiana, Clyde W. Henry

A-1-1-4-1-1 m. 2nd 12 Jun 1894, Marion Co., Indiana, Katie Fitzgibbon

A-1-1-4-1-1-4 William Addington, b. 28 Jul 1893

m. 7 Jan 1913, Marion Co., Indiana, Elizabeth Ochiltree

A-1-1-4-1-1-5 Morris Addington, b. 3 Dec 1896

m. 4 Mar 1918, Marion Co., Indiana, Anna Hills

A-1-1-4-1 m. 2nd 20 Dec 1852, Wayne Co., Indiana, Sarah Jane Smith, d. 1857

A-1-1-4-1 m. 3rd 8 Jul 1857, Wayne Co., Indiana, Julie Ann Anderson, d. 1861

A-1-1-4-1 m. 4th 24 Nov 1861, Wayne Co., IN, Mary Caroline Burdsall, b. 1843, Ohio, d. 15 Dec 1920

A-1-1-4-1-2 Sheriden Addington, b. 13 Dec 1865, d. 26 Mar 1914

A-1-1-4-1-3 Alta Addington, b. 9 Nov 1867, d. 13 Mar 1886, Wayne Co., Indiana

A-1-1-4-1-4 Martin Luther Addington, b. 15 Sep 1869

m. 8 Feb 1893, Wayne Co., Indiana, Freda Ricka Bescher

A-1-1-4-1-4-1 Herbert Addington, b. 7 Sep 1894, Wayne Co., IN

A-1-1-4-1-4-2 Lena Addington, b. 4 Aug 1899

A-1-1-4-1-4-3 Rosella Addington, b. 12 Dec 1902

A-1-1-4-1-5 Ursula Addington, b. 22 Sep 1871

m. I. W. Humphrey

A-1-1-4-1-5-1 Freda Humphrey, b. 15 Aug 1897, m. ? Ogle

A-1-1-4-1-5-1-1 Theodore Ogle

A-1-1-4-1-5-1-2 June Ogle

A-1-1-4-1-5-2 Orville Humphrey, b. 25 Apr 1899

A-1-1-4-1-6 Nellie Addington, b. 26 Aug 1875

m. 29 Dec 1897, Wayne Co., Indiana, Clarence M. Hunt

A-1-1-4-2 Benjamin Addington, b. 1824, Indiana
  m. 12 May 1852, Randolph Co., Indiana, Louisa (Gray)
  (Atkinson) Addington, widow of A-1-1-4
A-1-1-4-3 Kathern Addington, b. 1826, d. 27 Feb 1913
  m. 29 Mar 1846, Wayne Co., Indiana, Madison Sullivan, b.
  1823, d. 1903
A-1-1-4-3-1 Wesley Sullivan
A-1-1-4-3-2 Albert Sullivan
A-1-1-4-4 William Addington b. 1825/35 (?1880 Union Co., KY)
  m. Mary ?
A-1-1-4-4-1? Katie B. Addington, b. c1862, Indiana
A-1-1-4-4-2? Alice Addington, b. c1871, KY
A-1-1-4-4-3? John Addington, b. c1873, KY
A-1-1-4-5 Elizabeth Addington, b. 1831, Indiana
  m. 27 Oct 1861, Wayne Co., Indiana, Freeman Burdsall
A-1-1-4-5-1 Josephine Burdsall, m. ? Reeder
A-1-1-4-5-2 Alliho Burdsall
A-1-1-4-6 Drusila Addington, m. 6 Oct 1850, William G. Bundy
A-1-1-4-7 Nacon Addington, b. 1839
  m. 9 Oct 1862, Wayne Co., Indiana, Anna Burdsall
A-1-1-4-8 John Addington, Jr., b. 1842, d. ? 12 Sep 1864, Civil
  War, 84th Indiana Reg.
A-1-1-4 m. 2nd 18 Apr 1845, Randolph Co., Indiana, Louisa
  (Gray) Atkinson, b. c1820, Ohio
A-1-1-4-9 Susan Addington, b. 1847
A-1-1-4-10 Miriam Lucretia Addington, b. 1849
A-1-1-5 Jacob Addington (only listed in HMA, I I)
A-1-1-6 William Addington, b. 1807, Indiana, d. 1859/60
  m. 1828, Sudie (?Mary) White, d. 1847, Randolph Co., Indiana
A-1-1-6-1 Joel Addington, b. 17 Nov 1830, Richmond, Indiana,
  d. 19 Jul 1921, Portland, Oregon (1852 to Oregon)
  m. 12 Feb 1860, Lane Co., Oregon, Mary Jane Lewellen, b. 14
  Apr 1843, Indiana, d. 16 Jun 1914, Lane Co., Oregon
A-1-1-6-1-1 Ella Olive Addington, b. c1861, Oregon, d. bef 1895
  ? m. 22 Jan 1879, Lane Co., Oregon, Charles L. Williams
A-1-1-6-1-2 Minnie Lillas Addington, b. 19 Feb 1866, Linn Co.,
  Oregon, d. 26 Feb 1945, Portland, OR
  m. 16 Feb 1887, Lane Co., Oregon, Robert Ellis Callison
A-1-1-6-1-3 Louis Leuwellen Addington, b. 4 Dec 1872, Oregon,
  d. 7 Sep 1948, Oakridge, OR, m. Frances Octavia Stiers
A-1-1-6-1-3-1 Lucille Lena Addington, b. 6 Feb 1901, Lane Co.,
  Oregon, m. B. W. Pettijohn
A-1-1-6-1-3-2 Louis Leonard Addington, b. 7 Mar 1905, Lane Co.,
  Oregon, d. 12 Jan 1929, Marcola, OR, m. Wilma ?

A-1-1-6-1-3-2-1 Patty Lou Addington
A-1-1-6-1-4 Leroy Kipling Addington, b. 16 Sep 1875, Oregon, d.
15 Oct 1955, Dexter, OR, dnm
A-1-1-6-1-5 Alva Bernard Addington, b. 12 Mar 1880, Oregon, d.
6 Apr 1964, Multnomah Co., OR, m. Margit Hanson
A-1-1-6-1-6 Winella Grace Addington, b. 17 Mar 1883, Oregon,
d. 15 Nov 1954, Eugene, OR
m. Munsey Goddard, 4 children, m. 2nd Charles Hoag, 1 ch.
A-1-1-6-2 Bishop Addington, b. Nov 1833, Indiana, d. Tazewell
Co., Illinois (1880 Tazewell Co., Illinois)
m. 29 Mar 1857, Tazewell Co., Illinois, Lucinda Falcor
A-1-1-6-2-1 Charles W. "Oscar" Addington, b. Feb 1859, IL
m. 3 Oct 1878, Rachel Hay, b. Nov 1858, Ohio
A-1-1-6-2-1-1 Bessie Addington, b. Jul 1881, Illinois
A-1-1-6-2-1-2 George Addington, b. Nov 1883, Illinois
A-1-1-6-2-1-3 Nellie Addington, b. Nov 1887, Illinois
A-1-1-6-2-1-4 Willie Addington, b. Feb 1893, Illinois
A-1-1-6-2-2 Emma J. Addington, b. Jan 1860, Illinois
m. John Jones, b. c1859, Illinois
A-1-1-6-2-2-1 Walker Jones, b. May 1894, Illinois
A-1-1-6-2-3 Gracie Addington, b. c1866, m. Charles Pratt
A-1-1-6-2-3-1 Lee Pratt, b. Dec 1886, Illinois
A-1-1-6-2-4 Fannie Addington (twin), b. c1866
A-1-1-6-2-5 Mary Alice Addington, b. c1867
A-1-1-6-2-6 George Addington, b. c1872 (1900 Logan Co., IL, Carl
Addington, b. Oct 1872)
A-1-1-6-2-7 Laura Addington, b. Nov 1876, Illinois
A-1-1-6-2-8 Harry Addington, b. Feb 1881, IL, m. Anna M. ?
A-1-1-6-3 Louis "William" Addington, b. Apr 1839, d. 1908,
(1900 Marion, Indiana)
m. 1 Sep 1866, Randolph Co., Indiana, Elizabeth Ullom, b.
1837, Ohio
A-1-1-6-3-1 Oliver Bishop Addington, b. 4 Sep 1867, Indiana, d.
20 Feb 1949
m. 15 Feb 1891, Jay Co., Indiana, Emma Retta Brown, b. 5 Jun
1870, d. 14 Dec 1938
A-1-1-6-3-1-1 Orville Edgar Addington, b. 9 May 1894, Jay Co.,
Indiana, d. 9 Jun 1971
m. 12 Jan 1921, Grace Edna Miller, b. 21 Sep 1892, d. 8 Jan 1975
A-1-1-6-3-1-1-1 Wilma Jean Addington, b. 23 Nov 1921
A-1-1-6-3-1-1-2 Jay Wendell Addington, b. 30 Jul 1928
m. 8 Apr 1951, Betty Jane Chalk, b. 18 Mar 1933
A-1-1-6-3-1-1-2-1 Jay Randall Addington, b. 19 Apr 1952
m. 24 Oct 1970, Rose Free

A-1-1-6-3-1-1-2-1-1 Jennifer Ann Addington, b. 5 Apr 1971
  m. 4 May 1991, Larry Brown
A-1-1-6-3-1-1-2-1-2 Debra Marie Addington, b. 12 Mar 1972
  m. 13 Jul 1991, Kirk Jetmore
A-1-1-6-3-1-1-2-1-3 Jeffrey Randall Addington, b. 3 Apr 1977
A-1-1-6-3-1-1-2-2 Connie Jean Addington, b. 22 Aug 1953, d. 4
  Aug 1954
A-1-1-6-3-1-1-2-3 Brian Lynn Addington, b. 20 Jul 1956
  m. 4 Sep 1977, Janis Stanley
A-1-1-6-3-1-1-2-3-1 Brooke Lyn Addington, b. 27 Feb 1978
A-1-1-6-3-1-1-2-4 Jone Elaine Addington, b. 3 Feb 1958
  m. 12 Jul 1980, Robin Snider
A-1-1-6-3-1-1-2-4-1 Austin Jay Snider, b. 4 Dec 1987
A-1-1-6-3-1-1-2-5 Nancy Jane Addington, b. 25 Jan 1959
  m. 3 Jul 1982, Bruce Fulkerson
A-1-1-6-3-1-1-2-5-1 Paul Michael Fulkerson, b. 4 May 1983
A-1-1-6-3-1-1-2-5-2 Marc Alan Fulkerson, b. 3 Feb 1987
A-1-1-6-3-1-2 Caude Lewis Addington, b. 5 Oct 1897, Jay Co.,
  Indiana, d. 15 Jun 1986
  m. 2 Jun 1921, Edith Rae Miller, b. 3 Dec 1899, d. 26 Dec 1969
A-1-1-6-3-1-2-1 Erma Janette Addington, b. 4 Mar 1925
  m. John Crow, b. 10 Mar 1924
A-1-1-6-3-1-2-1-1 Mark Crow, m. Diane Zachary
A-1-1-6-3-1-2-1-2 Jay Crow
A-1-1-6-3-1-2-2 Ilah Rosmond Addington, b. 16 Dec 1926
  m. 7 Jul 1945, Howard Roberts, b. 10 Feb 1927
A-1-1-6-3-1-2-2-1 Craig Roberts, b. 26 May 1946
  m. 1979, Nancy Fich
A-1-1-6-3-1-2-2-1-1 Edon Basil Lee Roberts, b. 13 Oct 1981
A-1-1-6-3-1-2-2-1-2 Robyn Roberts, b. 8 Oct 1983
A-1-1-6-3-1-2-2-2 Lyle Roberts, b. 7 May 1953
  m. 27 Mar 1976, Mary Hasker, b. 14 Aug 1952
A-1-1-6-3-1-2-2-2-1 Lindsay Diane Roberts, b. 9 Oct 1982
A-1-1-6-3-1-2-2-2-2 Ashley Nicole Roberts, b. 11 Sep 1985
A-1-1-6-3-2 John W. Addington, b. 1869, d. 21 Jan 1888, Jay Co.,
  Indiana
A-1-1-6-3-3 Addie C. Addington, d. young
A-1-1-6-3-4 Rose E. Addington, b. 1873
A-1-1-6-3-5 Charles W. Addington, d. 2 Apr 1882
A-1-1-6-3-6 William O. Addington, b. 1877, d. ? 8 Dec 1896,
  Muncie, Indiana
A-1-1-6-3-7 Clemie Estus Addington, b. 1878
A-1-1-6-3-8 Herman L. Addington, b. 1880, Indiana
A-1-1-6-4 Matilda Addington, b. c1842

?? m. 11 Jun 1853, Henry Dodd
A-1-1-6-5 Elizabeth Addington, b. c1843
   m. 17 Jun 1860, Randolph Co., Indiana, Samuel Turner
A-1-1-6-6 Zachariah Addington, b. Feb 1849, d. 1908
   m. 2 Jun 1872, Susan Lefevre, b. 14 Mar 1847, d. 1925 (Susan
     m. 2nd 13 Feb 1912, Thomas Mason)
A-1-1-6-6-1 Lesley(son) L. Addington, d. 15 Feb 1879, age 3
A-1-1-6-6-2 Daisy Addington, b. c1874 (?adopted)
   m. 11 Nov 1896, Randolph Co., Indiana, Virgil Macy
A-1-1-6 ?m. 2nd 18 Oct 1853, Randolph Co., Indiana, Nancy
   Rash, b. c1820, d. 31 May 1883
A-1-1-6-7 William Addington, b. c1855, Indiana
   m. ? 11 Aug 1879, Delaware Co., Indiana, Savana Dudelston
A-1-1-6-7-1 George Addington, b. 1884
   m. 6 Feb 1905, Delaware Co., Indiana, Emma McGuire
A-1-1-6-7-1-1 dau. b. 5 May 1907
A-1-1-6-7-1-2 son, b. 11 Nov 1912
A-1-1-6-7-1-3 Howard Paul Addington, b. 4 Sep 1913, Delaware
   Co., Indiana
A-1-1-6-7-1-4 dau. b. 25 Jul 1914
A-1-1-6-7-2 Hazel Addington, b. 5 Oct 1890
   m. 24 Oct 1908, Delaware Co., Indiana, Grover Irelan
A-1-1-7 Elsie Addington, b. 1808, Wayne Co., Indiana
   m. 24 Jan 1830, James Seagraves
A-1-1-8 Elizabeth Addington, b. 1809, d. 1877, Winchester, IN
   m. 22 Mar 1832, Wayne Co., Indiana, Martin Seagraves, b.
   1808, NC, d. 1875
A-1-1-8-1 William Seagraves, b. c1834
A-1-1-8-2 Martha J. Seagraves, b. c1840
A-1-1-8-3 James M. Seagraves, b. c1842
A-1-1-8-4 Sarah E. Seagraves, b. c1844
A-1-1-8-5 Anna Seagraves, b. c1846
A-1-1-8-6 John C. Seagraves, b. c1852, m. Emma L. Boltz
A-1-1-8-6-1 John A. Seagraves, m. Myra Kimball
A-1-1-8-6-1-1 Bobby B. Seagraves, m. 1950, Joan Seiss
A-1-1-8-6-1-1-1 Mark F. Seagraves, b. 1954
A-1-1-8-6-1-1-2 Bruce A. Seagraves, b. 1958
A-1-1-8-7 Preston Seagraves
A-1-1-8-8 Mason Seagraves
A-1-1-8-9 Lizzie Seagraves
A-1-1-9 Joab Addington, b. 28 Aug 1814, Wayne Co., IN, d. 6 Feb
   1853, Randolph Co., IN, bur. Old Ridgeville Cemetery
   m. 2 Feb 1843, Elizabeth Edwards, d. 1845/7

A-1-1-9-1 Polly or "Molly" Ann Addington, b. 15 Jul 1845, d. 16 Jan 1871, Ridgeville, Indiana
m. 6 Dec 1863, Oliver Young Sackman, b. 11 Jul 1842, Preble Co., Ohio, d. 6 Feb 1922, Genesee Co., Michigan
A-1-1-9-1-1 William Norton Sackman, b. 5 Oct 1864, Preble Co., Ohio, m. 4 Jan 1924, Celina Stebbins
A-1-1-9-1-2 Olivia "Viola" Sackman, b. 18 Mar 1866, d. 24 Apr 1929, m. 14 Jun 1894, Jacob Elwood Pearson
A-1-1-9-1-2-1 Elvah Pauline Pearson, b. 16 Nov 1896, Wabash Co., Indiana, d. 7 Oct 1978, Mishawaka, Indiana
m. 3 Dep 1925, Sherman Tecumceh Deo, b. 14 Sep 1890, d. 22 Mar 1976
A-1-1-9-1-2-1-1 Janis Deo, b. 29 Nov 1927, Mishawaka, Indiana
m. 1 Dec 1948, Robert Gabriel Klute, b. 4 Jan 1925
A-1-1-9-1-3 Ida May Sackman, b. 10 Jun 1869, Ridgeville, IN
m. 1918, Lincoln Richardson Boylston
A-1-1-9 m. 2nd 17 Jun 1847, Randolph Co., Indiana, Barbara A. Harshman, b. 15 Feb 1826, d. 3 Dec 1876, McDonald Co., Missouri, (Barbara, m. 2nd 19 Feb 1855, John Wilson)
A-1-1-9-2 Elizabeth Addington, b. 1848
m. 11 Sep 1864, Christian Miller
A-1-1-9-3 Malinda Alice Addington, b. 7 Oct 1849, Ridgeville, Indiana, d. 30 Jan 1927, Pineville, Missouri
m. 24 Oct 1869, McDonald Co., Missouri, John Dudley Noel, b. 10 Mar 1849, Pineville, MO, d. 24 Feb 1914, Pineville, MO
A-1-1-9-3-1 John Willard Noel, b. c1870, d. c1930, ni
A-1-1-9-3-2 Charles Clinton Noel, b. 25 Dec 1873, d. 29 Apr 1955, m. Bertha ?
A-1-1-9-3-3 Ernest Noel, b. 14 Nov 1875, d. 1 Oct 1902
A-1-1-9-3-4 Vera "Mink" Noel, b. 1 Sep 1876, Pineville, MO
m. May 1900, Alice Victoria Studivan
A-1-1-9-3-4-1 Cleo Marine Noel, b. 8 Feb 1911, Pineville, MO
m. 26 Jun 1929, Ray Glenn Eslick
A-1-1-9-3-4-1-1 Akuce Colleen Eslick, b. 6 Feb 1930, Sedon, KS
m. 28 Sep 1946, San Francisco, California, Carl Duain West
A-1-1-9-3-4-1-1-1 Michael West, b. 19 Apr 1947
A-1-1-9-3-4-1-1-2 Virginia West, b. 21 Apr 1949
A-1-1-9-3-4-1-1-3 Glen West, b. 5 Jul 1950
A-1-1-9-3-4-1-1-4 Shannon West, b. 26 Oct 1952
A-1-1-9-3-4-1-1-5 Dayna West, b. 27 Dec 1953, d. 9 Apr 1954
A-1-1-9-3-4-1-1-6 Kevin West, b. 29 Mar 1955
A-1-1-9-3-4-1-1-7 Donald West, b. 5 Jun 1956
A-1-1-9-3-4-1-1 m. 2nd 2 Nov 1961, Reno, NV, Alvin Eszler
A-1-1-9-3-5 George Earl Noel, b. 15 Dec 1880, d. 26 Jan 1951

A-1-1-9-3-6 Vadis Noel, b. Nov 1887, m. Beulah Staley

A-1-1-9-3-7 Lillie D. Noel, b. Jun 1883, m. ? Sullivan

A-1-1-9-4 John W. Addington, b. c1851, d. 1875/6,
  m. 10 Aug 1873, prob. Pineville, Missouri, Mary Elizabeth
  Roberts, b. 11 May 1858, d. 23 Sep 1917 (Mary m. 2nd 15 Mar
  1878, McDonald Co., Missouri, Simon Brooks)

A-1-1-9-4-1 Joab Addington, b. 18 Jun 1874, Pineville, Missouri,
  d. 14 Jul 1944, Lewiston, Idaho
  m. 1 Jul 1905, Colorado, Blanche Gould Ebbert, b. 5 Apr 1868,
  d. 3 Oct 1952

A-1-1-9-4-1-1 Lucille Ebbert Addington, b. 23 Apr 1906,
  Rockford, Colorado, d. 20 Oct 1930, Montana
  m. 16 Jun 1929, Montana, Ernest Omar, ni

A-1-1-9-4-1-2 Cornelia Blanche Addington, b. 11 Jul 1908,
  Rockyford, Colorado
  m. 22 Jul 1927, Lewiston, Idaho, Lawrence Sassaman, div.
  1932, ni
  m. 2nd 9 Nov 1933, Calgary, Alberta, Earl Lee Johnson, div.

A-1-1-9-4-1-2-1 Joanne Johnson, b. 26 Dec 1936, Calgary
  m. 22 Sep 1956, Calgary, Gordon L. Moulton

A-1-1-9-4-1-2-1-1 Theresa Lynn Moulton, b. 1957
  m. Lloyd George Schinnour

A-1-1-9-4-1-2-1-2 Larry Moulton, d. 1980

A-1-1-9-4-1-2-1-3 Melanie Moulton, m. David Marshall

A-1-1-9-4-1-2-2 Barbara Jean Johnson, b. 9 Apr 1942, Lewiston,
  Idaho
  m. Jul 1960, Rockyford, Weldon Henke

A-1-1-9-4-1-2-2-1 Leah Louise Henke, b. 1961, m. Kevin Keene

A-1-1-9-4-1-2-2-2 Shelley Lynn Kenke, b. 1962
  m. Thomas William Samuel

A-1-1-9-4-1-3 Mary Adele Addington, b. 19 Jul 1910, Cortez,
  Colorado, d. 16 Apr 1988, Spokane, Washington
  m. 21 Jan 1930, Lewiston, Idaho, Theodore Hinsdale Clark

A-1-1-9-4-1-3-1 Roberta Lucille Clark, b. 19 Oct 1931, Lewiston,
  Idaho
  m. 16 Nov 1950, Calgary, Edward Christensen
  m. 2nd 15 Apr 1981, Frank Joseph Richter

A-1-1-9-4-1-3-2 Theodore Richard Clark, b. 2 May 1937, Calgary,
  Alberta, m. 28 Dec 1960, Olive Larsen

A-1-1-9-4-2 John Calvin Addington, b. 11 Jan 1876, Pineville,
  Missouri, d. 5 Sep 1934, LaJunta, Colorado
  m. 14 Jun 1918, Crowley Co., Colorado, Helen Gould Russell,
  b. 28 Apr 1894, d. 1978

A-1-1-9-4-2-1 Clarabeth "Clara" Addington, b. 11 Mar 1918, Rockyford, Colorado
m. 25 May 1941, John Wadhams

A-1-1-9-4-2-2 Mary Evelyn Addington, b. 20 Apr 1920, Rockyford, Colorado
m. 2 Aug 1938, Pueblo, Colorado, Gerry Atwood

A-1-1-9-4-2-2-1 John Atwood, b. 18 Oct 1940, Turlock, CA
m. Nov 1961, Turlock, California, Beverly Jessee, div.

A-1-1-9-4-2-2-1-1 Joni Atwood, b. Aug 1962, Turlock, CA

A-1-1-9-4-2-2-1-2 Lori Atwood, b. Oct 1963, Turlock, California
m. 12 Jan 1985, David Bruce Ferrari

A-1-1-9-4-2-2-1-2-1 Adam David Ferrari, b. 13 Nov 1985, Montague, Maine

A-1-1-9-4-2-2-1-3 Christie Atwood, b. Sep 1971, Texas

A-1-1-9-4-2-2-2 Gerry David Atwood, b. 14 Mar 1942, Turlock, CA, m. 31 Jan 1963, Diane Calou

A-1-1-9-4-2-2-2-1 Brian Michael Atwood, b. 10 Sep 1964, Lafayette, California

A-1-1-9-4-2-2-2-2 Jeannie Marie Atwood, b. 23 Jul 1968, Lafayette, California

A-1-1-9-4-2-2-3 Rita Ann Atwood, b. 23 Apr 1949, Kingsburg, California, m. Aug 1972, Randy Johnson

A-1-1-9-4-2-2-4 William Steven Atwood, b. 31 Jan 1953, Fresno, California, m. 4 Jul 1971, Carrie Sparks

A-1-1-9-4-2-3 Helen Esta Addington, b. 15 May 1922, Rockyford, Colorado, m. 22 Mar 1941, Joe Davis Phillips

A-1-1-9-4-2-3-1 Helen Phillips, b. 13 Sep 1942, Turlock, CA
m. 1969, Claud Kendall

A-1-1-9-4-2-3-2 Barbara Phillips, b. 6 Jan 1946, LaJunta, CO
m. 1966, Frederick Warren Walls

A-1-1-9-4-2-3-2-Misty Walls, b. 11 Mar 1967, Modesto, CA

A-1-1-9-4-2-3-2 Suni Lee Walls, b. 31 Jul 1974, Tracy, California

A-1-1-9-4-2-3-3 Mary Phillips, b. 14 Jan 1948, LaJunta, Colorado
m. 1979, Wes Olsen

A-1-1-9-4-2-3-4 Donald Phillips, b. 17 Feb 1950, LaJunta, CO
m. 1979, Tina Perez

A-1-1-9-4-2-3-5 James Phillips, b. 1 Aug 1953, Modesto, CA

A-1-1-9-4-2-4 Jamie Aline Addington, b. 24 Jun 1928, Rockyford, Colorado, m. 16 Jun 1946, Wayne Daley

A-1-1-9-4-2-4-1 Darryl Wayne Daley, b. 16 Jun 1947, Fort Collins, Colorado, m. 2 Aug 1970, Marilyn Reikem

A-1-1-9-4-2-4-2 Carryl Aline Daley, b. 3 Aug 1950, Caldwell, ID
m. 15 Nov 1969, Leroy Klein, div.

A-1-1-9-4-2-4-3 Helen Elizabeth Daley, b. 13 Oct 1953, Grangeville, Idaho, m. 5 May 1973, Kurt Jack Sage

A-1-1-9-4-2-4-3-1 Troy Eric Sage, b. 27 Oct 1976, Denver, CO

A-1-1-9-4-2-4-3-2 Korie June Sage, b. 4 Apr 1977, Idaho Falls, ID

A-1-1-9-4-2-4-4 Charles William Daley, b. 9 May 1956, b. Grangeville, Idaho, m. Cindy Caldwell

A-1-1-9-4-2-4-4-1 Krishnan William Daley, b. 21 Mar 1985, Calcutta, India

A-1-1-9-4-2-4-5 Jamie Ann Daley, b. 6 May 1961, Blackfoot, ID

A-1-1-9-4-2-5 Bernice Cornelia Addington, b. 21 May 1931, Rockyford, Colorado, m. 6 May 1950, Harold Hammerquist

A-1-1-9-4-2-5-1 Dyanne Hammerquist, b. 27 Dec 1950, Fort Collins, Colorado

A-1-1-9-4-2-5-2 Eddy Hammerquist, b. 19 May 1952, Fort Collins, Colorado, m. 26 Jun 1976, Barbara Bachman

A-1-1-9-4-2-5-2-1 Michael Hammerquist, b. 4 Mar 1980, Cadwell, Idaho

A-1-1-9-4-2-5-3 Mahlon Hammerquist, b. 29 May 1953, Fort Collins, Colorado, m. 20 Nov 1982, Janet Ralphs

A-1-1-9-4-2-5-4 Lee Hammerquist, b. 2 Jul 1955, Twins Falls, ID m. 1 Sep 1979, Emma K. Fairbanks

A-1-1-9-4-2-5-4-1 Mark Hammerquist, b. 24 May 1981, Albuquerque, New Mexico

A-1-1-9-4-2-5-4-2 Julie Hammerquist, b. 23 Sep 1982, Twin Falls, Idaho

A-1-1-9-4-2-5-4-3 Gregory Hammerquist

A-1-1-9-4-2-5-5 David Hammerquist, b. 4 Oct 1957, Twin Falls, Idaho

A-1-1-9-4-2-5-6 Carolyn Hammerquist, b. 22 Jun 1960, Twin Falls, Idaho
m. 24 Nov 1980, Jim Kodesh, Jr., div.

A-1-1-9-4-2-5-7 Bernice Hammerquist, b. 14 Jul 1962, Twin Falls, Idaho, m. 20 Mar 1982, David Michael Davis

A-1-1-9-4-2-5-7-1 Andrea Davis, b. Twin Falls, Idaho

A-1-1-9-4-2-5-7-2 Timothy David Davis, b. 13 Mar 1984

A-1-1-9-4-2-5-7-3 Tara Bernice Davis

A-1-1-9-5 Joanna Addington, b. 13 Jan 1853, Randolph Co., Indiana, d. 11 Jan 1884, McDonald Co., Missouri
m. 6 Feb 1868, Pineville, Missouri, James Meranda, b. 17 Mar 1846, d. 3 Aug 1886

A-1-1-9-5-1 Mercy Ann Meranda, b. 25 May 1870, McDonald Co., Missouri, d. 1959, m. 1892, Samuel Bullock

A-1-1-9-5-2 Minerva Alice Meranda, b. 18 Oct 1872, McDonald Co., Missouri, d. 15 Jan 1963

m. 19 Oct 1890, John Abraham Carder

A-1-1-9-5-2-1 John Palmer Carder, b. 14 Feb 1892, Jay Co., IN
m. 14 Apr 1917, Nettie Burtner

A-1-1-9-5-2-2 Oerbact Nae Carder, b. 12 Feb 1894, Jay Co., IN
m. Elmer Shafer, m. 2nd Jacob Ford

A-1-1-9-5-2-3 Maggie Rea Carder, b. 19 Jun 1896, Jay Co., IN
m. 19 May 1919, John Lambert

A-1-1-9-5-2-4 Rosemary Carder, b. 25 Nov 1899, Jay Co., Indiana,
d. 16 Jul 1984
m. 29 Sep 1917, Clarence L. Tharp, b. 5 Jun 1894, Jay Co.,
Indiana, d. 27 May 1974

A-1-1-9-5-2-4-1 Francis Raymond Tharp, b. 3 Feb 1921, Jay Co.,
Indiana, m. 24 Jun 1944, Donna Marie Corle

A-1-1-9-5-2-4-2 Celia Elma Tharp, b. 28 Apr 1923, Delaware Co.,
Indiana, m. 14 Nov 1944, Joseph Castelo

A-1-1-9-5-2-4-3 Cecil Edwin Tharp, b. 28 Apr 1923, Delaware Co.,
Indiana, m. 21 Sep 1946, Mary Jane McKinley

A-1-1-9-5-2-4-3-1 Sharon Sue Tharp, b. 16 Jul 1947, Delaware
Co., Indiana, m. 11 Dec 1965, Richard Allen Morris

A-1-1-9-5-2-4-3-2 Cynthia Jane Tharp, b. 18 Apr 1950, Hartford
City, Indiana, m. 25 Apr 1970, Richard L. Marquell

A-1-1-9-5-2-4-3-3 Edwin Leroy Tharp, b. 20 Apr 1951, Delaware
Co., Indiana

A-1-1-9-5-2-4-3-4 Theresa Ann Tharp, b. 18 Sep 1955, Delaware
Co., Indiana, m. 29 Jun 1974, Michael Bundy

A-1-1-9-5-2-4-3-5 Lynden Kinley Tharp, b. 27 Mar 1961,
Delaware Co., Indiana, m. 5 Sep 1981, Diedra Smith

A-1-1-9-5-2-4-4 Thelma Roberta Tharp, b. 18 Feb 1930, Delaware
Co., Indiana, m. 1 Jan 1949, Jack Linsmeyer

A-1-1-9-5-2-5 Chester Lee Carder, b. 3 Jul 1904, Jay Co., Indiana,
m. Edna Hinton

A-1-1-9-5-2-6 Delver Fremont Carder, b. 5 Feb 1907, Jay Co., IN
m. 24 Aug 1930, Isabelle Welling

A-1-1-9-5-2-7 Dale Carder, b. 20 Mar 1906, Jay Co., Indiana
m. 31 Oct 1937, Wilma Lewis

A-1-1-9-5-3 Effie Elizabeth Meranda, b. 31 Mar 1875, McDonald
Co., Missouri, d. 29 Jan 1957
m. 28 Mar 1894, George W. McKitrick

A-1-1-9-5-4 Rose Altha Meranda, b. 16 Aug 1877, McDonald Co.,
Missouri, b. 31 Jan 1931, m. 2 Dec 1897, Robert Rozzell

A-1-1-9-5-5 James Delver Meranda, b. 19 Oct 1880, d. 7 Mar 1957
m. 16 Jan 1915, Kate Andell

A-1-1-9-5-6 Lona Dale Meranda, b. 12 Aug 1883, (twin). adopted
by James Addington (A-1-1-9-5), d. 7 May 1960

m. 2nd 6 Nov 1906, John Mitchell

A-1-1-9-5-7 Lawson Meranda (twin), b. 12 Aug 1883, d. Dec 1883

A-1-1 m. 2nd 23 Nov 1840, Randolph Co., IN, Sarah Norton, b. 1787, NC, d. 25 Oct 1864, bur. Ridgeville Cemetery

A-1-2 Alice Addington, b. 8 Mar 1773, d. bef 1833
m. 1790, Joab Garrett

A-1 m. 2nd 3 May 1775, Newberry Co., SC, Elizabeth Heaton, d. bef 1830, Chester, Indiana

A-1-3 Joseph Addington, b. 21 Jul 1776, d. 20 Feb 1836, (20 Feb 1836 on gravestone, 9 Feb 1836 in Sparrow Creek MM records), bur. Sparrow Creek Cemetery, Randolph Co., IN
m. 21 Dec 1799, Rachel Randel, b. 27 Dec 1783, Union Co., South Carolina, d. c1806, Indiana

A-1-3-1 John Randel Addington, b. 18 Oct 1800, 96 District, South Carolina, prob. d. 1812/34, ni

A-1-3-2 William Randel Addington, b. 25 Aug 1802, d. 5 Mar 1875, Randolph Co., Indiana
m. 28 Sep 1825, Dorcus Mendenhall, b. 1808 Tennessee, d. 6 Sep 1869, Randolph Co., Indiana

A-1-3-2-1 Jesse L. Addington, b. Mar 1827, Indiana, d. 7 Dec 1908, Modoc Co., CA (1850 Fulton Co., IN; 1860, Iowa; 1870 Walla Walla Co., Washington; 1880 Lake Co., Oregon, 1900 Modoc Co., California)
m. Martha Ann Harshman, b. 16 Oct 1832, OH, d. 16 Oct 1901

A-1-3-2-1-1 Rachel Addington, b. 1850, MO, m. Richard ?

A-1-3-2-1-2 Elvira Addington, b. 8 Apr 1853, d. 13 Nov 1921
m. Richard C. Clark

A-1-3-2-1-3 Isaac Addington, b. 23 Apr 1856, Missouri, d. 1 Feb 1904, Cedarville, California
m. 1 Jan 1882, Sarah Odis, d. 17 Apr 1883
m. 27 Jan 1884, Agnes DeLauenaux, b. 14 Jun 1863, OR

A-1-3-2-1-3-1 Rosa Etta Addington, b. 27 Oct 1884, California
m. ? Bordwell

A-1-3-2-1-3-2 Oley Addington, b. 22 Jan 1886, California, d. 8 Dec 1952, Butte Co., California
m. 4 Jul 1909, Ellen May St. John, b. c1894, California

A-1-3-2-1-3-2-1 Ruby Addington, b. 1915, Modoc Co., CA

A-1-3-2-1-3-2 m. 2nd Edith M., b. 1884, d. 27 Nov 1931, Butte Co., California

A-1-3-2-1-3-3 Isaac Addington, b. 21 Jan 1888, California, d. 23 Aug 1937, Stanislaus Co., California
m. 19 Oct 1914, Myrtle B. Morgan

A-1-3-2-1-3-3-1 Marie E. Addington, b. 10 May 1915

A-1-3-2-1-3-4 Stella Addington, b. 16 Mar 1890, California

A-1-3-2-1-3-5 Walter Addington, b. Nov 1891, California
A-1-3-2-1-3-5-1 Alice A. Addington, b. 14 Apr 1914, Modoc Co.,
    California
A-1-3-2-1-3-6 Pearl Addington, b. 23 Nov 1892, California
A-1-3-2-1-3-7 Gracie Addington, b. 6 Aug 1896, California
A-1-3-2-1-3-8 Elsie A. Addington, b. Jan 1898, California
A-1-3-2-1-3-9 Jacob Addington, b. Jan 1899, California, d. 28 Nov
    1958, Stockton, California
  m. 22 Dec 1922, Mary Elizabeth Wortman
A-1-3-2-1-3-9-1 Jacob M. Addington, b. 19 Oct 1923
A-1-3-2-1-3-9-2 Loda L. Addington
A-1-3-2-1-3-10 Miram P. Addington, b. c1900, California
A-1-3-2-1-3-11 Infant, b. & d. 1902
A-1-3-2-1-4 Joseph William Addington, b. 19 Apr 1859, Iowa, d.
    26 Jun 1911, Modoc Co., California
  m. 28 Nov 1880, Emma A. Schaffer, b. 27 Dec 1862, d. 25 Jun
    1954
A-1-3-2-1-4-1 Lizzie Addington, b. 5 Nov 1881, California
  m. ? Metzher
A-1-3-2-1-4-2 Josie May Addington, b. 19 Apr 1883, m. ? Shedd
A-1-3-2-1-4-3 Diehless Undine Addington, b. 12 Sep 1885,
    Modoc Co., California
  m. 13 Feb 1907, Modoc Co., CA, Amasa Reynolds Dollarhide
A-1-3-2-1-4-3-1 Gerald Dollarhide, b. c1908, Modoc Co., CA
A-1-3-2-1-4-3-2 Lily B. Dollarhide, b. c1910, Modoc Co., CA
A-1-3-2-1-4-4 Joseph William Addington, b. 23 Mar 1887, d. 9
    Dec 1893
A-1-3-2-1-4-5 Jesse Edward Addington, b. 1 May 1889, Modoc
    Co., California, d. 13 Dec 1948, Modoc Co., California
  m. 21 Jun 1921, Sadie P. Cannon
A-1-3-2-1-4-5-1 Harrold O. Addington, b. 16 Aug 1923
A-1-3-2-1-4-5-2 Ernest L. Addington, b. 24 Aug 1924
A-1-3-2-1-4-6 Henry Earl Addington, b. 26 Aug 1891, CA, d. 30
    Nov 1961, Alturas, California, dnm
A-1-3-2-1-4-7 Leslie Orville Addington, b. 17 Dec 1894, CA, d. 10
    Aug 1969, Modoc Co., California, m. Frances L. Griffith
A-1-3-2-1-4-7-1 Emma E. Addington, b. 12 Mar 1922
A-1-3-2-1-4-8 Persie Pearl Addington, b. 11 Nov 1897, d. Nov
    1897
A-1-3-2-1-4-9 Clara Belle Addington, b. 7 Jun 1899, California
  m. 28 Mar 1915, Herman Jason Dollarhide
A-1-3-2-1-4-10 Lilly Louise Addington, b. 27 Apr 1900, CA
  m. 5 Jul 1918, Henry William Dollarhide
A-1-3-2-1-4-11 Frank Hubert Addington, b. 19 Feb 1902, CA

m. May Cannon
A-1-3-2-1-4-12 Louis Oren Addington, b. 22 Mar 1906, CA
A-1-3-2-1-4-13 Alma Addington, d. age 15 mo.
A-1-3-2-1-5 Mary Cordelia Addington, b. 6 Feb 1861, Iowa
   m. Joel Crawford Allen
A-1-3-2-1-6 Abraham Addington, b. Feb 1863, Washington, d. 8
   Aug 1936, Modoc Co., California, dnm
A-1-3-2-1-7 Henry Addington, d. young
A-1-3-2-1-8 Margaret Jane Addington, b. 14 Sep 1867,
   Washington, d. 15 Sep 1895, Cedarville, Ca
   m. 1883, Peleg Chase, b. 14 May 1848, NY, d. 27 Apr 1900, CA
A-1-3-2-1-8-1 Elsie J. Chase, b. c1894, California
A-1-3-2-1-8-1-1 John Nolal Griener, b. 1 Feb 1920, Modoc Co.,
   CA, m. Kimball, NE, Lois Marie Dyke, b. 1 Jan 1923, CA
A-1-3-2-1-8-2 Harvey D. Chase, b. c1895, California
A-1-3-2-1-9 Annie Addington, b. Dec 1869, Washington
   m. ? Poujay
A-1-3-2-1-10 Lydia Addington, b. 9 May 1872, Washington, d. 11
   Dec 1880
A-1-3-2-2 Joseph Mendenhall Addington, b. 6 Oct 1829, Wayne
   Co., IN, d. 3 Feb 1898, Randolph Co., Indiana, dnm (1870
   Lane Co., Oregon)
A-1-3-2-3 Rachel Addington, b. 1831, Wayne Co., Indiana
   m. 5 Sep 1850, Randolph Co., Indiana, Julian Green
A-1-3-2-3-1 Malissa Green, b. c1851, Indiana
A-1-3-2-3-2 William Green, b. c1853, Indiana
A-1-3-2-3-3 Jonathan Green, b. c1855, Indiana
A-1-3-2-3-4 Absolum Green, b. c1857, Indiana
A-1-3-2-3-5 Elisha Green, b. c1859, Indiana
A-1-3-2-4 Absolum Addington, b. c1832, Wayne Co., Indiana, d.
   26 Sep 1864, Boise, Idaho
   m. Martha J. Mendenhall
   m. 11 Jun 1854, Linn Co., OR, Hannah L. Lewellen
A-1-3-2-5 James M. Addington, b. 9 Mar 1834, d. 5 Oct 1912
   m. 27 Sep 1863, Rand. Co., Indiana, Sarah Ann Tharp, b. 12
   Jan 1837, Indiana, d. 21 Mar 1907
A-1-3-2-5-1 Adopted Lona D. (Meranda) Addington, b. 1883,
   Missouri
   m. John B. Mitchell (lived in Andover, Ohio)
A-1-3-2-5-1-1 Robert A. Mitchell, b. c1908
A-1-3-2-5-1-2 L. Paul Mitchell, b. c1909
A-1-3-2-6 John Addington, b. c1836, nfi
A-1-3-2-7 Warren Addington, d. bef. 1850
A-1-3-2-8 Thomas M. Addington, b. 1839, nfi

A-1-3-2-9 Sarah J. Addington, b. c1843, ? m. Liberty Penney
A-1-3-2-10 Elizabeth "Betsey" Addington, b. c1843
  m. 8 May 1867, Nelson Barnesly
A-1-3-2-11 Elmira Addington, b. c1854, nfi
A-1-3-3 Joseph Randel Addington, b. 28 Feb 1804, Union Co.,
    South Carolina, d. 3 May 1889, Pilot Grove, Lee Co., Iowa
  m. 26 Oct 1825, Wayne Co., Indiana, Mary Barker, b. 8 Jan
    1807, NC, d. 28 Jun 1888, Pilot Grove, Iowa
A-1-3-3-1 Isaac Barker Addington, b. 21 Oct 1826, d. 13 Feb 1914,
    Farmland, Indiana, bur. Hopewell Cem.
  m. 25 Sep 1873, Nancy J. Flood, b. 10 Feb 1838, d. 10 May 1915,
    bur. Hopewell Cem.
A-1-3-3-1-1 Ivery H. Addington, b. 28 Jun 1874, m. ? West
A-1-3-3-1-1-1 Gussie B. West, b. 1895
A-1-3-3-1-2 Ida P. Addington, b. 24 Jun 1876
  m. 19 Jul 1894, Randolph Co., Indiana, James H. West
  ??m. William O. Lang
A-1-3-3-1-3 Irena V. Addington, b. 16 Nov 1879, d. 1880
A-1-3-3-2 Rachel Addington, b. 29 Nov 1828, nfi
A-1-3-3-3 Louise (or Louisa) Addington, b. 9 Feb 1830
  ? m. ? Benford
A-1-3-3-4 Celia Addington, b. 9 Jun 1832, d. 2 Nov 1899, bur.
    Kendrick, Idaho
A-1-3-3-5 William J. Addington, b. 21 Nov 1835, Chester,
    Wayne Co., IN, d. 17 Sep 1917, Randolph Co., Indiana (1860
    Henderson Co., IL, 1880 Montgomery Co., Kansas)
  m. 16 Feb 1869, (Sparrow Creek MM records) Annis L. or
    Aner Jane "Jennie" Pike, b. 7 Nov 1850, d. 16 May 1935,
    Randolph Co., Indiana
A-1-3-3-5-1 Edwin Kester Addington, b. 6 May 1870, Iowa, d. 18
    Aug 1955, bur. Maxville Cem.
  m. 6 Oct 1894, Randolph Co., Indiana, Minnie P. Green, b.
    1876, d. 23 Sep 1942, bur. Maxville Cemetery
A-1-3-3-5-1-1 Emma Marie Addington, b. 18 Feb 1896, Indiana,
    d. 198?
  m. 27 Nov 1913, Wayne Co., Indiana, Earl Baldwin Ozbun
A-1-3-3-5-1-1-1 Frances Amerilias Ozbun, b. 8 Mar 1915
  m. Edward Fodge
A-1-3-3-5-1-1-1-1 Kathleen Marie Fodge, m. Raymond Malpede
A-1-3-3-5-1-1-1-1-1 Christopher Edward Malpede, b. 1987
A-1-3-3-5-1-1-1-1-2 Daniel William Malpede
A-1-3-3-5-1-1-2 Mabel Elizabeth Ozbun, b. 9 Mar 1917, d. 1938
  m. Joe Locke
A-1-3-3-5-1-1-3 Edwin Albert Ozbun, m. ? Teen

A-1-3-3-5-1-1-3-1 Roger Ozbun
A-1-3-3-5-1-1-3-2 Key Ozbun
A-1-3-3-5-1-1-3-3 David Ozbun
A-1-3-3-5-1-1-3-4 Joyce Ozbun
A-1-3-3-5-1-1-4 Charles Delmont Ozbun, m. Virginia ?
A-1-3-3-5-1-1-4-1 Theresa Ozbun
A-1-3-3-5-1-1-4-2 Denise Ozbun
A-1-3-3-5-1-1-5 Bernice Rose Ozbun, b. 13 Mar 1924
  m. Talmadge Thompson
A-1-3-3-5-1-1-5-1 Donald Thompson
A-1-3-3-5-1-1-5-2 Floyd Thompson
A-1-3-3-5-1-1-6 Elvin Ozbun, b. 9 Jul 1926, m. Elizabeth ?
A-1-3-3-5-1-1-6-1 Diana Ozbun
A-1-3-3-5-1-1-6-2 Larry Ozbun
A-1-3-3-5-1-1-6-3 Randy Ozbun
A-1-3-3-5-1-1-7 James Earl Ozbun, b. 5 Feb 1928, m. Violet ?
A-1-3-3-5-1-1-7-1 Marsha Kay Ozbun
A-1-3-3-5-1-1-7-2 Robin Denise Ozbun
A-1-3-3-5-1-2 Henry Taylor Addington, b. 23 Aug 1897
  m. 17 Feb 1921, Randolph Co., Indiana, Bernice Borsey, b. Dec
  1896, d. 20 Jun 1938
A-1-3-3-5-1-2-1 Jean Warren Addington, b. 7 Mar 1922
  m. Nina Oberender
A-1-3-3-5-1-2-2 Robert Brosey Addington, b. 30 Apr 1924
  m. Irene Eades
A-1-3-3-5-1-2-2-1 Stephen Duane Addington, b. 24 Mar 1949
  m. Janet Patton
A-1-3-3-5-1-2-2-1-1 Robert Todd Addington, b. 4 Feb 1973
A-1-3-3-5-1-2-2-1-2 Carrie Susan Addington, b. 8 Jul 1977
A-1-3-3-5-1-2-2-2 David Allen Addington, b. 16 Jan 1954
  m. Debbie Burge
A-1-3-3-5-1-2-2-2-1 Scott Allen Addington, b. 1 Sep 1980
A-1-3-3-5-1-2-2-2-2 Brian David Addington, b. 13 May 1984
A-1-3-3-5-1-2-3 David Addington, b. 14 Jul 1929 (stillborn)
A-1-3-3-5-1-2-4 Charles Duane Addington, b. 22 Oct 1933
  m. Ruth Anderson
A-1-3-3-5-1-2-4-1 Michael Duane Addington, b. 30 Mar 1956
  m. Joy Robbins
A-1-3-3-5-1-2-4-2 Marilyn Louise Addington, b. 22 Jun 1957
  m. Virgil Bird
A-1-3-3-5-1-2-4-2-1 Angela Denise Bird, b. Jan 1979
A-1-3-3-5-1-2-4-3 Thomas Eugene Addington, b. 18 Nov 1965
A-1-3-3-5-1-2-5 Clayton Lee Addington, b. 17 Jan 1937
  m. Sharon ?

A-1-3-3-5-1-2-5-1 Diana Addington, b. 13 Sep 1956
m. ? Woodings
A-1-3-3-5-1-2-5-1-1 Lori Beth Woodings
A-1-3-3-5-1-2-5-2 LaConda Jo "Connie" Addington, b. 14 Nov 1959, m. ? Reynolds
A-1-3-3-5-1-2-5-2-1 Johnny Lee Reynolds
A-1-3-3-5-1-2-5-3 Teresa Marline "Terri" Addington, b. 14 Feb 1961, m. Richard Foudray
A-1-3-3-5-1-2-5-3-1 Lori Ann Foudray
A-1-3-3-5-1-2 m. 2nd Helen Ester Willis, b. 7 Jul 1909, d. 23 Nov 1988
A-1-3-3-5-1-2-6 Henry Taylor Addington, Jr., b. 2 Oct 1940
m. Louise Simon
A-1-3-3-5-1-2-6-1 Norman Lee Addington, b. 1 Sep 1962
m. Mary Byer
A-1-3-3-5-1-2-6-1-1 Paul Taylor Addington, b. 16 Nov 1989
A-1-3-3-5-1-2-6-1-2 Bethany Louise Addington, b. 10 Dec 1990
A-1-3-3-5-1-2-6-2 Tamara Louise Addington, b. 6 Aug 1964
A-1-3-3-5-1-2-6-3 Rhoda Jane Addington, b. 23 Sep 1965
A-1-3-3-5-1-2-6-4 Rosalyn Kay "Rosie" Addington, b. 12 Dec 1971
A-1-3-3-5-1-2-7 Anita Mae Addington, b. 18 Jan 1942
A-1-3-3-5-1-3 William M. Addington (twin), b. 23 Aug 1897, d. 1903
A-1-3-3-5-1-4 Bernice M. Addington, b. Jul 1899, d. 7 May 1925
A-1-3-3-5-1-5 James Edwin Addington, b. 27 Nov 1909, d. 30 Nov 1988
m. Reva Huffman, b. 15 Nov 1909
A-1-3-3-5-1-5-1 James Allen Addington, b. 17 Aug 1933
m. Margaret Suttle
A-1-3-3-5-1-5-1-1 Kathleen Reva Addington, b. 3 Jun 1956
m. Leon Knox
A-1-3-3-5-1-5-1-1-1 Jeremy D. Knox, b. 27 Nov 1982
A-1-3-3-5-1-5-1-1-3 Meghan Leon Knox, b. 5 Feb 1989
A-1-3-3-5-1-5-1-2 James Allen Addington, Jr., b. 20 Oct 196?
A-1-3-3-5-1-5-1-3 Charles Michael "Chuck" Addington, b. 5 Feb 196?
A-1-3-3-5-1-5-2 Laura June Addington, b. 13 Oct 1935
m. Boyd Stephens
A-1-3-3-5-1-5-2-1 Jeffrey Dale Stephens, b. 10 Dec 1955
m. Cathy Mathews
A-1-3-3-5-1-5-2-1-1 Amy Lynn Stephens, b. 12 Dec 1986
A-1-3-3-5-1-5-2-1-2 Mathew Stephens, b. 2 Jun 1988
A-1-3-3-5-1-5-2-2 Jay Edwin Stephens, b. 14 Jun 1957

m. Mindy Lee

A-1-3-3-5-1-5-2-2-1 Caroline Lee Stephens, b. 26 Jun 1983

A-1-3-3-5-1-5-2-2-2 Jason Stephens, b. 29 Nov 1985

A-1-3-3-5-1-5-2-2-3 Anna Beth Stephens, b. 25 Jan 1990, stillborn

A-1-3-3-5-1-5-2-3 Sandra Lynn Stephens, b. 26 May 1961

A-1-3-3-5-1 m. 2nd Hattie Clevenger

A-1-3-3-5-2 Adam Franklin Addington, b. 15 Nov 1871, Iowa, d. 10 Oct 1952

m. 16 Mar 1895, Randolph Co., Indiana, Luzena M. Baker

A-1-3-3-5-2-1 Clovis Addington

A-1-3-3-5-2-2 Orla Addington

A-1-3-3-5-2-3 Myrtle Addington, b. 26 Aug 1905, Randolph Co., Indiana

A-1-3-3-5-2-4 Celia Addington

A-1-3-3-5-2-5 Aner Marie Addington

A-1-3-3-5-2 m. 2nd Claudia Leotta Brown, b. 7 Jan 1882, d. 30 Dec 1949, Randolph Co., Indiana

A-1-3-3-5-2-6 Adam F. Addington, Jr., b. 25 Oct 1908

m. 27 Oct 1927, Randolph Co., IN, Sylvia Genell Driskoll

A-1-3-3-5-2-7 Anna Marie Addington, b. 29 Apr 1911, Wayne Co., Indiana

m. 9 Apr 1927, Randolph Co., Indiana, Irven Wales

A-1-3-3-5-3 Julia Anna Addington, b. 27 Nov 1873, Iowa

m. ?? 3 Dec 1891, David Davis

m. 26 Sep 1896, Randolph Co., Indiana, Herbert Murray

A-1-3-3-5-3-1 Pauline Murray

A-1-3-3-5-3-2 Raymond Murray

A-1-3-3-5-3-3 Glen Murray

A-1-3-3-5-4 Effie Lue Addington, b. 7 Nov 1877, Iowa, d. 28 Apr 1898

m. 4 Apr 1896, Randolph Co., Indiana, Boyden Murray

A-1-3-3-5-5 Mary Ella Addington, b. 18 Sep 1882, d. 4 Mar 1923

m. Ora Brown

? m. 10 Apr 1902, Delaware Co., Indiana, Frank Cavender

A-1-3-3-5-5-1 Everett Brown

A-1-3-3-5-5-2 Mabel Brown

A-1-3-3-5-5-3 James Brown

A-1-3-3-5-5-4 Annabelle Brown

A-1-3-3-5-5-5 Lester Brown

A-1-3-3-5-6 William Lewis Addington, b. 30 Apr 1885, d. 1 Aug 1947

m. 24 Jul 1906, Clara Alice Hutchens

A-1-3-3-5-6-1 Pearl Lucille Addington, b. 22 Oct 1906

m. Joseph R. Greene, d. 11 Oct 1986, bur. Maxville Cemetery

A-1-3-3-5-6-1-1 Alice Mae Greene
   m. 1946, Norman Wesley Watson
A-1-3-3-5-6-1-1-1 Cheryl D. Watson, m. ? Sipe
A-1-3-3-5-6-1-1-1-1 Lisa Renee Sipe, b. 4 Oct 1965
A-1-3-3-5-6-1-1-1-2 Chad Matthew Sipe, b. 8 Aug 1972
A-1-3-3-5-6-1-1-1 m. 2nd Tom Zell
A-1-3-3-5-6-1-1-2 Carla Jennine Watson, b. 14 Jun 1953
   m. 6 Jun 1975, Gregory Eugene Younts, b. 29 Oct 1948
A-1-3-3-5-6-1-1-2-1 Brad Michel Younts, b. 8 Oct 1976
A-1-3-3-5-6-1-1-2-2 Joseph Noel Younts, b. 3 Dec 1979
A-1-3-3-5-6-1-2 Joseph R. Greene, Jr., b. 12 Mar 1928
   m. Evelyne Eileen Greene
A-1-3-3-5-6-1-2-1 Gary Joe Greene, b. 4 Nov 1950
   m. 21 Aug 1969, Sherry Bonewit
A-1-3-3-5-6-1-2-1-1 Brian Joe Greene, b. 21 Mar 1970
A-1-3-3-5-6-1-2-2 Robin Scott Greene, b. 4 Sep 1952
   m. 16 Dec 1977, Paulette Pesola
A-1-3-3-5-6-1-2-2-1 Nathan Scott Greene, b. 12 Dec 1979
A-1-3-3-5-6 m. 2nd 26 Jul 1916, Marion Co., Indiana, Mary L.
   Adams, b. 1897, d. 1976
A-1-3-3-5-6-2 Raymond Lewis Addington, b. 24 Apr 1918
A-1-3-3-5-6-3 Richard North Addington, b. 28 May 1920
A-1-3-3-5-6-4 Leland Addington, b. 1924, d. 1968, m. Vera G. ?
A-1-3-3-5-7 Rosa Estella Addington, b. 16 Jan 1889, d. 11 Aug
   1900, Randolph Co., Indiana
A-1-3-3-5-8 Hazel R. Addington, b. 7 Nov 1892, d. Nov 1917
   m. 17 Dec 1912, Randolph Co., IN, Leland Lester Harshman
A-1-3-3-5-8-1 Charles Harshman
A-1-3-3-5-9 Arthur M. Addington, b. 7 Nov 1892, d. 11 Jan 1954,
   Randolph Co., Indiana
   m. 29 Feb 1912, Randolph Co., IN, Azora Celcelia Wisener, d.
   19 Sep 1940
A-1-3-3-5-9 m. 2nd Emma Morehouse
A-1-3-3-5-10 ?? twin daughter, b. 7 Nov 1892, d. as infant
A-1-3-3-6 Willis G. Addington, b. 31 Oct 1838, Wayne Co., IN, d.
   17 May 1919, Riverside, California (1880 Columbia Co.,
   Washington, 1900, Nez Perce Co., Idaho)
   m. 21 Feb 1864, Mary Melissa Jessup, b. 4 Jan 1843, Iowa, d. 28
   Feb 1925, Riverside, California
A-1-3-3-6-1 Alice Mille Addington, b. c1865, Iowa, m. ? Lewis
A-1-3-3-6-2 Emma M. Addington, b. c1868, Kansas
   m. ? Hammer, m. 2nd ? Walkenshaw
A-1-3-3-6-3 Mina Addington, b. c1870, Kansas, m. ? Travis

A-1-3-3-6-4 Oscar Tilton Addington, b. 13 Jun 1873, Topeka, KS,
   d. 6 Dec 1948, San Bernardino, CA (1880 Columbia Co.,
   Washington, 1900 Shoshone Co., ID)
   m. 4 Jun 1895, Lincoln Co., Washington, Beva Sara Crockett
A-1-3-3-6-4-1 Orval Raymond Addington, b. 12 Mar 1897,
   Dayton, WA, d. 1 Apr 1971, Riverside, California
   m. Rachel Applington
A-1-3-3-6-4-1-1 Raymond Orval Addington, b. 29 Sep 1919,
   Yakima, Washington, d. 14 Mar 1990
   m. Wanda Garnett, m. 2nd Hazel ?
A-1-3-3-6-4-1-2 son, b. 20 Apr 1921, Yakima, WA, d. 1 May 1921
A-1-3-3-6-4-1-3 Robert Addington
A-1-3-3-6-4-1-4 Jean Addington
A-1-3-3-6-4-1-5 Judith Ann Addington, b. 1 Jan 1946
   m. 13 Jun 1964, William Stanley Warren
A-1-3-3-6-4-2 Mabel Addington, b. Dec 1898, Idaho
A-1-3-3-6-4-3 Percy D. Addington, b. 30 May 1901, d. 28 May
   1973, Stanislovis Co.
A-1-3-3-6-4-4 Harold Oscar Addington, b. 29 Sep 1905, d. 27 Sep
   1983, San Bern. Co., California
   m. Mabel I. Hall, m. 2nd Della ?
A-1-3-3-6-4-4-1 James Addington
A-1-3-3-6-4-5 Donald O. Addington, b. 9 Sep 1909, Idaho, d. 1
   Sep 1964, Colton, California, m. 12 Sep 1930, Lura E. Vigus
A-1-3-3-6-4-5-1 Roger Lee Addington, b. 12 Jul 1934, CA
   m. 7 Mar 1959, Barbara A. Dynes
A-1-3-3-6-4-5-1-1 Carl M. Addington, b. 4 Jan 1961, LA Co., CA
A-1-3-3-6-4-5-1-2 Christina A. Addington, b. 17 May 1963, CA
A-1-3-3-6-4-5-2 John Edward Addington
A-1-3-3-6-4-5-3 Dona Rae Addington, b. 26 Feb 1939, Orange Co.,
   California, m. 5 Aug 1956, Kenneth J. Dixon
A-1-3-3-6-4-6 Hazel S. Addington, m. ? Strickler
A-1-3-3-6-4 m. 2nd 8 Feb 1928, Anna I. Myers
A-1-3-3-6-5 Burton Addington, b. 28 Dec 1874, Kansas, d. 14 Jan
   1927, Riverside, California
A-1-3-3-6-5-1 Floyd E. Addington, b. 24 Jul 1900, d. Nov 1960
A-1-3-3-6-6 Mary Ruth Addington, b. Nov 1879, Columbia Co.,
   Washington, m. James H. Denny
A-1-3-3-7 Hannah Anne Addington, b. 14 Nov 1841, d. young
A-1-3-3-8 Amos T. Addington, b. 29 Apr 1845, Wayne Co., IN, d.
   26 Feb 1891, Tacoma, Washington (1880 Lee Co., Iowa)
   m. 8 Apr 1866, Elizabeth Jessup, b. 7 Dec 1847, Indiana, d. 16
   Apr 1924, Spokane, Washington (1900, Spokane, WA)

A-1-3-3-8-1 Ida C. Addington, b. 25 Feb 1867, Lee Co., Iowa, d. 14 Mar 1948, Spokane, Washington
  m. 25 Apr 1886, William D. Jackman
A-1-3-3-8-1-1 Walter Jackman, b. 18 Feb 1887, m. 1906, Anna ?
A-1-3-3-8-1-1-1 Lillian Jackman
A-1-3-3-8-1-1-2 Nadine Jackman, m. John Robertson
A-1-3-3-8-1-1-2-1 Douglas Robertson
A-1-3-3-8-1-1-2-2 Bruce Robertson
A-1-3-3-8-1-1-3 Shirley Jackman, m. Wally Nelson
A-1-3-3-8-1-1 m. 2nd Marie ?
A-1-3-3-8-1 m. 2nd Robert Camp
A-1-3-3-8-2 Anna J. "Connie" Addington, b. 15 Dec 1868, Lee Co., Iowa, d. 15 Nov 1957, Mason City, Iowa
  m. 22 Dec 1889, Charles Thomas
A-1-3-3-8-2-1 Ira Thomas, b. 3 Mar 1891, d. young
A-1-3-3-8-2-2 Orin Thomas, b. 13 Feb 1895, m. 1915, Addie ?
A-1-3-3-8-2-2-1 Charles Thomas, b. Iowa
A-1-3-3-8-2-2-1-1 Ray Thomas, b. Iowa
A-1-3-3-8-2-2-1-1-1 Lanny Thomas
A-1-3-3-8-2-2-1-1-2 Charles Thomas
A-1-3-3-8-2-2-1-1-3 Edward Thomas
A-1-3-3-8-2-2-1-1-4 Blaine Thomas, b. 14 Mar 1960
A-1-3-3-8-2-3 Mable Thomas, b. 25 Jun 1906, m. Gerald McGee
A-1-3-3-8-3 Asa Addington, b. 20 Apr 1871, KS, d. 4 Mar 1884
A-1-3-3-8-4 Albert "Alva" Lee Addington, b. 23 Feb 1873, Kansas, d. 12 Jan 1933, Spokane, Washington
  m. 26 Dec 1897, Lela M. Stroup, b. 1879, WA, d. 1957, Kansas
A-1-3-3-8-4-1 Lynn Roy Addington, b. 6 Feb 1900, d. 12 Dec 1967, Spokane, Washington, m. Jessie Pearl Hampton
A-1-3-3-8-4-1-1 Celesta May Addington, b. 6 Sep 1924, WA
  m. ? Fron
A-1-3-3-8-4-1-2 Carolyn June Addington, b. 27 May 1929, WA
  m. ? Crews
A-1-3-3-8-5 Emery E. Addington, b. 9 Jan 1876, Iowa, d. 8 Mar 1886, Iowa
A-1-3-3-8-6 Linnie M. Addington, b. 21 Jun 1879, Iowa, d. 1975
  m. 13 Feb 1897, Harry Polson, d. 1946
A-1-3-3-8-6-1 Leroy Polson, b. 31 May 1898
A-1-3-3-8-6-1-1 Farrell Polson, d. 1946
A-1-3-3-8-6-1-2 Cheree Polson
A-1-3-3-8-6-2 Loren Polson, b. 5 May 1900, d. 18 Feb 1905
A-1-3-3-8-6-3 Infant, b. 2 Oct 1903, d. 30 Oct 1903
A-1-3-3-8-6-4 Cecil Polson, b. 19 Feb 1906, m. Francis ?
A-1-3-3-8-6-4-1 Loren Polson, m. Helene ?

A-1-3-3-8-7 Perry A. Addington, b. 28 Jun 1882, WA, d. 22 Mar
1969, Seattle, WA, m. 1 Mar 1902, Myrtle Stroup
A-1-3-3-8-7-1 Clare LaVern Addington, b. 12 May 1903, m.
Eleanor ?
A-1-3-3-8-7-2 Bernadine Opal Addington, b. 13 Sep 1907
m. Harris Graham
A-1-3-3-8-7-2-1 Judy Graham, b. 1938, m. 1958, David Clouse
A-1-3-3-8-7-2-1-1 Kenneth Clouse, b. May 1960
A-1-3-3-8-7-2-1-2 Cynthia Clouse, b. Jan 1962
A-1-3-3-8-8 Orie E. Addington, b. 17 Sep 1887, Lee Co., Iowa, d.
26 Apr 1938, San Francisco, California, m. Bertha ?
A-1-3-3-8-9 Infant, b. 2 May 1889, Lee Co., Iowa d. young
A-1-3-3-9 Alfred Benjamin "Fred" Addington, b. 25 Dec 1849,
Iowa (1880 Lee Co., IA, 1900 Dallas Co., IA), d. 14 Sep 1923,
Arnett, Oklahoma
m. Rosanne Jessup, b. 4 Oct 1854, Warren Co., Iowa, d. 9 Jul
1888, Colby, Kansas
A-1-3-3-9-1 Carrie Breatha Addington, b. 21 May 1875, Lee Co.,
Iowa, d. 26 Apr 1962, Wichita, Kansas
m. Von Holloway
A-1-3-3-9-1-1 Herchall Holloway, b. 11 Dec 1898, d. 21 Jun 1964
A-1-3-3-9-1-2 Velma Holloway, b. 21 Sep 1906
A-1-3-3-9-2 Leonard Cole Addington, b. 27 Jun 1878, Pilot
Grove, Iowa (1910 Ellis Co., Oklahoma)
m. 28 Feb 1905, Edna Luella Duncanson
A-1-3-3-9-2-1 Margaret Faye Addington, b. 17 Jun 1909, Arnett,
Oklahoma, m. 8 Mar 1933, Elmer Deward Sult
A-1-3-3-9-2-2 Chloe Wilma Addington, b. 12 Jun 1913, Arnett,
Oklahoma, m. 14 Aug 1934, Forrest Dale Lewright
A-1-3-3-9-2-2-1 Linden Dale Lewright, b. 19 May 1937, Shattuck,
Oklahoma, m. 16 May 1965, June Squires
A-1-3-3-9-2-2-2 Marilou Lewright, b. 22 Dec 1939, Shattuck, OK
m. 28 Dec 1959, Clifford Morris Town
A-1-3-3-9-2-3 Esther Marie Addington, b. 15 Aug 1915, Arnett,
Oklahoma, m. 27 Jun 1934, Wesley Willard Bishop
A-1-3-3-9-2-3-1 Patricia Lou Bishop, b. 17 Jan 1935, Shattuck, OK
m. 19 Sep 1952, Ronald J. Miller
A-1-3-3-9-2-3-1-1 Russell Loy Miller, b. 17 Jan 1955, Shattuck,
Oklahoma
A-1-3-3-9-3 Luther James Addington, b. 17 Nov 1879, Pilot
Grove, Lee Co., Iowa, d. 5 Aug 1964, Jackson Co., Oregon
m. 3 Mar 1900, Dallas Co., Iowa, Loretta Mae Keltner
A-1-3-3-9-3-1 Lena Mae Addington, b. 8 Jul 1901
m. 26 May 1920, Bend, Oregon, Earl Harry Clark

A-1-3-3-9-3-1-1 Lyal Gene Clark, b. 30 Jun 1921, Snoqualmie
Falls, WA, d. 26 Oct 1922, Modesto, California
A-1-3-3-9-3-1-2 Earl Harry Clark, Jr., b. 14 Nov 1922, Don Pedro,
California, m. 11 Mar 1944, Patricia J. Williams
A-1-3-3-9-3-1-2-1 Earl Harry Clark, III, b. 6 Jan 1945, Elko, NV
A-1-3-3-9-3-1-2-2 Michele Ann Clark, b. 23 Oct 1946, NV
A-1-3-3-9-3-1-2 m. 2nd 22 Jun 1954, Irma Anne Nendigate
A-1-3-3-9-3-1-3 Robert Dale Clark, b. 5 Dec 1924, Don Pedro, CA
m. 18 Jan 1946, Shirley Louise, Lilley
A-1-3-3-9-3-1-3-1 John Addington Clark, b. 7 Dec 1956, San
Diego, California
A-1-3-3-9-3-1-3-1 Mark Keltner Clark, b. 9 Apr 1958, San Diego
A-1-3-3-9-3-1-4 Charles Seevera Clark, b. 2 Mar 1930, Modesto,
California, m. 5 Sep 1953, Marlene May Moore
A-1-3-3-9-3-1-4-1 Linda Sue Clark, b. 6 May 1954, Boulder City,
NV, m. 24 Jun 1972, Kenneth James Berri
A-1-3-3-9-3-1-4-1-1 Angela Marie Berri, b. 6 Jun 1975, Yuba City,
California
A-1-3-3-9-3-1-4-2 Shirlanne Clark, b. 12 Aug 1955, San
Fernando, CA, m. 19 Oct 1974, Perry Dennman Pasquale
A-1-3-3-9-3-1-4-3 Nancy Lynn Clark, b. 7 Apr 1959, Hollywood,
California
A-1-3-3-9-3-1-4-4 Patricia Dale Clark, b. 14 Mar 1960, Van Nuys,
California
A-1-3-3-9-3-1-4-5 Constance Marie Clark, b. 13 May 1964, Encino,
California
A-1-3-3-9-3-2 Melvin Elmer Addington, b. 6 Dec 1902, d. 16 May
1965, Red Bluff, California
m. 13 Jul 1922, Modesto, California Mattie Belle Ray
A-1-3-3-9-3-2-1 Ermah Frona Addington, b. 13 Nov 1922
m. Chester William Ballard
A-1-3-3-9-3-2-2 June Talitha Addington, b. 13 Sep 1924
m. Franklin C. Dement
A-1-3-3-9-3-2-3 Melvin Elmer Addington, Jr., b. 19 Jul 1926
m. 12 Jun 1948, Elva Margaret Chesnut
A-1-3-3-9-3-2-4 James Franklin Addington, b. 9 Aug 1931
m. Dixie Bebb
A-1-3-3-9-3-2-5 Joseph Addington, b. 9 Aug 1931, d. 9 Aug 1931
A-1-3-3-9-3-2-6 Sharon Loverna Addington, b. 11 Jan 1943
m. Carroll Ray Otten Ross
A-1-3-3-9-3-3 Lola Cophene Addington, b. 21 Nov 1907
m. 1 Jan 1929, Burns, Oregon, Lester Elverton Tyler
A-1-3-3-9-3-3-1 Lyle Elverton Tyler, b. 1934, m. Mary Voss
A-1-3-3-9-3-3-2 Lesley Leroy Tyler, b. 1943, m. Sarah Dunten

A-1-3-3-9-3-4 Virgil Orval Addington, b. 4 Sep 1915
A-1-3-3-9-3-5 Vera Naomi Addington, b. 7 Jul 1919
  m. Louis Albert Wagner, b. 1914
A-1-3-3-9-3-5-1 Laurence Alvin Wagner, b. 1939, m. Rita Olson
A-1-3-3-9-3-5-2 Neil Ray Wagner, b. 1940, m. Judith Ann Lyons
A-1-3-3-9-4 Cora Cophene Addington, b. 7 Nov 1882, d. 9 Jan
  1971, Portland, Oregon
  m. Clarence Swartz, m. 2nd William Gibbons
A-1-3-3-9 m. 2nd 1890, Dallas Co., Iowa, Margaret Hammer
A-1-3-3-10 Albert David Addington, b. 25 Dec 1849, Iowa, d. 1
  Oct 1875, Lee Co., Iowa,
  m. Mary Elizabeth Jessup, b. 1854, (Mary ? m. 2nd Gilbert
  Coats)
A-1-3-3-10-1 Martha E. Addington, b. c1874, Iowa, d. young
A-1-3-3-10-2 Albert David Addington, Jr., b. 27 Sep 1875, Lee
  Co., Iowa (1900 Cherokee Co., KS)
A-1-3 m. 2nd 22 Dec 1808, Preble Co., Ohio, Celia Townsend, b.
  22 Feb 1785, d. 5 Mar 1852, bur. Sparrow Creek Cemetery,
  Randolph Co., Indiana
A-1-3-4 Rachel Addington, b. 19 Mar 1810, Preble Co., Ohio, d.
  bef. 1850, bur. Sparrow Creek Cemetery, Randolph Co., IN
  m. 3 Nov 1828, Wayne Co., Indiana, Seth Elliott, b. 1807
A-1-3-4-1 Jonathan Elliott, b. 1834
A-1-3-5 Thomas Addington, b. 14 Jul 1811, d. c1840, bur.
  Sparrow Creek Cemetery, Randolph Co., Indiana
  m. 16 May 1833, Wayne Co., Indiana, Beulah Hunt, d. c1838
A-1-3-5-1 Anna E. Addington
  ? m. 6 Sep 1867, Wayne Co., Indiana, William Medearis
A-1-3-5-2 Hanna Addington
A-1-3-5-3 Kentia E. Addington, m. ? Fert
A-1-3-5-4 Henry Addington, b. 1834, (raised by Celia) d. 7 Oct
  1863, Nashville, Tenn. while in 84th Indiana Regiment
  m. 25 Jul 1855, Sophia A. Bolinger, b. c1839, d. 1871
A-1-3-5-4-1 Anne Eliza Addington, b. 1856 (lived Missouri)
  m. 4 Jul 1872, Randolph Co., IN, Benjamin Franklin Harris
A-1-3-5-4-1-1 Florence Rosella Harris, b. 1873
  m. Benjamin G. Maughmer, b. 1865
A-1-3-5-4-1-1-1 Frederic H. Maughmer, b. 1873
  m. Ruth Miriam Hine
A-1-3-5-4-1-1-2 Eva Maughmer, m. Charles Raymond Miller
A-1-3-5-4-1-2 Naomi May Harris, b. 1875
  m. Robert Lee Wilson Daily
A-1-3-5-4-1-2-1 Mary Annie Daily, m. Charles Ernest Farrow
A-1-3-5-4-1-2-1-1 Flora Naomi Farrow, b. 1915

A-1-3-5-4-1-2-1-2 Charles Daily Farrow, b. 1919, m. Elaine Beck
A-1-3-5-4-1-2-1-2-1 Charlaine Farrow, b. 1942
A-1-3-5-4-1-2-1-2-2 Carolyn Farrow, b. 1946
A-1-3-5-4-1-2-1-2-3 Lonnie Charles Farrow, b. 1951
A-1-3-5-4-1-2-1-3 Julia Neva Farrow, b. 1921
  m. Aubrey Dale Kirk, b. 1907
A-1-3-5-4-1-2-1-4 Betty Lou Farrow, b. 1923
  m. Harvey Aloin McKee, b. 1919
A-1-3-5-4-1-2-1-4-1 Thomas H. McKee, b. 1947
A-1-3-5-4-1-2-1-4-2 Judith A. McKee, b. 1948
A-1-3-5-4-1-2-1-4-3 John A. McKee, b. 1956
A-1-3-5-4-1-2-1-4-4 Geoffrey L. McKee, b. 1958
A-1-3-5-4-1-2-1 m. 2nd Theodore R. Chenoweth
A-1-3-5-4-1-2-1-5 Teresa Marie Chenoweth, b. 1927
A-1-3-5-4-1-2-1-6 Robert Chenoweth, b. 1928
A-1-3-5-4-1-2-1-7 Paul L. Chenoweth, b. 1930
  m. Grace Kikue Shimizu
A-1-3-5-4-1-2-1-7-1 Timothy L. Chenoweth, b. 1952
A-1-3-5-4-1-2-1-8 Frank Leroy Chenoweth, b. 1934
  m. Mildred Boyer, b. 1936
A-1-3-5-4-1-2-1-8-1 Carla Sue Chenoweth, b. 1959
A-1-3-5-4-1-2-1-8-2 Carl Dean Chenoweth, b. 1961
A-1-3-5-4-1-2-1-8-3 Cheryl Ann Chenoweth, b. 1962
A-1-3-5-4-1-2-1-8 m. 2nd Ellen Marie Berthiaume
A-1-3-5-4-1-2-2 Julia Florence Daily, b. 1901, m. Harry L. Lowe
A-1-3-5-4-1-3 Rebecca Jane Harris, b. 1877
  m. Wilson Lee Gates Daily, b. 1874
A-1-3-5-4-1-3-1 Allen Harris Daily, b. 1898
  m. Maude Anna Martin, b. 1897
A-1-3-5-4-1-3-1-1 Allen Harris Daily, Jr., b. 1931
  m. Jacquelin M. Arthur, b. 1929
A-1-3-5-4-1-3-1-1-1 Kit Allen Daily, b. 1957
A-1-3-5-4-1-3-1-1-2 Tad Elton Daily, b. 1958
A-1-3-5-4-1-3-2 Wilson Lee Gates Daily, b. 1900
  m. Ada Sontheimer
A-1-3-5-4-1-3-2-1 Infant, b. 1922, d. young
A-1-3-5-4-1-3-2-2 Kathleen Emma Jane Daily, b. 1923
  m. Elvin Jones Payne, b. 1918
A-1-3-5-4-1-3-2-2-1 Elvin Dale Payne, b. 1943
A-1-3-5-4-1-3-2-2-2 Chadwin Jay Payne, b. 1946
  m. Marsha Ann Kelly, b. 1952
A-1-3-5-4-1-3-2-2-2-1 Kelly Kathleen Payne, b. 1978
A-1-3-5-4-1-3-2-2-2-2 Jared Tyler Payne, b. 1984
A-1-3-5-4-1-3-2-2-2-3 Lorin Nicole Payne, b. 1986

A-1-3-5-4-1-3-2-2-2-4 Alexa Brooke Payne, b. 1989
A-1-3-5-4-1-3-2-2-2-3 Vernon Lee Payne, b. 1949
  m. Joan Ernestine Harwood, b. 1955
A-1-3-5-4-1-3-2-2-3-1 Vernon Lee Payne, Jr., b. 1974
A-1-3-5-4-1-3-2-2-3-2 Dustin Neil Payne, b. 1976
A-1-3-5-4-1-3-2-2-3-3 Gina Anne Payne, b. 1978
A-1-3-5-4-1-3-2-2-3-4 Valerie Renne Payne, b. 1980
A-1-3-5-4-1-3-2-2-3-5 Haley Elizabeth Payne, b. 1987
A-1-3-5-4-1-3-2-2-4 Kathy Lynn Payne, b. 1951
  m. Brent Burton Sandstrom, b. 1950
A-1-3-5-4-1-3-2-2-4-1 Stacey Lynn Sandstrom, b. 1975
A-1-3-5-4-1-3-2-2-4-2 Jill Allison Sandstrom, b. 1977
A-1-3-5-4-1-3-2-2-4-3 Lori Elaine Sandstrom, b. 1979
A-1-3-5-4-1-3-2-2-5 Karen Sue Payne, b. 1953
  m. Allen Joseph Hunsaker, b. 1949
A-1-3-5-4-1-3-2-2-5-1 Wendy Hunsaker, b. 1973
A-1-3-5-4-1-3-2-2-5-2 Benjamin A. Hunsaker, b. 1977
A-1-3-5-4-1-3-2-2-5-3 Jed Dale Hunsaker, b. 1980
A-1-3-5-4-1-3-2-3 Carolyn June Daily, b. 1930
  m. Robert Francis White, b. 1927
A-1-3-5-4-1-3-2-3-1 Mary Margaret White, b. 1948
  m. Richard Douglas Deshon, b. 1947
A-1-3-5-4-1-3-2-3-1-1 Wendy Suzette Deshon, b. 1967
  m. Karl Roger Kirschbaum
A-1-3-5-4-1-3-2-3-1-1-1 Jhett L. Kirschbaum, b. 1989
A-1-3-5-4-1-3-2-3-1 m. 2nd Raymond Edward Cline, b. 1945
A-1-3-5-4-1-3-2-3-1-2 Amy Leanne Cline, b. 1975
A-1-3-5-4-1-3-2-3-1-3 Sara Dianne Cline, b. 1976
A-1-3-5-4-1-3-2-3-2 Robert Francis White, Jr., b. 1949
  m. Carol Ann Lorenz, b. 1950
A-1-3-5-4-1-3-2-3 m. 2nd Donald Richard Garver, b. 1929
A-1-3-5-4-1-3-2-4 Wilson Lee Gates Daily, III, b. 1931
  m.Patricia June Pope, b. 1935
A-1-3-5-4-1-3-2-4-1 Debra Sue Daily, b. 1955
  m. William L. Coldwell, b. 1951
A-1-3-5-4-1-3-2-4-1-1 Richard Lee Coldwell, b. 1981
A-1-3-5-4-1-3-2-4-1-2 Genni Ada Coldwell, b. 1988
A-1-3-5-4-1-3-2-4-2 Rebecca Jean Daily, b. 1957
  m. Kenneth Blane Ramage, b. 1956
A-1-3-5-4-1-3-2-4-2-1 Richard Wilson Ramage, b. 1982
A-1-3-5-4-1-3-2-4-2-2 Elizabeth Ramage, b. 1987
A-1-3-5-4-1-3-2-4-3 Melanie Kathleen Daily, b. 1965
  m. Curtis Grant Van Orman, b. 1962
A-1-3-5-4-1-3-2-4-3-1 Bradley Mark Van Orman, b. 1991

A-1-3-5-4-1-3-2-4-4 Wilson Lee Pope Daily, b. 1967
A-1-3-5-4-1-3-2 m. 2nd Geneva M. Richards, b. 1908
A-1-3-5-4-1-3-2-5 Richard Arthur Daily, b. 1935
m. Dixie Deane Maugh, b. 1936
A-1-3-5-4-1-3-2-5-1 Richard Arthur Daily, Jr., b. 1955
m. Patricia Ann Curtis, b. 1954
A-1-3-5-4-1-3-2-5-1-1 Ashley Ann Daily, b. 1977
A-1-3-5-4-1-3-2-5-1-2 Curtis David Daily, b. 1980
A-1-3-5-4-1-3-2-5-1-3 Christopher B. Daily, b. 1983
A-1-3-5-4-1-3-2-5-2 Terri Lynn Daily, b. 1956
m. Joseph Michael Rock
A-1-3-5-4-1-3-2-5-2-1 Joseph Michael Rock, Jr., b. 1979
A-1-3-5-4-1-3-2-5-2-2 Kevin Scott Rock, b. 1982
A-1-3-5-4-1-3-2-5-3 Timothy Allen Daily, b. 1973
m. Kuuipo Marie Kalama, b. 1973
A-1-3-5-4-1-3-2-5-3-1 Keilani Marie Daily, b. 1991
A-1-3-5-4-1-3-2-6 Charles Thomas Daily, b. 1940
m. Rosa Marie Oliver, b. 1942
A-1-3-5-4-1-3-2-6-1 Brigide Lorraine Daily, b. 1961
A-1-3-5-4-1-3-2-6-2 Roxanne Margaret Daily, b. 1963
m. Mohammed S. Abu/Koush
A-1-3-5-4-1-3-2-6-2-1 Jessica M. Abu/Koush, b. 1989
A-1-3-5-4-1-3-2-6-2-2 Josef Abu/Koush, b. 1990
A-1-3-5-4-1-3-2-6-3 Charles Thomas Daily, Jr., b. 1964
A-1-3-5-4-1-3-2-6-4 Michael Anton Daily, b. 1971
A-1-3-5-4-1-3-2-6 m. 2nd Emilee Millsap
A-1-3-5-4-1-3-2-6 m. 3rd Sherrie Elosie Sanet
A-1-3-5-4-1-3-3 Mary Helen Daily, b. 1903
m. Harry Lovell Wright, b. 1893
A-1-3-5-4-1-3-3-1 Richard Lee Wright, b. 1928
A-1-3-5-4-1-3-3-2 Janie Sue Wright, b. 1934
m. Richard A. Priester, b. 1934
A-1-3-5-4-1-3-3-2-1 Stephanie L. Priester, b. 1958
A-1-3-5-4-1-3-3-2-2 Stephen Lee Priester
A-1-3-5-4-1-3-4 Anna Naomi Daily, b. 1905
m. Otis Elbert Wells
A-1-3-5-4-1-3-4-1 Robert Lee Wells, b. 1932
m. Marie A. Berube, b. 1929
A-1-3-5-4-1-3-4-1-1 Diane Louisa Wells, b. 1955
A-1-3-5-4-1-3-4-1-2 Paula Marie Wells, b. 1956
A-1-3-5-4-1-3-4-2 Mary Ann Wells, b. 1935
m. Bruce A. Bishop
A-1-3-5-4-1-3-4-2-1 Scott Allen Bishop, b. 1973
A-1-3-5-4-1-4 Mazania Grace Harris, b. 1880

m. Lawrence Victor Sexton, b. 1881
A-1-3-5-4-1-4-1 Clifford B. Sexton, b. 1905
A-1-3-5-4-1-4-2 Thelma H. Sexton, b. 1906
m. Herrold Allen Millen, b. 1902
A-1-3-5-4-1-4-2-1 Clarice Carolyn Millen, b. 1931
m. Joseph William Rioux, b. 1926
A-1-3-5-4-1-4-2-1-1 Steven Crane Rioux, b. 1960
A-1-3-5-4-1-4-2-1-2 Moira Leigh Rioux, b. 1964
A-1-3-5-4-1-4-2-1-3 Jennifer Grace Rioux, b. 1966
A-1-3-5-4-1-4-2-2 Pauline Elaine Millen, b. 1934
m. Bernard L. Elming, b. 1931
A-1-3-5-4-1-4-2-2-1 Gregory Bernard Elming, b. 1960
A-1-3-5-4-1-4-2-2-2 Mark Millen Elming, b. 1963
A-1-3-5-4-1-4-2-2-3 Douglas Charles Elming, b. 1965
A-1-3-5-4-1-5 William Frederick Harris, b. 1883
m. Adelia Grace Wright, b. 1882
A-1-3-5-4-1-5-1 William Harold Harris, b. 1906
m. Essie Louise Cooley, b. 1909
A-1-3-5-4-1-5-2 Annah Lucille Harris, b. 1912
m. Howard McDonald
A-1-3-5-4-1-5-2-1 Virgil Lee McDonald, b. 1935
m. Sandra McVey
A-1-3-5-4-1-5-2-1-1 Kelley Lea McDonald, b. 1958
A-1-3-5-4-1-5-2-1 m. 2nd Mary Ruth Noonan
A-1-3-5-4-1-5-2-1-2 David Lee McDonald
A-1-3-5-4-1-5-2-1-3 Danny McDonald
A-1-3-5-4-1-5-2-1-4 Danielle McDonald
A-1-3-5-4-1-5-2-1 m. 3rd Faye Williams
A-1-3-5-4-1-5-3 James Wilson Harris, b. 1916
m. Yvonne Malson, b. 1916
A-1-3-5-4-1-5-3-1 Betty Josephine Harris, b. 1936
m. Richard A. Hellerich, b. 1936
A-1-3-5-4-1-5-3-1-1 James Paul Hellerich, b. 1959
A-1-3-5-4-1-5-3-1-2 Jennifer L. Hellerich, b. 1960
A-1-3-5-4-1-5-3-1-3 Richard R. Hellerich, b. 1962
A-1-3-5-4-1-5-3-2 JoAnn Harris, b. 1938, m. Robert Lee Herring
A-1-3-5-4-1-5-3-2-1 Shelia Renaie Herring, b. 1957
A-1-3-5-4-1-5-3-2-2 Nancy Doreatha Herring, b. 1958
A-1-3-5-4-1-5-3-2-3 Kristi E. Herring, b. 1962
A-1-3-5-4-1-5-3-2-4 Robert Scott Herring, b. 1963
A-1-3-5-4-1-5-3-2 m. 2nd Franklin C. Meadows
A-1-3-5-4-1-5-3-2-5 Glynnda Gay Meadows, b. 1965
A-1-3-5-4-1-5-3-2-6 Anne Carliese Meadows, b. 1968
A-1-3-5-4-1-5-3-2-7 Jodi Lin Meadows, b. 1971

A-1-3-5-4-1-5-4 Willard B. Harris, b. 1923
A-1-3-5-4-1-6 Stephen Henry Harris, b. 1885
A-1-3-5-4-1-7 Laurabell Abigal Harris, b. 1888
  m. Carl Levi Jessup, b. 1889
A-1-3-5-4-1-7-1 Alice Lea Jessup, b. 1915
  m. Clive Dail Halbert
A-1-3-5-4-1-7-1-1 Carl Dale Halbert, b. 1952
A-1-3-5-4-1-7-1-2 Elaine Gail Halbert, b. 1959
A-1-3-5-4-1-7-1-3 Mathew Halbert
A-1-3-5-4-1-8 Flora Anna Harris, b. 1888
  m. Bruce Ralston Cassidy, b. 1883
A-1-3-5-4-1-8-1 Nile Milford Cassidy, b. 1912
A-1-3-5-4-1-8-2 Florence R. Cassidy, b. 1916
  m. James Gordon Coffin, b. 1912
A-1-3-5-4-1-8-2-1 James Ivan Coffin, b. 1935
A-1-3-5-4-1-8-2-2 Allen Wayne Coffin, b. 1941
A-1-3-5-4-1-8-3 Murrel Maxine Cassidy, b. 1919
A-1-3-5-4-1-8-4 Raymond Dale Cassidy, b. 1930
A-1-3-5-4-1-9 Carl Benjamin Harris, b. 1894
  m. Bertha Leora Farrow Lea, b. 1896
A-1-3-5-4-1-9-1 Juanita Jean Harris, b. 1923
  m. Herrold Allen Millen, b. 1902
A-1-3-5-4-1-9-1-1 Marvin Lloyd Harris, b. 1926
A-1-3-5-4-1-9-1-2 Winona Lucille Harris, b. 1928
A-1-3-5-4-2 Hannah M. Addington, b. 24 Jan 1858, d. 21 Jun 1936
  m. 30 Jun 1876, Randolph Co., Indiana, William Richard
    Herron, b. c1852
A-1-3-5-4-2-1 Leo Nina Herron, b. 1878, m. ? Thornburg
A-1-3-5-4-2-2 John Leroy Herron, b. 23 Apr 1881, d. 13 Sep 1956
  m. Pearl Christina Freidline
A-1-3-5-4-2-2-1 Howard Raymond Herron, b. 24 Sep 1913,
    Union City, Ohio
  m. 11 Jun 1938, Phyllis Eileen Miller
A-1-3-5-4-2-2-1-1 Anne Sherril Herron, b. 1 Jun 1941
  m. 19 Jun 1960, Jon Paul Hinshaw
A-1-3-5-4-2-2-1-2 Jerome Miller Herron, b. 28 Apr 1946
A-1-3-5-4-2-2-1-3 Angela Eileen Herron, b. 8 Aug 1949
  m. 10 Apr 1981, Michael B. Soper
A-1-3-5-4-2-2-1-3-1 Ryan Miller Soper, b. 25 Jun 1983
A-1-3-5-4-2-3 Charles E. Herron, b. 1886
A-1-3-5-4-2-4 Opal Herron, b. 1890, m. ? Moore
A-1-3-5-4-3 Kitina Ella Addington, b. c1860
  m. 24 Dec 1881, Randolph Co., Indiana, Albert Collier (lived
    in Muncie)

A-1-3-5-4-4 Henry Taylor Addington, Jr., b. 22 Mar (or 3 Feb) 1863, Indiana, d. 16 Sep 1932, bur. Maxville Cemetery
  m. 1 Nov 1885, Randolph Co., Indiana, Christina Green
A-1-3-5-4-4-1 Clara Mary Addington, b. 23 May 1888, Indiana
  m. 18 Sep 1906, Randolph Co., Indiana, Milton Rinard
A-1-3-5-4-4 m. 2nd Loretta ?, b. 1865, d. 1941
A-1-3-6 Jonathan Addington, b. 18 Mar 1813, Indiana, d. 15 Sep 1891, Randolph Co., Indiana
  m. 4 Jul 1839, Randolph Co., Indiana, Sarah Ruble, b. 11 Aug 1817, Ohio, d. 7 May 1899
A-1-3-6-1 Louise Addington, b. 1839
  m. 26 Aug 1860, John McIntyre
A-1-3-6-2 Henry T. Addington, b. 19 Sep 1844, Nr. Ridgeville, Indiana, d. 3 Sep 1911, bur. Maxville Cemetery
  m. 2 Aug 1865, Emily C. Green, b. 10 Mar 1848, d. 12 May 1876, bur. Maxville Cemetery
A-1-3-6-2-1 Lilly Addington, b. 1869, d. aft. 1933
  m. 20 Jun 1885, Randolph Co., IN, Charles Moyer (or Myers)
A-1-3-6-2-2 Ellsworth Elmer Addington, b. 1871, d. 1943
  m. 24 Dec 1894, Randolph Co., Indiana, Gertrude Hunt, b. 1878, d. 1908
A-1-3-6-2-2-1 daughter, b. 14 Mar 1894
A-1-3-6-2-2-2 daughter, b. 6 May 1897
A-1-3-6-2-2-3 Ralph H. Addington, b. 20 Jun 1899, d. Aug 1919, bur. Maxville Cem.
A-1-3-6-2-2-4 Garnet Rebecca Addington, b. 26 Feb 1907, Randolph Co., Indiana
  m. 15 Oct 1927, Randolph Co., IN, Ray Marcus Davissen
A-1-3-6-2-3 Minnie Addington, b. 1873
  m. 14 Feb 1891, Randolph Co., Indiana, Albert McGuire
A-1-3-6-2-3-1 Neal Webster McGuire, b. 6 Dec 1896
  m. Rosina Bolinger
A-1-3-6-2 m. 2nd 29 Mar 1877, Nannie E. Edgar, b. 21 Apr 1850, d. 9 Jun 1933, South Bend, Indiana, bur. Maxville Cem.
A-1-3-6-2-4 Bertha R. Addington, b. c1878,
  m. 3 Jul 1894, Randolph Co., Indiana, Marion Conyers
  m. ? 2nd 1 Dec 1899, Delaware Co., Indiana, Albert Fuller
A-1-3-6-2-5 Harry (or Henry) Rolla Addington, b. Dec 1880, Indiana, d. 20 Jul 1937, bur. Maxville Cemetery
  m. Jennie M. Patty, b. 1882, d. 1976, bur. Maxville Cemetery.
A-1-3-6-2-5-1 son, b. 13 Nov 1901
A-1-3-6-2-5-2 Curtis B. Addington, b. 23 Mar 1908, Delaware Co., Indiana

A-1-3-6-2-6 Edward C. Addington, b. 13 Dec 1887, d. 8 Apr 1940
(lived in Marion)

A-1-3-6-2-7 Laura B. Addington, b. 29 Apr 1891, d. aft 1933
m. 15 Nov 1910, Randolph Co., Indiana, Hovey Thornburg

A-1-3-6-2-8 Russell Addington, b. 1896, Indiana (lived South
Bend)

A-1-3-6-3 Robert G. Addington, b. 1846, d. 1944
m. 27 Jan 1878, Sarah Angeline Brickley, b. 1850, d. 9 Oct 1922,
Randolph Co., Indiana

A-1-3-6-3-1 (adopted?) Mamie Addington, b. 5 Feb 1891
m. 18 Jun 1912, Randolph Co., Indiana, Roy Pursley

A-1-3-6-4 Benjamin Addington, b. Oct 1849, d. 1936
m. 1878, Salina W. Lewis, b. Feb 1855, d. 18 Apr 1931,
Randolph Co., Indiana

A-1-3-6-4-1 Gussie E. Addington, b. Jun 1880, d. 17 Apr 1904

A-1-3-6-5 Sarah A. Addington, b. c1850

A-1-3-6-6 Ida Belle Addington, b. May 1860, Randolph Co., IN

A-1-3-7 Elvira Addington, b. 20 Apr 1815, Wayne Co., Indiana,
d. 30 Aug 1837, Wayne Co., Indiana
m. 30 Apr 1834, Wayne Co., IN, Robert Cox, b. 1814, d. 1890

A-1-3-7-1 Joseph Cox, b. 5 Mar 1835, d. 1912

A-1-3-7-2 Celia Cox, b. 3 Jul 1836, m. ? Boyd

A-1-3-7-3 Elvira Cox, b. 19 Aug 1837, d. 2 Feb 1838

A-1-3-8 Elisha Addington, b. 11 Sep 1817, d. 4 Mar 1839, bur.
Sparrow Creek Cemetery, Randolph Co., Indiana

A-1-3-9 Elihu Addington, b. 21 Jan 1820, d. 17 Feb 1898, Grant
Co., Indiana
m. 1 Sep 1842, Hannah Cox, b. 15 Nov 1824, d. 19 Apr 1859

A-1-3-9-1 Ruth Ellen Addington, b. 1844, Indiana

A-1-3-9-2 Martha Ann Addington, b. 1846
m. 3 Oct 1867, Randolph Co., Indiana, Joel May

A-1-3-9-3 Lindsey Addington, b. 15 Apr 1848, Indiana, d. 3 Feb
1920, Marion, Indiana (1880, Worth Co., Missouri)
m. 7 Apr 1870, Worth Co., Missouri, Angeline Scott

A-1-3-9-3-1 Albert M. Addington, b. c1872, Missouri, d. 28 Mar
1892, Grant Co., Indiana

A-1-3-9-3-2 Lewis K. Addington

A-1-3-9-4 Wilson Addington, b. May 1851 (1900 Marion, IN)
m. Oct 1874, Katie M. Law
m. 2nd 31 Oct 1878, Grant Co., In, Mary A. Brandon

A-1-3-9-5 Mary S. Addington, b. c1854
m. ? Hiatt (lived Grand City, MO)

A-1-3-9-6 Lilly Addington, b. c1856

A-1-3-9 m. 2nd 25 Nov 1860, Delaware Co., Indiana, Eliza
Branson, b. 1832, Ohio, d. 29 Nov 1897
A-1-3-9-7 Minnie E. Addington, b. 1863, d. aft. 1920,
m. 21 Jun 1883, Randolph Co., Indiana, Elmer W. Jay
A-1-3-9-8 Ellsworth Addington, b. 1864 (1900 Cook Co., IL)
A-1-3-9-9 Burtie Lee Addington, b. Feb 1868
m. 28 Sep 1890, Melva Carolina Long, m. 2nd Ollie L. ?
A-1-3-9-9-1 Mertal Addington, b. c1890, m. Henry Carroll
A-1-3-9-9-2 Gertrude Addington, b. 9 Apr 1892, Prudy, Barry
Co., Missouri, m. Samuel Sanders Haddock
A-1-3-9-9-2-1 Warren G. Haddock, b. 11 Feb 1921, Barry Co., MO,
m. 22 Feb 1941, Jennie Mooney
A-1-3-9-9-2-1-1 Donna R. Haddock, b. 12 Jan 1942, Barry Co.,
Missouri, m. George C. Cooper
A-1-3-9-9-2-1-1-1 Jamie Shawn Cooper, b. 7 Apr 1964
A-1-3-9-9-2-1-1-2 Tracy Denise Cooper, b. 3 Oct 1967
A-1-3-9-9-3 Lottie B. Addington, b. 1897, m. ? Douthilt
A-1-3-9-10 Waldo Addington, b. c1870
A-1-3-10 Stephen Addington, b. 12 Jan 1822, d. 1 Mar 1839, bur.
Sparrow Creek Cemetery, Randolph Co., Indiana
A-1-3-11 Benjamin Robert Addington, b. 28 Jun 1824, Wayne
Co., Indiana, d. 6 Nov 1906, Randolph Co., Indiana
m. 30 Oct 1850, Randolph Co., Indiana, Rebecca Harold, b. 2
Aug 1828, d. 4 Mar 1876
A-1-3-11-1 Cornelius M. Addington, b. 15 Mar 1852, d. 1897
(lived Geneva, IN)
m. 1 Jan 1878, Mary "Mollie" Walker (1900 Adams Co., IN)
A-1-3-11-1-1 Celia Alice Addington, b. 4 Jan 1879, d. 11 Nov
1948, ni (lived at Geneva)
m. 21 Sep 1905, William A. Wells
A-1-3-11-1-2 Arthur Warren Addington, b. 25 Jan 1882, d. 1 Jul
1956
m. 1 Sep 1911, Rosa Della Betz, b. 10 Feb 1889, d. 30 Dec 1961
A-1-3-11-1-2-1 James Ernest Addington, b. 10 Feb 1913,
Randolph Co., Indiana, d. 5 Dec 1939, dnm
A-1-3-11-1-2-2 Floyd Roger Addington, b. 24 Feb 1915, Randolph
Co., Indiana, d. 21 Jan 1980
m. 13 Jan 1940, Ruth E. Swartz
A-1-3-11-1-2-2-1 Ernest Wayne Addington, b. 8 Apr 1942
m. 1965, Judith Guyton
A-1-3-11-1-2-2-1-1 Lynn Andria Addington, b. 23 Sep 1967
A-1-3-11-1-2-2-1-2 Jason Christopher, b. 11 Dec 1970
A-1-3-11-1-2-2-1-3 Eric Jacob Addington, b. 12 Nov 1972
A-1-3-11-1-2-2-2 Robert Lee Addington, b. 9 Jun 1953

m. 1973, Connie Bauer, div

A-1-3-11-1-2-2-2-1 Courtney Douglas Addington, b. 20 Oct 1973

A-1-3-11-1-2-2-2-2 Nathaniel Damien Addington, b. 13 Sep 1981

A-1-3-11-1-2-3 Florence Lucille Addington, b. 24 Oct 1918, Randolph Co., Indiana

m. 27 Oct 1938, James H. Teeters, b. 2 Sep 1913

A-1-3-11-1-2-3-1 James H. Teeters, Jr., b. 27 Sep 1939

m. 6 Jun 1964, Karon Cortrecht, b. 23 Dec 1945

A-1-3-11-1-2-3-1-1 Jama Kristine Teeters, b. 2 Apr 1967

A-1-3-11-1-2-3-1-2 Kelly Leight Teeters, b. 2 Sep 1969

A-1-3-11-1-2-3-1-3 James Harvey Teeters, b. 1 Jun 1980

A-1-3-11-1-2-4 Elizabeth Ann Addington, b. 21 Nov 1920

m. 25 Dec 1941, Richard J. Fiely, b. 28 Apr 1922, d. 5 Jun 1981

A-1-3-11-1-2-4-1 Shirley Fiely, b. 13 Jul 1943

m. 18 Apr 1964, Charles D. Acheson, b. 17 Sep 1937

A-1-3-11-1-2-4-2 Richard A. Fiely, b. 22 Sep 1945

m. 13 Sep 1969, Janice Bickel, b. 13 Jul 1945

A-1-3-11-1-2-4-3 J. Michael Fiely, b. 12 Sep 1948

m. 18 Apr 1970, Kathy Tucker, b. 8 Dec 1950

A-1-3-11-1-2-4-4 Linda Fiely, b. 16 Jan 1951

m. 11 Nov 1978, Michael McCoy, b. 20 Nov 1948

A-1-3-11-1-2-4-5 Donna Fiely, b. 23 May 1953

m. 26 Nov 1981, Gregory Mannia, b. 20 Jan 1951

A-1-3-11-1-2-4-6 Barbara Fiely, b. 3 Mat 1956

m. 7 Jun 1986, Troy Shaffer, b. 23 Sep 1957

A-1-3-11-1-2-4-7 Joseph Alan Fiely, b. 5 Jul 1958

A-1-3-11-1-2-4-8 Harold W. Fiely, b. 8 Aug 1963

m. 22 Aug 1987, Kimberly Bonvillian, b. 17 Oct 1965

A-1-3-11-1-3 Lula Addington, b. 3 Feb 1887, d. 1978, dnm

A-1-3-11-1-4 Ernest Benjamin Addington, b. 3 Sep 1889, d. 13 Nov 1930

m. 6 May 1911, Randolph Co., Indiana, India Miller, b. 4 Mar 1893, d. 8 Mar 1964

A-1-3-11-1-4-1 Mary Alice Addington, b. 11 Nov 1911

m. 27 Feb 1932, Gerald Fisher, b. 14 Dec 1911

A-1-3-11-1-4-1-1 Jack M. Fisher, b. 29 Nov 1934

m. 25 Apr 1955, Joyce Ann Lawrence, b. 14 Nov 1935

A-1-3-11-1-4-1-1-1 Gerald Lewis Fisher, b. 5 Nov 1956

m. 1 Sep 1989, Pamela Sue Loney, b. 14 Apr 1960

A-1-3-11-1-4-1-1-1-1 Jack Daniel Fisher, b. 28 Sep 1990

A-1-3-11-1-4-2 Hugh Richard Addington, b. 20 Dec 1913, Randolph Co., Indiana

m. 20 Nov 1940, Garnet L. Burton, b. 19 Jun 1920, d. 23 Aug 1965

A-1-3-11-1-4-2-1 Patricia Sue Addington, b. 12 Aug 1941, CA
  m. 20 Oct 1962, Richard Wilson, b. 23 May 1940
A-1-3-11-1-4-2-1-1 Stephen Michael Wilson, b. 15 Sep 1965
  m. 1 Sep 1990, Cheryl Lynn Davis, b. 4 Jan 1966
A-1-3-11-1-4-2-1-2 Susan Ann Wilson, b. 15 Nov 1969
  m. 29 Dec 1989, Jason Lynn Cox, b. 16 Mar 1970
A-1-3-11-1-4-2-1-1 Ashley Marie Cox, b. 23 Apr 1987
A-1-3-11-1-4-2-1-3 Kenneth Scott Wilson, b. 7 Jun 1971
A-1-3-11-1-4-2-2 Hugh Richard Addington, Jr., b. 11 Oct 1945,
  California
  m. 25 Sep 1964, Jeanne Smith, b. 27 Jul 1946
A-1-3-11-1-4-2-2-1 Cheri Lynn Addington, b. 14 Mar 1967
  m. 2nd 29 Aug 1981, Sylvia Marie Brian, b. 31 Dec 1955
A-1-3-11-1-4-2-2-2 Hugh Richard Addington, III, b. 1 Nov 1982
A-1-3-11-1-4-2-2-3 Summer Marie Addington, b. 24 Jun 1989
A-1-3-11-1-4-2-3 Alfred Arthur Addington, b. 7 Feb 1953, CA
  m. 5 Aug 1972, Debbie Henry, b. 8 Jan 1953
A-1-3-11-1-4-2-3-1 Amber Addington, b. 28 Feb 1973
  m. 19 Apr 1990, Larry Dale Booth, Jr., b. 30 Jan 1971
A-1-3-11-1-4-2-3-2 Brian Addington, b. 15 Jan 1977
A-1-3-11-1-4-2-3-3 Casey Addington, b. 21 Sep 1978
A-1-3-11-1-4-3 Marjorie Addington, b. 11 Mar 1918
  m. 31 May 1935, J. Woody Campbell, b. 31 Jul 1908, d. 26 Mar
  1943
A-1-3-11-1-4-3-1 Ronald W. Campbell, b. 4 Dec 1937
  m. 25 Jul 1959, Judith Arthur, b. 6 Jul 1940
A-1-3-11-1-4-3-1-1 Christopher Charles Campbell, b. 6 Sep 1970
A-1-3-11-1-4-3-1 m. 2nd 17 Dec 1988, Susanne Bailey
A-1-3-11-1-4-3 m. 2nd 5 Feb 1944, Charles F. Clear, b. 14 Aug
  1912, d. 11 Oct 1988
A-1-3-11-1-4-3-2 Charles Rick Clear, b. 17 Nov 1953
A-1-3-11-2 Sylvester Addington, b. 25 Dec 1853, d. 30 Jan 1908
  m. 24 Jan 1877, Randolph Co., Indiana, Eliza A. Walker, b.
  c1855, d. 1945
A-1-3-11-2-1 Ira Addington, b. 1880, d. 1951, m. 1910, Pearl ?
A-1-3-11-2-1-1 Earl Addington
A-1-3-11-2-1-2 Herman Addington
A-1-3-11-2-1-3 Donald Addington
A-1-3-11-2-1-4 Lebur Addington
A-1-3-11-2-1-5 Lois Addington
A-1-3-11-2-1-6 Mary Addington, m. Matthew Marierrison
A-1-3-11-2-1-7 Phyllis Addington, m. R. C. Ferneyhough
A-1-3-11-2-2 Oliva "?Allie" Addington, b. c1881
  m. 14 May 1898, Randolph Co., Indiana, Edward Dull

A-1-3-11-2-3 Grace Addington, b. c1885
A-1-3-11-2-4 Gale Walker Addington, b. 24 Feb 1888
  m. 11 Jun 1913, Randolph Co., Indiana, Hazel Smithson, b. 20 Jan 1892
A-1-3-11-2-4-1 Edward L. Addington, b. 3 Oct 1915, Randolph Co., Indiana, d. 3 Oct 1918
A-1-3-11-2-4-2 daughter, b. 7 Jul 1920, Randolph Co., Indiana
A-1-3-11-2-5 Lorena A. Addington, b. 10 Oct 1891
  m. 25 Mar 1911, Randolph Co., Indiana, Hoke Wall
A-1-3-11-3 Milfred W. Addington, b. 3 Dec 1855, d. 7 May 1911
  m. 3 Aug 1879, Randolph Co., Indiana, Sarah S. Milner, b. 14 Feb 1857, d. 13 Aug 1935
A-1-3-11-3-1 Noel Edgar Addington, b. 19 Jan 1882, d. 27 Apr 1962
  m. 24 Jul 1909, Jay Co., Indiana, Myrtle May Green, b. 9 Aug 1884, d. 11 May 1925
A-1-3-11-3-1-1 Elsie Juanita Addington, b. 13 Jun 1910, ni
  m. 25 Apr 1936, Jay Craw, b. 18 Aug 1907, d. 2 Nov 1973
A-1-3-11-3-1-2 J. Milfred Addington, b. 4 Feb 1912, Randolph Co., Indiana, d. 13 Oct 1972
  m. 5 Aug 1935, Osa V., Caylor, b. 9 Jun 1919
A-1-3-11-3-1-2-1 Jaetta Sue Addington, b. 9 Dec 1938
  m. 10 Jun 1956, Donney L. Roberts, b. 3 Jan 1936
A-1-3-11-3-1-2-1-1 Jill Ann Roberts, b. 19 Apr 1957
  m. 24 Jun 1977, Larry J. Golliher, b. 29 Oct 1955
A-1-3-11-3-1-2-1-1-1 Travis J. Golliher, b. 23 May 1980
A-1-3-11-3-1-2-1-2 Doreen Sue Roberts, b. 20 Jun 1961
  m. 17 Jul 1982, Gary Conn, b. 14 May 1957
A-1-3-11-3-1-2-1-3 Tina Lynn Roberts, b. 1 Sep 1965
  m. 17 Sep 1988, Lary Kent KcKissick, b. 26 Jul 1964
A-1-3-11-3-1-2-2 Danny Lee Addington, b. 16 Apr 1942
  m. 30 Jun 1961, Carol L. Vannatter, b. 22 Jul 1944
A-1-3-11-3-1-2-2-1 Douglas Alan Addington, b. 21 Jan 1962
  m. 17 May 1986, Ramona Rumph, b. 1 Apr 1963
A-1-3-11-3-1-2-2-2 Aimee Dawn Addington, b. 30 Apr 1966
  m. 7 Oct 1989, Mark Davis, b. 5 Aug 1965
A-1-3-11-3-1-2-2-3 Holly Michelle Addington, b. 23 Feb 1971
  m. Sean Anderson, b. 5 Apr 1971
A-1-3-11-3-1-2-2-3-1 Alexander James Anderson, b. 12 Jan 1991
A-1-3-11-3-1-2-3 Edgar Alan Addington, b. 6 Dec 1945
  m. 21 Feb 1969, Terry Kay Albertson, b. 5 Apr 1946
A-1-3-11-3-1-2-3-1 April Renee Addington, b. 21 Feb 1973
A-1-3-11-3-1-3 Sarah Sophia Addington, b. 13 Nov 1914, Jay Co., Indiana, d. 12 Aug 1979

m. 1 Dec 1947, Walter Thomas Younts, b. 19 Jan 1917, d. 2 Jun 1988

A-1-3-11-3-1-3-1 Gregory Eugene Younts, b. 29 Oct 1948
m. 6 Jun 1975, Carla Jeannine Watson, b. 14 Jun 1953
A-1-3-11-3-1-3-1-1 Brad Michael Younts, b. 8 Oct 1976
A-1-3-11-3-1-3-1-2 Joseph Noel Younts, b. 3 Dec 1979
A-1-3-11-3-1-3-2 Douglas Jay Younts, b. 1 Jul 1950
A-1-3-11-3-1-3-3 Dianna Kay Younts, b. 1 Jul 1950
m. Jerry Duane Williams, b. 13 Apr 1949, div.
A-1-3-11-3-1-3-3-1 Chad Duane Williams, b. 23 Sep 1972
A-1-3-11-3-1-4 Mildred Edna Addington, b. 6 Jun 1922, d. 20 Apr 1982, m. Gilbert Mullen
A-1-3-11-3-1-4-1 Robert V. Mullen, b. 22 Oct 1945
m. 17 Feb 1968, Linda F. Jones, b. 6 Oct 1946
A-1-3-11-3-1-4-1-1 Anita Faye Mullen, b. 21 Mar 1969
A-1-3-11-3-1-4-1-2 Ryan Nicholas Mullen, b. Nov 1978
A-1-3-11-3-1-4-2 Geradine Mullen, m. Joe Garringer
A-1-3-11-3-1-4-2-1 Lori Garringer
A-1-3-11-3-1-4-2-2 Mike Garringer
A-1-3-11-3-1-4-2-3 Lisa Garringer
A-1-3-11-3-1-4-2-4 Rick Garringer
A-1-3-11-3-2 Edna Laura Addington, b. 12 Mar 1884, d. 1968 dnm
A-1-3-11-3-3 Forest Morris Addington, b. 20 Aug 1888, d. 1941 (lived in Muncie)
m. 25 Jan 1915, Delaware Co., Fleety Gladys Bolinger, b. 1888
A-1-3-11-3-3-1 Forest K. Addington, b. 21 Dec 1919, Delaware County, Indiana
A-1-3-11-3-3-2 Margaret Louise Addington, b. 15 Oct 1923, Muncie, Indiana, d. 15 Oct 1923
A-1-3-11-3-4 Asa Everet Addington, b. 7 May 1893, d. 28 Aug 1924, Farmland, Indiana
A-1-3-11-4 Elvia C. Addington, b. 11 Apr 1858
m. 10 Dec 1875, Randolph Co., Indiana, Thomas Overman
A-1-3-11-4-1 Minnie Overman
A-1-3-11-4-2 Gerald Overman
A-1-3-11-5 Emma Addington, b. 8 Oct 1860
m. 6 Oct 1883, Valentine Stanley
A-1-3-11-5-1 Emma Stanley
A-1-3-11-5-2 Ethel Stanley, m. ? Wheeler, m. 2nd ? Choral
A-1-3-11-5-3 Delmar Stanley, m. Clessey
A-1-3-11-6 Henry Lincoln Addington, b. 22 Mar 1863, d. young
A-1-3-11-7 Asa Robert Addington, b. 28 Dec 1865, d. 2 Feb 1941

m. 30 May 1889, Lillie Pearl Bolinger, b. 29 May 1873, d. 2 Jul 1931

A-1-3-11-7-1 Perry Orvil Addington, b. 8 Mar 1890, d. 13 Feb 1967

m. 22 Dec 1911, Randolph Co., Indiana, Mae Veirl Jones

A-1-3-11-7-1-1 son, b. 7 Feb 1913, Randolph Co., Indiana

A-1-3-11-7-1-2 daughter, b. 8 Oct 1915

A-1-3-11-7-1-3 son, b. 23 May 1917, d. 23 May 1917

A-1-3-11-7-1-4 Rebecca Claire Addington, b. 20 Dec 1921, Randolph Co., Indiana

A-1-3-11-7-2 Cleo Louisa Addington, b. 22 Mar 1895, d. 6 Dec 1904

A-1-3-11-7-3 Kathleen Rebecca Addington, b. 28 Sep 1897, Randolph Co., Indiana, d. 28 Jan 1986, Clawson, Michigan

m. 27 Aug 1919, Randolph Co., Indiana, George Russell Patterson, b. 28 Aug 1891, Jay Co., Indiana, d. 26 Jun 1958, Plainwell, Michigan

A-1-3-11-7-3-1 Joseph Milton Patterson, b. 31 Dec 1921, Jay Co., Indiana

m. 6 Jan 1944, Orlando, Florida, Marjorie Jean Decker

A-1-3-11-7-3-1-1 Lucinda Kathleen Patterson, b. 17 Oct 1944, Fresno, California

m. 3 Apr 1965, Orlando, FL, Henry Pardee Bedford III

A-1-3-11-7-3-1-1-1 Tera Lynn Bedford, b. 11 Aug 1967, Winter Park, Florida

A-1-3-11-7-3-1-1-2 Jason Todd Bedford, b. 18 Aug 1971, Winter Park, Florida

A-1-3-11-7-3-1-2 Joseph Milton Patterson, Jr., b. 20 Nov 1948, Lansing, Michigan

m. 18 Apr 1969, Orlando, Florida, Jeanne L. Giddens

A-1-3-11-7-3-1-2-1 Cassandra E. Patterson, b. 12 Aug 1969

A-1-3-11-7-3-1-2 m. 2nd 12 Jul 1986, Kim Michelle Rolly

A-1-3-11-7-3-1-2-2 Justin M. Patterson, b. 20 Jan 1987

A-1-3-11-7-3-1-2-3 Nicole C. Patterson, b. 9 Oct 1988

A-1-3-11-7-3-1-3 James Kingsley Patterson, b. 9 Jan 1952, Lansing, Michigan

m. 12 Jun 1973, Orlando, Florida, Cynthia J. Mishko

A-1-3-11-7-3-1-3-1 Sara M. Patterson, b. 1 Jun 1977

A-1-3-11-7-3-1-3-2 Amy N. Patterson, b. 4 Apr 1979

A-1-3-11-7-3-1-3-3 Clayton J. Patterson, b. 17 Jun 1988

A-1-3-11-7-3-1-4 Jayne Ann Patterson, b. 24 Nov 1953, Lansing, Michigan

m. 14 Jun 1975, Winter Park, Florida, William Lewis Gierke

A-1-3-11-7-3-1-4-1 William N. Gierke, b. 9 Dec 1979

A-1-3-11-7-3-1-4-2 Jeffrey M. Gierke, b. 31 Aug 1983
A-1-3-11-7-3-1-4-3 Katie Ann Gierke, b. 25 Apr 1985
A-1-3-11-7-3-2 Lois Patricia Patterson, b. 24 Nov 1926, Plainwell,
    Michigan
    m. 23 Aug 1952, Plainwell, Michigan, Jack Ryan
A-1-3-11-7-3-2-1 Michele P. Pyan, b. 29 May 1955, Royal Oak, MI
    m. Jul 1980, Royal Oak, Michigan, Jeffrey J. Phillips
A-1-3-11-7-3-2-1-1 Katherine P. Phillips, b. 24 Oct 1983
A-1-3-11-7-3-2-1-2 Joseph K. Phillips, b. 25 Jan 1986, Evanston, IL
A-1-3-11-7-3-2-2 Kevin P. Ryan, b. 9 Jul 1957, Royal Oak, MI
    m. 16 Jun 1990, Royal Oak, Michigan, Kristin Sue Farlow
A-1-3-11-7-3-2-3 Timothy J. Ryan, b. 21 Jul 1959, St. Josephs, MI
    m. 1 Oct 1988, E. Lansing, Michigan, Felicia G. Anselmo
A-1-3-11-7-3-2-4 Sarah E. Ryan, b. 27 Jun 1961, Royal Oak, MI
    m. 20 Aug 1988, Royal Oak, Michigan, John J. Wysocki
A-1-3-11-7-3-2-5 Daniel M. Ryan, b. 21 Feb 1963, Royal Oak, MI
A-1-3-11-7-4 Paul O. Addington, b. 14 Nov 1905, d. 12 Nov 1905
A-1-3-11 m. 2nd Jun 1878, Sarah Jane Day, b. 1842, d. 26 Jun 1902
A-1-3-12 David Addington, b. 9 Mar 1828, Wayne Co., Indiana,
    d. 19 Jul 1902, Randolph Co., Indiana, bur. Maxville Cem.
    m. 27 Nov 1851, Randolph Co., Indiana, Huldah Ruth
    Bolinger, b. Nov 1830, Pennsylvania, d. 18 Sep 1907 (ae 76-9-
    29), bur. Maxville Cemetery
A-1-3-12-1 Mary Elizabeth Addington, b. Dec 1852, d. 20 Jan
    1943, bur. Maxville Cemetery
    m. 1870, James M. Pursley, b. May 1849, Indiana, d. 24 Nov
    1912, bur. Maxville Cemetery
A-1-3-12-1-1 Nora Bell Pursley, b. 1871
    m. Andrew Jackson, d. bef. 1910
A-1-3-12-1-1-1 Eldon Jackson, b. 1891
A-1-3-12-1-1-2 Orel R. Jackson, b. 1892
A-1-3-12-1-1-3 Hattie G. Jackson, b. 1896
A-1-3-12-1-2 Ruth Myrtle Pursley, b. c1874, m. Orla Amburn
A-1-3-12-1-3 Nellie B. Pursley, b. c1876, m. Jesse W. Jackson
A-1-3-12-1-3-1 Norval Jackson, b. 1894
A-1-3-12-1-3-2 Rolland Jackson, b. 1899
A-1-3-12-1-3-3 Miltie Jackson, b. 1901
A-1-3-12-1-3-4 Edith Jackson, b. 1904
A-1-3-12-1-4 Mattie Jackson, b. 1878, m. J. Clinton Jackson
A-1-3-12-1-4-1 Idris Jackson, b. 1901
A-1-3-12-1-4-2 Opal Jackson, b. 1905
A-1-3-12-1-4-3 Horner Jackson, b. 1907
A-1-3-12-1-5 Ernest Pursley, b. 1880, IN, m. Emma ?, b. 1880
A-1-3-12-1-5-1 Vanda Pursley, b. 1899, Indiana

A-1-3-12-1-6 David E. Pursley, b. 2 May 1887
m. 19 Jan 1907 Opal Fodrea
A-1-3-12-1-6-1 Robert D. Pursley, b. c1908
A-1-3-12-1-6-2 Roger V. Pursley, b. c1910
A-1-3-12-2 Cecilla Addington, b. 1854/6, d. age 2
A-1-3-12-3 Joseph Leander Addington, b. Feb. 1858, Randolph
Co., Indiana, d. 11 Oct 1935, Randolph Co., Indiana, bur.
Maxville Cemetery
m. 10 Feb 1880, Randolph Co., Indiana, Dora Elizabeth
Feagans, b. 24 Oct 1862, Randolph Co., Indiana, d. 19 Mar
1944, Randolph Co., bur. Maxville Cemetery
A-1-3-12-3-1 David "Cressie" Addington, b. 3 Jan. 1881, d. 1966,
bur. Maxville Cemetery
m. 25 Nov 1911, Randolph Co., Indiana, Jeanetta Clevenger,
b. 3 Mar 1886, d. 11 Jan 1946
A-1-3-12-3-1-1 Floyd Addington, b. 2 Jan 1913, d. 10 Nov 1977
m. Ethel Green, b. 1919
A-1-3-12-3-1-1-1 Linda Addington, m. ? Riley, div.
A-1-3-12-3-1-1-1-1 son
A-1-3-12-3-1-1-1-2 daughter
A-1-3-12-3-1-1-1 m. Danny Retz, div.
A-1-3-12-3-1-1-1-3 daughter
A-1-3-12-3-1-1-1 m. ? Wolfe
A-1-3-12-3-1-1-2 Robert Addington, b. 1945, d. 1978, bur. New
Castle, Indiana, m. Doris ?
A-1-3-12-3-1-1-3 Michael (Mickey) Addington
A-1-3-12-3-1-1-4 Judy Addington, m. Gary Simmons
A-1-3-12-3-1-1-5 Tammy Addington, m. ? Moore
A-1-3-12-3-1-2 Doris Addington, b. 17 Sep 1915, Randolph Co.,
Indiana
A-1-3-12-3-1-3 Mildred Addington, b. 6 Feb 1917, Randolph Co.,
Indiana, m. Bud Oliver
A-1-3-12-3-1-3-1 Marlene Oliver
A-1-3-12-3-1-4 Gerald (Bill) Addington, b. 9 Dec 1919, White
River T., Randolph Co., Indiana
m. 12 Sep 1937, Ruth Potter, b. 1 Oct 1918, Darke Co., Ohio
A-1-3-12-3-1-4-1 Nila Mae Addington, b. 7 Apr 1939, Mercer Co.,
Ohio, m. 1957, Keith Shoal, div.
A-1-3-12-3-1-4-1-1 Lisa Diane Shoal, b. 6 Mar 1962, Union City,
Indiana
m. 24 Sep 1983, Andreis Jaymon McGhee
A-1-3-12-3-1-4-1-1-1 Andrea McGhee, b. 28 Feb 1986, Ft.
Campbell, Kentucky

A-1-3-12-3-1-4-1-1-2 Carmon Alisha McGhee, b. 24 Dec 1989, Indianapolis, Indiana

A-1-3-12-3-1-4-1-2 Lyle Kent Shoal, b. 22 Aug 1963, Union City, Indiana

A-1-3-12-3-1-4-2 Ardith Ann Addington, b. 12 Sep 1940, Randolph Co., Indiana

m. 23 May 1959, Jerome (Jerry) Leroy Rohrer

A-1-3-12-3-1-4-2-1 Jerome Leroy Rohrer, Jr., b. 3 Feb 1961

A-1-3-12-3-1-4-2-2 James Patrick Rohrer, b. 17 Feb 1962

m. 24 Oct 1982, Deborah Luanne Gant, b. 29 Jan 1964

A-1-3-12-3-1-4-2-2-1 Nathaniel James Rohrer, b. 1 Oct 1989

A-1-3-12-3-1-4-2-3 Gary Allen Rohrer, b. 8 Dec 1963

m. 11 Apr 1986, Portland, IN, Kay Ellen Lynch, b. 1 Sep 1964

A-1-3-12-3-1-4-2-4 Paul Joseph Rohrer, b. 3 Jan 1965

m. 24 Dec 1984, Union City, Indiana, Janet Ann Parker, b. 21 May 1966

A-1-3-12-3-1-4-2-4-1 Daniel Glenn Rohrer, b. 8 Apr 1985

A-1-3-12-3-1-4-2-4-2 Jessica Ann Rohrer, b. 11 Jun 1987

A-1-3-12-3-1-4-2-5 Nicholas William Rohrer, b. 24 Jul 1970

A-1-3-12-3-1-4-3 William (Bill) Addington, b. 13 Oct 1942, Randolph Co., Indiana

m. Kay LeMaster, div.

A-1-3-12-3-1-4-3-1 William Lee Addington, Jr., b. 16 Jul 1962, Union City, Indiana, m. Candy Byrum

A-1-3-12-3-1-4-3-1-1 son

A-1-3-12-3-1-4-3-2 Todd Phillip Addington, b. 5 Sep 1963, Union City, Indiana

A-1-3-12-3-1-4-3-3 Christie Dawn Addington, b. 12 Jan 1969, Jay Co., Indiana

A-1-3-12-3-1-4-3-4 Mathew Trent Addington, b. 19 Jan 1974, Jay Co., Indiana

A-1-3-12-3-1-4-3 m. 2nd Dorinda Joyce Boyter

A-1-3-12-3-1-4-4 Marilyn Sue Addington, b. 16 Nov 1944, Randolph Co., Indiana

m. 7 Jul 1963, Bill Jessop, div.

A-1-3-12-3-1-4-4-1 Timothy Lee Jessop, b. 11 Apr 1966

A-1-3-12-3-1-4-4-2 Bradley William Jessop, b. 26 Aug 1971

A-1-3-12-3-1-4-4 m. 2nd 27 Sep 1974, James Lee Sullenbarger

A-1-3-12-3-1-4-5 Sandra Kay Addington, b. 21 Mar 1950

m. 14 Feb 1976, William Keith Immel, b. 27 Jan 1950

A-1-3-12-3-1-4-5-1 Michelle Lynn Immel, b. 19 Aug 1977

A-1-3-12-3-1-4-6 David Russell Addington, b. 17 Dec 1951

m. 21 Jan 1972, Linda Sue Garland, div.

A-1-3-12-3-1-4-6-1 David Russell (Rusty) Addington II, b. 5 Aug 1975

A-1-3-12-3-1-4-6-2 Kendra Noel Addington, b. Greenville, OH

A-1-3-12-3-1-4-6-3 Benjamin Lucas Addington, b. 28 Mar 1978, Greenville, Ohio

A-1-3-12-3-1-4-6 m. 2nd 3 Sep 1983, Rebecca (Jean) Brooks Lusterm

A-1-3-12-3-1-4-7 Mark Allen Addington, b. 15 Apr 1961, Jay Co., Indiana

m. 25 Feb 1984, Cathy Newman, b. 18 Dec 1957

A-1-3-12-3-1-4-7-1 Mark Clinton Addington, b. 16 Sep 1984, Huntingburg, Indiana

A-1-3-12-3-1-4-7-2 Katie Rachelle Addington, b. 21 Aug 1987, Union City, Indiana

A-1-3-12-3-1-5 Dora Alice Addington, b. 2 Nov 1921, Randolph Co., Indiana

m. 26 Apr 1941, Howard Thornburg, b. 3 Oct 1920, Randolph Co., Indiana

A-1-3-12-3-1-5-1 Vern Allen Thornburg, b. 31 May 1943, d. Nov 1952

A-1-3-12-3-1-5-2 Luetta Sue Thornburg, b. 18 Mar 1945

m. Jul 1964, Garry Lee Campbell, b. 21 Sep 1945

A-1-3-12-3-1-5-2-1 Gregory Scott Campbell, b. 2 Nov 1969

A-1-3-12-3-1-5-2-2 Bradley Dean Campbell, b. 19 Sep 1971

A-1-3-12-3-1-5-2-3 Ryan Troy Campbell b. 3 Nov 1972

A-1-3-12-3-1-5-3 Lew Edward Thornburg, b. 4 May 1949, Winchester, Indiana

m. Aug 1968, Rebecca J. Morrison

A-1-3-12-3-1-5-3-1 Vernon Lewis Thornburg, b. 19 Sep 1978

A-1-3-12-3-1-5-3-2 Amy Michelle Thornburg, b. 28 Jan 1985

A-1-3-12-3-1-5-4 Donna Jo Thornburg, b. 6 Feb 1954, Winchester, Indiana

m. Aug 1973, John (Mac) Orcutt

A-1-3-12-3-1-5-4-1 Monty Allen Orcutt, b. 10 May 1974, Muncie, Indiana

A-1-3-12-3-1-5-4-2 Myra Luann Orcutt, b. 13 May 1979, Muncie, Indiana

A-1-3-12-3-1-5-5 David Neil Thornburg, b. 14 May 1956

m. Karen Bosworth, b. 6 Mar 1958

A-1-3-12-3-1-6 Mary Alma Addington b. 13 Mar 1923, Randolph Co., Indiana

m. John Pavey, b. 30 Mar 1931

A-1-3-12-3-1-6-1 Alfred Lawrence (Larry) Pavey, b. 30 Oct 1953

m. Kim ?

A-1-3-12-3-1-6-1-1 Erice Brecka Pavey, b. 22 Dec 1973
A-1-3-12-3-1-6-1-2 Landon Lafayette Pavey, b. 21 Nov 1980
A-1-3-12-3-1-6-2 Stephen Harold Pavey, b. 1 Aug 1955
   m. Micki ?
A-1-3-12-3-1-6-2-1 Karen Pavey, b. 6 Mar 1977
A-1-3-12-3-1-6-2-2 Richard Stephen Pavey, b. 4 Apr 1978
A-1-3-12-3-1-6-3 Sue Ann Pavey, b. 23 Aug 1957, m. Mike Fisher
A-1-3-12-3-1-6-3-1 Shannon Brittany Fisher, b. 18 Jul 1986
A-1-3-12-3-1-6-3-2 Megan Lynette Fisher, b. 18 Jul 1986
A-1-3-12-3-1-6-3-3 Diana Michelle Fisher, b. 18 Jul 1986
A-1-3-12-3-1-6-4 Ronnie Pavey, b. 1 Jun 1959, d. 1 Jun 1959
A-1-3-12-3-1-6-5 Dale Pavey, b. 1 Jun 1959, d. 1 Jun 1959
A-1-3-12-3-1-6-6 Ronald William Pavey, b. 7 Sep 1960
A-1-3-12-3-1-6-7 Carol Jo Anne Pavey, b. 21 Dec 1961
   m. Eddie Byers, b. 1 Sep 1969
A-1-3-12-3-1-7 Gene Clay Addington, d. about age 49, bur.
   Maxville, Cem.
   m. June Shreves
A-1-3-12-3-1-7-1 Millie Addington
A-1-3-12-3-1-7-2 Ronnie Addington
A-1-3-12-3-1-7-3 Bruce Addington
A-1-3-12-3-2 Robert "Gilva" Addington, b. 4 Aug 1885, d. 18 Sep
   1971, Randolph Co., Indiana, bur. Maxville Cem.
   m. 28 Feb 1914, Mary Ermel Clevenger, b. 24 Nov 1890, d. 19
   May 1968, bur. Maxville Cem.
A-1-3-12-3-2-1 Dallas Eugene Addington, b. 22 Nov 1917, Parker
   City, Indiana
   m. 1 Nov 1940, Nell Oliver, b. 4 Dec 1918
A-1-3-12-3-2-1-1 Pamela Kay Addington, b. 26 Dec 1943
   m. Philip Reed
A-1-3-12-3-2-1-1-1 Christopher Reed, b. 6 Feb 1965
   m. May Marie Hamilton
A-1-3-12-3-2-1-1-2 Stacey Elizabeth Reed, b. 4 Dec 1967
   m. 3 Oct 1962, Greg Necessary
A-1-3-12-3-2-1-1-2-1 Joshua Necessary, b. 25 Nov 1986
A-1-3-12-3-2-1-1-2-2 Jacob Necessary, b. 5 Apr 1988
A-1-3-12-3-2-1-2 Kim John Addington, b. 16 Mar 1952
   m. Cathy Leeka
A-1-3-12-3-2-1-2-1 Joseph Wyatt Addington, b. 10 Sep 1978
A-1-3-12-3-2-2 Viola Elizabeth Addington, b. 7 Nov 1922
   m. 29 Feb 1948, Marvin Hart, b. 23 Apr 1908, d. 1 Jan 1972
A-1-3-12-3-2-3 Rosemary Addington, b. 22 Aug 1929
   m. Henry Haworth, b. 31 Dec 1921
A-1-3-12-3-2-3-1 Lowell Anthony Haworth, b. 10 Jan 1958

m. Arlene Wilkinson

A-1-3-12-3-3 Mabel Elizabeth Addington, b. 10 Jul 1890, d. 16 Oct 1977

m. Sylvester Starbuck, b. 17 Feb 1892, d. 28 Aug 1972

A-1-3-12-3-3-1 Murray L. Starbuck, b. 1919, d. infant

A-1-3-12-3-3-2 Glenn Starbuck, b. 4 May 1921, Indiana

m. Ester I. Davis, b. 26 Feb 1921, Union City, Indiana

A-1-3-12-3-3-2-1 Sandra Sue Starbuck, b. 16 Jan 1947

m. Anthony Joseph McConnell, b. 21 Jul 1945

A-1-3-12-3-3-2-1-1 Brian McConnell, b. 7 Mar 1974

A-1-3-12-3-3-2-1-2 Brett Anthony McConnell, b. 24 Jul 1979

A-1-3-12-3-3-2-2 Shirley Suzanne Starbuck, b. 10 Sep 1953

m. Larry Gene Pippin, b. 7 Jan 1952

A-1-3-12-3-3-2-2-1 Sheri Ann Pippin, b. 23 Aug 1974

A-1-3-12-3-3-2-2-2 Matthew Wayne Pippin, b. 22 Mar 1981

A-1-3-12-3-3-2-3 Sheldon Scott Starbuck, b. 10 Feb 1955

m. Carol Elizabeth Flanary, b. 21 Dec 1955

A-1-3-12-3-3-2-3-1 Samantha Ann Starbuck, b. 30 Jan 1989

A-1-3-12-3-3-3 Cecil Starbuck, b. 9 Sep 1922

m. 16 Feb 1952, Dora May Archer, b. 1 Apr 1929

A-1-3-12-3-3-3-1 Jerry Starbuck, b. 28 Mar 1954

A-1-3-12-3-3-4 Irwin Eugene "Pete" Starbuck, b. 11 Feb 1927, Winchester, Indiana

m. 31 Dec 1953, Bonnie Watson, div.

A-1-3-12-3-3-4-1 Stephen Starbuck, b. 18 Aug 1954

A-1-3-12-3-3-4-2 Dane Starbuck, b. 8 Nov 1956

A-1-3-12-3-4 Harry Vern Addington, b. 9 Mar 1893, Randolph Co., Indiana, d. 13 Aug 1930, bur. Maxville Cemetery

m. 30 Sep 1922, Alma Marguerite Chalfant, b. 9 Jun 1905, d. 18 Aug 1979, Muncie, Indiana, bur. Maxville Cemetery

A-1-3-12-3-4-1 Leo Vern Addington, b. 10 Apr 1923, Randolph Co., Indiana

m. 24 May 1946, Cowan, Indiana, Frances Louise Boggs, b. 17 Jun 1922, Farmland, Indiana

A-1-3-12-3-4-1-1 Ann Frances Addington, b. 11 Jun 1947, Winchester, Indiana

m. 24 Apr 1971, Grissom AFB, Indiana, Richard Irwin Abel, b. 11 Feb 1938, Newark, New Jersey

A-1-3-12-3-4-1-1-1 Amy Louise Abel, b. 6 Mar 1978, Kokomo, IN

A-1-3-12-3-4-1-2 David Vern Addington, b. 4 Aug 1948, Winchester, Indiana

m. 29 Dec 1979, Richardson, Texas, Dixie Carol Behr, b. 30 Jul 1952, Detroit, Michigan

A-1-3-12-3-4-1-2-1 Ashley Lynn Addington, b. 20 Nov 1982, Dallas, Texas

A-1-3-12-3-4-1-2-2 Carmen Elizabeth Addington, b. 1 Nov 1985, Dallas, Texas

A-1-3-12-3-4-1-3 Dale Lee Addington, b. 5 Dec 1950, Winchester, Indiana
  m. 10 Jun 1972, West Lafayette, Indiana, Mary Tammis "Tammi" Carson, b. 29 Jun 1951, Danville, Illinois

A-1-3-12-3-4-1-3-1 Stephen Carson Addington, b. 16 May 1982, Findlay, Ohio

A-1-3-12-3-4-1-3-2 James Michael Addington, b. 28 Aug 1984, Findlay, Ohio

A-1-3-12-3-4-2 Joseph Elsworth Addington, b. 3 Apr 1925, Stony Creek Tw., Randolph Co., Indiana
  d. 11 Aug 1990, Winchester, Indiana, bur. Maxville Cem., Randolph Co., Indiana
  m. 10 Mar 1949, Winchester, Indiana, Norma Jean Heniser, b. 14 Jun 1929

A-1-3-12-3-4-2-1 Wayne Alan Addington, b. 26 May 1954, Winchester, Indiana
  m. 19 Jul 1990, Judith Ann Goforth

A-1-3-12-3-4-2-2 Michael Dean Addington, b. 12 Feb 1957, Winchester, Indiana
  m. 16 May 1981, Peggy Lynn Himes, div.

A-1-3-12-3-4-2-2 m. 2nd 28 Sep 1990, Rebecca Ann McDavid

A-1-3-12-3-4-2-3 Kent Lee Addington, b. 8 Jun 1961, Winchester, Indiana
  m. 31 Mar 1983, Angie Pigg

A-1-3-12-3-4-2-3-1 Quinton Lee Addington, b. 4 Sep 1983, Winchester, Indiana

A-1-3-12-3-4-2-3-2 Brandon Joseph Addington, b. 17 Feb 1985, Winchester, Indiana

A-1-3-12-3-4-2-3-3 Kayla Corrine Addington, b. 9 Nov 1988, Winchester, Indiana

A-1-3-12-3-4-3 Murrie Alexander Addington, b. 19 Apr 1927, Stony Creek Township, Randolph Co., Indiana
  m. 16 Mar 1973, Muncie, Indiana, Eunice Annette Barnett, b. 26 Mar 1925

A-1-3-12-3-5 Cecil Lester Addington, b. Oct 1898, d. 30 Aug 1980, bur. Maxville Cem.
  m. 20 Sep 1922, Osa Emma Main, b. 19 Jan 1900, d. 11 Feb 1990, bur. Maxville Cem.

A-1-3-12-4 Nora Bell Addington, b. c1868, d. c1872

A-1-3-13 Celia Addington, (only mentioned in Tucker History of Randolph County, either an error or died young)

A-1-4 John Addington, Jr., b. 13 Oct 1777, 96 District, SC, d. 1857 (will recorded 15 Oct 1857), Hancock Co., Indiana
m. 1800/5, Rebecca ?

A-1-4-1 Silas B. Addington, b. c1807, d. Wayne County, Indiana (will in 1836)
m. 17 Nov 1828, Wayne Co., Indiana, Polly Davis (widow Polly m. 2nd 4 Jul 1838, Wayne Co., Indiana, Johnson Harrison)

A-1-4-1-1 Polly A. Addington, b. 1834 (1850 Grant Co., IN)

A-1-4-2 Delilah Addington, m. 1 Apr 1819, James Smith

A-1-4-3 Morgan Addington, d. 1842
m. 12 Sep 1822, Wayne Co., Indiana, Jane Mendenhall, b. 1806, TN (Jane m. 2nd 23 Apr 1843, Fulton Co., Indiana, Michael Moracy *or Morrison*)

A-1-4-3-1 Absalom Morgan Addington, b. 28 Sep 1824, Wayne Co., IN, d. 15 Feb 1913, Santa Clara Co., CA (1840 Green Co., WS, 1842 Fountain Co., IN, 1850 El Dorado Co., CA, 1880 Sacramento, CA)
m. 1852, Knoxsville, IL, Martha Jane Boyd, b. 3 Jul 1830, Ohio

A-1-4-3-1-1 David Morgan Addington, b. 9 Feb 1853, CA, d. 7 May 1933, Sutter City, CA
m. Abigail Yates, b. 1 Dec 1859, CA, d. 18 Jul 1928, Sutter City

A-1-4-3-1-1-1 Edward M. Addington, b. 24 May 1882, CA, d. 12 Aug 1968, Nevada Co., CA, m. Mary E. ?, b. 1879, d. 1953

A-1-4-3-1-1-2 Luella Jane Addington, b. 6 Mar 1884, California, d. 23 Dec 1952, Sutter Co., California
m. Lester George Moon, b. 24 Jun 1881, Illinois, d. 1917, Sutter Co., California
m. 2nd 16 Sep 1929, George "Scottie" Young

A-1-4-3-1-1-3 Charles B. Addington, b. Dec 1887, California, d. 20 Nov 1972, Sutter Co., California
m. Cora B. ?, b. 25 Sep 1892

A-1-4-3-1-1-3-1 Edwin Addington

A-1-4-3-1-1-4 David Morgan Addington, Jr., b. 22 Oct 1890, California, d. 23 Feb 1924, Sutter Co., California

A-1-4-3-1-1-5 Frederick W. Addington, b. 22 Oct 1890, d. 28 Jul 1920, Plumas Co., California

A-1-4-3-1-1-6 Royal M. Addington, b. Sep 1894, m. Willie ?

A-1-4-3-1-2 L. I. Addington, b. 1856, d. young

A-1-4-3-1-3 Augustus Amos Addington, b. 20 Mar 1857, Eden, Hancock Co., Indiana, m. Alice Patrick

A-1-4-3-1-3-1 John Edgar Addington, b. 1 Jan 1880, Ridgeway, Kansas
A-1-4-3-1-4 Anna B. Addington, b. 19 Jul 1859, California
m. William Beaugner
A-1-4-3-1-5 Thomas Melvin Addington, b. 15 Feb 1862, California, d. 1 Dec 1933, Alameda Co., California
m. c1891, Rosa E. Drew
A-1-4-3-1-5-1 Ettie Addington, b. Mar 1892, California
A-1-4-3-1-5-2 Charles Melvin Addington, b. 11 Feb 1903, California, d. 25 Jun 1963, San Jose, California, m. Pearl ?
A-1-4-3-1-6 Charles Boyd Addington, b. 20 Nov 1870, Michigan Bar, California, d. 22 Mar 1941, Santa Clara Co., California
m. Lucia A. ?
A-1-4-3-2 Rebecca Addington
m. 21 Feb 1850, Fountain Co., Indiana, Alexander Beaver
A-1-4-3-3 Mary "Polly" A. Addington
m. 9 Sep 1852, Fountain Co., Indiana, James Beaver
A-1-4-3-4 Louisa Addington
? m. 24 May 1846, Fulton Co., Indiana, Samuel L. Lea
A-1-4-3-5 Sarah J. Addington, b. c1831 (1850 Fulton Co., IN)
A-1-4-3-6 James Addington, b. c1835 (1850 Fulton Co., IN)
A-1-4-3-7 Catherine Addington, b. c1837 (1850 Fulton Co., IN)
A-1-4-3-8 Margaret Addington, b. c1839 (1850 Fulton Co., IN)
A-1-4-3-9 Jesse Addington, b. c1843 (1850 Fulton Co., IN)
A-1-4-4 Charles Addington, b. 1808, Indiana d. aft. 1870 (1850-1870 Hancock Co., Indiana)
m. 10 Feb 1825, Wayne Co., Indiana, Elizabeth Hunt
A-1-4-4-1 Morgan Addington, b. Dec 1827, Indiana (1880 Hamilton Co., Indiana, 1900 Douglas Co., MO)
m. 2 Mar 1850, Hamilton Co., IN, Mariah Chew, b. 1822, OH
A-1-4-4-1-1 ? Henrita Addington, b. 1855, Hamilton Co., IN
A-1-4-4-1-2 Amos Addington, b. 1857, Hamilton Co., Indiana (?1900 Osage Co., Kansas), m. Alice ?
A-1-4-4-1-2-1 John E. Addington, b. c1880, Indiana
A-1-4-4-1-2-2 A. Addington (female), b. c1882, Kansas
A-1-4-4-1-3 Joseph A. Addington, b. 1859, Hamilton Co., IN
A-1-4-4-1-4 Emory Addington, b. 1861, Indiana, m. Martha ?
A-1-4-4-1-4-1 Rosa Addington, b. c1888, Missouri
A-1-4-4-1-4-2 Anna Addington, b. c1889, Missouri
A-1-4-4-1-4-2 Ethel Addington, b. c1891, Kansas
A-1-4-4-1-4-4 George Addington, b. c1897, Kansas
A-1-4-4-1-4-5 Arneta Addington, b. c1899, Kansas
A-1-4-4-1-4-6 Clark Addington, b. c1900, Kansas

A-1-4-4-1 m. ? 2nd 24 Oct 1865, Hancock Co., Indiana, Rachel A. Grow

A-1-4-4-1 m. ? 3rd 24 May 1870, Hancock Co., Indiana, Mary M. Barnes

A-1-4-4-1-5 William Addington, b. c1872, Indiana
m. 26 Sep 1897, Marion Co., Indiana, Della May Evans

A-1-4-4-1-5-1 John Addington, b. Apr 1899, Marion Co., IN

A-1-4-4-1-6 Chester Addington, b. Feb 1880, Indiana
m. 5 Apr 1907, Marion Co., Indiana, Mary Newton

A-1-4-4-1 m. 4th 27 Apr 1879, Hamilton Co., Indiana, Elma McCarty, b. 1833, Ohio

A-1-4-4-2 Rebecca Addington, b. c1831, Indiana
m. 16 Nov 1865, Hancock Co., Indiana, Leroy Brizendine

A-1-4-4-3 Louisa Addington, b. c1835, Indiana
m. 22 Nov 1865, Hancock Co., Indiana, Henry H. Barnes

A-1-4-4-4 Youtha A. Addington, b. c1838, Indiana
m. 22 Sep 1859, Hancock, Co., Indiana, Francis M. Wilson

A-1-4-4-5 John M. Addington, b. c1840, Indiana, d. 24 Aug 1907, Hancock Co., Indiana, m. 12 Jul 1860, Hancock Co., Indiana, Elizabeth A. Simms, b. 1839, NC

A-1-4-4-5-1 Charles D. Addington, b. c1867, d. 15 Jan 1919, Hancock, Indiana

A-1-4-4-5 ?m. 2nd 13 Oct 1885, Hancock Co., IN, Mary Andrews

A-1-4-4-6 Amy "Lucy" Addington, b. c1842, Indiana
m. 13 Feb 1877, Hancock Co., Indiana, Albert T. Roberts

A-1-4-4-7 Rachel Addington, b. c1846, Indiana
m. 15 Aug 1862, Hancock Co., Indiana, Albert T. Roberts

A-1-4-4-7-1 Louis Roberts, b. c1864, Indiana

A-1-4-4-7-2 Charles Roberts, b. c1866, Indiana

A-1-4-4-7-3 George Roberts, b. c1867, Indiana

A-1-4-4-7-4 Mary Roberts, b. c1868, Indiana

A-1-4-4-8 (Charles) Eli Addington, b. c1848, Indiana
m. 16 Mar 1870, Hancock Co., IN, Harriet Harkrader, d. c1878

A-1-4-4-8-1? John H. Addington, b. Feb 1871, Indiana (1880 Hancock Co., IN, J O. Addington, 1900 Osage Co., Kansas)

A-1-4-4-8-2? Elizabeth Addington, b. c1872, IN (1880 Hancock Co., IN census)

A-1-4-4-8-3 Mary Addington, b. c1878

A-1-4-4-8 m. 2nd 10 Sep 1880, Hancock Co., Indiana, Elizabeth Tucker

A-1-4-4-8-4 Arthur Addington, b. 30 Mar 1885, Hancock Co., Indiana

A-1-4-4-8-5 Olive Pearl Addington, b. 24 Jul 1887, Indianapolis, Indiana

m. 17 Jul 1912, Indianapolis, Indiana, Forest S. Fisher, b. 1889, d. 24 Jan 1962

A-1-4-4-8-5-1 Mary Fisher, m. ? Colton

A-1-4-4-8-5-2 Alice Fisher, m. Harold Mack

A-1-4-4-8-5-3 Charles D. Fisher

A-1-4-4-8-6 Rose Addington, m. ? Reisinger

A-1-4-5 Mary Addington

m. 11 Dec 1828, Wayne Co., Indiana, Thomas Jordan

A-1-4-5-1 Rebecca Jane Jordan

m. 8 Sep 1858, Jackson Co., Indiana, John T. Overman

A-1-4-6 Rebecca Addington, b. ? c1816, Ohio,

m. 28 Feb 1833, Wayne Co., Indiana, James Walker, b. 1816

A-1-4-7 Noah Addington, b. c1818, Wayne Co., Indiana, d. 12 Feb 1863, Jefferson Barracks, Missouri (? died while in 4th Iowa Regiment)

m. 18 Jun 1837, Wayne Co., Indiana, Miriam Roberts, b. 1818, Ohio, d. 20 Jan 1856, Iowa

A-1-4-7-1 Branson Lee Addington, b. Mar 1838, Wayne Co., Indiana, d. 27 Dec 1900, nr Jefferson, Kansas, (1870 Cherokee Co., Kansas, 1900 Jefferson Co., Kansas)

m. 13 Apr 1856, Rebecca Cade, b. 1839, d. 1925

A-1-4-7-1-1 Jeremiah B. Addington, b. 22 Jun 1858, Iowa, d. 12 Jun 1928, Yakima, Washington

m. Olive Iowa Taylor, b. Dec 1859, Kansas, d. 11 Aug 1943, Yakima, Washington

A-1-4-7-1-1-1 Blanche L. Addington, b. Sep 1880, Kansas

A-1-4-7-1-1-2 Jesse Leroy Addington, b. Jun 1882, Kansas, d. 12 May 1867, Yakima, Washington

m. 2 Jun 1903, Mary Mabel Morrier

A-1-4-7-1-1-3 Nydia M. Addington, b. Dec 1883, Kansas

A-1-4-7-1-1-4 Rebecca Addington, b. 1887, Jefferson Co., Kansas

A-1-4-7-1-1-5 Ida R. Addington, b. Feb 1889, Kansas

A-1-4-7-1-1-6 William C. Addington, b. Apr 1891, Kansas

A-1-4-7-1-1-7 Maggie T. Addington, b. Dec 1893, Kansas

A-1-4-7-1-1-8 Ella B. Addington, b. Jun 1896, Kansas

A-1-4-7-1-1-9 Linda Lovella Addington, b. 27 Oct 1898, Kansas, d. 30 Aug 1909, Yakima, Washington

A-1-4-7-1-2 Ulysses Sherman Addington, b. 17 May 1864, Iowa, d. 7 Aug 1940, Yakima, Washington

A-1-4-7-1-3 Alexander Elsworth Addington, b. 28 Dec 1865, Iowa (1900 Morton Co., Kansas)

m. 1 Nov 1886, Anna E. Perry, b. 24 Nov 1867, Jefferson Co., Kansas, d. 3 Oct 1913, Kansas

A-1-4-7-1-3-1 Grace Addington, b. Mar 1888, Colorado

m. Norton J. Close

A-1-4-7-1-3-2 Mabel L. Addington, b. Nov 1889, Colorado
m. Alvy J. Posey

A-1-4-7-1-3-3 Emery Lee Addington, b. Mar 1891, Colorado
m. 1914, Lucile Charlotte Latham

A-1-4-7-1-3-3-1 Alden A. Addington, b. Aug 1916, Morton Co., Kansas

A-1-4-7-1-3-3-2 Richard Addington, b. Apr 1920, Morton Co., Kansas

A-1-4-7-1-3-3-3 William Hubert Addington, b. 8 Mar 1924, Elkart, Kansas
m. 17 Mar 1948, Donna Lorene McCalla

A-1-4-7-1-3-3-3-1 Mark Wayne Addington

A-1-4-7-1-3-4 Ethel Marie Addington, b. Jan 1893, Colorado
m. Jesse Williams

A-1-4-7-1-3-5 Walter Ben Addington, b. Oct 1895, Kansas
m. Anna ?

A-1-4-7-1-3-6 Bert M. Addington, b. Oct 1896, Kansas
m. Nola Fern Hirt

A-1-4-7-1-3-7 Roy Alexander Addington, b. 22 Nov 1898, Kansas

A-1-4-7-1-3-8 Claude V. Addington, b. 1902, Kansas

A-1-4-7-1-3-9 Elton E. "Buck" Addington, b. 1905, Kansas
m. Alma ?

A-1-4-7-1-3-10 Kenneth Jason Addington, m. Stella Watson

A-1-4-7-1-? (A. Robert Addington, b. c1855, Indiana, 1870 Cherokee Co., Kansas)

A-1-4-7-1-4?? Bert Addington, b. c1876, Iowa

A-1-4-7-2 Joseph Clinton Addington, b. 1840, prob. Howard Co., Indiana, d. 22 Jul 1865, Louisville, Kentucky, dnm

A-1-4-7-3 Louisa Addington, b. 1843, prob. Howard Co., Indiana, d. 1850/60

A-1-4-7-4 Sylvester H. Addington, b. c1846, Wayne Co., Indiana, d. 27 Feb 1863, Helena, Arkansas, dnm

A-1-4-7-5 Armis (Amasilla Teresa) Addington, b. 5 May 1851, Indiana (lived Oaksdale, Nebraska)
m. 5 Jun 1871, Worth Co., Missouri, Samuel McCord

A-1-4-7-6 Nathan or Nason Robert Addington, b. 8 Apr 1855, Marion, Indiana, d. c1878

A-1-4-7 m. 2nd 5 Jun 1856, Ringgold Co., Iowa, Mary Jane Garrett, b. 1846, Kentucky, d. Feb 1861, Iowa

A-1-4-7-7 Rachel Addington, b. 2 Oct 1858, Ringgold, Iowa, d. 16 Oct 1940, Kingsburg, California
m. 29 Jan 1875, Ray, Missouri, Charles Edward Halstead

A-1-4-7-7-1 Harrison Charles Halstead, b. 15 Nov 1875, Ray Co., Missouri, m. 27 Dec 1887, Josephine Elva Lewis

A-1-4-7-7-2 Henry Hiram Halstead, b. 1 Mar 18777, Ray Co., MO, d. 10 Dec 1918, m. 26 Jul 1902, Estella Roberts

A-1-4-7-7-3 James Noah Halstead, b. 13 Aug 1879, Ray Co., MO, d. 20 Sep 1955, m. Stella Miller

A-1-4-7-7-4 George Fillmore Halstead, b. 13 May 1884, Gilroy, California, d. 2 May 1892, dnm

A-1-4-7-7-5 Walter Clinton Halstead, b. 18 Jan 1890, Gilroy, CA m. 27 Jun 1915, Ella Funk

A-1-4-7-7-6 Bertha Mae Halstead, b. 13 Jul 1896, Kingsburg, CA m. 15 Feb 1911, George Lowry, d. 3 Jun 1922

A-1-4-7-7-6-1 Leonard Anderson Lowry, b. 25 Jun 1912, Kingsburg, California, d. 20 Apr 1948
m. 10 Apr 1939, Eleanor Semas

A-1-4-7-7-6-2 Grace Ruth Lowry, b. 14 Feb 1915, Kingsburg, CA m. Rufus Dorsey, m. 2nd Norris Elmer Jobe
m. 2nd 2 Jun 1924, Ray J. Baker

A-1-4-7-7-6-3 Milton Robert Baker, b. 24 Apr 1926, Hanford, CA m. 11 Jun 1946, Pernilla LaVelle Parris

A-1-4-7-7-6-3-1 Pernilla LaVelle Baker, b. 18 Nov 1947, Stockton, California

A-1-4-7-7-6-3-2 Barbara Annamary Baker, b. 17 Mar 1950, Stockton, California, m. 26 Jul 1970, Donald Albert Benight

A-1-4-7-7-6-3-2-1 John Matthew Benight, b. 25 Sep 1972, Salt Lake City, Utah

A-1-4-7-7-6-3-2-2 Wanda Jean Benight, b. 16 Sep 1974, Oregon City, Oregon

A-1-4-7-7-6-3-3 Dianna Lynnray Baker, b. 21 Sep 1951, Boyes Hot Springs, California

A-1-4-7-7-6-3 m. 2nd 22 Dec 1966, Angela Belli Whitney

A-1-4-7-7-6-4 Gladine Rayella Baker, b. 3 Dec 1927, Hanford, CA, m. 26 Feb 1946, Fred Scott, m. 2nd Joseph Martin Newmann

A-1-4-7-7-6-5 Henry Fillmore, b. 16 Jun 1937, Hanford, CA m. 19 May 1958, Florence Forte

A-1-4-7-7-6 m. 3rd 1 Mar 1947, John Lutjens

A-1-4-7-7-7 Gertrude Marian Halstead, b. 1 Feb 1899, Fresno Co., California, m. 2 Mar 1918, George Sagaser, m. 2nd Lewis Jones, m. 3rd Kelly Adams

A-1-4-7-8 son, b. c1861, nfi

A-1-4-7 m. 3rd 4 Jul 1861, Phoebe Ann Roberts, b. c1843, d. c1912, Indiana

A-1-4-7-9 Clara Melissa Addington, b. 31 Mar 1862, Ringgold Co., Iowa

A-1-4-8 John Addington, b. 1 Mar 1820, Wayne Co., Indiana, d. 27 Apr 1908, Chester, Indiana
m. 3 Mar 1844, Wayne Co., Indiana, Sabrah Ann Sails, b. c1826, South Carolina, d. 1896, Wayne Co., Indiana
A-1-4-8-1 Daniel Elwood Addington, b. c1846, Indiana, d. ? young
A-1-4-8-2 Burgess Addington, b. c1849, d. young
A-1-4-8-3 Angie or Anise Addington, b. 1854, Indiana
m. ? 11 Mar 1875, Wayne Co., Indiana, Henry Hodgin
A-1-4-8-4 Julius Addington, b. c1859, Indiana, nfi
A-1-4-8-5 Benton Charles Addington, b. May 1860, Indiana, d. 21 Dec 1932, Chicago, IL (1900 Kenton Co., KY, 1910 Hamilton Co., Ohio)
m. 27 Oct 1887, Martha Benham
A-1-4-8-5-1 Sarah Addington, b. 6 Apr 1891, d. 7 Nov 1940, Cincinnati, Ohio, m. 20 Mar 1917, Howard Carl Reid
A-1-4-8-6 Leah Addington, b. 14 Mar 1862, d. 1942
m. 2 Oct 1912, Wayne Co., Indiana, Charles Crawford
A-1-4-8-7 William Dayton Addington, b. c1868, Indiana
m. 21 Oct 1899, Wayne Co., Indiana, Ida Hall
A-1-4-9 Martin S. Addington, b. c1823, Indiana,
m. 19 Sep 1844, Preble Co., Ohio, Nancy King, b. c1825, TN, d. 23 Sep 1882, Richmond, Indiana
A-1-4-9-1 Mary Elizabeth Addington, b. c1847, Eaton, Indiana, d. 1936, Galveston, Indiana
m. 1865, Jerome, IN, John Quincy Symons, b. 1843, d. 1929
A-1-4-9-1-1 Martin Van Meter Matthew Symons, b. 1865, Jerome, Indiana, d. 1944, Danville, Illinois
m. 1892, Kokomo, Indiana, Dora Alice Martz
A-1-4-9-1-2 Charles Edward Symons, b. 1867, Cedar Falls, Iowa, d. 1931, Sharon, PA, m. Emma Jane Leonard Queer
A-1-4-9-1-3 Schuyler Sydney Symons, b. 1869, Cedar Falls, Iowa, d. 1948, Washington, D.C., m. Jennie Elberta Mendel
A-1-4-9-1-4 Oliver Everett Symons, b. 1872, Jerome, IN, d. 1893
A-1-4-9-1-5 Edna Diana Symons, b. 1878, Jerome, IN, d. 1893
m. 1905, Galveston, IN, Frank Beeson
A-1-4-9-1-6 John Henry Symons, b. 1879, Jerome, IN, d. 1882
A-1-4-9-2 Delilah Addington, b. c1851, Indiana
m. ? 6 Dec 1868, Howard Co., Indiana, James Nicholas
A-1-4-10? Elizabeth "Betsey" Addington
m. 18 Apr 1822, Ichabod Gifford
A-1-4-11? Alice Addington ? m. 24 Jan 1830, James Graver
A-1-4-12? Louisa Addington, m. 23 Dec 1833, Nason Roberts

A-1-4 m. 2nd 25 Jan 1837, Chester, Wayne Co., Indiana, Rebecca
Johnson Thornton, b. 1795, South Carolina, d. 21 Aug 1862,
bur. Maxville Cemetery
A-1-5 Thomas Addington, b. 1 Dec 1778, 96 District, South
Carolina, d. 8 Mar 1839, Randolph Co., Indiana, bur.
Sparrow Creek Cemetery, Randolph Co., Indiana
  m. 11 Oct 1807, Mary Smith, b. 18 Jan 1786, NC, d. 25 Apr 1845,
  bur. Sparrow Creek Cemetery, Randolph Co., Indiana
A-1-5-1 Hannah Addington, b. 15 Nov 1808, d. 1854, dnm
A-1-5-2 Matilda Addington, b. 29 Aug 1810, d. 15 Mar 1811
A-1-5-3 David Smith Addington, b. 24 Feb 1812, d. 25 Feb 1813
A-1-5-4 Jesse Addington, b. 22 Jun 1814, Indiana, d. 24 Oct 1891
  m. 17 Jul 1834, Wayne Co., Indiana, Margaret Sullivan, b. 2
  Feb 1815, NC, d. 22 Aug 1892
A-1-5-4-1 Thomas Addington, b. 1836, d. 15 Jun 1854, bur. New
  Dayton Cem.
A-1-5-4-2 James M. Addington, b. Feb 1839, d. 11 Nov 1918
  m. 11 Jul 1857, Henrietta Holloway, b. 25 Dec 1838, Ohio, d. 16
  Sep 1905, Randolph Co., Indiana
A-1-5-4-2-1 Solomon H. Addington, b. Mar 1859, IN, d. 1930
  m. 22 Jan 1879, Jay Co., Indiana, Lucinda Munthenk
A-1-5-4-2-2 Thomas Jefferson Addington, b. c1860, Indiana
  m. 11 Sep 1877, Randolph Co., Indiana, Mary A. James, b.
  1859, Ohio
A-1-5-4-2-2-1 Luther M. Addington, b. 1879, Indiana
  m. 14 Nov 1907, Jay Co., Indiana, May Mowery
A-1-5-4-2-2-1-3 Evelyn Addington, b. 16 Jun 1913, Randolph
  Co., Indiana
  m. 20 May 1931, Randolph Co., IN, Othal Ronald Marsh
A-1-5-4-3 Robert Addington, nfi
A-1-5-5 James Addington, b. 12 Jul 1816, Indiana, d. 1881/2,
  Hancock Co., Indiana, bur. New Dayton Cem.
  m. 12 May 1836, Randolph Co., Indiana, Susan Kelly, b. 1815,
  Virginia, d. 23 Aug 1870
A-1-5-5-1 Mary Addington, b. 6 Nov 1837
  m. 1860, James Curtis Dodd, b. c1839, d. 23 Dec 1920,
  Winchester, Indiana
A-1-5-5-1-1 Lizzie Susan Dodd, b. c1862
A-1-5-5-1-2 James Dodd, b. c1867
A-1-5-5-1-3 William Dodd
A-1-5-5-1-4 Priscella Dodd, m. Lewis Payne
A-1-5-5-1-4-1 ? Russell Payne, b. c1899
A-1-5-5-1-5 ? Jane Estie Dodd, m. Kester Pike

A-1-5-5-2 William S. Addington, b. 1839, d. Feb 1893, Billbeck, Illinois, (1880 Butler Co., Kansas)
m. 28 Aug 1867, Randolph Co., Indiana, Mary L. Underwood, b. c1841, Indiana
A-1-5-5-2-1 Charles G. Addington, b. c1869, Indiana, d. Jun 1912, Winchester, Indiana, bur. Gas City, Grant Co., Indiana
m. 3 Feb 1894, Randolph Co., Indiana, Kate St. Clair
A-1-5-5-2-1-1 Marie Addington, b. c1897
m. 22 Feb 1913, Grant Co., Indiana, C. F. Lemaster
A-1-5-5-2-1-2 George Addington, b. c1898
m.. 22 Aug 1923, Grant Co., Indiana, Eulalie Gillam
A-1-5-5-2-1-3 Lillian Addington, b. 1900, prob. Grant Co., IN
A-1-5-5-2-1-4 Robert Addington, b. c1907
A-1-5-5-2-2 Frank Harold Addington, b. 24 Sep 1870, d. 26 Jan 1936, Indianapolis, Indiana
m. 14 Apr 1906, Jay Co., Indiana, Roxy Allen, div. c1921
A-1-5-5-2-2-1 Frank H. Addington, b. 22 Dec 1907, d. 4 Aug 1976, Tualatin, Oregon
m. 1935, Portland, OR, Valeria Gwendola Van Hyning
A-1-5-5-2-2-1-1 James Preston Addington, b. 5 Mar 1936, Washington Co., Oregon
m. 14 Nov 1958, Portland, Oregon, Yvonne Loretta Saarinen, b. 9 Mar 1940
A-1-5-5-2-2-1-1-1 Maxine Kay Addington, b. 8 Mar 1961
m. 13 Apr 1991, David Paul Box
A-1-5-5-2-2-1-1-2 Randall Glenn Addington, b. 29 May 1962, Hillsboro, Oregon
m. 18 Feb 1989, Laura Ann Robertson
A-1-5-5-2-2-2 James Allen Addington, b. 6 Nov 1916, Peoria, Illinois, d. 197?, Portland, Indiana
m. Lillian ?, m. 2nd Lucille Brown
A-1-5-5-2-3 Ottis (or Odes or Ola) Addington, b. c1873, d. March 1916, Union City, Indiana
m. 2 Nov 1895, Randolph Co., Indiana, Cora Gandy
A-1-5-5-3 George Wesley Addington, b. Oct 1844, d. 29 Dec 1917, bur. Maxville Cemetery
m. 1865, Rachel J. Burres, b. 1847, d. 1879, bur. Maxville Cem.
A-1-5-5-3-1 Effie L. Addington, b. 1868. d. aft 1924
m. 20 Jul 1893, Randolph Co., Indiana, Schuyler Williams
A-1-5-5-3-1-1 Doris Williams, b. c1896, m. 1916, Fred Wright
A-1-5-5-3-2 Edward A. Addington, b. 1871, d. 10 Feb 1921, Martinsville, Indiana
m. Edith Sears, b. 16 Oct 1872, Brantford, Ontario, d. 20 Sep 1913 Winchester, Indiana

A-1-5-5-3-2 m. 2nd Bessie ?

A-1-5-5-3 m. 2nd 19 Aug 1880, Randolph Co., Indiana, Magdalena Laura Gettle, b. 1852, Ohio

A-1-5-5-3-3 Ethel L. Addington, b. 23 May 1883
   m. 16 May 1906, Randolph Co., Indiana, John Hoover (lived at Dunkirk)

A-1-5-5-3-4 George Earl Addington, b. 25 Jan 1890, d. 15 Jul 1931, bur. Maxville Cem.
   m. 1 May 1913, Opal Edwards, b. 18 Sep 1893
   m. 2nd 1 Jul 1929, Randolph Co., IN, Anne Lee Armstrong

A-1-5-5-4 John Kelly Addington, b. 6 Jun 1853, Indiana, d. 20 Dec 1926
   m. 13 Mar 1880, Randolph Co., Indiana, Irene (Bond) Whitaker, b. 3 Jan 1854, NC (Irene, 1910 Montgomery Co., Ohio)

A-1-5-5-4-1 Clara L Addington (dau. of Irene), b. 1873, Indiana, m. Clarence Whitaker

A-1-5-5-4-2 Mabel G. Addington, b. 13 Apr 1886, Marion Co., IN
   m. ? Woodard (lived San Francisco)

A-1-5-6 Mercy Addington, b. 12 May 1819, d. 1894/5
   m. Littleberry Diggs, b. 11 Feb 1820, d. Dec 1849

A-1-5-6-1 Calvin Diggs, b. 13 Sep 1843
   m. 28 Oct 1877, Harriet Edgar

A-1-5-6-1-1 Bessie Diggs, d. young

A-1-5-6-1-2 Nellie E. Diggs

A-1-5-6 m. 2nd Joseph Hawkins

A-1-5-7 Joseph Addington, b. 10 Dec 1820, d. 12 Oct 1871
   m. 31 Oct 1845, Wayne Co., Indiana, Susan Sullivan, b. 12 Aug 1821, NC, d. 18 Dec 1896, Randolph Co., Indiana

A-1-5-7-1 Calvin Addington, b. 1846, d. 1849

A-1-5-7-2 Martha Ellen Addington, b. 12 Dec 1847, d. aft. 1922
   m. Elias Wright

A-1-5-7-3 Robert Nelson Addington, b. 10 Aug 1850, Randolph Co., Indiana, d. 14 Jul 1889
   m. Rebecca Jane Wright, b. 16 Aug 1855, Indiana, d. 1927

A-1-5-7-3-1 Rev. George Elvin Addington, b. 15 Aug 1874, d. 1970
   m. Lola Mabel Friar, b. 1884, d. 1957

A-1-5-7-3-1-1 Ruth Laurain Addington, b. 16 Jun 1903
   m. 26 Mar 1923, Randolph Co., IN, Henry Pickett Douglas

A-1-5-7-3-1-2 Opal Alice Addington, b. 25 Oct 1904, d. 25 Oct 1906

A-1-5-7-3-1-3 Roberta Leon Addington, b. 27 Jan 1907
   m. 11 Jul 1925, Randolph Co., Indiana, Charles Heston

A-1-5-7-3-1-3-1 Patricia Ann Heston, m. Roger Waltz

A-1-5-7-3-1-3-1-1 Karen Sue Waltz

A-1-5-7-3-1-4 Joseph Harold Addington, b. 21 Jan 1912, d. 30 Jul 1931, bur. New Dayton Cem.

A-1-5-7-3-1-5 Charles Harvey Addington, b. 11 Apr 1918, d. 1954, bur. Hopewell Cem.
m. Thana Alice Shafer, b. 1919

A-1-5-7-3-1-5-1 Chalene Jane Addington

A-1-5-7-3-1-5-2 Larry Lee Addington

A-1-5-7-3-1-5-3 Danny Joe Addington

A-1-5-7-3-1-6 George Elbert Addington, b. c1923, d. 30 Jul 1931, bur. New Dayton Cem.

A-1-5-7-3-2 Charles Wesley Addington, b. 1876
m. Mabel Hiatt

A-1-5-7-3-2-1 Chella Elena Addington, b. 9 Feb 1903
m. Harry Morgan

A-1-5-7-3-2-1-1 Cordellia Morgan

A-1-5-7-3-2-1-2 Francis Morgan

A-1-5-7-3-2-1-3 Chris Morgan

A-1-5-7-3-2-2 Carol Addington, b. 3 Jun 1904, m. Lyle Russell

A-1-5-7-3-2-2-1 Carolyle Russel

A-1-5-7-3-2-2-2 Barry Russell

A-1-5-7-3-3 Luther Elsworth Addington, b. 23 Dec 1878
m. 23 Dec 1899, Randolph Co., Indiana, Elsie W. Waltz

A-1-5-7-3-3-1 Lawrence Addington, b. 16 Sep 1901

A-1-5-7-3-3-2 Robert Nelson Addington, b. 24 Sep 1903, d. 1905

A-1-5-7-3-3-3 Basil Donnald Addington, b. c1905

A-1-5-7-3-3-4 Mahlon Addington, b. 15 Mar 1907

A-1-5-7-3-3-5 Esther Addington, d. 19 Apr 1912, Howard Co., Indiana (age 10)

A-1-5-7-3-4 Russell Wilson Addington, b. 4 Dec 1882
m. 16 Dec 1903, Randolph Co., Indiana, Nora Billman

A-1-5-7-3-4-1 Geraldine "? Constance Addington, b. 30 Mar 1906
m. 21 Aug 1924, Randolph Co., Indiana, Chloe Life

A-1-5-7-3-4-2 Wallace Addington, b. 3 Nov 1904

A-1-5-7-3-4-3 Harold W. Addington, b. 28 Sep 1917, Randolph Co., Indiana

A-1-5-7-3-5 Lena Gertrude Addington, b. 17 Feb 1887
m. Raymond Armstrong

A-1-5-7-3-5-1 Robert Nelson Armstrong, b. 1910, m. Rachel ?

A-1-5-7-3-5-1-1 Howard Armstrong

A-1-5-7-3-5-1-2 Raymond Armstrong

A-1-5-7-3-5-2 Rebecca Armstrong, d. young

A-1-5-7-3-5 m. 2nd Guy Friar

A-1-5-7-4 Franklin Madison Addington, b. 5 Dec 1853, d. 24 Oct
   1923, Randolph Co., Indiana, bur. New Dayton Cem.
   m. Anna Vanilla Wright, b. Jan 1859, d. 6 Jul 1925
A-1-5-7-4-1 John "Rufus" Addington, b. 17 Oct 1876, d. 1953
   m. 1902, Jeanetta Pearl Pogue, d. 3 Dec 1910, Randolph Co., IN
A-1-5-7-4-1-1 Marjorie Estella Addington, b. 1904, d. 1984, bur.
   Hopewell Cem.
   m. 25 Jun 1927, Randolph Co., Indiana, Delbert Baird, d. 1974
A-1-5-7-4-1-1-1 (stepdaughter) Mary Elizabeth Baird
   m. Herschel Taylor
A-1-5-7-4-1-1-1-1 Marlene Taylor, m. John Hershberger
A-1-5-7-4-1-1-1-2 David Taylor, m. Debra ?
A-1-5-7-4-1-1-1-3 Denny Taylor, m. Diana ?
A-1-5-7-4-1-1-1-4 Darlene Taylor, m. Mark Murphy
A-1-5-7-4-1-2 Lester Raymond Addington, b. 31 Jul 1905, d. 1986
   m. 28 Dec 1925, Randolph Co., Indiana, M. J. Elizabeth Lasley,
   b. 1902, d. 1983
A-1-5-7-4-1-2-1 William Lee Addington, b. 14 Aug 1926
   m. Teola Gulley
A-1-5-7-4-1-2-2 Jeanetta Addington, b. 1928
   m. Robert Smiley
A-1-5-7-4-1-2-2-1 Sarah Lee Smiley, b. 12 Apr 1957
   m. 6 Aug 1977, Dean Garringer
A-1-5-7-4-1-2-2-1-1 Erika Dawn Garringer, b. 5 Mar 1980
A-1-5-7-4-1-2-2-1-2 Justin Robert Garringer, b. 10 Aug 1981
A-1-5-7-4-1-2-3 Francis "Frank" Addington, b. 18 Apr 1931
   m. 3 Sep 1950, Anna Warnes, b. 5 Aug 1933
A-1-5-7-4-1-2-3-1 Michael Leroy Addington, b. 8 Oct 1951, d. 23
   Apr 1977
   m. Jun 1971, Sandy LeMay
A-1-5-7-4-1-2-3-2 Kina Ann Addington, b. 13 Jun 1954
   m. 29 Nov 1974, Mooreland, Indiana, Leslie Cunningham, b.
   19 Jul 1956
A-1-5-7-4-1-2-3-2-1 Hannah Beth Cunningham, b. 11 Jul 1976,
   Delaware Co., Indiana
A-1-5-7-4-1-2-3-2-2 Rhett Lester Cunningham, b. 6 Nov 1979,
   Delaware Co., Indiana
A-1-5-7-4-2 Harry C. Addington, b. 1879, d. 26 Dec 1899,
   Saratoga, Indiana
A-1-5-7-4-3 Hattie Maude Addington, b. 1881, d. 1955
   m. 15 Sep 1900, Randolph Co., IN, Jesse Cox, b. 1878, d. 1941
A-1-5-7-4-3-1 Everett R. Cox, b. 1909, d. 1989
   m. Elizabeth Sickles
A-1-5-7-4-3-1-1 Merrit L. Cox, b. 1909, d. 1989

m. Wilma Jean Pegg

A-1-5-7-4-3-1-1-1 Rebecca Sue Cox, b. 5 Aug 1958 (see A-1-5-7-4-6-2-2)

A-1-5-7-4-3-1-2 Marieta Cox, m. ? Willis

A-1-5-7-4-3-1-3 Hattie Ann Cox, m. ? Ludrick

A-1-5-7-4-3-1 m. 2nd Winifred Powers Elliott

A-1-5-7-4-3-1-4 Robert Cox

A-1-5-7-4-3-1-5 Jack Elliott Cox

A-1-5-7-4-3-2 Mildred Cox, m. Paul Heston

A-1-5-7-4-3-2-1 Melvin Lee Heston, m. Daisy ?

A-1-5-7-4-3-2 m. 2nd Bob Smith

A-1-5-7-4-3-3 Willard Albert Cox, m. Martha Ann Byrum

A-1-5-7-4-3-3-1 Ronald Cox

A-1-5-7-4-4 Earl Addington, b. 17 Mar 1883, d. 2 Jan 1884

A-1-5-7-4-5 Esta Addington, b. 14 Dec 1884, d. 11 Mar 1962
  m. 5 Nov 1906, Randolph Co., Indiana, Harry B. Woodbury,
  d. 1958

A-1-5-7-4-5-1 Floyd R. Woodbury, b. 2 Oct 1907, d. 5 Mar 1968
  m. Edna Swanson

A-1-5-7-4-5-2 George Clarence Woodbury, b. 9 Feb 1911, d. 1 Oct
  1984, m. Addaline Shaffer, d. 24 Oct 1911

A-1-5-7-4-5-2-1 Keith Eugene Woodbury, b. 12 Feb 1933
  m. Geneviere James

A-1-5-7-4-5-2-1-1 Dennis Eugene Woodbury, b. 9 Aug 1953
  m. Vicky Dillon

A-1-5-7-4-5-2-1-2 Connie Sue Woodbury, m. Randel Hoover

A-1-5-7-4-5-2-1-2-1 Erin Lyn Hoover, b. 24 Aug 1973

A-1-5-7-4-5-2-1-2-2 Katie Sue Hoover, b. 5 Mar 1980

A-1-5-7-4-5-2-1-2-3 Chase Randal Hoover, b. 29 Oct 1985

A-1-5-7-4-5-3-1-3 David Woodbury, b. 22 Oct 1962
  m. Stacey McCord

A-1-5-7-4-5-3-1-3-1 David Zachery Woodbury, b. 18 Jan 1986

A-1-5-7-4-5-3-1-3-2 Dustin Zane Woodbury

A-1-5-7-4-5-3-1-4 Dean Woodbury, b. 1 Aug 1964, m. Kelly ?

A-1-5-7-4-5-3-1-4-1 Alice Ann Woodbury

A-1-5-7-4-6 Willard Clayton Addington, b. 25 Jan 1891, d. 20 Jul
  1978
  m. 23 Nov 1921, Velma Fern Coats, b. 30 Jun 1894, d. 12 Mar
  1986

A-1-5-7-4-6-1 Chester Luther Addington, b. 6 Nov 1922
  m. Dorthy Frances Armistead

A-1-5-7-4-6-1-1 Paul Luther Addington, b. 1946
  m. Linda Dennis

A-1-5-7-4-6-1-1-1 Paul L. Addington, Jr., b. 1967, m. Gina ?

A-1-5-7-4-6-1-1-1-1 Brandon Addington, b. 1985
A-1-5-7-4-6-1-1-1-2 Megan Addington, b. 1986
A-1-5-7-4-6-1-1 m. 2nd Sherry Mannon, b. 1949
A-1-5-7-4-6-1-1-1-3 Shawn David Addington, b. 1972
A-1-5-7-4-6-1-1-1-4 Shelby Lee Addington, b. 1974
A-1-5-7-4-6-1-1-2 John Charles Addington, b. 1952
  m. Margaret Klosterman
A-1-5-7-4-6-1-1-2-1 John Charles Addington, Jr., b. 1978
A-1-5-7-4-6-1-1-2-2 Gretchen Ann Addington, b. 1981
A-1-5-7-4-6-1-1-3 Patricia Ann Addington, b. 1958
  m. William Johnson
A-1-5-7-4-6-1-1-3-1 William (Billy) Johnson, b. 1983
A-1-5-7-4-6-1-1-3-2 Julie Ann Johnson, b. 1985
A-1-5-7-4-6-2 Esta May Addington, b. 26 Jun 1926
  m. 10 Jun 1945, Howard Eugene Cunningham, d. 20 Nov 1976
A-1-5-7-4-6-2-1 Carol Lynn Cunningham, b. 1950
  m. 16 Aug 1970, William O. Hinshaw, b. 1947
A-1-5-7-4-6-2-1-1 Mark William Hinshaw, b. 9 Dec 1973
A-1-5-7-4-6-2-1-2 Greg Paul Hinshaw, b. 25 Jan 1975
A-1-5-7-4-6-2-2 Dean Howard Cunningham, b. 11 May 1954
  m. 22 Apr 1979, Rebecca Sue Cox
A-1-5-7-4-6-2-2-1 Matthew Dean Cunningham, b. 16 Nov 1979
A-1-5-7-4-6-2-2-2 Melissa Ruth Cunningham, b. 20 Jun 1982
A-1-5-7-4-6-2-2-3 Sarah Jo Cunningham, b. 17 Oct 1988
A-1-5-7-4-6-3 Melva Esther Addington, b. 16 May 1928
  m. 12 Aug 1951, James Olin Armistead, b. 26 Apr 1929
A-1-5-7-4-6-3-1 Deborah Kay Armistead, b. 20 Jan 1960
  m. Robert Wayne Zimmerman
A-1-5-7-4-6-3-1-1 Jessica Lynn Zimmerman, b. 16 Dec 1986
A-1-5-7-4-6-3-1-2 Robert James Zimmerman, b. 5 Dec 1988
A-1-5-7-4-6-3-2 James Franklin Armistead, b. 16 Nov 1961
  m. Pamela Suzanne Grigo, b. 26 Feb 1962
A-1-5-7-4-7 Lyra Addington, b. 8 Jul 1893, Randolph Co.,
  Indiana, d. 17 Nov 1970
  m. 1916, Eli Hiatt, b. 1893, d. 1967
A-1-5-7-4-7-1 Agnes Ireda Hiatt, b. 1918, m. Marvin E. Macy
A-1-5-7-4-7-1-1 Carolyn Sue Macy, b. 1938, m. John Chambers
A-1-5-7-4-7-1-2 Gail Edward Macy, b. 1940, m. Linda Chalfant
A-1-5-7-4-7-1-2-1 Abigail L. Macy
A-1-5-7-4-7-1-2-2 Michael E. Macy
A-1-5-7-4-7-1-3 Stephen Allan Macy, b. 1948, m. Judi Ross
A-1-5-7-4-7-1-4 Kenneth Armfield Macy, b. 1952
  m. Linda Chalfant, m. 2nd Sandra Streit
A-1-5-7-4-7-1-5 Martha Ruth Macy, b. 1953, m. Douglas Ruhe

A-1-5-7-4-7-2 Ruth Ann Hiatt, b. 1920, d. 1948

A-1-5-7-4-7-3 Richard Ollen Hiatt, b. 1922
m. Helen N. Wilson

A-1-5-7-4-7-3-1 Virginia Mae Hiatt, b. 1946

A-1-5-7-4-7-3-2 Elizabeth Ann Hiatt, b. 1947
m. Steven Hendrickson

A-1-5-7-4-7-3-2-1 Lurena Hendrickson

A-1-5-7-4-7-3-2-2 Benjamin Hendrickson

A-1-5-7-4-7-3-2-3 Stephanie Hendrickson

A-1-5-7-4-7-3-2-4 Marjorie Hendrickson

A-1-5-7-4-7-3-2-5 Stuart Hendrickson

A-1-5-7-4-7-3-3 Joyce Elaine Hiatt, b. 1948
m. Charles Lee Beard

A-1-5-7-4-7-3-3-1 Daniel W. Partain

A-1-5-7-4-7-3-4 Rachel Louise Hiatt, b. 1950
m. Rev. Wayne Stanhope

A-1-5-7-4-7-3-4-1 Jessica Stanhope

A-1-5-7-4-7-3-5 Rebecca Sue Hiatt, b. 1954

A-1-5-7-4-7-4 Norma Lee Hiatt, b. 1930, m. Ivan D. Bar

A-1-5-7-4-7-4-1 Beverly Kay Barr, b. 27 Jun 1950
m. Elvan Lamb

A-1-5-7-4-7-4-2 David Wayne Barr, b. 1 Aug 1951
m. Nancy Martin

A-1-5-7-4-7-4-3 Larry Allan Barr, b. 1953

A-1-5-7-4-7-4-4 Lois Ann Barr, b. 6 Aug 1954, m. Jerry Skinner

A-1-5-7-4-7-4-5 Sharon Darlene Barr, b. 20 Dec 1955
m. ? Christenberry

A-1-5-7-4-7-4-6 Amy Lise Barr, b. 21 Sep 1971

A-1-5-7-5 Mary Jamima Addington, b. 21 Oct 1856, Indiana
m. 5 Aug 1882, Randolph Co., Indiana, George Williams

A-1-5-7-5-1 Charles Williams, d. in Texas

A-1-5-7-6 George Emerson Addington, b. Nov 1859, d. 16 Apr
1922, ni
m. Indiana Rose Bolinger, b. 1862, d. 23 Dec 1920

A-1-5-7-7 Carrie Oscar Addington, b. 1861, d. 24 Mar 1881, bur.
New Dayton Cem.

A-1-5-7-8 Alvin Waldo "Wal" Addington, b. 23 Jan 1865, d. 29
Jul 1896, Randolph Co., Indiana, bur. Buena Vista Cem.
m. 4 Apr 1893, Randolph Co., Indiana, Laura May Allen, b. 18
Jan 1864, d. 1 Mar 1894

A-1-5-7-8-1 Archie Rombaugh Addington, b. 23 Feb 1894, d. 18
Sep 1972, Fresno, California
m. 30 Aug 1916, Saratoga, Indiana, Mary Frances Hitchcock

A-1-5-7-8-1-1 Madona Faye Addington, b. 26 Nov 1917, Bloomington, Indiana

m. 17 Jan 1941, Reno, NV Robert Noel Hansen, b. 27 May 1916, Sanger, California

A-1-5-7-8-1-1-1 Charlotte Lee Hansen, b. 28 Jul 1942, Sacramento, California

m. 8 Aug 1965, Berkley, California, Justin Albion Roberts

A-1-5-7-8-1-1-1-1 Bryce Albion Robert, b. 5 Mar 1973, Berkley, California

A-1-5-7-8-1-1-2 Kenneth Robert Hensen, b. 10 Aug 1948, Sacramento, California

m. 2 Jan 1971, Sacramento, California, Nancy Ann Housh

A-1-5-7-8-1-1-2-1 Kimberly Ann Hansen, b. 6 Dec 1972, Chico, California

A-1-5-7-8-1-1-2-2 Jeffrey Robert Hansen, b. 12 May 1980, Chico, California

A-1-5-7-8-1-1-2-3 Kristen Nicole Hansen, b. 30 Nov 1990, Chico, California

A-1-5-7-8-1-2 William W. Addington, b. 5 Oct 1919, Bloomington, Indiana

A-1-5-7-8-1-3 Elmer Louis Addington, b. 18 Sep 1922, Bloomington, Indiana, d. 13 May 1923, Bloomington, Indiana, bur. Buena Vista Cem.

A-1-5-7-8 m. 2nd 2 May 1896, Randolph Co., IN, Ida Alice Kelly

A-1-5-8 George Addington, b. 19 Sep 1822, d. 9 Apr 1885

m. 6 Apr 1854, Priscilla Horn, d. c1856

A-1-5-8 m. 2nd 11 Jul 1857, Priscilla Clinton, b. 5 Mar 1838, Ohio, d. 18 Jun 1900

A-1-5-8-1 Mercy Ellen Addington, b. 14 May 1858

m. Elvin L. Smithson, b. 1853

A-1-5-8-1-1 Lena G. Smithson

A-1-5-8-1-2 Harry W. Smithson, b. 1880, m. ni

A-1-5-8-1-3 Emma Smithson, b. 1885, m. ? Stettson

A-1-5-8-1-3-1 Max Stettson

A-1-5-8-1-4 Hazel D. Smithson, b. 1891

A-1-5-8-2 Nora R. Addington, b. 14 Oct 1860

m. 17 Oct 1878, Randolph Co., Indiana, Granville Barnes

A-1-5-8-2-1 Carl Barnes, m. Pearl Clevenger

A-1-5-9 Mary Addington, b. 23 Jan 1825, Wayne Co., Indiana, d. 22 Jun 1895, Hamilton Co., Indiana

m. 4 Mar 1844, Randolph Co., Indiana, William Roberts (lived Oaks Landing, IN), b. 22 Dec 1820, d. 26 Apr 1896, Hamilton Co., Indiana

A-1-5-9-1 Amy Roberts, b. 21 Jan 1845, Randolph Co., Indiana, d. 11 Sep 1845

A-1-5-9-2 Charles C. Roberts, b. 7 Nov 1846, Randolph Co., Indiana, d. 28 Mar 1931, Elgin, Nebraska
m. 30 Jan 1870, Mary Catherine Wenrick

A-1-5-9-3 Jeremiah S. Roberts, b. 25 Feb 1848, d. 22 Apr 1934, Oakland, California
m. 7 Nov 1872, Sarah Adams, m. 2nd 10 Jan 1895, Mrs. Clara E. Baker

A-1-5-9-4 Joseph P. Roberts, b. 11 Jun 1850, d. 17 Dec 1914, Hamilton Co., Indiana
m. 19 Jan 1871, Sarah Kepner
m. 2nd 14 Nov 1890?, Lena Honway

A-1-5-9-5 William Watson Roberts, b. 24 Aug 1852, d. 1 Aug 1886, m. 14 Jan 1877, Sarah Wasson

A-1-5-9-6 Martha Matilda Roberts, b. 27 Mar 1854, d. 11 Nov 1913, Hamilton Co., Indiana
m. 25 Jul 1872, John Zook, m. 2nd James Horace Beaver

A-1-5-9-7 Thomas T. Roberts, b. 26 Feb 1856, d. 1921
m. Lulu Ackman

A-1-5-9-8 Alpheus Lincoln Roberts, b. 15 Oct 1857, d. Mar 1929
m. 11 Aug 1880, Naomi Wasson
m. 2nd 18 Jun 1892, Mary Ann Redmond

A-1-5-9-9 Mercy Leota Roberts, b. 10 Jun 1859, d. Marion Co., IN
m. 24 Nov 1878, Thomas A. Silvey

A-1-5-9-10 Mary Alice Roberts, b. 10 Jan 1861, d. 4 Oct 1949, Hamilton Co., Indiana
m. 25 Nov 1883, William Pfaff, m. 2nd 31 Jul 1885?, John Gardner

A-1-5-9-11 Elvira "Ella" Roberts, b. 5 Aug 1862, d. 1959, CA
m. 29 Jan 1886, Charles Fearey
m. 2nd Henry Leander Conway

A-1-5-9-12 Samuel Ulyses Roberts, b. 19 Mar 1864, d. 1904
m. Myrtle Yancy

A-1-5-9-13 Sherman Roberts, b. 8 Apr 1867, Hamilton Co., Indiana, d. 27 Apr 1947, Indiana
m. 27 Apr 1892, Frances Rumell, m. 2nd Florence ?

A-1-5-9-14 Lily Mae Roberts, b. 12 Nov 1869, Hamilton Co., Indiana, d. 23 Jun 1940, Indianapolis, Indiana
m. 9 Jun 1895, Robert Donley Gatts, m. 2nd John Lewallyn

A-1-5-10 Elizabeth Addington, b. 28 Sep 1827, d. 25 Dec 1903, Winchester, Indiana
m. 26 Sep 1851, Randolph Co., Indiana, Marshall W. Diggs, b. 3 Oct 1824, d. 28 Sep 1897 (lived Fort Recovery, Ohio)

A-1-5-10-1 Ella Diggs, b. c1852
A-1-5-10-2 Calvin W. Diggs
A-1-5-10-2-1 Mary Jane Diggs, b. c1884
A-1-5-10-3 Albert B. Diggs
A-1-5-10-4 Elizabeth E. "Lybbie" Diggs
A-1-5-10-5 William Seward Diggs, b. 10 Feb 1862, Cincinnati,
  Ohio, m. 26 Sep 1886, Fremont, Ohio, Emma C. Hensel, b. 25
  Oct 1862
A-1-5-10-5-1 Ethel E. Diggs
A-1-5-10-5-2 Mary Ione Diggs
A-1-5-10-6 Marshall W. Diggs, Jr.
A-1-5-10-7 Mary E. Diggs
A-1-5-10-8 Mercy I. Diggs
A-1-5-10-9 Cora E. Diggs
A-1-5-11 (Rev.) Thomas Addington, b. 5 Dec 1829, d. 1 Feb 1912,
  bur. Bear Creek Cem.
  m. 8 Feb 1851, Randolph Co., Indiana, Martha Ann Hughes, b.
  1832, Ohio, d. 25 Mar 1885
A-1-5-11-1 Zeruiah J. Addington, b. c1852, d. aft. 1922
m. John E. Terrell
A-1-5-11-1-1 Morton Terrell, b. c1868
A-1-5-11-1-2 Margaret (Ada) "Elizabeth" Terrell, b. 1870
A-1-5-11-1 m. 2nd 12 Jun 1875, Randolph Co., Indiana, John W.
  Malott (lived West Fort, AR)
A-1-5-11-1-3 Estella Malott
A-1-5-11-1-4 Josie Malott, m. ? Asa Freel
A-1-5-11-1-5 Raymond Malott
A-1-5-11-1-6 Ruth Mallot
A-1-5-11-1-7 child, d. infancy
A-1-5-11-2 Alfred M. Addington, b. Nov 1854, IN, d. 23 Feb 1928
  m. 12 Jun 1875, Amerian P. McKee, b. Aug 1854, Indiana, d. 10
  Mar 1927
A-1-5-11-2-1 Minnie Esta Addington, d. infancy
A-1-5-11-2-2 Clyde W. Addington, b. 1877, Indiana, d. aft. 1928
  m. Flora Martin
A-1-5-11-2-2-1 Helen Addington, b. 28 Apr 1903
  m. 9 Jun 1922, Ivan Ernest Clear
A-1-5-11-2-2-1-1 Francis Clear
A-1-5-11-2-2-1-2 Gene Clear
A-1-5-11-2-2-2 Cecil T. Addington, b. c1907/8, d. 1980
  m. Varda Huffer
A-1-5-11-2-2-2-1 Marcia Addington, b. 19 May 1947
  m. Terry Roberts
A-1-5-11-2-2-2-1-1 Jennifer Robert, b. Aug 1974

A-1-5-11-2-2-2-1-2 Thomas Roberts, b. Jan 1976
A-1-5-11-2-3 Cora P. Addington, b. c1879, Indiana, d. aft. 1928
   m. 19 Aug 1899, Randolph Co., Indiana, Cecil C. Fisher
A-1-5-11-2-3-1 Guy Fisher
A-1-5-11-2-3-2 Ermin Fisher
A-1-5-11-2-3-3 Ralph Fisher
A-1-5-11-2-3-4 Margery Fisher
A-1-5-11-3 Emerson H. Addington, b. 1858, Indiana, d. aft 1922,
   (1922 New Orleans)
   m. 1 Jan 1885, Randolph Co., Indiana, Grace A. Watts
A-1-5-11-3-1 Constance Grace Addington, b. 26 Apr 1886
   m. Frank Bynner Davenport
A-1-5-11-3-1-1 Mary Elizabeth Davenport, m. ? Marsh
A-1-5-11-3-1-2 Ruth Davenport
A-1-5-11-3-1-3 Thomas Davenport
A-1-5-11-3-1-4 John E. Davenport
A-1-5-11-3-1-5 Katherine Davenport
A-1-5-11-3-1-6 Benjamin Davenport
A-1-5-11-4 Calvin T. Addington, b. Jun 1862, IN, d. aft. 1922
   m. 9 Oct 1884, Randolph Co., Indiana, Isadora Ray, b. 25 Apr
   1865, d. 19 Feb 1920
A-1-5-11-4-1 Inez Addington, b. 30 Jul 1885
   m. 14 Mar 1905, Randolph Co., Indiana,. Everett Gantz
A-1-5-11-4-1-1 Son
A-1-5-11-4-1-2 Adopted Daughter
A-1-5-11-4-2 Evert Ray Addington, b. 15 Nov 1893, d. 1924
   m. 31 Dec 1915, Randolph Co., Indiana, Edith Lasley
A-1-5-11-4-2-1 Isadora Addington, ? b. 1922, m. Francis Beck
A-1-5-11-5 Jesse M. Addington, b. 1868, Indiana, d. 24 Sep 1891,
   Ridgeville, Indiana
   m. 1 Nov 1890, Randolph Co., Indiana, Rose Ward
A-1-5-11-5-1 Roberta Zoe Addington, b. 5 Aug 1891
   m. 9 Feb 1912, Marion Co., Indiana, Wetzel Swartz
A-1-5-11-5-1-1 Martha Star Swartz
A-1-5-11-5-1-2 Addie Ann Swartz
A-1-5-11-5-1-3 W. Emerson Swartz
A-1-5-11 m. 2nd 11 Sep 1887, Margaret (Ellis) Painter, b. Sep
   1841, d. 13 Jul 1922
A-1-5-12 d. in infancy
A-1-5-13 d. in infancy
A-1-6 Mary Addington, b. 2 Nov 1780, d. 12 Mar 1866, Hancock
   Co., Indiana
   m. 26 Sep 1801, Thomas Roberts, b. 1780, d. 1831, Wayne Co.,
   Indiana

A-1-6-1 Martha Roberts, b. 1803
A-1-6-2 Joseph Roberts, b. 1805
A-1-6-3 Elizabeth Roberts, b. 1807
A-1-6-4 William Roberts, b. 1809, m. Mary Addington
A-1-6-4-1 Clara Belle Roberts, b. 16 Jul 1871, Noblesville, In, d. 6
    May 1965, m. 13 Sep 1893, James Carpenter
A-1-6-4-1-1 Mary Alma Carpenter, b. 14 Apr 1895, d. 30 Dec 1896
A-1-6-4-1-2 Maggie Mabel Carpenter, b. 9 Oct 1897, Nebraska, d.
    28 Sep 1983, m. 12 Dec 1917, Cornelius Floyd Bollacker
A-1-6-4-1-3 Gladys Alice Carpenter, b. 10 Dec 1899, Nebraska, m.
    29 Jun 1921, J. Elmer Yost
A-1-6-4-1-4 John Herald Carpenter, b. 15 Apr 1902, Nebraska, d.
    21 Jul 1913
A-1-6-4-1-5 Andrew Ralph Carpenter, b. 15 Dec 1904, Blair,
    Nebraska, d. 7 Mar 1905
A-1-6-4-1-6 Dorothy Irene Carpenter, b. 14 Oct 1909, Blair,
    Nebraska, m. 17 Jun 1931, Richard Oliver Woodin
A-1-6-4-1-7 Gertrude Adelle Carpenter, b. 24 Dec 1911, Blair,
    Nebraska, d. 8 Aug 1917
A-1-6-4-2 Arza Roberts, b. 26 Jul 1873, Noblesville, Indiana
A-1-6-4-3 Otha Arthur "Otto" Roberts, b. 16 Mar 1876, Cicero,
    IN, d. 18 Apr 1937, m. 27 Mar 1903, Stella Mae Sward
A-1-6-4-4 Alma Maud Roberts, b. 11 Feb 1879, Looking Glass,
    Nebraska, d. 28 Sep 1969, m. Earl ?
A-1-6-4-5 Grace Mabel Roberts, b. 14 Jul 1881, NE, d. 1 Mar 1919
    m. Al Evans
A-1-6-4-6 Robert Edward Roberts, b. 23 Apr 1884, Elgin,
    Nebraska, d. 4 Jul 1945, m. Jun 1905 Grace Mae Camp
A-1-6-4-7 Emma Roberts, b. 23 Apr 1887, Nebraska, d. 2 Dec
    1968, m. 12 Sep 1904, Jonah Gleason Totten
A-1-6-4-8 Cecila Hazel Roberts
A-1-6-4-9 William D. Roberts, b. 16 Nov 1891, Nebraska, d. 8
    Nov 1976, m. Buelah Round
A-1-6-5 Sarah Roberts, b. 1810
A-1-6-6 Jesse Roberts, b. 1812, d. 1870
A-1-6-7 Mary "Polly" Roberts, b. 1814, d. 1892
    m. 1835, John Walker, b. 1813, d. 1871
A-1-6-7-1 Melissa Walker, b. 1837, d. 1839
A-1-6-7-2 William Walker, b. 1839, d. 1909
    m. Lavina Personnett, b. 1842, d. 1867
A-1-6-7-2-1 Raleigh Clinton Walker, b. 1865, d. 1946
    m. 1899, Mary Idessia Moore, b. 1882, d. 1948
A-1-6-7-2-1-1 H. Ray Walker, m. M. Grace Brown
A-1-6-7-2-1-1-1 Garfield Walker

A-1-6-7-2-1-1-2 Howard E. Walker
A-1-6-7-2-1-1-3 Mary M. Walker
A-1-6-7-2-1-1-4 John R. Walker
A-1-6-7-2-1-1-5 Edgar A. Walker
A-1-6-7-2-1-2 Raleigh Walker, Jr.
A-1-6-7-2-1-3 Bertha Walker
A-1-6-7-2-1-4 Doris Walker
A-1-6-7-2-1-5 Carl Walker
A-1-6-7-2-1-6 Robert Walker
A-1-6-7-2-1-7 Martha Walker
A-1-6-7-2-1-8 Herbert Walker
A-1-6-7-2-1-9 Donnabelle Walker
A-1-6-7-2-1-10 Glen Walker
A-1-6-7-2-1-11 Calvin Walker
A-1-6-7-2-1-12 Glen Walker
A-1-6-7-2-1-13 Mary Walker
A-1-6-7-3 Winford Walker, b. 1843, d. 1891
A-1-6-7-4 Martha Walker, b. 1845, d. 1860
A-1-6-7-5 Jimmy Walker, b. 1848, d. 1860
A-1-6-7-6 Sarah Walker, b. 1851, d. 1882
A-1-6-7-7 Mary D. Walker, b. 1856, d. 1871
A-1-6-8 Thomas Roberts, Jr., b. 1816, d. 1878
   m. 31 Oct 1839, Martha Hart
A-1-7 Sarah Addington, b. 12 Sep 1783, Union Co., South
   Carolina, d. 26 Aug 1814
   m. 6 Nov 1806, Phineas Roberts, b. 16 Aug 1782, d. 21 May
   1836, Chester, Indiana
A-1-7-1 Martha Roberts, b. 14 Oct 1808, Chester, Indiana
A-1-7-2 John Roberts, b. 6 Apr 1810, Chester, Indiana
A-1-7-3 Phineas Roberts, Jr., b. c1811, Ohio (1850 Grant Co., IN)
A-1-7-3-1 Martha Roberts, b. c1842, Ohio
A-1-7-4 Elijah Roberts, b. 1 Dec 1812, Chester, Indiana
   m. Elizabeth ?
A-1-7-4-1 Wilson Roberts, b. 1835
A-1-7-4-2 Ambrose Robert, b. 1838
A-1-7-4-3 Ruth A. Roberts, b. 1841
A-1-7-4-4 Mahala Roberts, b. 1846
A-1-7-4-5 Joseph Roberts, b. 1849
A-1-7-5 Elizabeth Roberts, b. 9 Jan 1814, d. 5 Jan 1836, Chester,
   Indiana
A-1-8 Elizabeth Addington, b. 9 Feb 1787, d. 8 Mar 1841, Wayne
   Co., Indiana
   m. 1 Oct 1807, Warren Co., Ohio, James Martindale, b. 18 Mar
   1778, d. 28 May 1850, Wayne Co., Indiana

A-1-8-1 John A. Martindale, b. 13 Apr 1809, Wayne Co.,
   Indiana, d. 30 Mar 1850
   m. Lydia Hatfield, b. 24 Jan 1810, d. 9 May 1892
A-1-8-1-1 James William Martindale, b. 5 Dec 1829, d. 1916
   m. 20 Nov 1848, Lydia King
A-1-8-1-2 Sarah J. Martindale, m. William F. Dean
A-1-8-1-3 Elizabeth Adeline Martindale, m. George Davis
A-1-8-2 William Addington Martindale, b. 11 Jun 1814, Wayne
   Co., Indiana, d. 14 Feb 1873, Duncan, Washington Co., UT,
   m. Mahala Stigelman
A-1-8-2-1 William Clinton Martindale, b. 10 Jul 1834, d. 9 Jul
   1911, Oakley, Idaho
   m. 5 May 1854, Matilda Jane McMurray
   m. 2nd 30 Oct 1871, Lydia Marilla DeHart
   m. 3rd 22 Jul 1885, Mary Ellen Bagley
A-1-8-2-2 Martha Jane Martindale, b. 1 Feb 1837, Wayne Co.,
   Indiana, m. William Allred
A-1-8-2 m. 2nd Elizabeth Bunnell
A-1-8-2-3 Henrietta Martindale, m. Joseph McCollough
A-1-8-2 m. 3rd Rebecca Ann Haynes
A-1-8-2 m. 4th Caroline Smith, div., 1858
A-1-8-2 m. 5th Isabelle Ufrasia Pratt
A-1-8-2-4 Alonzo Pratt Martindale, b. 30 Apr 1859, d. 27 Apr
   1920, SLC, Utah
   m. 4 Feb 1882, Mary Elizabeth McIntosh
   m. 2nd Josephine Carver
A-1-8-2-5 John Albert Martindale, b. 5 Jul 1862, Grantsville,
   Utah, d. 1941/4 Pocatello, Idaho
A-1-8-2-6 Susannah Isabella Martindale, b. 26 Mar 1864, Utah
   m. 31 Dec 1883, James Keller Dayley
A-1-8-2-7 William Lyman Martindale, b. 18 Jan 1867, Virgin
   City, Utah, d. 13 Jan 1905, Oakley, Idaho
   m. 2 Apr 1891, Helen Agnes Civilla Lewis
A-1-8-2-8 Minnie Martindale, b. c1869, Virgin City, Utah
A-1-8-2-9 Athan Thomas Martindale, b. 18 Jan 1871, d. 12 Aug
   1949, m. 1902, Angeline McMurray
A-1-8-2 m. 6th 6 Jul 1867, Kindness Ann Haynes
A-1-8-2-10 Rebecca Ann Martindale, b. 30 Apr 1869, Duncan
   Retreat, Utah, d. 2 Feb 1959, Mills, Utah
   m. 8 Apr 1890, Albert Russell
A-1-8-2-10-1 Eva Russell, b. 1 Apr 1891, Grafton, Utah
A-1-8-2-10-2 Alvaretta Russell, b. 1 Mar 1894, Grafton, Utah
   m. Matthew Emauel Hartley
A-1-8-2-10-3 Flora May Russell, b. 26 Feb 1896, Grafton, Utah

m. William Chester Wright

A-1-8-2-10-4 Ellis Alonzo Russell, m. Estella Roundy

A-1-8-2-10-5 Wayne Russell, b. 23 Nov 1901, Hinckley, Utah

A-1-8-2-10-6 Hortense Russell, b. 28 Oct 1902, Grafton, Utah
m. Lindau Foremaster

A-1-8-2-10-7 Rowena Russell, b. 3 Jan 1906, Grafton, Utah

A-1-8-2-10-8 William Cyril Russell

A-1-9 James Addington, b. 6 Feb 1789, South Carolina, d. Oct
1860, Anderson, Co., Kansas
m. 15 Jun 1809, Preble Co., Ohio, Nancy Lewallyn, b. 1792,
Pennsylvania, d. 9 Nov 1851,Randolph Co., Indiana

A-1-9-1 John Lewallyn Addington, b. 1810, d. 1 Mar 1878,
Hardin Co., Iowa (1860 Anderson Co., Kansas)
m. 8 Nov 1832, Randolph Co., Indiana, Sally (or Sarah)
Stephens, d. 13 Dec 1847

A-1-9-1-1 James Alexander Addington, b. 11 Dec 1833, late 1880
to Kansas City, d. 29 Apr 1886, Missouri
m 1 Dec 1855, Nancy Kelly, b. 1 Jan 1831, Virginia, d. 1907,
Kansas City, Missouri

A-1-9-1-1-1 Jasper Addington, b. 18 Aug 1856, Indiana, d. 1910
(1900 Carroll Co., IN, 1910 Jackson Co., MO)
m. ? 1st Martha ?, d. bef 1910

A-1-9-1-1-1-1 Carl Addington, b. c1881, Indiana
m. Maud Gossett

A-1-9-1-1-1-1-1 Martin R. Addington, b. 1903, Missouri
m. 1928, Elizabeth Hays

A-1-9-1-1-1-1-2 Hiatt C. Addington, b. 1905, Missouri
m. 1923, Miram U. Ketchem

A-1-9-1-1-1-1-2-1 Carl Addington, Jr.
m. 1932, Eleanor J. Marshall

A-1-9-1-1-1-1-2-1-1 Sally Jo Addington, b. 26 Oct 1932

A-1-9-1-1-1-1-2-2 Lester C. Addington, m. Rea Neeley

A-1-9-1-1-1-1-2-2-1 Stephen Addington

A-1-9-1-1-1-1-2-2-2 Michael Addington

A-1-9-1-1-1-1-2-3 Alfred G. Addington, m. 1946, Vera Johnson

A-1-9-1-1-1-1-2-4 Nancy E. Addington, m. J. Lereok, 3 children

A-1-9-1-1-1-1-3 Carl Addington, Jr., b. 1907, Nebraska

A-1-9-1-1-1-1-4 Mary Lee Addington, b. 1908, Missouri, d. 1910

A-1-9-1-1-1-1-5 Lester C. Addington, b. 1912

A-1-9-1-1-1-1-6 Alfred G. Addington, b. 1914

A-1-9-1-1-1-1-7 Nancy E. Addington, b. 1915

A-1-9-1-1-1 m. 2nd 1884, Eva Hiatt, d. 1901

A-1-9-1-1-1-2 Winona Addington, b. c1885, Indiana
m. ? Edward Mutt

A-1-9-1-1-1-3 Dortha Addington, b. c1891, Missouri
m. 1911, Sherman Kilmer
A-1-9-1-1-1-4 Gernsie Addington, b. c1894, Iowa, d. 1953
m. 1912, Lawrence Miller
A-1-9-1-1-1-4-1 Melborn Miller, b. 1913, m. Lucile Burgess
A-1-9-1-1-1-4-1-1 Judith Ann Miller, b. 1934
m. Jeffrey Scott, two sons
A-1-9-1-1-1-4-1-2 Andrea Miller, b. 1935
A-1-9-1-1-1-4-1-3 Larry Miller, b. 1941
A-1-9-1-1-1-5 Joseph Addington, d. in infancy
A-1-9-1-1-2 Newton Addington, b. 5 Sep 1858, Kansas
m. Sadie Vincent, b. 1863, Michigan
A-1-9-1-1-2-1 Floyd Addington, b. 1887, d. 1898
A-1-9-1-1-2-2 d. in infancy
A-1-9-1-1-2-3 Hazel Addington, b. 1889, d. 1924
m. 4 Dec 1910, Howell Co., Missouri, Walter Alsup
A-1-9-1-1-2-3-1 Merrie Alsup
A-1-9-1-1-2-3-2 Flinton Alsup
A-1-9-1-1-2-3 m. 2nd ? Johnson
A-1-9-1-1-2-3-3 Hazel Johnson, b. 1924
A-1-9-1-1-2-4 James Addington, m. Merie Enyard
A-1-9-1-1-2-4-1 Newton Addington
A-1-9-1-1-2-4-2 Maxine Addington
A-1-9-1-1-2-4 m. 2nd Eva Anderson
A-1-9-1-1-2-4-3 James V. Addington, b. 1934
m. 1953, Marity McTernan
A-1-9-1-1-2-4-3-1 Mark Stevens Addington, b. 1956
A-1-9-1-1-2-4-3-1-1 Ashley Marie Addington, b. c1983
A-1-9-1-1-2-4-3-1-2 Lindsay Addington, b. c1983
A-1-9-1-1-2-4-3-2 Cynthia Lee Addington, b. 1957
A-1-9-1-1-2-5 Annetta Addington, m. 1937, Walter Ludwig
A-1-9-1-1-2-6 Roe Addington, m. Charlotte Vestel
A-1-9-1-1-2-6-1 Rosemary Addington
A-1-9-1-1-2-7 Raymond Addington, b. 18 Dec 1903, Randolph
Co., Indiana, m. Frances Urrell
A-1-9-1-1-2-7-1 Raymond Lee Addington
A-1-9-1-1-2-7-1-1 Helen Addington, b. 1958
A-1-9-1-1-2-7-2 Irean Addington
A-1-9-1-1-3 Alice Addington, b. 19 Apr 1861, Indiana,
m 6 Nov 1882, Randolph Co., Indiana, Albert Watterman
? m. c1888, Thomas Kelly, adopted Roscoe Kelly, b. 1889
A-1-9-1-1-4 William Marion Addington, b. 16 Jun 1863,
Indiana, d. 26 Jan 1912

m. 26 Oct 1886, Rebecca Miltida Herd, Kansas City, Missouri, d. 28 Sep 1942

A-1-9-1-1-4-1 Blanche Addington, b. 19 Jul 1889
  m. 16 Aug 1910, Walter J. Sanders
A-1-9-1-1-4-1-1 Walter Sanders, b. Oct 1917
  m. 1 Aug 1946, Frances Lepold
A-1-9-1-1-4-1-1-1 William Leroy Sanders
A-1-9-1-1-4-1-2 William J. Sanders, b. 12 Oct 1918
  m. 12 Sep 1938, Blanche Volchaster
A-1-9-1-1-4-1-2-1 Robert Sanders, d. at age 3
A-1-9-1-1-4-1-2-2 Eddie Lee Sanders, b. 5 Dec 1951
A-1-9-1-1-4-1-3 Noma Marian Sanders, b. 10 Jan 1921
  m. 12 Apr 1941, Samuel Hammond, div.
A-1-9-1-1-4-1-4 Lula Jane Sanders, b. 1922, d. 1923
A-1-9-1-1-4-1-5 Francis L. Sanders, b. 4 Jan 1924
  m. 15 Jan 1947, Elnora DeVault
A-1-9-1-1-4-2 Florence Addington, b. 26 Oct 1891, d. Feb 1949
  m. 1917, Harry Cornman, ni
A-1-9-1-1-4-3 Joy Addington, b. 1894
  m. Raymond O. Mountain
A-1-9-1-1-4-3-1 Elaine Mountain, b. 28 Feb 1916
  m. 1935, Louis V. Portesi
A-1-9-1-1-4-3-1-1 Louis V. Portesi, Jr., b. 18 Mar 1936
A-1-9-1-1-4-3-1-2 Patricia E. Portesi, b. 15 Oct 1939
A-1-9-1-1-4-3-1-3 Marlena M. Portesi, b. 28 May 1942
A-1-9-1-1-4-3-2 Eilene Mountain, b. 28 Feb 1916
  m. 1934, Robert P. Bartine
A-1-9-1-1-4-3-2-1 Margie Joy Bartine, b. 26 Mar 1936
A-1-9-1-1-4-3-2-2 Roberta P. Bartine, b. 29 Apr 1938
A-1-9-1-1-4-3-2-3 Shirley E. Bartine, b. 28 May 1943
A-1-9-1-1-4-3-3 Raymond O. Mountain, Jr., b. 1 Nov 1919
  m. 10 May 1941, Verball Garbutt, 3 children
A-1-9-1-1-4-3-4 Harold Mountain, b. 20 Sep 1922, dnm
A-1-9-1-1-4-3-5 Betty Mountain, b. 11 Feb 1925
  m. 6 Dec 1946, Charles Cox
A-1-9-1-1-4-3-5-1 Pamilia J. Cox
A-1-9-1-1-4-3-5-2 Charlene M. Cox
A-1-9-1-1-4-3-5-3 Stephen Cox
A-1-9-1-1-4-3-6 Netty Mountain, b. 11 Feb 1925
  m. Ernie Potts, 3 children
A-1-9-1-1-4-3-7 Francis J. Mountain, b. 16 Jul 1926
  m. 14 Feb 1948, Margie Hickman
A-1-9-1-1-4-3-7-1 Larry Mountain, b. 30 Oct 1949
A-1-9-1-1-4-3-7-2 Cheryl Mountain, b. 25 Jan 1954

A-1-9-1-1-4-3-8 Leon J. Mountain, b. 15 May 1928
m. 12 Jun 1948, Jacqelyn K. McClure
A-1-9-1-1-4-3-8-1 Randy J. Mountain, b. 12 Aug 1949
A-1-9-1-1-4-3-8-2 Arnold R. Mountain, b. Sep 1952
A-1-9-1-1-4-3-9 Lenora J. Mountain, b. 15 May 1928
m. 1947, George Wilson
A-1-9-1-1-4-4 Myrtle Addington, b. 27 Oct 1896
m. 10 Jan 1921, Francis B. Foster, ni
A-1-9-1-1-4-5 Carrie Addington, b. 9 Jul 1899
m. Mar 1925, Arthur Scott, no children
A-1-9-1-1-5 Annetta Addington, b. 5 Oct 1865, Indiana
m. 17 Aug 1884, Jay. Co., Indiana, Augustus Brown
A-1-9-1-1-5-1 Maud Brown, b. 12 Dec 1884
m. 1907, Porter Murry
A-1-9-1-1-5-1-1 Leon Murry, m. 1932, Geraldine Drew
A-1-9-1-1-5-1-1-1 Jerry Lee Murry
A-1-9-1-1-5-1-1-2 Keith Murry
A-1-9-1-1-5-1 m. 2nd c1935, Clark Brooks
A-1-9-1-1-5 m. 2nd Leon Worthimer
A-1-9-1-1-6 Rosetta Addington, b. 5 Oct 1865, Indiana, d. c1941,
St. Louis, Missouri
m. c1890, Samuel Hayes (1900 Jackson Co., MO)
A-1-9-1-1-6-1 Paul Hays
A-1-9-1-1-6-2 Phillip Hays
A-1-9-1-1-7 Florence Addington, b. 30 May 1868, IN, d. 1948
m. 1890, Charles Crosley, d. 1949
A-1-9-1-1-7-1 Carrie Crosley, b. 1891, m. 1909 Joseph Brennen
A-1-9-1-1-7-1-1 Joseph Brennen, Jr.
A-1-9-1-1-7-1-2 Margaret Brennen
A-1-9-1-1-7-1-3 Robert Brennen
A-1-9-1-1-7-2 Gail (Ted) Crosley, b. 1894, m. Halcyon Saterfield
A-1-9-1-1-7-2-1 Gail Crosley, Jr., b. 1916
m. 1939, Mildred Reynolds
A-1-9-1-1-7-2-1-1 Gary Crosley
A-1-9-1-1-7-2-1-2 Linda Kay Crosley
A-1-9-1-1-7-2-1-3 Bernard G. Crosley
A-1-9-1-1-7-3 Celo Crosley, m. William Hartley
A-1-9-1-1-7-3-1 Pauline Hartley
A-1-9-1-1-7-3-2 Robert Hartley
A-1-9-1-1-7-3-3 Billy Hartley
A-1-9-1-1-7-4 Charles Crosley, Jr., m. Celest ?, ni
A-1-9-1-1-7-5 Athein Crosley, b. 1903, m. ? Moore
A-1-9-1-1-7-6 Van Horn Crosley, b. 1906, dnm, d. 1958
A-1-9-1-1-8 Olive Addington, b. 30 Aug 1870, Indiana, d. 1919

m. 1887, ? Miller

son, b. 1899 adopted to her oldest sister

A-1-9-1-1-9 Carrie Addington, b. 1 Apr 1873, Indiana, d. 1880

A-1-9-1-2 Matilda A. Addington, b. c1835,

  m. 1 Dec 1855, Randolph Co., Indiana, Charles S. Jones

A-1-9-1-2-1 Anna B. Jones, b. c1858, Indiana

A-1-9-1-3 Francis L. or S. "Stephen" Addington, b. c1837,
  Indiana (1880 IN census, palsied)

  m. 15 Dec 1859, Hannah J. Mansfield, b. 1839, Indiana

A-1-9-1-3-1 Bertha C. Addington, b. c1861

  m. 16 Feb 1882, Delaware Co., Indiana, Diedrich Hartge

A-1-9-1-3 m. 2nd 8 Mar 1865, Delaware Co., Indiana, Elizabeth
  Ashery (or A. Sherry), b. c1842

A-1-9-1-3-2? Homer or "Albert" Addington, b. c1866 (? 1900
  Cook Co., IL), ? m. Mary ?, b. 1859

A-1-9-1-3-2?-1 Carl Addington, b. Apr 1890, Illinois

A-1-9-1-3-2?-2 Bertha Addington, b. Oct 1891, Illinois

A-1-9-1-3-2?-3 Homer Addington, Jr., b. Mar 1894, Illinois

A-1-9-1-3-3? Lone Addington, b. c1870, Randolph Co., Indiana

A-1-9-1-3 m. 3rd c1882, Rebecca Fleffler, b. 1854, Ohio

A-1-9-1-3-4 John Lewis Addington, b. 10 Sep 1883, d. 31 Mar
  1969, m. Elsie Wale Elkins, b. 1886

A-1-9-1-3-5 Cora Addington, b. 18 Mar 1886, d. 1 Apr 1886

A-1-9-1-3-6 Nora Addington, b. 18 Mar 1886, d. 26 Mar 1953
  m. John Elmer Dean, b. 8 Nov 1873, d. 25 Apr 1928

A-1-9-1-3-6-1 Cecelia May Dean, b. 25 Feb 1908, d. 16 Nov 1989
  m. Leonard Witts, b. 25 Jan 1904, d. 16 Nov 1989

A-1-9-1-3-6-2 John Elmer Dean, b. 9 Oct 1909, d. 13 Sep 1979
  m. Rosemary Fanchon Barrum, b. 14 Jan 1915

A-1-9-1-3-6-2-1 John Elmer Dean, b. 9 Oct 1933
  m. Johann Emily Dean, b. 13 Feb 1938

A-1-9-1-3-6-2-1-1 Douglas Scott Dean, b. 11 Apr 1963
  m. Deborah Ann Richter, b. 15 May 1963

A-1-9-1-3-6-2-1-2 Grant Matthew Dean, b. 23 Jan 1968

A-1-9-1-3-6-2-1-3 Brett Madison Dean, b. 5 Mar 1970

A-1-9-1-3-6-2-2 Larry Joseph Dean, b. 27 Sep 1947

A-1-9-1-3-6-3 Charles Roscoe Dean, b. 7 Nov 1912, d. 26 Jan 1975
  m. Wanda Lucille Honn, b. 28 Apr 1915, d. 21 Apr 1974

A-1-9-1-3-6-3-1 Charles Duane Dean, b. 9 Aug 1941
  m. Karin Jutta Puchalla, b. 23 May 1947

A-1-9-1-3-6-3-1-1 Randal Charles Dean, b. 5 Nov 1974

A-1-9-1-3-6-3-1-2 Michael Thomas Dean, b. 5 Dec 1977

A-1-9-1-3-6-3-2 Letha Deanna Dean, b. 9 Feb 1947

A-1-9-1-3-6-3-2-1 Ashley Renee Dean, b. 14 Jul 1990

A-1-9-1-3-6-3-3 Sheila Tahoa Dean, b. 30 Sep 1948, d. 26 Nov
    1966
A-1-9-1-3-6-3-4 Sherri Lynn Dean, b. 9 Dec 1951
A-1-9-1-3-6-3-5 Debbie Dorita Dean, b. 1 Jun 1954
    m. David Allen Cobble
A-1-9-1-3-6-3-5-1 Dana Marie Cobble, b. 5 Feb 1977
A-1-9-1-3-6-3-5-2 Amy Lynn Cobble, b. 14 Sep 1979
A-1-9-1-3-6-4 Francis Forrest Dean, b. 12 Jan 1915, d. 25 Dec 1970
    m. Ollie Francis Boles, b. 19 May 1908, d. 30 Dec 1989
A-1-9-1-3-6-5 Anna Louise Dean, b. 8 Feb 1919, d. 30 Nov 1921
A-1-9-1-3-6-6 Marie Dean, b. 1 Jan 1921, d. 2 Jan 1921
A-1-9-1-3-6-7 Nora Rowena Dean, b. 9 Oct 1922
    m. George Dunster
A-1-9-1-3-6-7-1 Pearl Deane Dunster, b. 8 Jun 1946
A-1-9-1-3-6-8 Rebecca Maxine Dean, b. 31 May 1927
    m. Neely Ray Brown
A-1-9-1-4 Eli Nathan Addington, b. c1839, Indiana, d. ? 9 Oct
    1884, bur. New Dayton Cem.
    m. 6 Mar 1863, Sarah Elizabeth Williams, b. 3 Aug 1845, d. 27
    Apr 1916, Richmond, Indiana, bur. New Dayton
A-1-9-1-4-1 Lulla Addington, b. c1866
    m. 1 Jan 1888, Randolph Co., Indiana, Orlando Flood
A-1-9-1-4-2 Eva Addington, b. 1871, d. 1945
A-1-9-1-4-3 Melvin C. Addington, b. 1877
    m. 1 Jan 1898, Randolph Co., Indiana, Hermia A. Booher, b.
    1879, d. 1958 Adpt. 2
A-1-9-1-4-3-1? son b. 30 Mar 1898, Delaware Co., Indiana
A-1-9-1-4-3-2 Harriet Addington, m. Wesley DeLong
A-1-9-1-5 Nancy Alice Addington, b. 17 Jun 1842, d. aft. 1910
    m. 20 Dec 1867, William W. Macy
A-1-9-1-5-1 Orla A. Macy, b. c1870
A-1-9-1-5 raised nephew Albert H. Addington, b. c1867 (?son of
    Stephen A-1-9-1-3)
    m. Eleanore Beck
A-1-9-1-3-1-1 Helen Belle Addington, b. 9 Sep 1886,
    m. 19 Oct 1907, Carl Edward Leavy
A-1-9-1-3-1-2 Ruth E. Addington, d. 12 Dec 1900
A-1-9-1-6 Mary J. Addington, b. 1844
    m. ? 21 Mar 1868, Randolph Co., Indiana, Caleb Sanders
A-1-9-1-7 William B. Addington, b. c1845, IN, d. ? bef. 1875
    m. ? 7 Jan 1865, Randolph Co., Indiana, Sabina Hiatt (Sabina
    m. 2nd Eliho Lambert)
A-1-9-1-8 George Wesley Addington, b. 6 Dec 1847, nfi

A-1-9-1 m. 2nd 7 May 1848, Randolph Co., IN, Nancy Fansher, b. 1823, Tenn., d. 9 Mar 1878, Hardin Co., Iowa

A-1-9-1-9 Samuel L. Addington, b. Apr 1849, Indiana, (1900 Polk Co., Kansas)
m. Josephine ?, b. 1849, Indiana

A-1-9-1-9-1 Frank J. Addington, b. c1872, Nebraska

A-1-9-1-9-2 Lenora Addington, b. c1879, Iowa

A-1-9-1-9-3 Earl Addington, b. c1882, Iowa

A-1-9-1-9-4 Waine Addington, b. c1884, Iowa

A-1-9-1-9-5 Ray Addington, b. c1888, Iowa

A-1-9-1-10 Thomas F. Addington, b. 1854, Indiana, (1873/9 in Texas, 1910 Canadian Co., Oklahoma)
m. 2nd 1883, Myrtle Maxey, b. Illinois

A-1-9-1-10-1 Max Addington, b. c1887, Texas

A-1-9-1-10-2 Lucille Addington, b. c1891, Oklahoma

A-1-9-1-10-3 Arnie Addington, b. c1893, Oklahoma

A-1-9-1-11 John LaSalle Addington, b. 8 Oct 1856, Randolph Co., Indiana, d. ? Clay Co., Iowa (1900 Reynolds Co., Kansas)
m. 6 Apr 1881, Mary Crist, b. Aug 1858, WS, d. 25 Jan 1901

A-1-9-2 William Lewallyn Addington, b. 1818, d. 4 Aug 1853 (lightning), bur. Old Ridgeville Cem.
m. 22 Sep 1840, Randolph Co., Indiana, Mary Hughes, b. 1820, Virginia

A-1-9-2-1 Nancy A. Addington, b. 1841, Indiana

A-1-9-2-2 Isaac H. Addington, b. 1843, Indiana (1880 Crawford Co., KS), d. ? 21 Jan 1903, Muncie, IN, bur. Farmland, IN
m. Jennie S. Bryan, b. c1842, Maine

A-1-9-2-2-1 Bertha Addington, b. c1875, Kansas
m. 25 Sep 1894, Delaware Co., Indiana, William Neal

A-1-9-2-2-2 William "Wiley" Addington, b. c1878, Missouri

A-1-9-2-3 David Addington, b. 1846, Indiana, d. Miami Co., Ohio (1880 Miami Co., Ohio), bur. Red Key, Indiana
m. 13 Jun 1870, Mary C. Aspinall, b. 1846, Ohio

A-1-9-2-3-1 Orry (son) Addington, b. c1871, Ohio

A-1-9-2-3-2 Bertha Addington, b. c1879, Ohio, m. J. P. Wilkeirson (Huntington, WV)

A-1-9-2-4 Meshach Lewellen Addington, b. 11 May 1849, Indiana, d. 5 Mar 1889, bur. Mt. Hope Cem., Deerlodge, TN
m. 28 Mar 1875, Miami Co., Ohio, Sarah Angeline Aspinall

A-1-9-2-4-1 Charles Milton Addington, b. c1876, Ohio,
m. Jesse Maud Smith

A-1-9-2-4-1-1 Mabel Eunice Addington, m. Trowbridge

A-1-9-2-4-1-1-1 Kenneth Eugene Trowbridge, m. Vera ?

A-1-9-2-4-1-1-1-1 Kenneth Eugene Trowbridge, Jr.

A-1-9-2-4-1-1-1-2 Michael Trowbridge
A-1-9-2-4-1-1-1-3 Lee Trowbridge
A-1-9-2-4-1-1-2 Carl Trowbridge, m. Elizabeth ?
A-1-9-2-4-1-1-2-1 Marcia Trowbridge
A-1-9-2-4-1-1-2-2 Sheila Trowbridge
A-1-9-2-4-1-1-3 Lyle Trowbridge, m. Shirley ?
A-1-9-2-4-1-1-3-1 Vanessa Trowbridge
A-1-9-2-4-1-2 Lola May Addington, m. Harold Jackson
A-1-9-2-4-1-2-1 Juanita Jackson
   m. ? Sideris, m. 2nd Russell Look
A-1-9-2-4-1-2-1-1 Mark Sideris, m. Susan
A-1-9-2-4-1-2-1-2 Evan Sideris
A-1-9-2-4-1-3 Harold Kenneth Addington, m. Margaret ?
A-1-9-2-4-1-3-1 Marcia Addington, m. Richard Liddiard
A-1-9-2-4-1-3-1-1 Donna Lynn Liddiard
A-1-9-2-4-1-3-2 Sheila Addington
A-1-9-2-4-1-4 Carol Addington, m. Channing Hornbeck
A-1-9-2-4-1-5 Loyal Randolph Addington, b. 28 May 1903
   m. 15 Nov 1927, Rose Goldie Wopat
A-1-9-2-4-1-5-1 Elizabeth Rose Addington, b. 2 Sep 1928
   m. John L. Ford
A-1-9-2-4-1-5-1-1 Christopher Lawrence Ford
A-1-9-2-4-1-5-1-2 David Randall Ford
A-1-9-2-4-1-5-1-3 Barbara Ellen Ford
A-1-9-2-4-2 Randolph Addington, b. 28 Feb 1878, Ohio, bur.
   Somerset, Kentucky
   m. Martha Jones
A-1-9-2-4-2-1 Bernice Addington, m. ? Lindle
A-1-9-2-4-2-1-1 Betty Jean Lindle, m. Donald Chatham
A-1-9-2-4-2-2 Glenice Addington, m. ? Jackson
A-1-9-2-4-3 Barbara Eunice Addington, b. 26 Jun 1884, Ohio,
   bur. Somerset, Kentucky, ni
   m. Carl W. Crane
A-1-9-3 Rachel Addington, b. ? 5 Apr 1814, d. 31 Dec 1896,
   Anderson Co., Kansas
   ?m. 27 Dec 1838, Randolph Co., Indiana, David Wilson, b. 4
   Apr 1815, Virginia, d. Feb 1875, Kansas
A-1-9-3-1 Sarah Wilson, m. c1860, Jacob Meyers
A-1-9-3-2 Elizabeth Wilson, b. 6 Dec 1842, d. 20 Feb 1888,
   Anderson Co., Kansas
   m. 1862, Ridgeville, Indiana, David Brown
A-1-9-3-3 Martha Wilson, b. 13 Dec 1849, d. 19 Feb 1890, dnm
A-1-9-3-4 Meribeth Wilson, b. c1852, d. 27 Mar 1892, m. Jim
   Knight

A-1-9-3-5 William Allen Wilson, b. 2 Oct 1853, d. WA aft 1935
m. 15 Sep 1880, Martha Ellen Efaw
A-1-9-3-6 Thomas Jefferson Wilson, b. 2 Oct 1853, d. 13 Dec
1935, Denver, Colorado
m. 25 Dec 1877, Sarah Amanda Sevrens
A-1-9-4 Benjamin Lewallyn Addington, b. 2 Dec 1826, Wayne
Co., Indiana, d. 1885, Sibley, Ford Co., Illinois (1860
Anderson Co., Kansas)
m. 22 Jan 1846, Randolph Co., IN, Margaret Mariah Hughs
A-1-9-4-1 Randolph Addington, b. 1846, Indiana, d. ? 1899,
Norway (1880, Will Co., Illinois), m. Eunice ?
A-1-9-4-1-1 Mary Addington, b. c1868, Illinois
A-1-9-4-1-2 Robert Addington, b. c1871, Illinois, m. Edna ?, b.
1876, Ohio (1900 Cuyahoga Co., Ohio, 1910 Cook Co., IL)
A-1-9-4-1-3 Annie Addington, b. c1873, Illinois
A-1-9-4-2 Elizabeth Addington, b. 1850, Indiana
A-1-9-4-3 Nancy Addington, b. 1852, Indiana
A-1-9-4-4 James Monroe Addington, b. 14 Sep 1858, Anderson
Co., Kansas, d. 29 Oct 1925, Riverside, California (1887 to
MN, 1900 Lincoln Co., MN)
m. 31 Aug 1881, Eliza Nebengers, b. 1859/60, Illinois, d. 17 Apr
1931, Riverside, California
A-1-9-4-4-1 Zoe Addington, b. 2 Apr 1884, Sibley, Illinois
m. Jes Hamstreet
A-1-9-4-4-2 Muriel Addington, b. 31 May 1885, Seymour,
Illinois
m. Gilbert Hainline (lived Oceanside, California)
A-1-9-4-4-3 Nelle Addington, b. 1 Nov 1888, Lake Benton,
Lincoln Co., MN, m.? Ziesloff (live San Bern., California)
A-1-9-4-4-4 Virgie Addington, b. 3 Jan 1896, Lake Benton, MN
m. Harry F. Antrobus (lived Riverside, California)
A-1-9-5 Thomas Lewallyn Addington, b. 26 Jan 1829 Wayne
Co., Indiana, d. 7 May 1914
m. 11 Sep 1852, Margaret Woodward, d. 7 Sep 1854
A-1-9-5-1 Melissa Addington, b. 1854, d. aft 1914
m. 6 May 1875, Randolph Co., Indiana, John Warren
A-1-9-5-1-1 Bessie Warren, d. young
A-1-9-5-1-2 Orla Warren, m. Minnie Henkle
A-1-9-5-1-3 Pearl Warren, m. ? Teagarden, m. 2nd Tom Pierce
A-1-9-5-1-4 Carl Warren, m. Gladys Sperce
A-1-9-5-1-4-1 John Curtis Warren
A-1-9-5-2 William Addington, b. c1854, (1914 in Indianapolis),
d. ? 10 Jun 1918, Muncie, Indiana
m. 20 May 1880, Delaware Co., Indiana, Josephine Pierce

A-1-9-5-2-1 Arthur Addington, b. 1884, d. 29 Mar 1888
A-1-9-5-2-2 Della V. Addington, b. 30 Oct 1889
A-1-9-5-2-3 Lee Addington, b. 16 Mar 1895, Randolph Co.,
    Indiana
A-1-9-5-2-3-1 Charles W. Addington
A-1-9-5-2-4 Josephine Addington, m. Eston Stump
A-1-9-5 m. 2nd 26 Jul 1857, Nancy Alice Pierce, d. Sep 1884
A-1-9-5-3 Marybeth Addington, b. 1858, d. bef. 1870
A-1-9-5-4 Elizabeth F. Addington, b. 18 Aug 1859, Jay Co.,
    Indiana, d. 16 Feb 1942, Indiana
    m. 15 Apr 1880, Randolph Co., IN, Richard A. "Osborn" Fraze
A-1-9-5-4-1 Ora Fraze, m. Lona Hetsler
A-1-9-5-4-2 Gertrude Fraze, b. c1886
A-1-9-5-4-3 Edna Fraze, m. Warren Middleton
A-1-9-5-4-4 Fae Fraze, b. c1893, m. Von Gemmil
A-1-9-5-4-5 Mirrilla Fraze, b. c1899
A-1-9-5-5 Elmer Elsworth Addington, b. 29 Jun 1861, d. 9 Jan
    1947, Randolph Co., Indiana, (lived Clarksville, WV)
    m. 2 May 1885, Nancy Almira Cox, b. 1 Apr 1862, d. 21 Jan
    1944, Randolph Co., Indiana
A-1-9-5-5-1 Inez Mable Addington, b. 23 Feb 1886, d. 1961
    m. Charles Ross, d. Dec 1955
A-1-9-5-5-1-1 Ralph Edgar Ross, b. 9 May 1917, m. 24 Oct 1945,
    Mary Lou Adams
A-1-9-5-5-1-1-1 Robert Elsworth Ross, b. 17 Aug 1946
A-1-9-5-5-1-1-2 John Adams Ross, b. 20 Aug 1949
A-1-9-5-5-1-1-3 Margo Eilson Ross, b. 24 Dec 1950
A-1-9-5-5-1-2 Verne Elouise Ross, b. Sep 1925
A-1-9-5-5-2 Mary Grace Addington, b. 25 Apr 1888
    m. 29 Aug 1911, Randolph Co., Indiana, Harry G. Warren
A-1-9-5-5-2-1 Raymond A. Warren, m. Jul 1935, Betty Ginor
A-1-9-5-5-2-2 Wallace Wayne Warren, m. 29 Jul 1939, Vauna
    Jean Wolf
A-1-9-5-5-3 Orvah Alfred Addington, b. 10 Feb 1899
    m. 8 May 1920, Randolph Co., Indiana, Eva Irene Edwards, b.
    4 Jun 1896, Randolph Co., Indiana
A-1-9-5-5-3-1 Deloris Irene Addington, b. 28 Nov 1921,
    Randolph Co., Indiana
A-1-9-5-5-3-2 Orvah Keith Addington, b. 21 Jul 1923, Ridgeville,
    IN, m. 1 Feb 1947, Rebecca Lois Riley, b. 31 May 1921, Iowa
A-1-9-5-5-4 Ralph Addington, b. c1899, d. 4 Sep 1919
A-1-9-5-6 Anthony (Jack) Addington, b. 16 Aug 1868, Indiana, d.
    3 Feb 1934, Los Angeles, California
    m. Mary Lou McLane, b. Apr 1871, Indiana, d. Jan 1920

A-1-9-5-6-1 Harry A. Addington, b. 6 Apr 1888, Randolph Co., Indiana, d. 13 Jul 1967, Anaheim, California, m. Mildred Mastny, b. 23 Mar 1888, d. 15 Jun 1967, Anaheim, California

A-1-9-5-6-1-1 Melvin John Addington, b. 12 Feb 1910, Indianapolis

A-1-9-5-6-1-2 Eveline Dorothy Addington, m. George Pritchard

A-1-9-5-6 m. 2nd 15 Oct 1905, Marion Co., Indiana, Agnes Huls

A-1-9-5 m. 3rd 28 Aug 1885, Randolph Co., Indiana, Hannah M. Ward

A-1-9-6 Isaac Lewallyn Addington, b. 20 Jan 1832, Wayne Co., Indiana, d. 9 May 1903, bur. New Dayton Cem.

m. 7 Dec 1854, Piety Horn, b. 1838, d. 27 Mar 1885

A-1-9-6-1 Sarah Ann Addington, b. 1856, d. aft 1932

m. 1 Feb 1885, Randolph Co., IN, George T. Riddlebarger

A-1-9-6-2 Benjamin Franklin Addington, b. Sep 1858, d. 30 Nov 1932

m. 23 Feb 1881, Wayne Co., Indiana, Ella Miller, b. 2 Sep 1862, d. 6 Apr 1890

A-1-9-6-2-1 Pearl Addington, b. ? 1 Sep 1882

A-1-9-6-2-2 (Isaac) Clayton Addington, b. 30 May 1884, d. 3 Nov 1962, bur. Maxville Cemetery

m. 29 Aug 1905, Randolph Co., Indiana, Nova Williams, b. 1886, d. 9 Jun 1966

A-1-9-6-2-2-1 Bernice Irene Addington, b. 19 Mar 1906, d. 6 Apr 1919

A-1-9-6-2-3 Ida Addington, b. 6 Sep 1886, m. Stephen Ringley

A-1-9-6-2 m. 2nd 20 Jun 1891, Jay Co., Indiana, Leverna J. Osburn, b. Oct 1871, d. aft 1932

A-1-9-6-2-4 Roy R. Addington, b. Jan 1893, Randolph Co., IN m. 1920, Mary Hacker Fleming

A-1-9-6-2-4-1 William F. Addington, m. 1945, Marjorie Marvin

A-1-9-6-2-4-1-1 Deborah Addington

A-1-9-6-2-4-1-2 William F. Addington, Jr.

A-1-9-6-2-4-1-3 Nancy Addington

A-1-9-6-2-5 Carl Addington, b. Jun 1895, Randolph Co., Indiana, d. 12 Jan 1920

m. 1914, Lavina "Bonnie" Smith, d. 14 Jan 1920

A-1-9-6-2-5-1 Vera Addington, b. 4 Jun 1913

A-1-9-6-2-5-2 son, b. c1918

A-1-9-6-2-6 Helen Addington, b. 11 Oct 1897, Randolph Co., IN

A-1-9-6-3 Jacob F. Addington, b. 26 Jun 1859, d. 29 Jun 1859, bur. Maxville Cemetery

A-1-9-6-4 Rose B. Addington, b. 1861

m. 16 Apr 1881, Randolph Co., IN, Edwin A. Cadwallader

A-1-9-6-5 Mary Addington, b. 3 Jan 1863, d. 27 May 1885
A-1-9-6-6 Flora (Florence) Addington, b. 1866, d. bef. 1910
  m. 25 Oct 1885, Randolph Co., IN, Samuel Elsworth Fraze
A-1-9-6-6-1 Olive Fraze, b. 1891
A-1-9-6-7 Cora Addington, b. 1868
  m. 16 Apr 1887, Randolph Co., Indiana, Louis Schlutzhauer
A-1-9-6-8 Minnie Addington, b. 1874, m. ? Pyle (1932 in
  Lawrence, Kansas)
A-1-9-6 m. 2nd 4 Sep 1886, Randolph Co., Indiana, Eliza Frances
  Pogue
A-1-9-7 Mary Addington, b. 1834
A-1-9-8 Nancy Addington, b. 1841
A-2 James Addington, b. c1751, Bucks Co., Pennsylvania, d.
  c1799 (will dated 28 Jul 1798)
  m. Jan 1776, Rebecca Garrett
A-2-1 Thomas Addington, b. 12 Feb 1777, m. Mary Stubbs
A-2-2 Mary Addington, b. 30 Sep 1778, m. Roberts
A-2-3 Sarah Addington, b. 6 Sep 1781, nfi
A-2-4 Henry Addington, b. 2 Jul 1784, d. 18 Aug 1855, Miami
  Co., Indiana
  m. 29 Mar 1804, Cane Creek MM, SC, Elizabeth Randel, b. 11
  Oct 1787, SC, d. 18 Aug 1856, Miami Co., Indiana
A-2-4-1 Ann Addington, b. 1 Nov 1804, d. young
A-2-4-2 Rachel Addington, b. 5 Apr 1814, d. young
A-2-4-3 Rebecca Addington, b. 19 Apr 1815, Darke Co., Ohio
  m. 29 Aug 1837, Preble Co., Ohio, William O. Smith, Jr.
A-2-4-3-1 William Stubbs Robbins, b. 1842, d. 1887
A-2-4-4 Sarah (Sally) Addington, b. 6 Jun 1816, Darke Co., OH
  m. 6 Apr 1837, Preble, Co., Ohio, Scott Freeman
A-2-4-5 Lydia Addington, b. 6 Dec 1817, Darke Co., Ohio, d. 3
  Mar 1906, Sedan, Kansas
  m. 22 Feb 1838, Grant Co., Indiana, Jacob Page Robbins
A-2-4-5-1 William Stubbs Robbins, b. 1842, d. 1887
A-2-4-6 Hannah Addington, b. 15 May 1819, Darke Co., Ohio,
  m. 25 Apr 1840, Grant Co., Indiana, Benjamin Small
A-2-4-7 Thomas Addington, b. 3 Aug 1820, Darke Co., Ohio, d.
  15 Oct 1896, Henry Co., Indiana
  m. 27 Feb 1840, Grant Co., Indiana, Mary Ann Mason, d. 18
  Dec 1894, Henry Co., Indiana
A-2-4-7-1 Mary Ann Addington, b. 2 Jun 1841, Grant Co., IN
  m 26 Nov 1856, Howard Co., Indiana, Nathan Draper
A-2-4-7-2 Isaac Addington, b. 25 Jun 1843, Jackson, Township,
  Miami Co., Indiana, d. 21 Nov 1926, Converse, Indiana
  m. 5 Nov 1862, Howard Co., Indiana, Sarah Herrington

m. 2nd 31 Oct 1865, Henry Co., Indiana, Mary Jane Shaw
A-2-4-7-2-1 Edward Addington, d. in childhood
A-2-4-7-2-2 Oliver Morton Addington, b. c1868
    m. Fannie May Collins
    m. ? 2nd 24 Dec 1904, Howard Co., Indiana, Jessie Sater
A-2-4-7-2-2-1 Jack Blackwell Addington, b. Oct 1900, Dallas, TX
A-2-4-7-2-3 William Sherman Addington, b. 1870, Indiana
    m. ? 11 Jan 1890, Howard Co., Indiana, Mattie Ray
A-2-4-7-2-4 John Milton Addington, b. Jan 1871, Iowa, d. 5 Feb
    1905, Miami Co., Indiana
    m. 18 Jun 1893, Howard Co., Indiana, Maggie L. Little
A-2-4-7-2-5 Benjamin Franklin Addington, b. Mar 1873, Henry
    Co., Indiana, d. 23 Mar 1939, Kokomo, Howard Co., IN
    m. 28 Jan 1899, Howard Co., IN, Ella Overman, b. May 1879
A-2-4-7-2-5-1 Ethel Marie Addington
A-2-4-7-2-5-2 Esther May Addington
A-2-4-7-2-5-3 Alice Mildred Addington, b. 9 May 1908
A-2-4-7-2-5-4 Paul Franklin Addington, b. 16 Sep 1914, Howard
    Co., Indiana
    m. 3 Sep 1936, Inez Elnora Rush
A-2-4-7-2-5-4-1 Alan Franklin Addington, b. 27 Nov 1938,
    Kokomo, Indiana, m. 7 Dec 1963, Kokomo, IN, Rose Burton
A-2-4-7-2-5-4-1-1 Lara Marie Addington, b. 25 Jul 1966
A-2-4-7-2-5-4-1-2 Brent Franklin Addington, b. 9 Oct 1968
A-2-4-7-2-5-4-2 Myrtle Jean Addington
A-2-4-7-2-6 Mary Belle Addington, b. 28 Mar 1870, Howard Co.,
    Indiana, d. 20 Dec 1969, Phoenix, AZ
    m. 14 Dec 1899, Cass Co., Indiana, Claude Masters, div.
    m. 2nd 27 Aug 1903, Cass Co., Indiana, Francis Marion Cook
    m. 3rd 12 Dec 1947, San Diego, California George Wardwell
A-2-4-7-2-7 Thomas Benton Addington, d. in childhood
A-2-4-7-3 Nathan "Nate" Addington, b. 23 May 1846, Miama
    Co., Ohio, d. 24 Feb 1929, Weld Co., Colorado
    m. 7 Jan 1866, Kokomo, Howard Co., IN, Susannah Perkins
A-2-4-7-3-1 William H. Addington, b. 16 Oct 1866, d. 1951,
    Sterling, Colorado
    m. 1 Jun 1887, Howard Co., Indiana, Effie Mae Winterroud
A-2-4-7-3-1-1 Odes L. Addington, b. c1888, Indiana
A-2-4-7-3-1-2 Cora Addington, b. c1892, IN, m. George Kellnar
A-2-4-7-3-1-3 Thera O. Addington, b. c1897, Iowa
A-2-4-7-3-1-4 Genevieve Addington
A-2-4-7-3-2 Clyde Kimball Addington, b. 12 Jun 1868, d. 13 Jun
    1931, Kokomo, Indiana
    m. 19 Nov 1888, Logansport, Cass Co., IN, Martha Alice Ronk

A-2-4-7-3-2-1 Virgil Addington, b. 26 Nov 1889, d. 29 Jun 1890
A-2-4-7-3-2-2 Urgal Decia "Dee" Addington, b. 26 Nov 1889, d.
25 Jan 1981, Orlando, Florida
m. 3 Jan 1907, Harry O. Spradling
m. 2nd c1946, Harley Hardin
m. 3rd c1958, Alex Pynowski
A-2-4-7-3-2-3 Clayton Forrest "Frosty" Addington, b. 12 Oct
1896, Howard Co., Indiana, d. 15 Oct 1948, Kokomo, Indiana
m. 24 Jan 1920, Indianapolis, Indiana, Margaret Cynthia
Thompson, b. 1903, d. 1941
A-2-4-7-3-2-3-1 Norma Louise Addington, b. 8 Oct 1921, Howard
Co., Indiana,
m. 21 Jan 1942, Hattiesburg, MO, Robert Ault Stanley, div.
m. 2nd 28 Feb 1964, Kokomo, Indiana Frank Finley Thomas
A-2-4-7-3-2-3-1-1 Deborah Lynne Stanley, b. 1947
m. Michael Manley Miller
A-2-4-7-3-2-3-2 Mary Joe Addington, b. 29 Jan 1928, Howard Co.,
Indiana, d. 25 Feb 1955
m. 22 Feb 1947, William Taylor "Juggy" Anderson, Jr.
A-2-4-7-3-2-3-3 Patricia Ann Addington, b. 10 May 1931, d. 30
Mar 1934
A-2-4-7-3-2-3 m. 2nd 7 Feb 1944, Ruth Obermeyer Bookmiller
A-2-4-7-3-4 Adopted David Kent Addington, b. 25 July 1942
A-2-4-7-3-3 Mary Jane Addington, b. 16 Feb 1870, Howard Co.,
Indiana, d. 1963, Iowa
m. 16 Jun 1893, Howard Co., Indiana, John Marion McGraw
A-2-4-7-3-4 Thomas Valentine Addington, b. 12 Feb 1871, bur.
Loveland, Colorado,
m. 7 Aug 1890, Howard Co., Indiana, Mamie Winterroud
A-2-4-7-3-4-1 Lena Myrth Addington, b. Jan 1891, Indiana
A-2-4-7-3-4-2 Mabel Addington, b. Jun 1893, Iowa
A-2-4-7-3-5 Ora E. Addington, b. 22 Aug 1873, Howard Co., IN,
d. 24 Sep 1951, Orange Co., California (1900 Monora Co.,
Iowa)
m. Mattie Flora Abbott
A-2-4-7-3-5-1 Beulah Addington, b. 1899, Iowa
A-2-4-7-3-6 Naomi F. "Oma" Addington, b. 18 Oct 1876, d.
Sterling, Colorado
m. 21 Sep 1895, Elmer Stewart
m. 2nd 1903, Cass Co., Indiana, Joseph A. Cavis
A-2-4-7-3-6-1 Oral Stuart, b. Mar 1897
A-2-4-7-3-7 Minne Belle Addington, b. 28 Mar 1879, d. 1969
m. Francis Marion Cook
A-2-4-7-3-7-1 Marion Francis Cook, b. 1919, m. Hazel Walker

A-2-4-7-3-8 Lorenzo Dow "Rengie" Addington, b. 22 Jul 1883, Howard Co., IN, d. 30 Jul 1963, New Castle, Weston Co., WY m. Blanche Dewey, m. 2nd Grace Hampton

A-2-4-7-3-8-1 Ora Addington, b. 28 Jan 1905, m. Elva Laree Long

A-2-4-7-3-8-2 Gerald Addington

A-2-4-7-3-8-3 Ervin Addington

A-2-4-7-3-8-4 Zola Addington

A-2-4-7-3-9 Cora Roxelle Addington, b. 5 Jun 1885

A-2-4-7-3-10 Tunis Guy Addington, b. 17 Feb 1889, Howard Co., Indiana, d. 4 Jan 1975, Orange Park, Florida

A-2-4-7-3-10-1 Irma Mae Addington, b. 29 Apr 1913

A-2-4-7-4 Elizabeth "Lizzie" Addington, b. 3 Nov 1848, Miami Co., Indiana
m. 17 May 1866, Henry Co., Indiana, Bryant Hosier

A-2-4-7-5 William L. F. Addington, b. 6 Jan 1851, Converse, Miami Co., Indiana, d. ?
m. 23 Jul 1871, Howard Co., Indiana, Cordelia Hinkle (4 Jun 1874, Howard Co., Indiana, Cordelia Addington married Havila Pearson)

A-2-4-7-6 Edith Caroline "Callie" Addington, b. 24 Sep 1854
m. 9 Aug 1883, Henry Co., Indiana, James Kinsey

A-2-4-7-7 Milton Freemont "Milty" Addington, b. 17 Sep 1856, d. 4 Jan 1934, New Castle, Henry Co., Indiana
m. 9 Dec 1880, Henry Co., Indiana, Lydia C. Miller

A-2-4-7-7-? son, b. 16 Nov 1882

A-2-4-7-8 Rebecca V. Addington, b. 25 Nov 1858, d. 24 Feb 1859

A-2-4-7-9 Lydia F. Addington, b. 1 Oct 1861, nfi

A-2-4-7-10 Malinda Arabelle "Belle" Addington, b. 2 Sep 1864
m. 30 Aug 1883, Henry Co., Indiana, Henry Hunt

A-2-4-8 Martha Ann Addington, b. Nov 1822, Darke Co., Ohio
m. 6 Jun 1839, Grant Co., Indiana, William Thomas

A-2-4-9 Mary Ann Addington, b. 17 Feb 1824, d. Oct 1844, Grant Co., Indiana
m. 15 Feb 1843, Converse Co., IN, Oliver Hazard Perry Macy

A-2-4-10 William Sherman Addington, b. 2 Dec 1826, Butler Co., Ohio, d. 17 Mar 1915, South Dakota, (1860 Pattensburg, IL, 1900 Hall River Co., SD)
m. 15 Apr 1853, Celia Moorman, d. 1855

A-2-4-10-1 Uriah Addington, b. 1848, Illinois

A-2-4-10 m. 2nd Hannah Lemons, b. 1825, Ohio, d. 1897, White Owl, South Dakota

A-2-4-10-2 William B. Addington, (1918, Indianapolis, IN)

A-2-4-10 m. 3rd 18 Apr 1898, Margaret Spencer, b. 1844, Wales

A-2-4-10-3 Sheriden Addington

A-2-4-11? Isaac R. Addington, b. 15 Jul 1828, Ohio
A-2-5 Rebecca Addington, b. 18 Jan 1787, nfi
A-2-6 Martha Addington, b. 28 Aug 1789
A-2-7 James Addington, b. 15 Jan 1792, d. 1869, Missouri
   m. Elizabeth ? (1850 St. Clair Co., Missouri)
A-2-7-1 Mary Ann Addington, b. c1815
   m. 27 Aug 1843, Darke Co., Ohio, William Grayham
   m. 2nd James Penny
A-2-7-2 John F. Addington, b. c1816
   m. 5 Apr 1838, Darke Co., Ohio, Sophia Kinkade
A-2-7-2-1 William D. Addington, b. 1839, Darke Co., Ohio, ? d.
   bef 1870, m. 21 Apr 1859, Cedar Co., Missouri, Lydia A.
   Neely (Lydia m. 2nd John Pearson)
A-2-7-2-2 A. Lewis Addington, b. 1840, Missouri
A-2-7-2-3 James Ray Addington, b. 1842, Missouri
A-2-7-2-4 William Jones Addington, b. 16 Feb 1844, Hickory Co.,
   MO, d. 12 May 1911, Bradford, Ohio (1910 Darke Co., Ohio)
   m. May 1868, Darke Co., OH, Susannah Penny, b. 1848, d. 1905
A-2-7-2-4-1 Clara A. Addington, b. 12 Aug 1870, Ohio
A-2-7-2-4-2 Lucinda Addington, b. 17 Oct 1873, Ohio
A-2-7-2-4-3 Alva Mars Addington, b. 7 Mar 1877, d. 17 Aug 1942,
   Darke Co., Ohio
   m. 24 May 1908, Darke Co., Ohio, Clara E. Morris
A-2-7-2-4-?-1 Dale Addington, b. 1895, Ohio (1910 Darke Co.)
A-2-7-2-4-4 Bertha Addington, b. 7 Mar 1879, d. 1 Jan 1958,
   Darke Co., Ohio
   m. 5 May 1903, Darke Co., Ohio, Clayton O. Smith
   m. 2nd 15 Jun 1915, Harry B. Schmidlapp
A-2-7-2-4-5 Henry Lawrence "Hank" Addington, b. 17 Sep 1881,
   Darke Co., Ohio, d. 4 Jul 1919, Richland Co., Ohio
   m. 6 Jun 1909, Butler Co., Ohio, Edith Wodley
A-2-7-2-4-6 Venge Fern Addington, b. 22 Jul 1890, Ohio, d. 1931
   m. Sylvester Oliver Goens
A-2-7-2-4-6-1 David Eugene Goens, b. 1924, d. 1981
   m. Margaret Patricia Gerbrack
A-2-7-2-4 m. 2nd 17 Jan 1907, Margaret Ann Seddomidge
A-2-7-2-5 David Nelson Addington, b. 1848
A-2-7-2 m. 2nd 29 Dec 1851, Darke Co., Ohio Mary L. White
A-2-7-2-6 Finis C. Addington, b. 5 Sep 1854, d. 29 Sep 1890,
   Miami Co., Ohio
   m. 12 Oct 1882, Clark Co., Ohio, Magena M. Tibbetts
A-2-7-2-6-1 ? Charles Addington, b. c1884, Ohio
A-2-7-2-6-2 ? Flora Addington, b. c1886, Ohio
A-2-7-2-6-3 ? Emma M. Addington, b. c1888, Ohio

A-2-7-2-6-4 ? Laura A. Addington, b. c1890, Ohio
A-2-7-2-7 Sabina P. Addington, b. 20 Apr 1855
A-2-7-2-8 Sarah E. Addington, b. 1857
   m. ? 22 Sep 1878, Cedar Co., Missouri, George Paulk
A-2-7-2-9 Samuel Addington, b. 1860, d. bef. 16 Apr 1884
A-2-7-2-10 Alice Addington
A-2-7-3 L. Addington, b. c1823, ?? m. 25 Mar 1847, Darke Co.,
   Ohio, James Snell
A-2-7-4 Elizabeth Addington, b. 1825
   m. c1848, Thomas Chiles
A-2-7-5 Henry Addington, b. 11 Mar 1827, Darke Co., Ohio, d.
   bef 1880
   m. 25 Jan 1849, Darke Co., Ohio, Susannah North, b. 1834, OH
A-2-7-5-1 William H. Addington, b. May 1850, Ohio, d. 23 Apr
   1908, Milton, Washington dnm
A-2-7-5-2 Henry R. Addington, b. c1852, Indiana
A-2-7-5-3 John E. Addington, b. Jun 1855, Indiana
A-2-7-5-4 Lina Addington, b. c1866, Iowa
A-2-7-5-5 Rosa Addington, b. c1874, Iowa
A-2-7-6 Nancy Addington, b. c1828, m. 28 Nov 1848, Darke Co.,
   Ohio, Layton North
A-2-7-7 Sarah Ann Addington, b. 1830, Darke Co., Ohio,
   m 4 Nov 1858, St. Claire Co., Missouri, George Vernon
A-2-7 m. 2nd 18 Nov 1855, St. Claire Co., MO, Anna Wright
A-2-8 Karenhappuch "Carrie" Addington, b. 5 Mar 1795, SC
   m. James Brown
A-2-9 John T. Addington, b. 2 May 1797,. d. 1888
   m. Margaret "Peggy" ?
A-2-9-1 ? Andrew Jackson Addington, b. 1815, VA
   m. Verlina Hutchinson
A-2-10 Rachel Addington, b. 1798
A-3 Henry Addington, b. c1755, Bucks Co., PA, d. c1807, SC, ni
A-4 Bethena Addington, b. c1757
   m. 1 Mar 1787, Union Co., South Carolina, John McClain
A-5 William Addington, b. c1759, Buck Co., Pennsylvania, d. 7
   Sep 1845, Union Co., Georgia
   m. 23 Dec 1784, Deliah Duncan
A-5-1 Jane Addington, b. Jan 1786, d. bet. 1845 and 1848
   m. ? Shettlesworth
A-5-2 John Addington, b. 10 Nov 1787, South Carolina, d. 30
   Aug 1861, Georgia
   m. 1 May 1808, Buncombe Co., Georgia, Rachel Miller, b. 1791
A-5-2-1 Delila Addington, b. 1809, m. Ledford
A-5-2-2 Hannah Addington, b. 1810, m. Harratt

A-5-2-3 William Addington, b. 27 Sep 1811. m. Elizabeth
A-5-2-4 Henry Addington, b. 1812, NC, m. Martha Ann Holt
A-5-2-5 Carolyn Addington, b. 1815, m. Wynn
A-5-2-6 Margaret Addington, b. Nov 1819, m. Ralston
A-5-2-7 Jesse R. Addington, b. 1820, NC, m. Mary Ann
A-5-2-8 Mary Addington, b. 1823, m. Ellington
A-5-2-9 John M. Addington, b. 1827, m. Sarah Ann
A-5-3 Henry Addington, b. 28 Feb 1789, Newberry Co., South
    Carolina, d. 19 Apr 1878
  m. 17 Jun 1818, Mary Weaver, b. 10 Mar 1795, d. 28 Aug 1859
A-5-3-1 Jacob Weaver Addington, b. 27 Aug 1819
  m. Mary L. Dobson
A-5-3-2 Susana Matilda Addington, b. 10 Mar 1821
  m. 20 Dec 1840, Joseph W. Dobson, d. 1841
A-5-3-3 John Hardy Addington, b. 1823, m. Elizabeth Bernard
A-5-4 Sarah Addington, b. 1793, m. Harrison
A-5-5 William Addington, b. 1795
A-5-6 Moses Addington, b. 1797
A-5-7 James Addington, b. 1799, NC, m. Winifred Woodfin
A-5-7-5 James M. Addington, b. April 1827
  m. Matilda Ann Bradley
A-5-7-5-3 Asa Addington, b. Mar 1851, Georgia
  m. Rebecca Thomas
A-5-8 March Addington, b. 1802
A-5-9 Delilah Addington, b. 1804, m. Huckaby
A-5-10 Martha Addington, b. 1806, m. Hicks
A-5-11 Polly Addington, b. 1808, m. Logan
A-5-12 Elizabeth Addington, b. 1810, m. Curtis
A-6 Martha Addington, b. c1762, d. 1787
  m. c1782, George Bruton
A-6-1 George Bruton, Jr. b. 1787
A-7 Sarah (Sally) Addington, b. 1 Mar 1767
  m. c1787, George Bruton
A-8 Elizabeth Addington, b. c1760, d. 1810/20
A-8-1 Benjamin Addington, b. c1785, d. 1842/50
A-8-1-1 Jesse Addington, b. 1814, d. 1902
A-8-1-2 Thomas Addington, b. 1820
A-8-1-3 Isaac Addington, b. 1821
A-8-2 Vardy Addington, b. c1790, d. 1820/30
A-8-2-1 Jason Addington, b. 1814
A-8-2-2 Joshua Addington, b. 1816
A-9 Charlota Addington, nfi

Unresolved references to Indiana Addingtons believed to be descendents of John Addington of Indiana

Wayne County, Indiana marriages, unknown descendent
24 Jan 1825   Alice Addington to James Graver
28 Feb 1833   Rebecca Addington to James Walker
24 Dec 1833   Louisa Addington to Nason Roberts
19 Jan 1851   John Addington to Sarah Citizen
6 Sep 1867   Anna Addington to William Medearis
27 Oct 1879   Cora Addington to Robert Morgan Rea
22 Sep 1898   Anna Addington to Benjamin Dallas

Randolph County, Indiana marriages, unknown descendent
26 Sep 1853   William Addington to Caroline Gray (no ret.)
16 Aug 1855   Elizabeth Addington to James Whitesell
20 Mar 1856   William Addington to Margaret Patterson
9 Feb 1858   Mary Addington to George Howard
18 Feb 1864   William Addington to Rebecca Frick
21 Mar 1868   Mary J. Addington to Caleb Sanders
31 Jan 1874   James S. Addington to Elizabeth Hollowell
             Laura B. Kennedy to Edwin Addington

Jay County, Indiana marriages, unknown descendent
20 Sep 1857   Mary Addington to William T. Jones

Howard County, Indiana marriages, unknown descendent
6 Dec 1868   Delilah Addington to James Nicholas
4 Dec 1869   Hiram O. Addington to Eldora Stockdale
4 Jun 1874   Cordelia Addington to Havila Pearson
24 Dec 1898   Mary Addington to Gaston Renbarger
2 Apr 1894   Wilson S. Addington to Hannah L. Sisson

Delaware County, Indiana marriages, unknown descendent
17 Jan 1881   Elizabeth Addington to William Baker
1890-1895   Libbie Addington to William Brumer
1 Dec 1899   Bertha E. Addington to Albert Fuller

Marion County, Indiana marriages, unknown descendent
31 Dec 1900   John Addington to Jennie M. Conners
5 Apr 1907   Chester Addington to Mary Newton
16 Jun 1909   Mary A. Addington to Oliver Davis
21 Nov 1916   Frederick Addington to Ruth Lyons
28 Jan 1917   Mary F. Addington to John Lup

Hancock County, Indiana, marriages unknown descendent
22 Sep 1859   Elizabeth Addington to Francis M. Wilson
10 Nov 1877   Jas. S. Addington to Martha Roberts
13 Oct 1885   John M. Addington to Mary Andrews
15 May 1901   Daniel Addington to Sarah Grow
8 May 1913   Thos Addington to Malissie Swords
14 May 1914   Malissie Addington to Scott Lawson
21 Nov 1914   Sarah J. Addington to Alpha Skinner

Hamilton County, Indiana, marriages unknown descendent
1 Feb 1873   Morgan Addington to Martha Olvey

Berrin Co., Michigan, marriages unknown descendent
1 Jul 1849   Sarah Addington (b. 1826, IN) to Wm. Bachtel

1850 Will Co., Illinois
John N. Addington, b. 1827, Indiana

Descendents of Jacob Bolinger
born 1808, Pennsylvania

B Jacob Bolinger b. 1808, b. Pennsylvania, d. 27 Dec 1860, Randolph Co., Indiana, bur. Maxville Cemetery
m. c1829, Pennsylvania, Mary Goshorn, b. 1808, Pennsylvania, d. 20 Oct 1875, Randolph Co., Indiana, bur. Maxville Cemetery
B-1 Huldah Ruth Bolinger, b. 20 Nov 1830 Pennsylvania, d. 18 Sep 1907, bur. Maxville Cemetery
m. 27 Nov 1851, David Addington, b. 9 Mar 1828, d. 19 Jul 1902
(see Addington Descendents, A-1-3-12)
B-2 Moses E. Bolinger, b. 17 May 1836, Pennsylvania, d. 4 Nov 1912, Randolph Co., Indiana
m. 22 Jul 1858, Randolph Co., Indiana, Mariah Louisa Miller, b. 10 Dec 1840, PA, d. 19 Dec 1894, Randolph Co., Indiana
B-2-1 Waldo Rosco Bolinger, b. 12 May 1861, Indiana, d. 1925, bur. New Dayton Cem.
m. 10 Jul 1888, Randolph Co., Indiana, Rosa Smith, b. 1870, d. 1939, bur. New Dayton Cem.
B-2-1-1 Carl Bolinger, b. 30 Jun 1891, d. 24 Jul 1892, bur. New Dayton Cem.
B-2-1-2 Hattie Opal Bolinger, d. 20 Jul 1894
B-2-1-3 Fleety G. Bolinger, b. 15 Dec 1892
m. 25 Jan 1915, Delaware Co., IN, Forest Morris Addington
B-2-1-4 Neal W. Bolinger, b. 14 Jan 1895
B-2-1-5 Wilbur Bolinger, b. c1901
m. Dorothy Current
B-2-1-5-1 Rosemary Marjorie Bollinger, b. 29 Jul 1928
B-2-1-6 Madonna Bolinger, b. 7 Oct 1902
B-2-1-7 daughter, b. 5 Jul 1904
B-2-1-7 Mildred Bolinger, b. c1903
B-2-1-8 Edith U. Bolinger, b. c1905
B-2-1-9 Louise Adaline Bolinger, b. 2 Dec 1907
B-2-2 Indiana Rosa Bolinger, b. 9 Aug 1863, Randolph Co., Indiana, d. 30 Dec 1920
m. 20 Jun 1887, Randolph Co., Indiana, George Emerson Addington, ni
B-2-3 Charles T. Bolinger, b. 30 Mar 1865, IN, d. 4 Oct 1912
m. 16 Jun 1887, Randolph Co., Indiana, Nettie A. Barnes
B-2-3-1 Ernest E. Bolinger, b. 5 Aug 1888, Indiana
m. Inez Wise

B-2-3-1-1 Wayne Leroy Bolinger, b. 30 Mar 1912, d. 15 Jan 1915
B-2-3-1-2 Charles Bolinger, b. 4 Nov 1914
B-2-3-1-3 daughter, b. 16 Mar 1916
B-2-3-1-4 daughter, b. 2 Jun 1917
B-2-4 Minnie E. Bolinger, b. 9 Aug 1867, Indiana, d. aft 1920
   m. 29 Mar 1889, Randolph Co., Indiana, Kelly S. Smithson
B-2-4-1 Ruby Smithson, b. 1891, d. 1983
   m. George Chalfant, b. 1890, d. 1961, 5 sons
B-2-5 Lilly Pearl Bolinger, b. 29 May 1873, Randolph Co.,
   Indiana, d. 2 Jul 1931, Randolph Co., Indiana
   m. 30 May 1889, Randolph Co., Indiana, Asa Robert
   Addington, b. 28 Dec 1865, d. 2 Feb 1941
   (see Addington Descendents list A-1-3-11-7)
B-3 Sophia A. Bolinger, b. c1839, Indiana, d. 1871
   m. 25 Jul 1855, Henry Addington, b. 1834, d. 1863 (Civil War)
   (see Addington Descendents list, A-1-3-5-4)
B-4 Hannah Bolinger, b. c1840
   m. 1866/68, Sylvester Williams
B-5 Elizabeth J. Bolinger, b. 1842, Indiana
   m. 3 Jan 1871, Elisha Mills
B-6 Martha E. Bolinger, b. 1845, Indiana
   m. 21 Jun 1866, Randolph Co., Indiana, Rufus King
B-7 Samuel R. Bolinger, b. 9 Oct 1846, Indiana, d. 12 Apr 1912,
   bur. Maxville Cem.
   m. 7 Nov 1874, Randolph Co., Indiana, Samatha Clevenger, b.
   1852
B-7-1 Lily G. Bolinger, b. 1873
B-7-2 Leuela Bolinger, b. 1875
B-7-3 Charles W. Bolinger, b. 1879
B-8 adapted daughter, Mary J. (Grow) Bolinger, b. 1825, PA
   m. 20 Dec 1851, Randolph Co., Indiana, Lucas Ullum

Descendents of Jesse Chalfant, Jr.
born 1794, Pennsylvania

C Jesse Chalfant, Jr., b. 1794, Pennsylvania, d. 16 Sep 1873, Delaware Co., Indiana
m. 21 Sep 1826, Ross Co., Ohio, Elizabeth Winders, b. 1806, Pennsylvania, d. 1896, Indiana

C-1 Albert Chalfant, b. 5 Aug 1827, Ohio
m. 1850, Rachel Beamer, b. c1829, Indiana, d. bef 1878

C-1-1 David B. Chalfant, b. c1851
m. 1870, Catherine Brown

C-1-1-1 Luellen Chalfant, m. 1891, David E. Vance

C-1-2 Mary "Molly" Chalfant, b. c1853
m. 29 Jun 1872, Thomas M. Oxley

C-1-3 Christina Chalfant, b. c1854
m. 24 Dec 1877, Marion E. Carey

C-1-3-1 John Carey

C-1-4 Ezekial R. Chalfant, b. Nov 1855
m. 19 Oct 1879, Lillie M. Rector

C-1-4-1 Ocie Edna Chalfant, b. May 1885
m. 10 Feb 1903, Clayton McCreary

C-1-4-2 Ira Chalfant, b. May 1890, m. Arthur Mullen

C-1-5 Rachel Elizabeth Chalfant, b. c1858
m. 10 Feb 1876, Marion J. Collins

C-1-6 Phebe Jane Chalfant, b. c1860
m. 1876, Walter Collins

C-1-7 Hester "Ester" A. Chalfant, b. c1862
m. 18 Jul 1882, William Moveland

C-1-8 Lydia E. Chalfant, b. c1864
m. 25 Nov 1880, Joseph Clevenger

C-1-9 Isabel Chalfant, b. c1866, m. John Roach

C-1-10 Emily P. "Emma" Chalfant, b. c1868
m. 6 Sep 1894, John Brimhall

C-1-11 Samuel Jesse Chalfant, b. c1869
m. 1900, Stella Ann Mittendorf

C-1-11-1 Effie Chalfant, m. ? Norton

C-1-11-2 James Lawrence Chalfant, b. c1902, m. Sarah ?

C-1-11-2-1 Maxine Chalfant, b. c1922

C-1-11-2-2 Lawrence Chalfant, b. c1924

C-1 m. 2nd 24 Oct 1878, Rebecca Ellen Clevenger(widow)

C-2 Joel Chalfant, b. 1828, Ohio, d. 11 Feb 1899, Delaware Co., Indiana
m. 30 Jan 1849, Cynthia Jackson, b. c1833, d. 1874

C-2-1 Martha Jane Chalfant, b. 1852, Indiana
  m. 1870, Riley Felton
C-2-2 Oribenella "Emma" Chalfant, b. 1855, Indiana
  m. 1872, John Harrold
C-2-3 Finley Hanaway Chalfant, b. Jun 1858, Indiana
  m. 13 Jun 1878, Phebe Bell Shaw
C-2-3-1 Joseph Memphis Chalfant, b. 19 Mar 1879
  m. 27 Jan 1906, Fronnie M. Campbell
C-2-3-1-1 Bernice Chalfant, b. 1 Sep 1906, m. Forest Foutz
C-2-3-1-2 Dorothy Chalfant, b. 24 Dec 1909, m. Harold Oren
C-2-3-1-3 Rexford "Delbert" Chalfant, b. 23 Jul 1912, m. Violet ?
C-2-3-2 Everett O. Chalfant, b. Mar 1882, d. 22 Apr 1954
  m. Eliza ?
C-2-3-2-1 Frederick Chalfant, b. c1904
C-2-3-2-2 Betty Chalfant, b. c1906, m. ? Winget
C-2-3-2-3 Morris Chalfant, b. c1908, m. Yvonne ?
C-2-3-3 Fronie M. Chalfant, b. c1886, d. 25 Jul 1953
  m. John Dotson
C-2-4 Olive Chalfant, b. 1862
  ?m. 13 Jun 1878, Clark J. Nelson
C-2-5 Viola Chalfant, b. c1866
  m. 4 Nov 1881, William R. Turner
C-2-6 Serena B. Chalfant, b. 1869, d. bef 1880
C-2 m. 2nd 17 Oct 1872, Nancy J. Gibson
C-2-7 Chadd B. Chalfant, b. 24 Nov 1876
  m. 6 Mar 1897, Gertrude Hutchings
C-2-7-1 Gailarard Chalfant, b. 11 Dec 1897, d. Apr 1965
  m. Elsie D. Rash
C-2-7-1-1 LaVaugh D. Chalfant, b. 21 Sep 1918
  m. 1941, Thelma A. Thornburg
C-2-7-1-1-1 Karen Chalfant, b. 8 Jun 1944
  m. 1974, Tim Olaerts
C-2-7-1-1-2 Madaline K. Chalfant, b. 18 Jun 1946
  m. 1965, Luther G. Waters
C-2-7-2 Olan Chalfant, b. Jan 1900, m. Chessie Stanley
C-2-7-2-1 Kenneth Ray Chalfant, b. 16 Nov 1932
  m. Mary Elizabeth Nickels, m. 2nd Joyce Ann Skelton
C-2-7-3 Ermal D. Chalfant, b. 1904, d. Sep 1976
  m. Gladys McAllister
C-2-7-3-1 Bernidien Chalfant, b. c1921, m. ? Feeney
C-2-7-3-2 Max Chalfant, b. c1922
C-2-7-3-3 Robert L. Chalfant, b. 28 Jul 1923, d. 16 May 1984
  m. Helen Moulton
C-2-7-3-3-1 Terri Chalfant, b. 17 Nov 1947, m. John Carter

C-2-7-3-3-2 Stephen Douglas Chalfant, b. 26 Jan 1952, d. 25 Jun
1984, m. Karen Davis
C-2-7-3-3-2-1 Joshua Chalfant, b. 2 Apr 1977
C-2-7-3-3-2-2 Stephanie Chalfant, b. 27 Jun 1979
C-2-7-3-3-3 Cathy Lynn Chalfant, b. 7 Mar 1961
C-2-8 Jesse G. Chalfant, b. c1879
m. 4 Oct 1902, Mary E. Johnson
C-2-9 Cynthia Chalfant, b. 1881, m. 1898, Gola Resse
C-2-10 Glennie C. Chalfant, b. 8 Mar 1886
m. 2 Feb 1907, Aretus Rees
C-2-11 Marshall Homer Chalfant, b. 22 Nov 1886
m. 20 Jun 1908, Estella Gibson
C-2-11-1 Lemmie Davis Chalfant, b. 13 Mar 1911
m. Violet Fehrenback
C-2-11-2 Mae Chalfant, b. c1913, m. Robert Younce
C-3 Robert Chalfant, b. 5 May 1830, Ohio
m. 3 Sep 1851, Priscilla Weir, d. 1854
C-3-1 Mary Elizabeth Chalfant, b. c1851
C-3 ? 2nd m. Zerulda ?
C-3-2 ??? Austin Chalfant, b. c1865, d. young
C-4 George Chalfant, b. 28 Oct 1832, Ohio, d. 25 Mar 1909, Henry
Co., Indiana
m. 7 Sep 1854, Julia Esther Hutchings, b. 1854, d. 1879
C-4-1 Wesley Franklin Chalfant, b. 9 Jun 1855, d. 28 May 1930
m. 12 Aug 1875, Elizabeth Johnson, d. bef. 1880
C-4-1-1 Elmer Chalfant, b. c1877, Delaware Co., Indiana
C-4-1-2 Ollie Chalfant, b. c1879, Delaware Co., Indiana
C-4-1   m. 2nd 5 Nov 1881, Melissa Jane Taylor, b. 28 Oct 1857, d.
19 Dec 1923
C-4-1-3 Ellsworth Chalfant, b. Feb 1883
m. 5 Oct 1901 Ida M. Tuttle
C-4-1-4 Adda Chalfant, b. 13 Dec 1884, d. 9 Jan 1971
m. 1913, Oliver Baker
C-4-1-5 Ora Chalfant, b. 19 Nov 1886, d. 1 Feb 1965
m. 22 Dec 1908, Earl Williams
C-4-1-6 Rosa Chalfant, b. Jul 1889, d. 26 May 1965
m. 20 May 1913, Walter Mills
C-4-1-7 Edna Chalfant, b. 24 Sep 1894, Henry Co., Indiana
C-4-1-8 Edgar Chalfant, b. 24 Sep 1894, d. 20 Dec 1894, Henry Co.,
Indiana
C-4-1-9 Ivan Chalfant, b. 11 May 1900, Delaware Co., Indiana
C-4-2 Mary Elizabeth Chalfant, b. 1857, m. Benjamin Benbow
C-4-3 Lois Jennette Chalfant, b. 1860, m. William O. Collins
C-4-4 Elnora Chalfant, b. 9 Feb 1862, m. James Frank Bryan

C-4-5 Jesse "Bailey" Chalfant, b. c1866, Indiana, d. 1940
m. Lavona Simmons, b. 1865, d. 1926
C-4-5-1 Ethel Chalfant, b. c1889
m. 18 Feb 1909, George E. Reitenour
C-4-5-2 George Chalfant, b. 22 Jun 1890, Delaware Co., Indiana,
d. 1961
m. 21 Feb 1912, Ruby Smithson, b. 4 May 1891
C-4-5-2-1 R. Lee Chalfant
C-4-5-2-2 Ronald Eugene Chalfant, b. 30 Sep 1914
C-4-5-2-3 Ralph Chalfant, b. 22 Feb 1916
C-4-5-2-4 Max Chalfant, b. 19 Aug 1921
C-4-5-2-5 Joe Chalfant
C-4-5-3 Ulyssis Chalfant, b. 20 Jan 1892
m. 20 Sep 1919, Edna Young
C-4-5-4 Ernest Lowell Chalfant, b. 24 Aug 1894
m. 14 Mar 1920, Edna Haley
C-4-5-5 ?"Veva" Vay Chalfant, b. c1898
?m. 6 Jun 1917, Burton Johnson
C-4-5-6 Charles Chalfant, b. c1900, m. Jessie, b. 1906
C-4-5-7 Jesse "Clarence" Chalfant, b. 12 Jun 1902
C-4-5-8 Willard Chalfant, b. 24 Sep 1904, d. 13 Sep 1905
C-4-6 Charles Wilson Chalfant, b. 1 Jan 1868, d. 1949
m. 14 Sep 1928, Randolph Co., Indiana, Annaelma Hollowell,
b. 17 Jun 1870, d. 1932
C-4-7 William Chalfant, b. Nov 1870, m. Emma ?
C-4-7-1 Morton Chalfant, b. 6 Oct 1891
m. 23 Dec 1916, Geraldine Smith
C-4-7-2 Melvin Chalfant, b. Feb 1894
m. 7 Apr 1917, Gladys Howell
C-4-7-3 Delwa Chalfant, b. May 1898
C-4 m. 2nd 1 Aug 1878, Zerilda Jackson
C-4-8 Anna May Chalfant, b. 20 Jan 1880
m. 29 Jan 1898, William A. Parks
C-4-9 Ollie Chalfant, b. Jul 1885
m. 20 Dec 1903, Frank B. Lacy
C-4-10 George Chalfant, b. 22 Jun 1890, d. 11 Aug 1961
m. Ruby M. Smithson
C-4-10-1 Leroy Chalfant, b. 31 Mar 1923
m. 1941, Rose Marie Gade
C-4-10-1-1 Rex Eugene Chalfant, b. 1949, m. Norma Hartman ,
C-4-10-1-2 Jerry Chalfant, b. 27 Oct 1951
C-4-10-1-3 Jack Lynn Chalfant, b. 16 Jun 1954, m. Ann Parks
C-4-10-1-4 Joyce Ann Chalfant
C-4-10-1-5 Kelly Maurice Chalfant, b. 7 Jan 1963

C-5 John Chalfant, b. 22 Sep 1834, Ohio, d. 14 Feb 1896, Muncie, Indiana

   m. 13 Dec 1853, Sarah Thackara, b. 1835, Ohio, d. 14 Jul 1911, Muncie, Indiana

C-5-1 John P. Chalfant, b. Sep 1854, Indiana

   m. 21 Aug 1879, Elizabeth Collins

C-5-1-1 Gertrude Chalfant, b. Sep 1882

   m. 27 Oct 1902, Eugene Sollan

C-5-1-2 daughter, b. 21 Feb 1887, Henry Co., Indiana

C-5-2 Albert P. Chalfant, b. c1858, Indiana, m. Carrie Craig

C-5-3 Laura Chalfant, b. c1861, Indiana, m. Ed Knott

C-5-4 Homer Chalfant, b. c1867, Indiana

C-5-4-1 Roland C. Chalfant, b. c1888

C-5-4-2 Herbert Chalfant, b. c1890

C-5-4-3 Gladys Chalfant, b. c1892

C-5-4-4 Clement Chalfant, b. c1894

C-5-5 Jesse Chalfant, b. c1870, Indiana

C-6 Rachel Ann Chalfant, b. 1837, Ohio

   m. 16 Aug 1855, Thomas Thornburg

C-7 Phoebe Jane Chalfant, b. 8 Feb 1839, Ohio

   m. ? 10 Sep 1870, Riley Felton

C-8 Alexander Chalfant, b. 14 Jan 1840, Ohio, d. 29 May 1930

   m. Elizabeth Templin 27 Jun 1858, Delaware Co., Indiana, d. 1 Apr 1870, bur. Union Cemetery

C-8-1 Ora Chalfant, b. c1859

C-8-2 Alice Melissa Chalfant, b. 5 Aug 1862

   m. 4 May 1881, Aldolph Hill

C-8-2-1 Lillian A. Hill

C-8-2-2 Bertha E. Hill

C-8-2-3 Orville L. Hill

C-8-3 Finley Ellsworth Chalfant, b. 18 Aug 1866, Randolph County, Indiana, d. 10 Feb 1940, bur Union Cemetery, Randolph County, Indiana

   m. 25 Jul 1888, Randolph Co., Indiana, Emma Alice Fitzpatrick, b. 26 Nov 1866, d. 14 Feb 1946

C-8-3-1 Pearl Maude Chalfant, b. 25 Jan 1886, Windsor, Randolph Co., Indiana, d. 19 May 1958

   m. 3 Sep 1904, Randolph Co., Indiana, Tessie Dudley, b. 1886, d. 1957, bur Union Cemetery

C-8-3-2 Shirl Milford "Pete" Chalfant, b. 26 Mar 1888, Windsor, Indiana, d. 25 Mar 1956, bur. Union Cem.

   m. 7 Aug 1909, Randolph Co., Indiana, Elsie Effie Gable, b. 31 Aug 1890, d. 21 Aug 1978

C-8-3-2-1 Ardith Emily Chalfant, b. 13 Jan 1910

m. 6 Apr 1929, Randolph Co., Indiana, Roy Albert Owens
C-8-3-2-2 Russell Lee Chalfant, b. 11 Jul 1911
   m. 23 Nov 1932, Charline Madonna Moon, div.
C-8-3-2-2-1 Shirl Thomas Chalfant, b. 1940, m. Marian ?
C-8-3-2-2-1-1 Shirl Thomas Chalfant, Jr. b. 17 Dec 1967
C-8-3-2-2 m. 2nd 11 Jun 1951, Lila Mae Ludwig, div.
C-8-3-2-2-2 Vicki Lynn Chalfant, b. 18 Mar 1952
   m. 1971, Danny Eugene Ellis
C-8-3-2-2 m. 3rd 28 Feb 1958, Eunice Annette Barnett, div.
C-8-3-2-2-3 Timothy Lee Chalfant, b. 13 Nov 1958
   m. Jennifer Jean
C-8-3-2-2-3-1 Timothy Brian Chalfant, b. 23 Mar 1985
C-8-3-2-2-3-2 Jacalyn Jean Chalfant, b. 17 Apr 1987
C-8-3-2-2 m. 4th Norma Gene McKinley
C-8-3-2-3 Ermel Glee Chalfant, b. 27 Aug (recorded 4 Sep) 1914
   m. 28 Oct 1933, Paul C. Ulrich
C-8-3-2-4 Wilbur Raymond Chalfant, b. 13 Sep 1915
   m. 12 Oct 1934, Olga Sunday, div.
C-8-3-2-4-1 Leo Vernon Chalfant, b. 4 Apr 1935, Randolph Co.,
   Indiana
C-8-3-2-4-2 Phyllis Chalfant, b. c1938
C-8-3-2-4-3 Gary Chalfant, b. c1940
C-8-3-2-4 m. 2nd 13 Nov 1948, Lillian Irene Shroyer
C-8-3-2-5 Ivan Ray Chalfant, b. 13 Sep 1917
   m. 1 Jun 1945, Randolph Co., Indiana, Mary Parkison
C-8-3-2-5-1 Robert Ray Chalfant, b. 2 Apr 1946
   m. 1964, Sharon K. Johnson
C-8-3-2-5-1-1 Tracy Chalfant, b. 3 May 1965
C-8-3-2-5-1-2 Tiffany Renee Chalfant, b. 15 Oct 1968
   m. 1987, Wes Briar, div.
C-8-3-2-5-1-2-1 Shea Michael Briar
C-8-3-2-5-2 Jack Eugene Chalfant, b. 22 Mar 1948
   m. 1965, Vicki Ullom
C-8-3-2-5-2-1 Charles Ray Chalfant, b. 27 Jan 1966
   m. Brook Perdue
C-8-3-2-5-2-2 Derek Andrew Chalfant, b. 12 Jun 1968
C-8-3-2-5-3 Susan Diane Chalfant, b. 20 Jun 1950
   m. 1974, Allen Gaines
C-8-3-2-6 Ethel Charlene Chalfant, b. 13 Feb 1920
   m. 17 Dec 1939, Granville Deckman
C-8-3-2-7 Merrill Warren Chalfant, b. 27 Jan 1922, d. 4 Nov 1979
   m. 2 Dec 1944, Pauline Ruth Dickey
C-8-3-2-7-1 Steven Lee Chalfant, b. 5 Mar 1946, m. Nancy ?
C-8-3-2-7-1-1 Ryan Chalfant, b. 8 Apr 1979

C-8-3-2-7-2 Debra Kay Chalfant, b. 2 May 1956, m. James Butcher
C-8-3-2-8 Leland Eugene Chalfant, b. 2 Feb 1924, d. 26 Jun 1980
  m. 25 Sep 1948, Mary Eunice Baker
C-8-3-2-8-1 David Wayne Chalfant, b. 11 Sep 1950
  m. 1977, Carolyn Louise Gray
C-8-3-2-8-1-1 Jeremy Allan Chalfant, b. 9 Dec 1984
C-8-3-2-8-1-2 Courtney Lynn Chalfant, b. 13 May 1989
C-8-3-2-8-2 Jerriam Chalfant, b. 7 Sep 1954
  m. 1971, Larry Freddie Wesley
C-8-3-2-9 Merritt Leroy Chalfant, b. 13 Jul 1926, d. 25 Oct 1950
  m. 24 Mar 1947, Zelda Marie King, d. 25 Oct 1950
C-8-3-2-9-1 Ted Chalfant (Hiatt), b. c1947
C-8-3-2-10 Richard Dale Chalfant, b. 13 Oct 1929
  m. 1 Sep 1947, Betty Lou Cassel
C-8-3-2-10-1 Gordon Lee Chalfant, b. 17 Sep 1947
  m. Myra Winningham
C-8-3-2-10-2 Sharon Lee Chalfant, b. 15 Oct 1948
  m. Gary Maynard
C-8-3-2-10-3 Cheryl Lynn Chalfant, b. 16 Nov 1954
  m. 1977, Patrick McNulty
C-8-3-2-10-4 Larry Richard Chalfant, b. 11 Jan 1947
  m. 1988, Donna Lawton
C-8-3-2-10-4-1 Michael Ray Chalfant, b. Jan 1990
C-8-3-2-10-5 James Alan Chalfant, b. 20 Mar 1960
C-8-3-2-11 Martha Joanne Chalfant, b. 22 Feb 1931
  m. 2 Nov 1951, John Eugene Ellis, b. 1951, d. 1969
C-8-3-2-12 Betty Lou Chalfant, b. 3 Feb 1935
  m. 10 Aug 1952, Wayne Cox
C-8-3-3 Earle Melvin Chalfant, b. 26 Jan 1891, Windsor, Indiana,
    d. 10 Jan 1947
  m. 21 Sep 1912, Randolph Co., Indiana, Lola Gunkie
C-8-3-3-1 Adopted Capitolia Chalfant, m. Herbert Pact
C-8-3-4 Mabel Meryl Chalfant, b. 22 Dec 1894, Windsor, Indiana,
    d. 1982
  m. 28 Dec 1912, Randolph Co., Indiana, William Richard
    Clevenger, b. 1887, d. 1964
C-8-3-4-1 Vernon Joseph Clevenger, m. Miriam Hill
C-8-3-4-1-1 Rick Clevenger
C-8-3-4-1-2 daughter
C-8-3-4-2 Emma Belle Clevenger
  m. Jimmy Alcorn (2 children)
C-8-3-4-3 Janice Clevenger, m. Robert Ruble (twin sons)
C-8-3-5 Verle Murtle Chalfant, b. 12 Oct 1897, Windsor, Indiana,
    d. 20 Apr 1970

m. 27 Apr 1914, Randolph Co., Indiana, Earl James, b. 4 Jan 1894, d. 1977

C-8-3-5-1 Claron James, m. Frances ? (1 son, 1 daughter)

C-8-3-5-2 Glenn James, m. Barbara Crouch

C-8-3-5-2-1 Mindy James

C-8-3-5-2-2 Tommy James

C-8-3-6 Marvin Hurley Chalfant, b. 3 Apr 1901, Parker, Indiana, d. 29 Jul 1974

m. 11 Jun 1921, Mary Ethel Winget, b. 1900, d. 1974

C-8-3-6-1 Mary Evelyn Chalfant, b. 3 May 1922

m. 1946, Ralph Acord, b. 1923

C-8-3-6-1-1 Alan Ray Acord, b. 4 Oct 1952

C-8-3-6-2 Douglas M. Chalfant, b. 1926, d. 1982, bur. Mt. Tabor Cemetery, dnm

C-8-3-7 Alma Marguerite Chalfant, b. 9 Jun 1905, Parker, Randolph Co., Indiana, d. 18 Aug 1979, Muncie, Indiana, bur. Maxville Cem., Randolph Co., Indiana

m. 30 Sep 1922, Randolph Co., Indiana, Harry Vern Addington, d. 13 Aug 1930

(see Addington Descendents, A-1-3-12-3-1)

C-8-3-7 m. 2nd 12 Oct 1932, Clarence Mason, div

C-8-3-7 m. 3rd 10 May 1960, Harry E. Puckett, b. 1890, d. 1965

C-8-3-8 Harry Marshall Chalfant, b. 14 Jan (or 23 Jan) 1911, Parker, Indiana, d. 8 Aug 1922, bur. Union Cemetery

C-8-4 Charles Chalfant, b. 1869, d. ? 24 Aug 1911

m. ? 30 Oct 1893, Sophia Schussler

C-8-4-1? Alpha R. Chalfant, b. 13 Feb 1909

C-8-4-2? Mary Chalfant, b. 17 May 1920, Henry Co., Indiana

C-8 m. 2nd 25 Oct 1870, Jay Co., Indiana, Susannah Puckett, d. bef 1880

C-8-5 Ethel Chalfant, b. 1873

C-8-6 LeRoy Chalfant, b. 1875

C-8-7 Edna Chalfant, b. 1877

C-9 Lavina Chalfant, b. 18 Apr 1842, Indiana

m. 8 Mar 1860, Thomas W. Newcomb

C-10 Elizabeth Chalfant, b. 12 Mar 1844, Indiana

m. 15 Dec 1859, Samuel Hutchings

C-11 Jesse Bailey Chalfant, b. c1846, Indiana, d. 17 Dec 1932

m. 1866, Pauline Benbow

C-11-1 Noah Chalfant, b. c1869, m. 27 Dec 1892, Clara E. Lee

C-11-2 Jesse E. Chalfant, b. Mar 1870, m. Adda

C-11-3 Marion F. Chalfant, b. 26 Jan 1875, Delaware Co., Indiana

m. 27 Jan 1897, Cora Maud Shaw, b. c1877, d. 23 Nov 1907, Delaware Co., Indiana

C-11-3-1 Hershal Chalfant, b. Jan 1898

C-11-4 Bindella Chalfant, b. Feb 1883, m. 2 Dec 1900,

C-11-5? Dema D. Chalfant, m. 3 Nov 1887

C-11-6 Edward Chalfant, b. Jan 1888, d. 29 Aug 1904, Delaware
    Co., Indiana

C-11-7? Amanda J. Chalfant, m. 3 Jul 1892

C-11-8? Emma Chalfant, m. 6 Sep 1894

C-11-9? Mary Chalfant, m. 27 Jan 1897

C-12 Levi Chalfant, b. 18 Apr 1848
  m. 8 Nov 1866, Sarah A. Felton

C-12-1 Frank Chalfant, b. 1871
  m. 1897 Jennie Morris

C-12-1 m. 2nd 15 Apr 1911, Nellie Essa Morris

C-12-2 Beverley Chalfant, b. c1885, m. Charles Beresford

C-12-3 Harly J. Chalfant, b. Jul 1880, m. ?

C-12-4 Alta Chalfant, m. 30 Oct 1885 Charles H. Carey

C-12-5 Ralph B. Chalfant, b. May 1886, m. 1910, Rozzie Johnson

C-12-6 Mark C. Chalfant, b. Sep 1887, m. Lenora ?

C-12-6-1 Barbara Chalfant, b. c1919

C-12-6-2 Lee Chalfant, b. c1921

C-12-7 Clayton Chalfant, b. c1887

C-13 John B. Chalfant, b. c1853
  m. 19 Jan 1872, Ellen Stanford (1880 Madison Co.)

C-13-1 Emery Chalfant, b. 1873
  m. 12 Apr 1896, Jessie Darnell

Descendents of James Figins
born about 1775, Virginia

F James Figins, b. c1775, prob. Fauquier Co., Virginia, d. c1835,
prob. Licking Co., Ohio

F-1 James H. Figins, b. 1814, VA, d. c1870, Randolph Co., IN
m. prob. Licking Co., Ohio, Rebecca McCracken, b. c1817, prob.
Licking Co., Ohio, d. c1838

F-1-1 Alexander Feagans, b. c1836, prob. Licking Co., Ohio
m. 14 Sep 1854, Randolph Co., Indiana, Rachel Moore, b. 19
Mar 1836

F-1-1-1 Rebecca Mahala Feagans, b. May 1855, Indiana, d. 18 Aug
1904, Randolph Co.
m. 2 Jul 1871, Randolph Co., Indiana, David Basil Strahan, b.
5 Mar 1844

F-1-1-1-1 George A. Strahan, b. Jul 1874, d. Apr 1876

F-1-1-1-2 Loren Parker Strahan, b. 2 Jan 1877
m. 28 May 1896, Maude Belle Halstead

F-1-1-1-2-1 Wilbur David Strahan, b. 1897, d. 1965
m. 24 Sep 1920, Erma Mae Fields

F-1-1-1-2-1-1 Mary Alice Strahan, b. 1921
m. 8 Apr 1944, Cedric Ira Benedict

F-1-1-1-2-1-1-1 Cheryl Ann Benedict, b. 1945
m. Konstation Georgiou

F-1-1-1-2-1-1-1-1 Maria Georgiou, b. 1975

F-1-1-1-2-1-1-1-2 Angie Rae Georgiou, b. 1978

F-1-1-1-2-1-1-2 Victoria Jo Strahan, b. 1947
m. 9 Aug 1975, Merle Robert Long

F-1-1-1-2-1-1-3 Dawn DeAnn Strahan, b. 1960
m. 19 Apr 1986, Kevin Rex James

F-1-1-1-2-1-1-3-1 Danielle Nicole James, b. 18 Oct 1988

F-1-1-1-2-1-2 Mildred Mae Strahan, b. 1924, d. 1972

F-1-1-1-2-1-3 Betty Irene Strahan, b. 1927, d. 1927

F-1-1-1-2-1-4 Ruth Marie Strahan, b. 1928, d. 1976

F-1-1-1-2-2 Raymond Harold Strahan, b, 1898, d. 1968

F-1-1-1-2-3 George Kenneth Strahan, b. 1901, d. 1966

F-1-1-1-2-4 Donald Parker Strahan, b. 1906, d. 1955

F-1-1-1-3 Egbert Jessie Strahan, m. Daisy Bright

F-1-1-1-4 Oren P. Strahan, b. Jan 1883, d. 23 Feb 1883

F-1-1-1-5 David Clayton Strahan, b. 18 Sep 1893
m. Frances Leatherford

F-1-1-2 George W. Feagans, b. c1858, Indiana

F-1-1-3 Mary E. Feagans, b. c1861, Indiana

F-1-2 Robert Wesley Feagans, b. 13 Nov 1836, Ohio, d. 8 May 1902, bur. Buena Vista Cem.

m. 26 Aug 1858, Randolph Co., Indiana, Mary Elizabeth Starbuck, d. ? 20 May 1861

F-1-2-1 Elizabeth Feagans, b. 1859

F-1-2-2 Mary E. Feagans, b. 30 May 1861, d. 22 May 1936, Farmland, Indiana, bur. Maxville Cem.

m. Isaac Smith, 4 children

F-1-2 m. 2nd 17 Jul 1862, Randolph Co., Indiana, Rebecca Jane Moore, b. 10 Oct 1842, Indiana, d. 20 May 1878, Randolph Co., Indiana, bur. Buena Vista Cem.

F-1-2-3 Dora Elizabeth Feagans, b. 24 Oct 1862, Randolph Co., Indiana, d. 19 Mar 1944, Randolph Co., Indiana, bur. Maxville Cemetery

m. 18 Feb 1880, Randolph Co., Indiana, Joseph Leander Addington

(see Addington Descendents, A-1-3-12-3)

F-1-2-4 Ella Feagans, b. 1863/69, m. ? Sayers, 5 children

F-1-2-4-1 Orville Sayers

F-1-2-5 Pearl Feagans, b. 1863/69, m. ? Powell

F-1-2 m. 3rd 1879, Indiana, Mary ?

F-1-2-6 Ottus A. Feagans, b. c1880, Indiana, d. 12 Nov 1970, bur. Maxville Cemetery

m. c1903, Ella J. Hick, b. 3 Mar 1865, d. 14 Jul 1922, bur. Maxville Cemetery

F-1-2-7 Burley Feagans, b. c1885, m. Bessie Huffman

F-1-2-7-1 son, b. 2 Sep 1905, Randolph Co., Indiana

F-1-2-8 Orvil Feagans, b. c1887

F-1-2-9 Iva K. Feagans, b. c1889

F-1-2-10 Claude Feagans, b. c1894

F-1 m. 2nd 15 Mar 1843, Randolph Co., Indiana, Julia Cowgill, b. 25 Mar 1838, d. Dec 1877

F-1-4 James H. Feagans, b. 1 Feb 1841, Indiana

m. 17 Mar 1863, Abigail Harris, b. 19 Oct 1846

F-1-4-1 Charles C. Feagans, b. 19 Sep 1865

F-1-4-2 Orin G. Feagans, b. 11 Aug 1867

F-1-3 Sarah E. Feagans, b. 12 Nov 1838, Indiana,

m. 20 Jul 1854, Randolph Co., Indiana, Levi Bond

F-1-5? Mary E. Feagans, b. 1848, d. 9 May 1931, bur. Maxville Cemetery, m. ? Gustin

Descendents of William Fitzpatrick
born 1815, North Carolina

F-1 William Fitzpatrick, b. 1815, North Carolina, d. 1856/60
   m. 25 Mar 1837, Wayne Co., Indiana, Hannah Seany, b. 1818,
   Indiana, d. 1856/60
F-1-1 William F. Fitzpatrick, b. c1839, Wayne Co., Indiana, d. 9
   Sep 1915, Randolph Co., Indiana, bur. Union Cemetery
   m. 22 Feb 1865, Randolph Co., Indiana, Jemima Emily Terrell,
   d. 7 Jun 1916
F-1-1-1 Emma A. Fitzpatrick, b. 1867, Indiana, d. 9 Feb 1940, bur.
   Union Cemetery, Randolph County
   m. 25 Jul 1888, Randolph Co., IN, Finley Ellsworth Chalfant
(see Chalfant descendents, C-8-3)
F-1-1-2 Sarah M. Fitzpatrick, b. 1875, Indiana
   m. ? Bailey (lived in Desoto)
F-1-1-3 George Wesley Fitzpatrick, b. 1879, Indiana, d. 8 Oct
   1951, Randolph Co., Indiana, bur. Union Cemetery
   m. Nancie Ann Wood, b. 1883, d. 14 Jan 1913
F-1-1-3-1 son b. 29 Jun 1904, Randolph Co., Indiana
F-1-1-3 m. 2nd 28 Feb 1916, Grace Myrtle Wood
F-1-2 John W. Fitzpatrick, b. 15 Dec 1842, Indiana, d. 11 Aug
   1922
   m. Mary L. Smith, b. 15 Mar 1843, d. 4 Jul 1923
F-1-3 Pleasant Fitzpatrick, b. c1849, Indiana, d. aft. 1923
F-1-4 Lewis Fitzpatrick, b. c1854, Indiana, nfi
F-2 James Fitzpatrick, b. NC
   m. Sallie Thomas, Delaware Co., Indiana

Descendents of William Terrell
born 1779, Virginia

TR William Terrell, b. 24 Mar 1779, Virginia, d. 1834, Highland
Co., Ohio
m. 25 Feb 1801, Campbell Co., Virginia, Jemima Smithson,
daughter of Drummond and Mary Smithson
TR-1 Drummond Terrell, b. 30 Aug 1803, Virginia, d. 1885,
Delaware County, Indiana, bur. Union Cemetery
m. 4 Oct 1825, Highland Co., Ohio, Judith Merrell, d. prob.
within a few years
TR-1 m. 2nd 25 Sep 1850, Clinton, Co., Ohio, Sarah Norah
Ratcliff
TR-1-1 John W. Terrell, b. 1853, Indiana
TR-2 George Wesley Terrell, b. 1804, Virginia, d. 22 Mar 1878,
Randolph Co., Indiana, bur. Union Cemetery
m. 27 Nov 1825, Highland Co., Ohio, Sarah Moore, b. 1804,
Virginia, d. 8 Jul 1884, Randolph Co., IN, bur. Union Cem.
TR-2-1 William Terrell, b. 13 Jul 1827, Indiana, d. 13 Jan 1915
m. 1st 22 Nov 1849, Randolph Co., IN, Rebecca Thornburg
TR-2-1-1 Lucinda J. Terrell, b. 8 Dec 1850
m. ? Halstead
TR-2-1-2 John W. Terrell, b. 19 Nov 1852
TR-2-1 m. 2nd 27 Mar 1856, Delaware Co., Indiana, Mary A.
Thornburg (Mary's will 11 Jun 1925)
TR-2-1-3 Margaret E. Terrell, b. 22 Oct 1858, m. ? Dudley
TR-2-1-4 Sarah E. Terrell, b. 10 May 1861
TR-2-1-5 George E. Terrell, b. 18 Jan 1866, d. 13 Mar 1888,
Windsor, Indiana
TR-2-1-6 Ulysses G. Terrell, b. c1868
TR-2-1-7 William "Grant" Terrell, b. 30 May 1869
m. Laura Bell Cline, b. c1872
TR-2-1-7-1 Jessie Terrell, b. 7 Aug 1892, Randolph Co., Indiana
TR-2-1-7-2 Hoover Terrell, b. 13 Mar 1894, Randolph Co., IN
TR-2-1-7-3 George Terrell, b. 20 Apr 1896
m. 15 Sep 1917, Alice Moon
TR-2-1-7-4 Velma Terrell, b. Jan 1898, Indiana
TR-2-1-7-5 Orville Terrell, b. May 1900, Indiana
TR-2-1-8 Susannah Josephine Terrell, b. 30 May 1871
TR-2-1-9 Maud B. Terrell, b. 7 May 1873
m. 2 Feb 1895, Delaware Co., Indiana, James Bailey
TR-2-1-9-1 Ethel Bailey

TR-2-1-9-2 Evert Bailey
TR-2-1-9-3 Clarence Bailey
TR-2-1-9-4 Anna O. Bailey
TR-2-1-10 Della May Terrell, b. 30 May 1875
   m. ? Warren
TR-2-1-11 Lydia Carey Terrell, b. 20 Dec 1878
   m. ? Cline
TR-2-1-11-1 Dessie Cline
TR-2-2 Martha Ann Terrell, b. c1830,
   m. 4 Apr 1850, Randolph Co., Indiana, John Tilman Cox, d.
   bef. 1860
TR-2-3 Jemima Emily Terrell, b. 3 Dec 1837, d. 7 Jun 1916, bur.
   Union Cemetery
   m. 22 Feb 1865, Randolph Co., Indiana, William F.
   Fitzpatrick, b. c1839, d. 9 Sep 1915, Randolph Co., Indiana,
   bur. Union Cemetery
TR-2-3-1 Emma A. Fitzpatrick, b. 1867, Indiana
   m. 25 Jul 1888, Randolph Co., IN, Finley Ellsworth Chalfant
   (see Chalfant descendents, C-8-3)
TR-2-3-2 Sarah M. Fitzpatrick, b. 1875, Indiana
TR-2-3-3 George W. Fitzpatrick, b. 1879, Indiana
   m. ? Ford
TR-2-3-3-4 Frances Lee Terrell, b. 1903, Randolph Co., Indiana
TR-2-4 George C. Terrell, b. c1842, d. 22 Mar 1865 (member of
   124th Indiana Infantry, Company H, died of wounds
   received in Battle of Goldsboro, NC on 21 Mar 1865)
   ?m. 30 Mar 1862, Delaware Co., Indiana, Sharon A. Glaze
TR-2-5 Lucinda Terrell, b. c1851
TR-3 ? Jemima Terrell
   m. 15 Sep 1825, Highland Co., Ohio, William Bell
TR-4 John M. Terrell, b. c1811, Virginia, d. 1899, Indiana, bur.
   Union Cem.
   m. 1 Aug 1833, Randolph Co., Indiana, Eliza Smithson, b.
   1818, Ohio
TR-4-1 William W. Terrell, b. c1835, Indiana, d. 16 Apr 1882,
   Windsor, Indiana, bur. Union Cem.
   ?m. 13 Jun 1855, Delaware Co., Indiana, Louisa Hart
   ?m. 2nd 24 Nov 1860, Delaware Co., Indiana, Jane Keeriese
TR-4-1-1 Eliza Alice Terrell, b. c1862, Indiana
   m. 3rd 8 Oct 1867, Randolph Co., Indiana, Elizabeth A.
   French, b. 1847
TR4-1-2 George W. Terrell, b. May 1873, Indiana, d. 1947
   m. Etta Ford
   m. 2nd 10 Feb 1913, Margaret Jane (Puckett) Robertson

TR-4-1-2-1 John Herbert Terrell, d. 28 May 1900

TR-4-2 Drummond S. Terrell, b. May 1837, Indiana, d. aft 1900 (1900 Huntington Co., Indiana)

m. 22 Feb 1859, Clinton, Co., Ohio, Louisa J. Taylor, b. 1841

TR-4-2-1 Blanche Terrell (adopted), b. c1877, Indiana

TR-4-3 Isaac Terrell, b. c1839, Indiana

?m. 3 Feb 1859, Delaware Co., Indiana, Lucinda Flinn

TR-4-4 Elizabeth A. Terrell, b. c1842, Indiana

m. ? 1 Sep 1862, Randolph Co., Indiana, Seth Conarrog

TR-4-5 John E. Terrell, b. c1849, IN, d. 1915, bur. Buena Vista

m. Gertrude ?, b. 1856

TR-4-5-1 Deanna M. Terrell, b. c1895

TR-4-6 George Harlin Terrell, b. 13 Dec 1858, Indiana,

m. 8 Nov 1879, Delaware Co., Indiana, Malindae Dudley

TR-4-6-1 Frank Terrell, b. Nov 1880, Indiana

TR-4-6-2 William Otis Terrell, b. 4 Sep 1882, Randolph Co., Indiana, d. 12 Apr 1883, Windsor, Indiana

TR-4-6-3 Joab Terrell, b. 1 Aug 1886, Randolph Co., Indiana

TR-4-6-4 Lenne C. Terrell, b. May 1897, Indiana

TR-4-6 m. 2nd 10 Feb 1913, Randolph Co., Indiana, Margaret Jane (Puckett) Robertson

Descendents of John Townsend
born 1725, Pennsylvania

John Townsend, b. c1725, Pennsylvania
  m. Elizabeth Pearson, b. 8 Dec 1726, Pennsylvania, dau of
  Enoch and Margaret (Smith) Pearson
T-1 James Townsend
  m. 6 Apr 1775, South Carolina, Mary Cook
T-2 Elizabeth Townsend
  m. 12 Apr 1775, Amos Cook
T-3 William Townsend, ? b. c1759, ? South Carolina, d.
  Greenville, Darke Co., Ohio
  m. Margaret ?
T-3-1 Joseph Townsend, b. ?1780-90, d. April 1843, Allen Co.,
  Indiana
T-4 John M. Townsend, b. 6 Nov 1763, Pennsylvania, d. 25 Aug
  1853, 89y, 8m, 19d, Fountain City, Indiana
  m. 6 May 1783, South Carolina, Elvira Cain, b. 7 Mar 1768,
  Edgecombe, NC, d. 11 Mar 1870, Elkton, Preble Co., Ohio,
  dau of Jonathan and Betty (Harold) Cain
T-4-1 Celia Townsend, b. 22 Feb 1785, d. 5 Mar 1852, bur.
  Sparrow Creek Cemetery, Randolph Co., Indiana
  m. Joseph Addington, b. 21 Jul 1776, d. 20 Feb 1836
(see Addington Descendents, A-1-3 2nd)
T-4-2 James Townsend, b. 17 Dec 1787
  m. 16 Dec 1807, Warren Co., Ohio, Rosannah Smith, b. 16 Sep
  1787, NC, d. 23 Jan 1854, West Grove, Indiana
T-4-2-1 Thomas Townsend, b. 3 Dec 1808
  m. 17 Jul 1828, Mary Hastings
T-4-2-1-1 William H. Townsend, b. 27 Nov 1832
T-4-2-1-2 Hannah Townsend, b. 16 Apr 1837
T-4-2-1-3 Isaac Townsend, b. 5 Jun 1843
T-4-2-2 Rachel Townsend, b. 7 Mar 1810, b. 22 Feb 1811
T-4-2-3 Celia Townsend, b. 10 Nov 1811
  m. 14 Apr 1831, Needham Reece
T-4-2-4 Charolotte Townsend, b. 27 Jul 1813
T-4-2-5 Isaac Townsend, b. 4 Aug 1815
  m. 16 Mar 1837, Wayne Co., Indiana, Lucinda McConkey
T-4-2-6 Hannah Townsend, b. 8 Mar 1817
T-4-2-7 David Townsend, b. 25 Feb 1819
  m. 16 May 1839, Syndey Maudlin
T-4-2-8 Elizabeth Townsend, b. 1 Jun 1823

T-4-2-9 Esther Townsend, b. 10 Jul 1825

T-4-2-10 Elvira Townsend, b. 27 May 1827

T-4-2-11 Nancy Townsend, b. 30 Jan 1830
 m. 8 Feb 1849, William J. Harbit

T-4-2-11-1 Henry Thomas Harbit, b. 1 Sep 1855
 m. Mary Alice Brown

T-4-2-11-1-1 William Russell Harbit, b. 12 May 1883, Wisconsin,
 d. 23 Nov 1947, Butte, MT

T-4-2-11-1-1-1 Henry Richard Harbit, b. 27 Jun 1904, Holst, MN,
 d. 13 Sep 1963, Boise, ID

T-4-2-11-1-1-1-1 Bonnie Jean Harbit, b. 19 Jul 1938, Nampa, ID
 m. Alfred Wallace Salo

T-4-2-12 Richard Townsend, b. 24 Dec 1841

T-4-3 Rachel Townsend, b. 29 Oct 1790
 m. 18 Dec 1807, William Harvey

T-4-4 Jonathan Townsend, b. 1793, d. 13 Jul 1862, Pilot Grove,
 Iowa
 m. 28 Sep 1814, Wayne Co., Indiana, Polly Clawson, b. 1791, d.
 27 Jul 1846, Pilot Grove, Iowa

T-4-4-1 Daniel Townsend, b. 22 Aug 1815, d. 28 Feb 1848, nr
 Pilot Grove, Iowa

T-4-4-2 John Townsend, b. 7 Dec 1817, d. 28 Jan 1821

T-4-4-3 Mahlon Townsend, b. 26 Sep 1819, d. 18 Mar 1848, nr
 Pilot Grove, Iowa

T-4-4-4 Amos Townsend, b. 13 Dec 1821, d. 28 Jan 1893, Salem,
 Iowa
 m. 18 May 1858, Pilot Grove, Iowa, Mary Amelia Groesbeck

T-4-4-5 Stephen Townsend, b. 2 Apr 1824, d. 28 Jan 1860, nr
 Pilot Grove, Iowa,
 m. 16 Nov 1848, Hannah Garretson

T-4-4-5-1 Stephen Townsend, b. 23 Feb 1850

T-4-4-6 James Townsend, b. 16 Jun 1826, d. 7 Aug 1826

T-4-4-7 Rebecca Townsend, b. 30 Jun 1827, d. San Diego, CA

T-4-4-8 William Townsend, b. 3 Oct 1829

T-4-5 Mary Townsend, b. 7 Mar 1794
 m. 29 Nov 1809, Isaac Commons

T-4-5-1 William Commons, b. 29 Jan 1811, d. 20 Feb 1811

T-4-5-2 Jonathan Commons, b. 2 Mar 1812, d. 15 May 1851
 m. Apr 1832, Mary Ann Moore

T-4-5-3 Hannah Commons, b. 25 Dec 1813
 m. 28 Apr 1831, Samuel Nicholson

T-4-5-4 Esther Commons, b. 8 Nov 1816, d. 7 Jun 1818

T-4-5-5 John Commons, b. 15 Dec 1818

T-4-5-6 Lydia Commons, b. 9 Aug 1821

T-4-5-7 Robert Commons, b. 2 Sep 1823
T-4-5-8 Elvira Commons, b. 25 Nov 1825, d. 4 May 1853
T-4-5-9 Joseph A. Commons, b. 3 Jul 1827
T-4-5-10 Isaac Commons, b. 22 Oct 1830
  m. 24 May 1855, Keziah Stubbs
T-4-5-11 Nathan Commons, b. 3 Nov 1830
T-4-6 William Townsend, b. 10 Apr 1795, d. bef. 1850
  m. 29 May 1816, Elizabeth Morrow
T-4-6-1 Eli Townsend, b. 20 Apr 1817, Indiana, d. 27 Mar 1883
  m. 29 Nov 1838, Wayne Co., Indiana, Rachel Moore, b. 16 Jun
  1818, Indiana, d. 2 Jan 1868
T-4-6-1-1 Hiram Townsend, b. 6 Apr 1840, m. Edith ?
T-4-6-1-2 Mary E. Townsend, b. 3 May 1842
  m. Abraham Symons
T-4-6-1-2-1 John E. Symons, b. 1 Jul 1871, d. Jun 1927
  m. Lillie M. Huston
T-4-6-1-2-2 Sarah E. Symons, b. 8 Oct 1874
T-4-6-1-3 Caldwell G. Townsend, b. 28 Jun 1844,
  m. 23 Sep 1863, Martha M. Hodgin, b. 1 Sep 1845
T-4-6-1-3-1 Lindley J. Townsend, b. 21 Jan 1865, d. 10 Mar 1865
T-4-6-1-3-2 William R. Townsend, b. 21 Sep 1866
T-4-6-1-3-3 Lillie M. Townsend, b. 12 Aug 1869
T-4-6-1-3-4 Elwood S. Townsend, b. 25 Mar 1872
T-4-6-1-3-5 Ira J. Townsend, b. 17 Oct 1878
T-4-6-1-3-6 Matilda E. Townsend, b. 30 Apr 1881
T-4-6-1-3-7 Clara A. Townsend, b. 30 Oct 1882
T-4-6-1-4 David W. Townsend, b. 30 Jun 1848, Indiana
  m. Martha Moyer, b. Oct 1852
T-4-6-1-4-1 Orla V. Townsend, b. 5 Feb 1877, d. 31 Dec 1882
T-4-6-1-4-2 Jeanetta F. Townsend, b. 22 Dec 1883
  m. Lloyd Cowgill
T-4-6-1-4-3 J. Neal Townsend, b. 4 Feb 1886
  m. Hattie Gladys Wright
T-4-6-1-4-3-1 Howard W. Townsend, b. 3 Oct 1910
T-4-6-1-4-3-2 Margaret Townsend, b. 27 Oct 1912
T-4-6-1-4-3-3 Martha Jean Townsend, b. 17 Jan 1921
T-4-6-1 m. 2nd Indiana Diggs
T-4-6-1-5 Lavina E. Townsend, b. 13 Jun 1872, Indiana
  m. Albert Vandergriff, b. Aug 1873, Indiana
T-4-6-2 Mary Townsend, b. 10 Nov 1818
T-4-6-3 Sarah Townsend, b. 24 Jun 1820
T-4-6-4 Elvira Townsend, b. 5 Jun 1822
T-4-6-5 Lydia Townsend, b. 1 Dec 1823, d. 2 Jan 1894, Richmond,
  Indiana

m. 23 Jan 1856, Abijah Moffitt
T-4-6-6 John M. Townsend, b. 7 Oct 1825, d. 1893
  m. 25 Nov 1852, Wayne Co., Indiana, Elizabeth Edgerton
T-4-6-6-1 Emily Jane Townsend, b. 31 Jan 1861
T-4-6-6-2 Albert Townsend, b. Jul 1853, Indiana, d. 1909
  m. Amelia Collins, b. 1854, NY
T-4-6-6-2-1 Mary Townsend, b. Oct 1876, Indiana
T-4-6-6-2-2 Carrie Townsend, b. Aug 1885, Indiana
T-4-6-6-2-3 Murray Townsend, b. Oct 1889, Indiana
T-4-6-6-3 Rawley W. Townsend
T-4-6-6-4 Rosa E. Townsend, b. 25 Aug 1866
T-4-6-6-5 William C. Townsend
T-4-6-7 Eliza Ann Townsend, b. 8 Jan 1828, d. 21 Jun 1854
T-4-6-8 Esther Townsend, b. 4 Jan 1830
T-4-6-9 Joel Townsend, b. Jun 1832, Indiana, m. Lydia E. ?
T-4-6-9-1 Anna R. Townsend, b. Mar 1879, Indiana
T-4-6-10 David William Townsend, b. 30 Jun 1848
T-4-7 Esther Townsend, b. 4 Feb 1798, d. 3 Sep 1832
  m. 1 Mar 1815, William Stubb
T-4-8 Sarah Townsend, b. 1801, m. 8 Apr 1818 Joseph Stubbs
T-4-9 John Townsend, b. 1804, Wayne Co., Indiana
  m. 8 Mar 1827, Wayne Co., Indiana, Martha Jones
T-4-9-1 William Townsend
T-4-9-2 George Townsend
T-4-9-3 James Townsend
T-4-10 Elizabeth Townsend, b. 28 Dec 1802
  m. 4 Sep 1819, Wayne Co., Indiana, Elisha Stubbs
T-4-11 Barbara Townsend, b. 6 Feb 1807
T-4-12 Stephen Townsend, b. 31 Dec 1810, d. 15 Jul 1884
  m. Mary Griffin
T-4-7-1 Elvira Townsend, b. 23 Oct 1836
T-4-7-2 Sarah G. Townsend, b. 16 Feb 1839
T-4-7-3 Jane Townsend, b. c1840
T-4-7-4 Jacob Townsend, b. c1843
T-4-7-5 Lydia E. Townsend, b. c1848
T-4-7-6 Lindsey Townsend, b. Jun 1850, m. Emma ?
T-4-7-6-1 Ethel Townsend, b. Apr 1880, Indiana
T-4-7-6-2 Harrison Townsend, b. Mar 1885, Indiana
T-5 Margaret Townsend
  m. 11 Feb 1789, Samuel Hunt
T-6 Sarah Townsend, m. ? Cain
T-7 Esther Townsend
  m. 1784, James Parnell

Bibliography

1. Addington, Brenda S., *Addington, A Search*, privately published, Ontario, Canada, 1982 (in Library of Congress).

2. Addington, Hugh M., *History of the Addington Family in United States and England*, Service Printery, Nickelsville, Virginia, 1931.

3. Addington, Hugh M., *Addington, Volume II, U.S.A. and England*, Franklin Publishing Company, Kingsport, Tennessee, 1960.

4. Addington, Rev. Thomas, *History of the Addington Family*, privately published, Randolph County, Indiana, 1910.

5. Barnhill, Cleste Jane Terrell, *Richmond, William and Timothy Terrell, Colonial Virginians*, Mitchell Company, 1934.

6. Belfield, Eversley M. G., *The Annals of the Addington Family*, Wykeham Press, Winchester, England, 1959.

7. Bollinger, Noah, *History and Record of the Clan of Rudolph Bollinger of Switzerland*, privately published, North Manchester, Indiana, 1951.

8. Bowen, A. W. and Company, *A Portrait and Biographical Record of Delaware and Randolph Counties, Indiana*, Chicago, 1894.

9. Carter, Marjorie H., *Goshorn Descendents of Johann Georg and Susannah Gansshorn of Shade Valley, Pennsylvania*, privately published, San Francisco, 1981.

10. Chalfant, Paul W., *Chalfant Family Tree, 1265-1987*, privately published, 1989.

11. Chalfant, Paul S., *The Chalfants*, 1959, papers in the Library of Congress.

12. Dicken, Emma, *Terrell Genealogy*, Naylor Corp., San Antonio, 1952.

13. Heaton, Dean, *The Heaton Families, 350 Years in America*, Gateway Press, Baltimore, 1982.

14. Helm, Thomas B., *History of Delaware County, Indiana*, 1881.

15. Ayres, Elsie Johnson, *Highland Pioneer Sketches and Family Genealogies*, H. K. Skinner & Sons, Springfield, Ohio, 1971.

16. Johnson, R, Winder, *Winders of America*, J. P. Lippincott, Philadelphia, 1902.

17. Kelsey, Mavis Parrott, *The Family of John Massie*, privately published, Houston, 1979.

18. Kemper, G. W. H., *History of Delaware County, Vol II*, Lewis Publishing, Chicago, 1908.

19. Murphy, Doris J., Bonnie Murphy, Olive M. Murphy and Ethel Murphy Burk, *The Matthew Moore Family*, privately published, 1978.

20. Patterson, Naomi and M. J. Edwards, *Addington, A Directory of the Descendents of Henry and Sarah Addington of South Carolina*, Heritage Books, Bowie, Maryland, 1989.

21. Pruitt, Susan L., *Some Descendents of Walter Chiles, the Immigrant in Virginia, Until About 1800*, privately published, 1984.

22. Randolph County Historical and Genealogical Society, *Randolph County, Indiana, 1818-1990*, Turner Publishing Company, Paducah, Kentucky, 1991.

23. Smith, Josiah B., *Historical Collections of Persons, Land, Business and Events in Newton, Bucks County, I-III*, Bucks Co. Historical Society, Doylestown, Pennsylvania, 1942.

24. Smith, and Driver, *Past and Present of Randolph County, Indiana*, 1914.

25. Templin, Ronald R., *The Templins of Indiana*, 1985.

26. Terrell, Joseph Henry, *Genealogy of Richmond and William Terrell*.

27. Townsend Society of America, Inc., Editor, Martha J. Burke, *The Townsend Newsletter* (Winter 1982, Winter 1983).

28. Tucker, Ebenezer, *History of Randolph County, Indiana with Illustrations and Biographical Sketches*, A. L. Kingman, Chicago, 1882.

29. Waters, Margaret R., *Roster of Soldiers and Patriots of the American Revolution Buried in Indiana*, Indianapolis, 1949, Supp., 1954.

Abbreviations and Numbering

aft	-	after
b.	-	born
bap.	-	baptized
bef	-	before
btw	-	between
bur.	-	buried
c	-	circa, about the time of (c often used with census data to indicate the approximate year of birth)
Co.	-	County
d.	-	died
dnm	-	did not marry
m.	-	married
MM	-	Monthly Meeting (Quakers organization)
nfi	-	no further information
ni	-	no issue, children
prob.	-	probably
Twp	-	Township
*	-	Indicates direct line ancestor
/	-	between the years
?	-	Indicates probable connection but some uncertainty in information
??	-	Indicates speculation on the information

Ancestral Chart, Numbering System - Father's name is always twice number of the offspring. Mother's name is twice the offspring's number plus one. Therefore, father's numbers are always even and mother's numbers are always odd.

Descendent's List, Numbering System - Letter refers to the earliest ancestor with which the list begins. Each subsequent dash indicates the next generation and the number refers to the order of the children in the next generation. Children are numbered in order of birth if that is known.

The US Postal Service two letter abbreviations for the states are used when any state name is abbreviated.

AZ	Arizona
CA	California
CO	Colorado
CT	Connecticut
DL	Delaware
FL	Florida
IA	Iowa
ID	Idaho
IL	Illinois
IN	Indiana
KS	Kansas
MD	Maryland
MI	Michigan
MN	Minnesota
MO	Missouri
NB	Nebraska
NC	North Carolina
NJ	New Jersey
NV	Nevada
NY	New York
OH	Ohio
OR	Oregon
PA	Pennsylvania
SC	South Carolina
SD	South Dakota
TX	Texas
UT	Utah
VA	Virginia
WA	Washington
WV	West Virginia
WS	Wisconsin

www.ingramcontent.com/pod-product-compliance
Lightning Source LLC
Chambersburg PA
CBHW070717280326
41926CB00087B/2404